Pelican Books
The Hothouse Society

Dr Royston Lambert was born in 1933, has been a Fellow of King's College, Cambridge, for the last six years, and was educated at State day schools and Cambridge. He has taught and researched in history and sociology at Oxford, at the London School of Economics, and as a Fellow of two Cambridge colleges. His publications include three works on social subjects, and numerous articles on history, sociology and education. In 1964 he initiated the research unit into boarding education and since then has lived, researched and taught in many schools. His unit is also undertaking five research projects for the Public Schools Commission. His collaborator in this volume, Spencer Millham, was also born in 1933, was educated at Cambridge, and taught in two boarding schools before joining the research team.

The Hothouse Society

An exploration of boarding-school life
through the boys' and girls' own writings

Royston Lambert
with Spencer Millham

Penguin Books

Penguin Books Ltd, Harmondsworth,
Middlesex, England
Penguin Books Australia Ltd, Ringwood,
Victoria, Australia

First published by Weidenfeld & Nicolson 1968
Published in Pelican Books 1974

Copyright © Royston Lambert, 1968

Made and printed in Great Britain by
Richard Clay (The Chaucer Press) Ltd, Bungay, Suffolk
Set in Monotype Ehrhardt

This book is sold subject to the condition that
it shall not, by way of trade or otherwise, be lent,
re-sold, hired out, or otherwise circulated without
the publisher's prior consent in any form of
binding or cover other than that in which it is
published and without a similar condition
including this condition being imposed on the
subsequent purchaser

For C. C. C. in gratitude

Contents

　　Acknowledgements 9
1　Introduction 11
2　Differences 20
3　Beginnings 59
4　The Pattern 87
5　'This Tiny Universe' – The House 150
6　A Place in the Sun – Power 170
7　The Outside World 210
8　The Inner World 242
9　The Underworld 266
10　Problems 294
11　Sex in Single-sex Schools 332
12　Sex in Coeducational Schools 377
13　Adaptations and Verdicts 394
　　Index 433

Acknowledgements

Without the warm cooperation of many headmasters the research of which this book is a by-product could never have been attempted. They welcomed us into their communities, gave us unrestricted freedom in them, housed and fed us, entertained us and gave us unremitting help, information, material and guidance, only to be subjected to a three to six hour interview themselves at the end of it all. Their staff, housemasters, other masters, chaplains, bursars, matrons, doctors and others, also put us up, gave us generous hospitality, access to documents and to their own experience, viewpoint and guidance, and also endured systematic cross-examination from us. Though their own contribution will appear in the companion sociological volume, their help was essential to this book. It would be invidious to single out any one of them; I can only offer them all my profound thanks.

The contribution of the thousands of boys and girls was vital. Besides answering our questionnaires, they too gave endless hospitality of Nescafé and toast, volunteered documents and other writings of many kinds, and gave us much insight into their school and personal experience in interview and in conversation. It was a delight to have met, heard and got to know so many under such privileged circumstances. Having intruded into the lives of so many people, received their confidences, assistance and hospitality, I feel I have a responsibility towards them to use the material they provided in a fair and constructive manner and not to betray identities. This book attempts to record their experience faithfully. Any merit it possesses comes from the boys and girls who contributed to it.

Of my research staff, Spencer Millham did most of the work on three chapters of this book, coordinated the initial transcription of the material, and provided unceasing and invaluable help in many other ways. Roger Bullock helped classify the material, criticized drafts and gave generous advice and encouragement. With Susan Stagg, they helped gather most of the vast mass of material of which this is a selection. Also helping collect or classify were Penelope Fitzgerald, Penelope Mellor, John Hipkin, Philip Powell and Maurice Punch. Carole Haine, Monique Turpin, Aileen Stein and Mrs Pullen coped valiantly with the transcription, and then the two latter typed splendidly from a most difficult manuscript. Penny Fitzgerald and Spencer Millham helped me cut the bulky manuscript to its present size. I am deeply grateful to them all.

Finally, I owe thanks to the Department of Education and Science for the grant to cover the research on which this, the companion volume, and other studies are based, and to my colleagues, the Provost and Fellows of King's College, Cambridge, for making available the facilities of the Research Centre and for help in several other ways.

November 1967
ROYSTON LAMBERT
King's College
Cambridge

1 Introduction

There are many books about boarding schools, but they are almost all written by adults presenting their individual experience or arguing their particular case. This book is different. It neither puts forward a case nor describes the experience of adults. It simply presents the life and operation of the hothouse society in the words of boys and girls who belong to it: an education system is explored through the eyes of those for whose welfare and development it exists.

Of the many unique features of our education system, there is none which has attracted so much controversy, passion and fascination as our boarding schools. Other countries have boarding schools too, and some have more children in them, but they attract no such interest or discussion. The reason is that only in England has boarding rather than day school been the style of education long favoured by the governing classes. 'Public schools', the schools in which for over a century the governing élite in our society have been educated, are largely boarding schools. To most people 'boarding education' is simply equated with public-school education. The essentially political issue of whether or not to keep an independent system of schools which serves one social group – the public-schools issue – has thus got inextricably mixed up with an educational one, whether residential education has merits which day education has not. The consequence is that in the voluminous and almost completely subjective literature which daily accumulates on the matter, proponents of the public school are usually pro-boarding and their antagonists almost always anti-boarding.

This book and its companion volume and related studies really began in 1954–6 when I, as an undergraduate educated at day schools, spent several vacations as an unpaid assistant in an approved school on the south coast. From this, my first taste of 'boarding', I derived an interest in the impact which residential communities, deliberately or otherwise, make on their members, and an awareness that 'boarding' education was not confined to the public-school classes, an awareness confirmed as I later learnt of the existence of the progressive and independent schools outside the public-school orbit, and more especially of the Foundation schools, direct-grant schools and the small body of LEA-maintained boarding schools which serve widely differing social groups and functions. It was not until 1963 that, stimulated by the institutional studies of Peter Townsend and others, and increasingly concerned at the absence of evidence on the educational issues underlying all the political turmoil over the public schools, I found the opportunity to begin research work on the subject. I then started work on my own, but in June 1964 the Department of Education and Science made a grant to cover the costs and establish a research unit.

Since then, my colleagues and I have been continuously living and researching in boarding schools. Our research has had two main objectives. First we wished to describe English boarding schools: what they were trying to do, how they operated, and with what effect. Using the theoretical perspectives and the methods of the sociology of complex organizations, we have examined the objectives, organizations and operation of a representative sample of schools for ordinary children, establishing their similarities and differences. Secondly, we wished to find out what effects, if any, residential education had on children, effects not produced by day-school education. To do this, we have made sociological and psychological comparisons between groups of similar children in schools similar in all things except that some were boarding and others were day schools. Unfortunately the original project was limited by the terms of the grant to secondary schools, and to boys' or coeducational schools. Preparatory schools and girls' schools were cut out. Since 1966, however, the grant has been extended to cover prep and girls' schools, and other research has begun: into the demand and 'need' for types of residential education in this country, into the ways children with such 'need' can best be suited, into various schemes of integration in public schools, and into the effects of 'progressive' education. All this work covers 155 boarding schools as well as numerous day schools, and work with parents and families.

Introduction 13

This particular book is based on the work done since 1964 into the original representative sample of 66 boys' and coeducational schools, though it does draw on some of the work recently done in preparatory schools.[1] The 66 schools were chosen from boarding schools for ordinary children in England and Wales recognized by the Department of Education and Science (there are no unrecognized schools represented in this book), and cover all the principal kinds of boarding in this country. They include 26 public schools (Headmasters' Conference schools) all over the country, nationally famous or obscure, Anglican, Catholic, non-conformist; 18 other independent schools,[2] some of which have LEA-assisted pupils and are called 'integrated' – this group as a whole includes *quasi* public schools, vocational schools and tiny family-run schools; 7 others are called progressive schools – coeducational and 'free' in style; 15 others are directly maintained by LEAs – some are grammar, some secondary modern, some vocational and some coeducational. All the schools in the sample, except 3 of the state schools, are mainly boarding schools. Of schools in England and Wales, the sample includes 1 in 3 of all Headmasters' Conference schools, 1 in 1·5 of all maintained schools, 1 in 3 of all progressive schools, and 1 in 5 of other independent schools which are secondary in age range and mainly boarding in composition. Of the schools we chose in our sample only two refused to cooperate; the 66 others

1. Three services schools abroad which we have studied have been excluded from these tabulations: we visited 69 schools in all.
2. The distinction between the terms 'public school' and 'independent school' as used in this book should be made clear. Technically, all schools which are not Direct Grant, Voluntary Aided or Controlled, or Maintained, are independent. In this book, 'public school' refers *only* to those boarding schools in membership of the Headmasters' Conference. To be elected to HMC, schools must have a certain academic standing, size of sixth form and university entry, as well as other attributes. Though the 84 boarding HMC schools are varied in many ways, as a group they are remarkably alike in values, style and structure. We use 'independent school' for any recognized independent school not on the HMC. Some of these schools are like HMC ones in structure and values and call themselves 'public schools'. Many others, however, are vastly different in all respects. The 'independent school' category in this book includes a much greater variety of approaches to boarding than does the 'public school' one.

have welcomed our work, giving most generous cooperation and support.

Our methods were these. First we stayed in the schools for as long as possible and lived their life, observing and participating, though never taking up any role except that of a researcher. We lived in most of the schools continuously for a week or more, the shortest stay being three nights, the longest fourteen weeks.

Length of stay	No. of schools
Three nights to one week	25
Up to two weeks	27
Up to three weeks	6
Over three weeks	8
	66

Sometimes two or three of the research team stayed in one school. Throughout the stay we attempted to get to know as much of the school and its life and flavour as possible, recording our own observations systematically. To do this, we remained in the schools day and night, going through the routine, eating school meals, attending chapel, exploring all the extra-curricular activities and sometimes doing a bit of classroom teaching. We have gone on cross-country runs, slogged on Field Days, milked cows at 6 a.m., rowed across a stormy estuary with the boys' mail boat at 5.30 a.m., taken prayers, made Bath buns. We made it clear that we were not staff, that we were not there to 'judge' the school, that no school or individual in it would suffer from our work whatever we found out and – this was and is an absolutely cardinal rule – that nothing told us by one person would ever be identifiably communicated to another, whether it was a governor telling about the head, the head about the staff, or vice versa, or the pupils about the staff or anyone else. In these small communities we rapidly got known, and our continued living inside and appearances at meals, in the classroom and every imaginable activity enabled staff and pupils to test us out, to watch and experiment to see if we really could be trusted. Once this testing period was over, people usually opened up and talked freely about themselves and their experience: we were endlessly entertained by staff, and by the pupils in their common rooms and studies, and frequently invited to witness (we puritanically refused to participate in) illicit activities. Confidential archives, books and documents were usually made available to us by heads, staff and pupils.

Besides our notes of observation on all this, we interviewed according to specially designed interview schedules the head (three hours), a sample of the housemasters (two to three hours each), a sample of other teaching and boarding staff, a sample of the matrons, the doctor or nurse, the chaplain and bursar: 752 staff in the schools were interviewed in this way. With a sample of pupils, structured or focused interviews were also completed, 829 being interviewed. The rest of the work with the children was done in class after they had had a chance to know us and what we were doing. Writing under exam conditions – to guarantee absolute privacy and no collusion – the selected age groups completed standard questionnaires, answered verbal questions, projective tests and so on, ranging in time from three quarters of an hour to three and a half hours. In addition, children were asked to keep a diary of two or three days, recording frankly and privately what happened to them, what they thought and how they felt throughout the day: 410 children kept such diaries, and 9,711 others wrote for us in the other ways, making 10,181 children in all or 53·1 per cent of all the children in the 66 secondary schools. In addition, we are using in this book material written by 1,650 prep-school pupils. As we were not sampling from *all* the children in the school but from defined age groups in each, our response was always over 80 per cent of all the groups sampled. The data is representative of the children, and the schools of the recognized secondary boarding boys' and coeducational schools in this country. The table on page 16 summarizes these facts.

All this mass of data on boarding education has been analysed, and a report on it is being prepared entitled *Boarding Education: A Sociological Study*, which will also include a full account of our methodology, sampling and response.[3] But in analysing the data, we realized that we could never quote even a fraction of the material, particularly the mass of contributions from the children. In our opinion their

3. A complete account of the sociological theory and method will appear in *Manual to the Sociology of the School* to be published by Weidenfeld & Nicolson, Spring 1969.

16 The Hothouse Society

	No.	Type of school	Interviews Staff	Interviews Pupils	No. of children writing	Total nos. in school	Percentage of pupils writing
	15	Maintained	145	165	2,148	3,090	69·5
	18	Independent	186	244	2,414	4,014	60·1
	7	Progressive	88	71	1,336	1,855	72·0
	26	Public Schools	333	349	4,283	10,204	42·0
Total Secondary	66		752	829	10,181	19,163	53·1
	20	Preparatory*	120	220	1,650	2,345	70·4
Total all	86		872	1,049	11,831	21,508	55·0

*Research is still in progress in the sample of 40 prep and primary schools.

writings, as descriptions of an unusual kind of experience, had considerable educational and social value, and frequently had intrinsic quality simply as writing. We decided therefore, while preparing our sociological study, to publish in this companion volume the children's view of their life and assessment of their experience.

This book is not an objective evaluation of boarding education. It is not the whole truth. It presents one consistent viewpoint – that of the children in their writings. No other material has been used in this book – none of our own material or the staff interviews, or the statistics, or, with a few exceptions, our interviews with the children. If the staff and interview material were added, or if our own sociological results and interpretation were given, the picture might be different. The children have their own perspective with its own slant and narrowness: some aspects of school life – change, decision-making, aspects of structure, interrelationships among staff, for example – scarcely appear in their writings, and in some cases, as we shall find, their judgement lacks distance and balance. But incomplete as is their perspective, and raw as is their judgement, it provides a penetration, a sensibility and a freshness of its own. This book unfolds what it is like to be a boarder through the first-hand experience of boys and girls in the schools now, in the belief that what children feel, think, do and undergo is of importance. After all, it is for them that the schools exist: not for the staff or for visiting sociologists.

Only a minute fragment of the writings by the 12,000 children is used here. Every effort has been made to ensure that the extracts are representative of the children, of the schools or situations or responses under discussion. We have rigorously excluded the atypical, even when it means eliminating the interesting, the comic or the picturesque. Anything which is atypical is always presented as atypical. If some of the writings seem sensational, the reader should remember that they are typical of the situations being described, or of that response: we have withheld far more sensational material.

Even so, how do we know the children wrote the truth about themselves? Given the usual conditions, the exam privacy and lack of collusion, the length of time demanded, those children who were uncooperative found it unprofitable to falsify: they simply stopped writing. Such children were less than 0·5 per cent of the sample. It is clear that the vast majority of children wrote frankly and truthfully about themselves – more frankly than we sometimes expected – and felt free enough to put down exactly what they felt about us, which was not always flattering. As we lived in the school and had our own observations and information and the evidence of many others to hand, it was not difficult to tell whether any piece of writing or a private diary was consistent with life in that society. There were virtually no deliberate falsifications, and deliberate exaggerations stand out plainly and again have been excluded from this book. Finally, some of the material we have used was not written for us or for publication at all – it was either private business writing, like the confidential letter books of the heads of house in public schools, or functional writing like the study chits or games notices, or intimate writing of the children themselves like the love letters and poetry. We have their permission to use these spontaneous documents. Our belief – a belief substantiated by the statistical results of our work – is that the experience presented in this book is a faithful expression of the actual life, feelings and attitudes of boarders in English schools.

Certain firm principles have been kept in the presentation, as part of our commitment to the schools and children not to break confidence.

(1) Though we provide an analytical framework, we do not present any views of our own, but we do sometimes refer to the results of our research to be found in the companion volume.

(2) All the material used was voluntarily given us on the explicit understanding that it might be used and published by us.

(3) All the material used was written by boys or girls in the school, with the exception of about five extracts from interviews. We have not drawn on any other of our data for this book.

(4) The vast majority of the writing has been done in recent years: these are schools and children as they are now, not as they were in the past.

(5) No individual person, child or adult, is identifiable – all proper names and descriptions which betray identity have been altered.

(6) No individual school is easily identifiable. Most schools are not referred to by name; a few are given fictitious names, because the school either produces a distinctive style of writing which deserves recognition, or has features which are unusual and should not be thought widespread, as would be the case if they appeared anonymously. Schools are mentioned according to their kind (public, progressive, direct grant, independent, integrated, maintained). *Cognoscenti* who still seek to identify particular schools should remember that in our sample there are relatively many of each type: the extract in question could come from any of them. Some few world-famous schools have distinctive practices or a private language which identify them to an outsider, and in these cases we have altered the text to render them anonymous.

The children's subject is *boarding*, so those aspects of their daily life which may not differ much from that of day schools (such as classroom teaching) are not given prominence. The type of material used alters as the book develops. It opens by illustrating the differences in style between schools by means of sustained extracts from intimate diaries written for us by children; it then analyses the process of starting boarding and the daily life of the boarder by more varied extracts from differing sources; presents the house life and power systems of schools largely through the hitherto never published house books kept by heads of house; illustrates relations with the outside and the inner world of the children from a diversity of sources; describes the problems, the sex-life and impact of single-sex and coeducational schools, partly from questionnaire material and partly from diaries and intimate private writings; and ends by assessing the whole experience from a wide variety of material. Some of the language may seem to the reader coarse, and some of the incidents and sentiments crude. It should be remembered that the writings come mainly from adolescent boys, who themselves come from a vast range of backgrounds, from the poorest homes in Foundation schools to those in the most expensive schools in the kingdom. Such language and incidents are included because they are true to the life of the people and of the school communities from which they come.

2 Differences

Boarding schools differ. This statement is not so devastatingly obvious as it at first seems. For to most people in this country the phrase 'boarding school' conjures up an image of a Victorian public school or prep school, Greyfriars or Eton, something stereotyped, archaic and remote, an image derived ultimately from Billy Bunter or *Tom Brown's Schooldays*. There are 166 public schools but 1,200 other schools with boarders. Great as the influence of the public schools has been, boarding education, it should be stressed, is not confined to them alone. In philosophy, organization and style, there is much greater and more far-reaching diversity among our various kinds of boarding schools, which cater for a minority of 160,000 children in all, than among our day schools, which cater for the majority of seven millions.

Outside the public schools there is a large miscellaneous group of secondary schools which we shall call independent, varying widely in approach. Among them is a small but influential band of 'progressive' schools, always coeducational, and trying to operate with more democratic forms and with less external pressures and restrictions on their pupils than more conventional schools. Equally small but equally distinctive is the small band of state boarding schools, run by local authorities and often with an ethos very much of their own: new styles of boarding are being nurtured in some of them. Yet other schools, which we will call integrated, have close associations with the state either through an intake of local-authority-financed pupils or because their charitable endowments enable them to take in numbers of pupils irrespective of the parents' capacity to pay the full fees. Among these are many independent schools, half a dozen public schools, and direct-grant schools. Finally, at the junior level, are 400 or so prep schools

Differences 21

with over 60,000 boarders, most of whom go on to public schools. The prep schools enjoy or suffer from the most inflexible and out-of-date public reputation of all: we have found among them, once again, considerable diversity in standards, operation and even aims.

As the book proceeds, the differences between kinds of school will become more clear, more subtle, more familiar. In this chapter a range of schools is being introduced in rapid succession by fragments of their pupils' lives, to bring home the variety, the richness, the sometimes amazing, even shocking contrasts which exist in this tiny part of our educational system.

To provide a basis for comparison, we start deliberately at an extreme: the harsh life at one independent school captured in the crude, vivid and poignant words of one typical boy's diary. The school we shall call Beauchamp Manor. Filling a bright modern building, it is not a public school but aspires to become one. It is a school where less bright boys who failed to get into public schools are being put through a stiff academic course, a place where life is an incessant round of organized activity from the compulsory morning run and cold shower to bedtime, where thirty-seven bells are rung each day to direct the boys what to do, and where rules, uniform and location isolate everyone from the world outside. The pressures and frustration of this regime generate an explosive, violent and bitter response. Several other schools in England are like this, though by no means most independent or public schools are similar: we start with the atypical to enable us to establish the norm later on. Brian Seymour, typical of many contributors from this school, sums up its particular life, the quality of response it breeds and some of the deeper anxieties of boarders like him everywhere, on one November day. He is sixteen and a half.

Wake up at 7.25 Aaah! Bloody morning run in 5 minutes. Got a full bladder, but I don't think there's time for a pee.

Clang clang clangclangclangclang.

5 more seconds then up. I'm in a curious state of non-thought; everything going too fast.

Out of the door – will it be cold, raining? Yes, both. Lovely pink-grey sky; ah, there's Tim. 'Wotcher!' Run round together; get a move on you bugger, it's cold; but loyal ties of friendship compel me to run with him. Into the shower, then out, upstairs. Still the brain's numb. Dress and downstairs.

Open the study door – surge of friend-feeling as I see Derek in the arm-chair. Into breakfast and cramming down toast and milk without thought at all. Out and upstairs to make bed; discuss homosexuality with Mark thinking: silly old stilted bugger, can't you see my point of view? Shockthought: do I really like Mark? Yes. Now the brain starts to thaw out as you sit in your study waiting for Chapel. Will the postman come before the bell? Perhaps there'll be one from my darling Penny. Penny has been blown up by separation and longing into a goddess. Reveries about last holidays and the party where I met her. Long, long slim legs in silk, and fingers intertwined in mine. Lovely word 'inter-twined', think of it draw it out in-ter-twined aaaaaaah!

The Bell; Oh fuck, now for twenty minutes of the chaplain. Into chapel with hands in pockets with Derek and Rob: Sit. Talk. Get dirty looks from Johnson, who's a head of house. Cor. Awesome. Bugger off, what I'm saying's important to me. Sing hymn without really concentrating. Sit. Listen. Pray; but if you asked me what had been said I couldn't tell you. Out of chapel.

Now the full shag begins to hit you. O god – sorry, you correct yourself, O God – 4 bloody lessons in a row. You feel very tired 'cos you never get enough sleep. Collect your books O where's my pen? Can't find the sodding pen. *Where's* my pen? Suddenly for very little reason you want to cry; don't be silly you can't cry. Up to lessons. Sit in the form-room. It's Maxwell's french first. O bugger I didn't do his test and there's Henry Patison feeling smug and asking everyone to test him 'cos *he* knows it all and he's glorying in the fear of everyone who hasn't prepared it, feeling goodygood. Imagine having him pegged out, with his legs open and kicking till his balls are a mass of – here's Maxwell, the master. You feel surprised at the vicious intensity of your own thoughts. 40 minutes pass. You're not really working – you know you're not going to pass your 'A' levels 'cos you just fritted away your time feeling I can't work there's no incentive. I wonder what Penny's doing now? I want a motorbike only the silly sod of a father I've got won't give me it. No he's not a silly sod really, be loyal. Christ Monday's are a shag you can only look forward to the oasis of your private study period sleep on thoughts and black bitter coffee time. O god – God – Maxwell's asked me a question. I'm going red, sweating there's dead silence he says 'What does it mean, Seymour?' ah shit that's not going to help you sod, hey Clark what did he say I can't ask you aloud but can't you feel my need? Clark sits. They all sit. Shocked falsely at my inability to answer. I'm bright red oh Christ say what the word was you bastard; then I can find it and guess. 'What does "acceuillir" mean, Seymour?' Thank God I know that already. Attention switches off me. Bell.

God will there be any of the pretty boys outside; if I look at the pretty boys I always blush. Am I queer? I ask myself this 1,000 times; I don't think so; I mean the thought of actually buggering a little boy is repulsive to me but they're just a substitute, something pretty to look at when there are no girls around. Collect up books and go outside yes there's Brightwell; quick avert eyes god he's *so* like a girl you're going red; don't don't don't screams your brain. Two more lessons pass in a daze what shitty SHITTY weather gray rain and mist why the hell was I born?

Bell. Down to break and you can hardly walk 'cos of a wave of tiredness that almost knocks you off your feet. Into the study ah god – God – there's Mark Dover; I can't STAND him but obviously shall have to as he's in our set. Here's a knock – postman? Yes. '2 for you, Seymour'. That means one from Mum and one from PENNY! Read Mum's first, this is the one saving link with the sane world outside. Lots of news, a good letter, mental thanks to Mum. Now, heart beats increase, rip open the envelope. How will she start? 'My darling Chris' SHITTTTTTTTT! Fab! Read it, you're going red but who cares a tup-penny bugger. What a letter! Ending coming up don't look or you'll spoil it for yourself 'My love, Penny'. My love MY love. Possessive and submissive. XXX. What a girl! Look out of the window. Wet green grass and a cold gray sky. Bump! Down to earth. Bell.

Oh god – God – the Chaplain's lesson. This is s'posed to be Divinity but it's just 40 minutes ballsing about his previous life. Goes quickly in thought and dreaming. Now, at last, a private study.

Sit in the armchair with a sigh, got some work but can't be buggered to do it. Here's Derek good. Talk with him on every imaginable subject. Thank Christ here's someone who can understand my point of view. Mentally we're alike. It's almost a love (but not sexual, reassure myself) between us. Bell. Pick up guitar wonder what sort of a day I'll have after lunch. Wish I was home.

Lunch. Cram food down. Discuss homosexuality with the world at large. Every buggers laughing 'cept for Derek and Rob. The silly fools can't understand, they all think I'm queer. Let them I don't give a fish's tit but deep inside I do care. After lunch look at the Games board what am I doing? Cross country run shitshitshit. Rest. Now downstairs. Another P.S. Got to work but I can't can't. Talk with Derek again but he wants to read; momentary irritation but never mind I can do my work. I try, but mind slips off it and I idle along with a gray mind half-thinking. That's how I shall always remember this dump – gray. Bell god – God – already? Up to Wilson's classroom, here comes the test. God I can't answer any of these I wish I'd done the work but I know I won't it'll be the same tomorrow. Always the same. The routine's invariable so boring – wake up, you've missed two questions. Now, mark it. Despair grows. Impossible impossible. 4 out of 25. O Christ how am I going to tell him. Red. '4 Sir'. God, He's understanding just looks at me but I know I'm going to my housemaster tonight for this. The black mood sets in.

Bell, down to change for run, 'Off games, Bodge?' (Bodge's me!) 'No'. 'I am'. FUCK. No Rob, no Derek. Round run in solitude part sweat heat. Wish I was out of this goddam hole. Showers are cold and there's too many people little boy holding his hands over his crotch poor little bugger wishing he had a bush. Out. No towel. Borrow Rob's and hope he won't mind but I bet he will, another shockthought do I like Rob? Yes, think of when you went home with him. There was a bond between you there.

Up to study. 'Time, Rob?' Slow slow hurry up you bugger. 'Two and a half minutes to five' That already. It's now raining and cold gray mist everywhere. You're in a real mood. Look. round. You can see Rob is as well. He catches your eye, smiles, knowing what's in your brain. You wish you could smash something. Bell. Bell. Bell.

Bell. Bell. Bell. Prep, haze, tipping chair back. *Got* to work. You don't. Fool with Derek, go mad: to let off steam. You can see Rob's suffering, wonder if he wants to join in? No, don't think so but we'd better stop. Think. Haze. God I want a drag. Drink. Freedom. PENN . . . Bell.

Supper. In with Derek and Rob. Cram the slush, uninterested. 'God I wouldn't give this shit to my pig', but you haven't got a pig anyway the swearings half-hearted, you're too floppy and lethargic to do anything but sit and 'ferment' as Derek says with his odd knack of getting the right word. Bell. Third prep. Bell. 'Sling something on to vibrate the needle' Derek says biting his fist, eyes screwed up. Rolling Stones; Searchers; Moonlight Sonata. The Moonlight really lifts you out of school and carries you away.

Door opens. 'Housemaster wants you'. Oh Christ here goes. Red. Heart-beat. Along to the study fearfear. 'Come in'. Talks about your work. Very severe. You give the appropriate softsoap answers, but don't really listen. You don't attend. Notice little things about him. Doesn't shave in the cleft of his chin. One eyebrow's fractionally higher than t'other. 'Yes sir I'll do better,' don't hit me. Bugger. Shall I tell him everything; an urge to let all the frustration and boredom flow out but the old cunt wouldn't understand. 'Yes, sir, I'll be a good boy sir, thank you sir, goodnight sir', but it's no use you won't do a fucking thing about it.

Bell. Up to bed. Last burst of companionship. 'Night, Dick. Night Rob. Night Derek' . . . 'Night Andrew'. Up to bed. Can't even be shagged to wash. Everyone else is. 'God you filthy pig'. 'Piss off' but he's right you know. Lights out. Into bathroom for conference with Mark. Twenty minutes of semi-listening to him about his girl friend, god – God – you're boring but I know you need to tell. So I fake interest, sometimes genuine. At last into bed. Shall I have a flog? No, too tired turn over thinking, wishing frustrated and then merciful release to sleep.

Meanwhile, in that same autumn, boys in other, more typical schools were penning their diaries: this time in full public schools. As these schools will figure largely in later chapters we confine ourselves here to three extracts from typical diaries.

26   The Hothouse Society

The first, by an eighteen-year-old prefect, comes from a well-known school near London. Cool, objective, impersonal, its very style exemplifies some public-school virtues. But it also quietly and succinctly introduces to some of the key features of these schools: the hierarchy among pupils and staff, the wide power and responsibility of senior boys (the prefects in this one actually being known as 'staff'), the stress on games, on the house unit and house life, the compulsory rituals of chapel, prayers and combined cadet force, the gregariousness and lack of privacy, the external formality of staff–pupil relations (the preordained appearances of the house tutor) accompanied by the quiet vigilance of the masters, the Conservative political tone, the high level of order and discipline and the stress on achievement at both work and play.

7.10 a.m. Get woken by a fellow in my dormitory by a sharp jab in the kidneys, it being one of his unofficial functions to wake me so as I can lie awake and meditate. Fag rings second bell – supposed to wake everyone up, (first bell having been rung at 7.00 by fag walking along a 100 yard stone corridor ringing hand-bell and calling 'first-bell'). Finally decide to get up and face the elements, inwardly cursing at having to get up so early.

Sit with another prefect and house tutor at the end of a table of over 20 boys. I prefer to read *The Times* so I let someone else dish out corn flakes etc. House tutor arrives for breakfast, and after returning good morning greeting relapses into his *Daily Telegraph*. Breakfast continues its pedantic course, conversation solely in monosyllables. Tutor says grace, I hastily down a last cup of tea and make for the exit before the 'rabble'. Proceed to make bed and converse with members of dormitory about coming election and Conservatives prospects, all of us being of a Conservative nature.

Downstairs to find a queue of a dozen people outside study waiting to pay their fines for leaving their common room in a mess. After having sorted them out, all members of the study eagerly wait for the post. Check up that fags have cleared up the dustbin area outside house, find that it has snowed during the night and retreat into study, which is still not warm.

8.30. Chapel, line up, proceed to late Victorian monstrosity for five minutes singing, five minutes listening to lesson and five minutes praying.

Back to house to collect books for first three lessons, discover I have double free, and trot off to the Library, where a dozen frozen individuals are huddled around coal fire. Custodian arrives to see that we are all working, no one is, but things settle down by 9.15. End of spell in the Library and I depart for economics.

11.00. Dart back to House to obtain one of the few mugs available for coffee, then took off to the tuck shop for some chicken rolls and more coffee; converse with other prefects in an exclusive room off the side of tuck shop. Back to house and prepare for two lessons of History, where I take notes and try unsuccessfully to fall asleep . . .

Lunch starts, and I dish out 'kangaroo' meat to table, tutor enters, takes one look at lunch, mutters something and departs hurriedly; he does not come back. End of lunch, again a quick exit is made and I collect some money from tutor, who safe-keeps everyones' money.

Off to 'quiet room' to read daily newspapers, magazines and punish boy for not observing silence.

Go around common-rooms and verbally force juniors to go on a cross-country run. Many complaints and excuses but they are of no avail. Don scarf and coat and go off to support senior house hockey, chat to hockey master on the way who talks about the elections.

Hockey finally finishes and everyone rushes back to house to de-freeze. Many depart to tuck shop to socialize, however I prefer to return to study, listen to records and catch up on some work.

Walk up to village post-office to obtain stamps, which also serves as a general store, so I decide to buy some sausages and packed bacon.

Change for a quick game of squash before tea.

6.40. I have to take prep in the senior common room in the House which has about 20 people in it. After a few questions are asked, absolute silence is maintained, usually, until prayers at 8.15. All prefects read the lesson for prayers in rotation, and I read an extract from Peter Dominic's book. *Britain and the Devil*, (Dominic being an old boy of the house), tutor says prayers and a few notices are announced. Everyone has snacks afterwards and one fills in time until 9.00 by cooking in fag's kitchen, working etc. I have to go into a senior study to tell them to turn their gramophone down as it can be heard at the other end of the corridor. Prep continues until 9.40.

Everyone then goes to bed except for prefects, commonly known as 'staff'. We socialize and listen to records, a few of us go around some of the dormitories and fraternize with the occupants until 10.30 when they are all told to be quiet. 10.45 Tutor is seen coming down corridor, flashing his torch, so I hurry off to bed.

From the other side of London, from one of the many public schools in the gin-and-tonic belt, comes another diary. It describes a very similar pattern of life: hard work, concern with values ('getting the most out of life' from the tutor), hierarchy, routine, games, a little of sex, and the rituals of religion. But this one comes not from the perspective of an Olympian prefect but that of a fifteen-year-old boy, typically self-conscious and slightly disaffected. The day starts with work, a touch of hierarchy and the pressures caused by lack of privacy on a sensitive boy.

Work never stops. Some people get up at 6 o-clock to work but today I am alright. By half past seven many people are beginning to say how much they detest this place and the work involved. Then a boy yells out 'five minutes to the bell'. You now have six minutes to dress and get down to breakfast, some people lie on in bed for a few minutes, I am one of them, and leave themselves too little time in which to comfortably dress. When the bell goes before they expect, they all (with a few exceptions) blame the duty fag. Everyone is so self centred and petty. One of the main troubles with dormitories is that one is forced to sleep in the close proximity of other boys some of whom are younger (literally). In my case most of them are younger mentally. The others enjoy 'jolly' chats in the evenings and 'very jolly' mobs on Sunday mornings. I hope that I will move into a cubicle next term, where I need only visit and be visited by the people I want.

It proceeds with routine and religion, which tend to get confused with each other.

Then we are back in the rush. Tidy your study, have it inspected, clean your shoes, do this do that. It all seems so futile. Then I am walking to chapel. I am waiting for the service to start. We sang some hymn, but the tune was not strong enough and hardly any sound came from our block at all, I cannot even remember what number it was. The lesson comes to an end and I almost stand up by mistake, my mind is so far away. I do not bother to open the school song book. I have heard it all before. Then the organ starts playing and we move slowly out.

Lessons follow and produce the same mixed reactions as in any kind of pupil. But lunch is more characteristic of the public school. We see the formality and informality of staff–pupil relations, feel the stress on 'effort' and values and glimpse a little sexual underlife:

Then it is lunch. The familiar greasy fish and chips smell greets you as you wait outside the dining room, engaged in polite 'small talk'. The bell goes and in we all troop. Then come the Prees then the senior house tutor with a loud 'click-clack click-clack'. One presumes that he wears those shoes to make himself look silly. But then he probably never thinks of anything like that, he is too busy worrying whether people are working to their utmost, getting the most out of life, doing well at games, having 'super' ideas and are not smoking or drinking or anything sinful like that. The funny thing is that no one gives a damn about him! The junior house tutor is rather different, he too cares about you and is pretty strict, but he doesn't snoop around and he has a strong and likeable personality. The lunchtime conversation is much the same as usual revolving round the morning dissection session (sickening!), the chemistry certain people are doing, music, homosexuality (feigned) that exceedingly pretty boy on the junior table in particular. Then there is the usual struggle over the peas, or any other rare commodity.

The day continues with games, work, culture and religion – a typical mixture – and ends with a warm flush of companionship.

After lunch I went to big school and read the magazines for a while and then went to play fives. This was a junior house match. I am hopeless and I lost hands down, the showers were cold, the final insult. I went up to the library for a few minutes and then to the music room for half an hour, most of which was spent talking to a friend, we talk mainly about music, we go back to his cubicle where the conversation moves on to cathedrals and places. Then I work for a while until tea. After tea we do little until prep when we are 'supposed' to work, some of the time I spend reading up my corps manuals for mock proficiency tests, they are hilariously funny in their seriousness. Then there is the awesome ritual of house prayers, it is a dismal hymn with the headmaster doing a solo in the first verse. Off to the senior house tutor to get permission to do second prep. 'Yes, certainly, with a will,' beaming.

Then in second prep there is a social with Tom, then Peter then both together, then in the bathroom with Peter and then to bed exhausted but reasonably happy.

Our final public-school diary was penned at a very well-known school on a summer's day clouded only by impending 'A' level. This time the boy is a seventeen-year-old prefect, in charge of games in the house. The now familiar lineaments of the public school reappear: but this time modified by features unique to this school and a few others: maids to look after the boys, study/bedrooms, a lesson before breakfast, the ritual cooked tea in boys' own rooms, the long stretches of free time in which the pupils are left to work or not at their own discretion. Our boy is contented and highly committed to his school.

'Good morning, Mr Berkley', says the boys'-maid.

The curtains open, and I am awoken by a blaze of sunlight. It is seven o'clock and I vaguely remember that I have early school (lesson) in half an hour; so when 'the man on the radio' informs me that it is 7.20, I arise. Unshaved, unwashed, and tired, very tired – I struggle along the road to my physics-room. Work at 7.30 a.m. is bad enough at any time, and physics-early-school tends to be ultra-difficult because my beak (master) is not very startling. Somehow I manage to keep one eye open but by eight o'clock my nose has smelt the eggs and bacon in the house over the road, and immediately this puts the master in a difficult position. How can he keep our interest and attention? Some succeed. Some fail – 75% fail.

Breakfast passes without any words being spoken. We are still recovering from early school. By the time I arrive at my room after breakfast, it has been tidied by my two young fags, and when they have left I have over an hour in which to amuse myself. Today I got down to some serious A-level work, but it would not be uncommon for me to have to go and talk to a few boys about their games, and perhaps I would have to organize a cricket game.

Chapel follows at ten. The traditional service consists of one psalm, one hymn, and one lesson, but this system has been changed recently and now the chapel services have been varied to the benefit of everybody.

As a boy rises to the top of the school he will be required to do unsupervised work in his room/study. This morning I had such a 'reading school' and I found it a marvellous opportunity to catch up on some revision, although I must admit that in not-so-pressing moments I have found such a time a marvellous opportunity to catch up on the reading of the morning paper. The 25-minute break between schools allows me to meet my friends for a chat upstairs, where the prefects have their own sitting room. Coffee and toast is laid on by a well-meaning boys' maid, and everybody finds that the twenty-five minutes is not long enough. Everything is done at the double. 'What's the time Martin?' 'Half past'. 'Blast, I'm late'.

After an hour and a half of strenuous chemistry, I was ready for a rest, and I got this during lunch and during the hour that followed before afternoon schools. Two 45-minute periods began at three o'clock.

From 4.30 until 8.00, I was free to do as I pleased. A cooked tea in the study took up nearly an hour, but then it was back to work. It is impossible to work for hours on end, so at seven I went round to visit the Dame (matron) in another house, whom I know particularly well from my private school and she (as I had hoped) invited me to look at her television which is a very rare luxury here. Supper and prayers conducted by the house master followed in quick time at 8.00 and 8.30 and then I was free to visit boys in the house, who by this time have to be in their rooms. This didn't take long this evening, and when I put my pen down, I will be back with my books.

Today has been a typical day in that I have had all the ingredients of school life except possibly one – games. House nets were organized this evening but games do not really get under way until the afternoons of a half-holiday.

From the great boys' public school we turn to the coeducational progressive schools, those places where:

> People think you're crazy going to this school and think you get raped every day and walk round with topless dresses also they think you are snobs.
> *Girl, fifteen, progressive school*

These schools deserve attention as they are less well known than public schools or known only by caricature, though they are now increasingly sought after and influential. They are coeducational, though there are other independent and state coeducational boarding schools which would not be placed in the 'progressive' group. Their stress is less on an absolute level of academic and social achievement than the unfettered development of personality at its own pace. External pressures and rules are kept low, considerable freedom and self-direction allowed and democratic machinery of authority and informal staff–pupil relations are encouraged. Women and pets play important roles in the child's emotional and pastoral development, and creative subjects have as high a status as the academic ones. The schools are secular, non-denominational or Quaker, and vary very much in their degree of 'progressiveness' or permissiveness. The following characteristic snatches illustrate some of these features.

First a fourteen-year-old girl at a relatively regulated coeducational school:

> The freedom is marvellous. We can go down town just by signing up. We watch tele sometimes and go swimming. On the weekends we are allowed to go to cinemas and fairs. Everyone is friendly on the whole and in the houses after school we have great fun in the Garden

where everyone joins in including the house father. We can call the staff by their first names and you can talk to them and they can join in with the children more. Obviously some staff are not popular. In summer you can have lessons outside. One of the best things is the fact that you can wear any clothes you like except for trousers for the girls (within reason) and on the weekend we can wear jeans. We can go Youth hostelling on the weekends and for long walks, besides learning we enjoy ourselves. We can wear any jewelry. There is a great mixture of people to meet and talk and there is a difference between day and boarders. The day have less fun than the boarders on the whole I would think, unless they had other friends out of school. There is too much stealing and breaking of windows and things like that but I suppose that happens everywhere today. People take advantage of the freedom we have here and then the staff have to make unnecessary rules.

Next a group of children from another school describe aspects of its ethos:

Don't call the staff 'miss' or 'sir' it flusters them apart from the fact that everyone will laugh. Social life comes first. Don't talk about work, talk about people, politics, anything else.

Boy, thirteen, progressive school

The many activities which go on, music, art, pottery, cooking, sewing, woodwork, metalwork, engineering, outdoor work, trampolining, etc. make the place always interesting. Also the less intellectual activities, dancing, films, plays and general enjoyment make life less like boarding school.

Although people are from well to do homes, I don't think we're in the least bit snobbish towards other schools. This term we had six people from the Bethnal Green secondary mod. We got on marvellously.

This place is great! Don't forget it.

Girl, sixteen, same school

Boys and girls here are fond of saying 'Up the workers and down the filthy capitalists', but this is, I feel, often out of a wish to be different rather than from a genuine wish to help the poor.

Boy, seventeen, same school

Somebody's whipped all the toast from top – so we pick holes in the bread and flick it at the prefects on the table next door – *we* won't have prefects when our age group is at the top of the school. We'll all refuse – a monitor system should be better – why should anyone be placed any higher than anyone else anyway?

Girl, fifteen, same school

A similar snatch follows from another school:

We had lovely baked beans and horrid toast. After breakfast I went up the hill to feed the pigs. We decided to take a long time and miss assembly we sat in the changing rooms and waited for them to come out then we went up to the form room. I read my book through morning school and finished it. I couldn't understand the ending it sounded a bit queer. We had fish for dinner it was awful. Glenda tipped her water over me and I got my skirt wet. We had french then double science it was great fun we were burning paper and spills on the bunsen.

Girl, thirteen, progressive school

Finally, a critical but perceptive footnote on the freedom at such schools:

There are some good things – The freedom, the relaxed atmosphere, strictly phoney but it's what everyone thinks. I have enjoyed myself a lot here at times. I'm glad it's not strict and that you can miss a class without too much trouble.

Boy, sixteen, progressive school

Our first serious glimpse of the progressive school comes from one with a reputation for being one of the most advanced, that is least concerned with externally imposed rules and regulations. We shall call it Stanton. Garry's diary (he was seventeen and a half) captures much of its essence: the apparently free pattern of life, casual and frank relations between the pupils and between the pupils and staff, an underlying anxiety about work, distinctive dress (almost an unofficial uniform), sudden bursts of spontaneous organization ('SESSION!' – a spontaneous evening dance), house *mothers* as pastoral agents, private bedsitters for everyone, a slight selfconsciousness about being a Stantonian.

Old Ted Pickering is actually the one who rings the bell at 7.30. He goes upstairs and downstairs in every house along the corridor and wakes up maybe twenty people altogether when he should wake up the whole school. But the bell usually takes quite a prominent spot in our morning dreams, and one can suppose that tradition is what makes Ted Pickering ring that bell at 7.30.

At 8.00 or so the few people who have woken up get their grams going (loud) and this is what really wakes people up. So at ten past eight approximately, a crowd of zombie-looking Stantonians cross a very dead courtyard and proceed to breakfast. So there's cornflakes, coffee, toast and sometimes a treat such as tomatoes on toast. But its very quiet at breakfast. No-one talks (fear of bad breath? mental inability?) No-one needs to talk. At 8.20 the doors of the kitchen close and the latecomer is doomed to go through an unbearable empty morning. But its summertime. The late guy can always find some leftover piece of toast or something.

8.45. Everyone's supposedly made their bed. The useful work bosses (pupils actually) go to every room, get everyone out there to do some work, sweeping or washing dishes or scavenging or something. But there is some sort of respect (if distant) between U.W. bosses and the U.W.'s.

9.15. Yes, we *do* go to classes. This morning its double English with Janet and we'll be doing bloody Sweeney Todd ('just to taste some Victoriana' she says), and bloody Pat will get the star part as usual and as usual will be very funny trying (in vain) to be humerous, and then Janet will tell us some background, some facts (actually she's young *and* enthusiastic, and if I may venture forth – INTERESTING!), and then we'll have an endless discussion on the matter and we'll go sailing away from the subject, but who cares, it's all culture and this *is* Stanton. And lots of last week's Shakespeare, bits of this week's Owen and Eliot.

And then a free period. So hurry up and do your prep before French. Put a Keep Out notice on your door but it doesn't seem to help so every ten minutes someone else comes in. So hop to the library and get it all down.

11.10. Break – tea, marmite sandwich, jam sandwich, borrow a fag 'till tomorrow' (eternal phrase).

11.30. In to double french with Maurice. Becket, Anouilh – double boredom – drone on 'Your turn' 'Eh?', 'Your turn' 'Page sixty two', 'Oh, bugger!', etc. Will one o'clock ever reach us? Twenty-to one, 'page sixty eight!', Quarter-to one, 'page seventy', Ten-to one, 'page seventy three!', 'line twenty one', five-to-one.

Bell – god – thank god.

1.00. Steak and kidney pudding, new potatoes, very clean water. 'Remember Tenors 1.15'.

1.15. 'All right, who's going to sing the solo at the concert? You're flat. A bit louder. If you don't stop mucking about, we won't get anywhere. Watch that F, you're flat.'

1.45. Classes: biology with Phil.

Proximal convuluted tubule; stomata; cortex, xylem; medulla...

'Phil, but if photosynthesis takes place in the...'

'I've just told you'.

'But surely its impossible for the stomata to...'

'Phil, for God's sake!'

'Radially symmetrical!'

'You remember the *Spirogyra* (capital letter; underline genus; species and how it reproduced in...'

'Phil its time'.

'You owe me a prep dear boy'.

'All right Philly, I'll have it in by suppertime'.

4.0. Tea – jam sandwich – broken plastic spoon. 'Could you clear up that table please?'

Out to Stanbury to get my shoes fixed, get some salami, look in the bookshop, look in the record shop. Depression. I've seen this main street so many bloody times. So secluded, insignificant, tiny, ugly. But its Barsetshire and this *is* Stanton.

Biology prep by seven.

7.00. 'Phil, I don't have time to do the prep, but I'll get it in by tomorrow'.

SUPPER: Eggs, sausages, chips, H.P. Ketchup. TASTY. 'Any seconds, please?'

At the dinner table – 'Meg was so stuuuuuupid today. Did you hear what Sara said about her?' Gossip, anecdotes, nasties, slips.

As the long hair, the pink shirts, the purple ties dip into the Krystal Ketchup, into the bowls of beans (on toast) of steaming stuck spaghetti.

As the tight jeans, the bare feet, the bright T-shirts, the dirty socks rush through a bright summer evening courtyard.

Where they are talking, discussing, arguing with a teacher whether or not free love should sprout, whether or not we should keep the television, whether Mike (the Head) should do this or that, someone throws a ball in the courtyard.

'Will you fuck off I'm trying to work . . .'

Temper . . .

Biros work frantically before the exams, the library's silence shattered by a scream in the courtyard:

'SESSION!'

The gramophone in the bank room yelling Rolling Stones. Inhibitions being lost in the dancing, in the frantic pulsations to the rhythm which holds us all together until its

10.00. House mother: 'Are you in your room?'

'Yeh'.

'Staying in? Mm?'

'Yes, thank you'.

'Goodnight'.

'Yes'.

And where does exhaustion come from? But its there, and you can't remember your head going down into the pillow and . . .

At 7.30 Ted Pickering's bell . . .

A girl of the same age provides a more critical, deeper and more personal insight into Stanton life, and into the complexities and abrupt changes of mood of adolescents in any boarding school:

I am woken up by 'radio Stanton', it is the only thing that makes waking up bearable. After breakfast I wait for the post. Letters mean a hell of a lot, they change the whole day. At my last boarding school the rush for the post was the same. If I haven't got a letter I might read somebody else's (with their permission) and that is almost as good.

Useful work doesn't take long. I think if I had to criticize the school I would criticize the selfishness of many of the people in it. It shows in the way the common room is left in a mess after people have watched television. It's laziness but that is selfishness I suppose.

The classes are interesting on the whole, because they are informal. This makes a great difference. Before I came here I went to a strict and very conventional girls' boarding school. Coming here was very difficult, but I like it here. The classes at my last school were formal. About thirty girls in one class, the staff were all uninspiring, catty spinsters. Here the staff are interesting people as well as good teachers and I don't find myself day-dreaming through all my classes which is apt to happen.

After classes I might go down to the teashop or sit and talk in somebody's room. Having single rooms is essential. Boarding is hell if there is no privacy. I might spend hours just pottering round my room doing things like moving the furniture around or putting up new pictures. Supper is the most chaotic meal. When the kitchen doors are open there is a stampede and the boys get in first, on the whole. Co-education is also essential, I think. If I have children, and I hope I have twelve, I will certainly send them to a mixed school. If I marry a millionaire I shall send them here. At supper everybody is arguing about how much work they've done, how much pocket money they get. Nobody listens to anybody else, but it doesn't matter.

After supper I join people in the courtyard. Some boys are playing football and there are a group of people sitting outside a window, watching. I watch too for a bit but soon I get restless and go indoors. I am beginning to get depressed. I go up to my room and try and work but I don't feel like staying in the same place. In the room opposite I can hear several people talking loudly and laughing. I would like to go in but haven't quite got the courage. It takes a lot of courage to go into a room full of people. I wander over to Cedar House. Everybody seems to be depressed. In one room five of my friends sit smoking and staring into space. I go in and they don't notice. After a bit they become livelier and we go off to find some fabulous boy! They eventually go to watch television and I go to the house-mothers room. It's warm in there and people are being amusing. The atmosphere is home-like and my depression begins to fade.

At ten o'clock I go upstairs. There are a group of people in the corridor. Gramophones are playing, people are flirting and fighting. One of the boys pays me a compliment and I suddenly wonder why I was ever depressed. This is something one can't get at home. This atmosphere – I can't describe it. Everything is warm, there are people one's own age around, but one has one's own room. This atmosphere I will hate leaving. The housemother comes up because we are making a noise; we disperse to our separate rooms. I go to sleep to the noise of 'Radio Stanton'.

One final comment from yet another school concludes this preliminary glimpse of progressive schools: a look at their distinctive staff–pupil relationships or pastoral care:

One of the most vital aspects of life here is the easy relationship between staff and pupils. We can call them by their Christian names and laugh openly at them if they make mistakes in class and they don't mind. Most staff are very young or have been here for years and years and this is important because those who are young are generally on our wave length and understand the extreme changes in our work and social life.

I have a marvelous tutor and if I can't and don't want to work he leaves me alone but if I can't work but want to, he'll listen, sympathize or say I'm wrong and he will help me. We talk a lot about everyday things but not about boyfriends although we do talk about home troubles. He knows I sometimes go drinking but he doesn't say much because he knows that I am fairly sensible and don't go just to get drunk.

You should never tell staff that you have been drinking or sleeping with someone because they will tell on you and the less they know about your social habits the better although one is often tempted to tell them because you feel they would understand.

Girl, seventeen, progressive school

Not all coeducational schools belong to the 'progressive' group, though they may allow more latitude than many single-sex schools. By way of illustration and light relief, here is the afternoon of a hulking hockey girl aged sixteen at such a coeducational school: we shall call her Brenda. This breathless gem of feminine cattiness and extroversion captures the informal out-of-class life and relationships of the pupils in a small, moderately free school in the country:

12.45. Just left Spencer Millham (one of research team) – he's quite a sweety-pops, good dress sense – Butch (my boyfriend) in a hurry to go, flipping impatience – rushed of to relieve himself then when I was ready to go decided there was time for a good necking session – after that it took five minutes to respectablize me – on the way down to lunch.

A fifth former asked me what games I was doing, swimming netball, or hockey. After a rather futile argument in which she persisted that I must play one of them, I insisted that she could go and screw herself, I managed to persuade her that I could not be found – which is the perfect excuse all round! After she'd gone, we tripped over Crosling, also in 5th form but a weedy little drip who's nick name is 'piss-pants' for obvious reasons – christ he's older than me too – ugh how pathetic can people be!

1.00. Stew, mash, carrots for lunch, quite disgusting, conversation flared over dying, work, the bomb, the pill, sociology, G.C.E. and work once more, me being at the top of the table, I've got Helen on one side, who is always willing to please but sickenly nondescript and characterless (and thats putting it tres kindly) then there is Diana ont'other side whos terribly good looking and a born introvert – so I can't really admit to having an extra-ordinary luncheon – still Apple pie for pudding so I stuffed myself on it.

1.45. Came up hill with Maxie and Buna (a coloured girl) whose getting on my pip, she's so infuriating, and its *not* because she's coloured – its because she's her and I'm me, and she's stupid. Up at the House, I found Janie taking over my job as House Leader, and bossing Juniors into entering for the Eistedffod. Butch saved her life by entering then, so I left her to stuff. After a rumpus caused by Butch trying to be romantic when I was trying to balance on a desk and fix my bra, we settled to work, not much done with both of us on same chair though! This lesson was P.S. (private study) near the end Simon (Head boy) and girls came in, we talked about Valentines decorations until Tania got narked at Simon and they had a row up! Tan was in the wrong and I've'd entered the fight just to prove her wrong only s'morning I promised Butch to reform and be nice to the world en masse.

To top this, Mick wandered in with the news that Janie and Buna were having one hell of a cat fight in the other room – I'm inclined to support Buna there, then neither of them inspire me to the heights but, Janie is such a loud, lying bigheaded prostitute and she smells, and she's got dyed hair and it seems to me that she's just dirt right throu' so Buna became definately preferable. Today's been rather grumpy so I'll rekon I'll sit behind the desk and read peacefully for the next 80 minutes and let life cool off a bit – I do hope this scrawl is legible . . .

4.00 – end of school, had to hang around for ages, waiting for Butch to come in from games, whilst Tan got more and more impatient when he came at last – we were together the long-time of ½ minute – a quick snog (I loathe that word, but its better than 'a kiss and a cuddle' which sounds terribly cissy) then Tan dragged me down to collect some money to spend at Brown's shop. In our Common Room we discovered that some more food had been stolen – this time a tin of salmon – this makes me really cross, but even when we report it like we did that last 4–5 times it occurred – what've they done? – the precise amount of *Nowt* – so whats the use – thieving seems to be the main hobby of some people round here.

Anyway, we looked for Miss Rider and had a quick sneak at the post too, to see if there was a letter for either of us, then wandered up to Browns. They must think us hell of a Guts – after buying an enormous tin of fruit, cream, Carnation, Mars, nougat, butter, cream crackers – I don't blame them – on the way down again we decided to make this a stinginess week – *not* giving stuff to anyone even if they ask! because we're both sick of giving away our food and getting nothing at all in return – especially when certain people sit and scoff without offering so much as a peanut, but if we mutter 'anyone want . . . ?' they'll chorus 'Yes please I would' before the blasted words are out of the mouth – so!!! After opening the tins in the kitchen and chatting to the Italian kitchen maids, we ate until we felt positively ill, and went for a bath, on the way swiping back the tin of marmalade and a kitchen tin from the cupboard that Miss Rider had swiped off us yesterday after going throu' our lockers – She reckoned she was going to give them to the cleaners – huh! I like that – they're a lot for a start they get a mass of money – and its a bit dodgy as to whether they're thieving rats or not. Still!

5.30 went to have a bath, water hot for once – but I was half way through washing when warning bell went – that gave me about five minutes – so panic – made it – just, looking cleaner, but thats about all – when the girls were going into tea – one revolting child was very rude – so I asked whether she *wanted* any tea – to which she replied some uncouth words which translated mean 'No' – so I told the top of her table to give her a large helping of everything (that being fritters and tomatoes, bread etc) and make her eat the lot that'll show her –!

After tea, had a 'mad' fit – much to Butch's disgust – but it serves him right! if he'd been nice and stopped talking about football and the opportunities of university (which I could repeat backwards to him) I might've been more human – this continued through prep – 6.30 to 8.30 and I couldn't work, so we larked around and Tan and I sang duets, and Butch got cross so I shut him up by sitting on him and then necking for a good 20 minutes – actually we're not usually the non-workers – but it was impossible tonight – went down after prep into the common room where we heard that Janie and Buna had had another cat fight in prep and now Janie was with Miss Rider!

Most people went to bed early, so only Candie and I were left in the Common Room. We talked about sex, death, Butch, petting and then how two-faced most of our form are. I felt most despondent and desperately wanted to smash a window or something. Finally went to bed about ten – couldn't be bothered to wash, but did Janie's back for her and massaged it also strained myself into cleaning my shoes. About 10.30, Mary (fifth former) came in and we talked until 11.45 and talked about lots of little nondescript things – like boyfriends and embarassing experiences and other impossibly weedy tho hilerously funny incidents like the girl who blushing madly and hysterically giggling admitted that 'he put his hand on my ... pants' when asked what she'd done she looked flabbergasted and said dimly 'nothing' AND BURST INTO TEARS ...

From that interlude we turn to a contrast between schools in one boy's life: a penetrating and moving contribution from a boy who used to go to a Quaker coeducational school. Now seventeen years old, he is at one of those dozen or more independent schools which prepare boys for a service career. This one we shall call Cromwell College. He analyses what the change has done to him and the extreme contrast of educational styles he has experienced: the one, as he sees it, instilling moral and social sensitivity but sapping the drive and energy which come from latent aggression, the other releasing these energies but at the expense of his concern for morals and for other people. But let him speak for himself:

My father left my mother and went off to Malta after he came out of the Forces. Everyone reckoned my brother and I seemed unhappy, suppose we were in a way, its rotten to have to tell people. So my mother sent us to a Quaker school. I was in Wood House and liked it, was relaxed, no drive at all, lots of art and music, I enjoyed painting; the girls were nice, had a new one every two weeks. I even liked the Meeting – much more than a dreary Church service, you sit in silence and think about your life and what you should do, I even liked the school uniform, wearing a cap on Sunday. I was in the choir, even learned four notes on the recorder, but it was a nice friendly place, and I am grateful to it.

You didn't get keyed up, but in this school you do – you get terribly tense. God knows why I came here, because I felt the glamour of action, its a great life and all that balls. But when I arrived I could hardly believe it, these loads of jerks marching everywhere. Everything was different; boys worked hard, played hard and punished hard, the senior boy was a right bastard, he used the 'tickle' (a rope knotted and hardened by brine) like a cat. But I enjoyed my first term there, it was great with the guns and games, but now I am sick to death of it, I only now enjoy the rugger and english. I've got a reserve cadetship but I'm not going, the glamour has gone I couldn't stand living with these people for the rest of my life. Most of the things we do here won't be done at war; the Forces have changed, these bums haven't been in for years, they all dropped out for one reason and another, in fact they are so damned 'pucker' just to make up for the fact that they failed, they're either blind or deaf or spastic and some of them are all three.

Funny I would never had said *spastic* at the Quaker school, I suppose because there were some there, but this place makes you like that. The Quakers did try to get you to do things for yourself even from the first few days but here you must do what everyone else does and nothing unless you are told. The tradition crushes everything even the boys. They think you're a mug if you try to change anything, 'it's not worth the trouble it won't get you anywhere'. I suppose its being stuck in here day after day.

I think its changed me a lot and not for the best, in some ways I'm not such a decent person. Before, if I had done something wrong, I felt rotten for two weeks or so, you felt everyone at school knew, you felt everyone was looking at you, you just couldn't tell a lie to get yourself out of things but now I can lie quite easily and wouldn't give a damn. I could tell the biggest lies right now just to save my skin, I could go outside and smash that bloody silly picture of Cromwell and come in and tell you I hadn't. I could look you straight in the eyes and say I hadn't. It's made me more brutal but it gives me much more spirit, much more drive, the trouble is it's against other people. They aren't interested in self discipline they couldn't give a damn what your really like, only what you appear to be like in that grey straight jacket. I've lost respect for people as people. You just want to take the piss all the time, anything that puts you one up on someone else.

Not all independent coeducational schools are as permissive as the ones we have seen so far. A girl aged fifteen at one such comments:

We can only wear our own clothes on Saturday evening and thats only for the 5ths and 6ths.

You can't go anywhere with your boyfriends alone in the evening and if you are caught kissing you've had it from staff for the rest of the term. You can't have long hair (girls) and if it is long you have to put it up, otherwise it needs to be short, above collar.

The school uniform is very limited and it doesn't fit us properly.

Some other independent schools are 'integrated' – they have a large proportion of children whose fees are paid by LEAs or from charitable endowments. This frequently affects their style and approach: they are often more free, more intimate and domestic than the traditional school but not so cosy or upper class (in speech, style and manners) as progressive schools.

A sixteen-year-old at a Catholic independent school in the north full of working-class boys puts his finger on some of its characteristics:

Being able to go outside and having bikes, no uniform after 4 o'clock making coffee and having a radio, this makes it more *homely*.

Another fifteen-year-old in a Cotswold school singles out a feature which becomes prominent in most integrated schools, lack of submissiveness to staff:

There are some good things in the school, such as the freedom of speech. We can refuse to some masters, if we want to, and have a fair argument. There is a good lot of freedom and a good lot of space, to walk in.

Not all such schools operate smoothly. One school which we shall call the Lady Margaret Foundation caters mainly for children with need for boarding who are paid for by local authorities. Some disturbing aspects of its life (aspects not found commonly in other schools) will appear later. Here are two, very typical, comments on its life by thirteen-year-old boys to compare with the styles of other schools and children:

46 The Hothouse Society

> Mr Tomkins is a dirty master. He is a horrible master. This school is horrible. This school is the worst I have been too. This school is full of smokers. This school has many sports. This school should get rid of the cane. I hate a boarding school. The school food is wrotten. They should have decent meals. To many boys are food poisoned.
>
> There are too many monitors. The food is not very good especally sasages they are always worst. You hardly get the things you like to. The desks are always broken and windoas. Every one takes every one else things. I have had 10 pens pinched and a watch.

One other Foundation school in the prosperous Midlands produces something of the same style of response. Compare this slightly disaffected fifteen-year-old, for instance, with our public-school diarist of the same age. We are in a different social world.

> At about 6.30 a.m. I woke up to find some silly burke tikling my feet and as I turned round (I was lying on my stomach) I rikked my neck.
>
> At breakfast we had Barnanas and roles not much cop or enough I think to have till dinner. When Mr Goodge summed me I told him what happened and he told me that me-ole-man was here, so we went to the Bull Hotel and had lunch and a few drinks.
>
> When we got back I just wandered around till tea then I just did some prep in the library till the films which were really Bleedin 'orrible, And so to bed.

Like several other Foundation schools, this one is enlarging its fee-payers and is adopting some of the style and routine of a public school. The addition of fee-payers to such an institution can sometimes cause problems. One extremist fifteen-year-old boy illustrates possible tensions:

> The end of the first prep came, and outside the back gate cars gathered full of filthy rich people, to collect their scholastic offspring, their daily labours done. The infernal parasites! Here they lie, sucking at the sacred blood, we made so pure and perfect, by our toil and teams, – and generations more before us! But mark what I

say, soon the rats will leave the ship, before the bones of discredit and disrepute, brought by them; cover us over. 'They came just in time to save us from extinction', they cry. Is it better for a school to close 'midst glory and majesty, in victory and triumph, than to last a little longer, and finally close empty, wasted, traditionless, unrespected, demoralized, ruined and broken?

I got up, and walked from the dorm, down the steps to supper.

State boarding schools are a relatively new growth, and are occasionally as fresh in approach as in age. Compared with public schools and some independent ones, they tend to allow more access to outside society, and to be more relaxed, varied and deliberately homely in their internal life. (There are, of course, some marked exceptions to this, as we shall find.) Unlike public, progressive and some other schools they sometimes make little attempt to influence their pupil's life outside the academic or vocational sphere and sometimes pass pastoral care back to the home, with which, in several cases, there is very close contact. The fact that recruitment is from the region or county makes ties with locality and home easier to maintain. Some, though not all, have a distinctive style, seemingly less 'cultural', rougher and tougher than that of other boarding schools but perhaps more closely adjusted to the background of the pupils, who are not from the upper middle classes.

Three sixth-form boys at a state boarding school bring out some of its distinctive attributes:

I thought it would be very strict with senior boys pushing you around and making you fag for them. There is no fagging and the restrictions, considering this is a boarding school, are light.

The other boys came from the same district as I did.

I remember reading about Eton and the cane and so I had a little apprehension as to what would happen. I thought it would consist of long dormitories with a great number of beds lining the walls. There is no cane, the dormitories are small; the whole is more homely.

The latter phrase should be contrasted with the following, very

48   The Hothouse Society

typical comment, from a fourteen-year-old boy at an independent school:

> Most of them haven't got much of a home and this isn't a home either.

A sixteen-year-old boy at a state boarding school for boys briefly recounts his Friday evening and Saturday. Compare this with the lives of the diarists who opened this chapter, and note how 'integration' and freedom in the locality goes beyond the visit to the local library, how his outside girl friend is brought back into school, and how the staff help.

> *Friday Night.* Went down to County library in the village to give in library books.
> Then rushed to Vicarage to see girl friend. Went for a walk around countryside with her until 7.30 p.m. Then returned to school, booked in. Played tennis from 8 o'clock to 10 o'clock with girl friend in the school court.
> Then did shower duty in new house until lights out.
> *Saturday morning.* Met girl friend and received a lift from master to Badley. There I got a birthday card and present for her. Then we had a cup of coffee each in a cafe then walked along Riverside, until 10.26 a.m. (time of bus).
> Arrived back at school 10.50, went in shop to buy watch-strap. Walked around countryside until dinner. Said goodbye and arranged to meet her at 1.30 in the afternoon.
> *Afternoon.* Went on Kenton road walking, listening to radio and 'snogging'. Stopping at several gates to fields. Found a quiet decent spot and stayed there till 4 o'clock. Then we arrived back for tea (had a cigarette each).
> After tea about 7 o'clock saw her again; we played tennis together (school courts) went over to Mack with her from 8.15 to 9 o'clock.
> Then did my shower duty until lights out.

Sometimes the schools have the flavour of progressive ones about them. Here is a fourteen-year-old girl boarding at a comprehensive in the south commenting on the fact that she has a house*master*:

Well, for a start our house master Mr Duncombe (Duncie as we call him) is fab! He is gorgeous looking. The only troubel is he is married, not that he would like me anyway. It's nice to live with people of your own age. I have quite a few good friends. The lessons aren't bad, in fact Geography (which is taken by our house master) is fab fun, not because he takes us but I just love geography and everything to do with it.

Some state boarding schools, unlike most others, provide vocational training. A thirteen-year-old boy has recently arrived at one in the country with an agricultural stress. His style ('my old man'), his surprise at having socks washed twice a week, his tractor driving and the rest of his piece communicate some of the essence of the state boarding life:

Before I came I was a bit scared, my old man said it would be very tough with a matron standing over me with a big cane, I thought you might get the cane about two times every day – thats what my old man said; well he didn't go to a boarding school so he doesn't know.

The people are much nicer than I thought they would be but the time we get up in the morning is very early and the first morning I was asleep when the bell went. Another strange thing was that we had to put our socks out twice a week and we had to do a queer tuck in at the bottom of our flipin bed. You get a better education being away because the day boys spend most of their time travelling. The farm is good but I was a bit shocked at first the animals are very rude they do things even if you are looking, the pig has a strong back, I was told just to support his balls, like some of the boys. I like milking the cows every night after school and seeing the calves, and driving the tractor around the farm and when you get in the third year you can take charge of the farm and the master makes it all very interesting.

I dont miss much being here, my mum sometimes, but I am away from my brothers that are always on at me, although we have a T.V. here I miss just going in and turning it on when I want to. I miss my friend Nick he and I used to raid gardens for peas strawberries rasberries broad beans and raid apple trees. The most serious thing

I dislike about boarding school is there is not much cake and I have to bring back nearly a cake shop and then you get your tuck tin raided or a rotten banana put in it. You long for a big slice all afternoon and when you get there all there is waiting for you is something that left the jungle years ago.

Not so far away is another state boarding school, this time with the building or constructive crafts as its focus. Its fate is uncertain, its buildings antiquated and scattered. (Bad buildings do not make a bad school, nor good buildings good ones.) The following typical comment sums up its approach, flexibility and achievement. It is from a boy who was thoroughly disaffected at his previous school and then only too anxious to leave. But there is little 'early leaving' at this school, as he explains:

When I came here I hoped the buildings would be like a 'with it' comprehensive and everything else would be the same as the other boarding school I was at. Really it was a crumbly trash heap as far as buildings go – miles to the local park where we play football – and nowhere to change. I felt the Gaffer (Headmaster) was a bit nutty always helping us lay bricks, and dancing with the local scrubbers when they came to dancing club, and there's a moody teacher who sends us on cross country runs when his niggled.

But apart from that the school is *great*, there's the set back that there are a few 'bums' in the dorm, but on the whole its great, everybody's okay, especially the masters. At the old school they used to be old Army Officers teaching you as a sort of favour but at this school they're with the boys. The 'trades' building things like plumbing laying bricks, plastering – there good cause they break up the day – dont get flaked out doing sentences and Algebra all the time, and in the evening there is a lot on, I'm making a canoe but you can jack out into the town if you feel in need of a bird. Trouble is I'm thick but if I get some Os or C.S.E. I'll stay on here with my mates.

Boy, fifteen, state boarding school

One longer contribution can close our preliminary glimpse of state boarding schools. The boy is again fifteen. Some of the things he describes are common to many kinds of boarding school (informal staff–pupil relations, boys running things themselves) but others are more prominent in this kind of school: the sometimes harsh initiation by prefects (not so much a characteristic of public schools as of some state and independent schools, as subsequent chapters illustrate), the dislike of some boys wielding large authority over others, the prominence of manual crafts, going home at weekends, the chip shop and football, and such duties as selling flowers outside the gates for funds.

When I came to this school I was the oldest in that year and I was frightened that I would not mix. I soon settled down though and the reasons I believe for this are the evening activities. The boys run them themselves and this I think gives a boy a sense of responsibility. He's got to trust other boys in the activities to maintain their smooth running and this I consider an ideal atmosphere for friendship and sure enough I think this is where the boys learn to trust each other.

The thing that I didn't like in the first year was the fact that the prefects picked on us a lot and gave us detentions for the slightest things, e.g. 5 mins. late for meal. Saturday all day detention. This went on right through the first half of my term here and resulted in me not going home on Sundays throughout that half of term. Instead I was doing detentions. My mother began to worry thinking I'd done something serious, like hanging the headmaster, which at that time I felt like doing for giving prefects the right to give out detentions so freely.

The thing I like about the school as far as learning is concerned is the fact that craft in between lessons breaks up the monotony of a school day. It seems to prevent you feeling 'done in' sort of thing and keeps your interest in lessons. Another thing is that a lot of lessons are helped by practical action as well as theory work. The atmosphere between pupil and master in the school is very informal and when you hit small snags in evening activities you turn to a master in place of your father for advice such as how to paint a model and etc. The masters in this school I find are always ready to help you with a problem, domestic and school work. Its this get togetherness I think that turns out well educated boys because they get to know the masters and give them their cooperation whereas day boys tend to mess around if not interested with a lesson.

Mind, you, as I have already said, everything in the garden is not lovely. The masters lose their tempers sometimes and make it rough for the boys. You can always tell when sir has not been re-picked for his local football team. The jobs on the Saturday are failed for minor things and the boys have to lose some of their free time to re-do their jobs and be ready for another inspection. Unfailingly they always pass the second time.

The boys in the school often do collections for local institutions in their free time, e.g. lifeboat and Famine Relief. This maintains the schools contact with the local community which I consider very important, but a thing I dislike is the headmaster getting boys to sell the school flowers outside the shop across the road in their free time. Admittedly I'm sure the boys of the school past and present have a lot to thank him for especially the existence of the school as it is today.

Another very old complaint is of course traditional School Dinners (Day) or Meals (Board). I'm sure if you asked the chip shop at the bottom of the drive you would find out that they do a roaring trade with us hungry boys down there. In fact I was once told they feel a heck of a draft when we go on our Summer holidays.

Boy, fifteen, state boarding school

Our opening review of secondary boarding styles is over. But many boys (and some girls) will have already boarded at a prep school, which provides such careful and subtle training for the public schools.

Colin Johnson, aged twelve and a half, at a school on the south coast, sums up the good English prep school. We savour its full life, its high academic expectations, its close staff–pupil relations, the scope it gives for this boy's vitality and imagination. We see too how the prep-school style matches that of the public schools which it exists to serve: the archaic Billy Bunter expressions and mannerisms; the formality of interaction (boys and staff are called by surnames); the secondary school kind of curriculum, with Latin prominent and exams and tests ever recurrent; the academic and sporting pressures; the prefect and house system and hierarchy again; the tightly controlled life with its strict routine.

Friday: 'Blip ... blop ... blip ... blop.'

That wretched tap ... it won't turn off ... What's that thing digging in my spine? ... crumbs I'm tired ... Yeowch! I suppose I'd better have a look ... now where is it? Ah, good, it's my watch ... still going I hope? Oh, yes. Five to seven, eh? Where's my rug? Ah, there it is, on the floor, no wonder I was cold.

'Blip ... blop ... blip ... blop ...'

I *am* tired. I'll sit up and put my glasses on, then I'll wake up. Now where on earth did I put my glasses is that them on the floor? Yes, yes, here they are. 'Johnson' says the dorm leader, 'lie down'. What?, oh, I see ... pity really, I'd just woken up.

What? The rising bell, oh gosh, now I've got to strip my bed. Why has this blanket got three corners, Now to wash, it's raining again, ugh, what a day. 'Hurry up, come on, you're all being slow'. Hurry, Oh, all right, I wish I was in Hawaii, or somewhere, where its always sunny. 'Hurry up'. I'd learn to swim, sky blue lagoons, sky blue sky. 'Hurry up'. Well come on, we're all dressed, go and tell the Master on Duty we're ready, glance in my diary – Friday, maths, oh no, that crummy maths prep back. French, another rotten prep. History, not bad, English, Latin, oh yes, that grammar exercise, not much hope for success in that. Greek, good. Scripture, O.K.; History and another Maths prep. Ugh. Well, I'm ready. I'll go down and clean my shoes, argument about polish again, line-up, I'm still tired.

Breakfast, ugh, porridge again, at least they call it porridge, still it looks worse than it tastes. Oh, no, I'm sitting next to Davis M.; the human sloth, eleven and still sucks his thumb, and lays on the table, and yawns and encourages his weedy brother to copy him. Still I can ignore Davis while talking to Mr Leggatt – super chap Mr Leggatt, so clever, a pleasant master and funny with it. Oh, oh – scrambled egg, more like yellow jellypaint. Davis M., is passing notes now. I'll ignore him and his silly notes.

Short break now, then we'll go into Martin Hall and almost fall asleep listening to Mr Marshall prattling away about house matches,

'House officers please put up their teams'. Good, the sun's come out, I think I'll fiddle with my penknife, I'm sure to drop it, and Mr Marshall will have finished waffling when I've found it and picked it up. 'House knockout, double sections, remember, that's Haig and Wellington'. Not long to go. Here come the masters. 'Hymn four hundred and thirty six, four, three, six', and then a reading, and then prayers, and then questions, and the Head getting muddled up about timetable changes and boys losing padlocks, and then bell, and first period maths, ugh.

'If a boy cycles at 10 m.p.h. to a village which is twenty miles away and his father starts from the village at one o'clock, an hour later than the boy left home, and goes by car at 35 m.p.h. draw a graph showing when the bicycle meets the car'. Gosh what a question. Poor Owen G., he's getting a rocket from Mr Trease for not listening. French, take a French book and go to the library. What now? Not a vocab test, as we haven't brought pens. Oh, good, a period with Miss Simmons.

History now, good, still in the library, looking at newspapers of 1900. Someone must have read this paper, some Victorian gentleman at breakfast with his wife. 'Shocking, m'dear. The Margate lifeboat sunk, seven killed . . . pass the marmalade'. A log fire burning in the grate. I say, 'set of false teeth on gold £1. 1s. 0d.' Quite a bit in those days. What now?

Break, I can get on with my diary in the library. Latin, please don't go through that learning prep. I didn't do much. Phew! Practice Scholarship Papers returned, relief. Bulb in projector next door breaks. Five minutes Latin wasted while Mr Unwin goes to look for a fuse, good, now I can finish my prep. Line up, lunch, super, still next to Mr Leggatt, food not too bad, rest. I'll go and ask to do some work, then I can continue my Friday 'diary'.

Games . . . Its cleared up, the sun's quite bright now, all to Martin Hall. If its free time I wonder what I'll do? I'll probably sit in my form room doodling. I love doodling; it takes my mind off everything else, and then I'll think of all the work I should be doing. When one gets to the top of the school its work, work all the way. Geography, History 'Johnson, Trapsall, Stone'. What? Me? Who? Where? Oh, I see. I often think about boarding school, but I can never talk freely about my opinion, except to my house officer, Peter Duncan. He's not exactly a friend, he's different. If I want to talk about anything, or argue even, I know he'll listen, he's that sort of boy. Round the four forty after the discussion, talking with Stone about karate, stamps, envelopes, the Meccano Magazine. Stone brings out the joke in anything, everything's funny to Stone.

Little tea now, how boring I never have anything to eat. Then Greek... Not much time to think, too much to learn. Scripture, I wish Mr Adcock would change his tone occasionally when talking, his voice makes concentration so difficult, parables, History prep continue reading about the cost of living in 1900. Too boring, I think I'll have a 'slow fight' with Johnston. (A slow fight consists of jabbing a boy in the back or turning over a page in the book he's reading or generally annoying him and then moving around the room slowly so that the master taking the period does not notice you. You chase each other in this fashion, for some time, the 'warfare' consisting of annoying things as before listed. These slow fights play a part in school life – they are always friendly, and hardly ever discovered). A bell rings, tea, but first line-up. Line-up has altered since I first came; then it was militarial 'Heads back, chests out, shoulders in, hands behind back, feet apart, STIFF', and above all, facing the front, staring at the chap in front's head so hard that your eyes nearly burst. Nowadays we still face the front with our hands behind our back, but no more are we stiff. Next to Davis C. now, but also next to Peter Duncan. Talk about various things including favourite animals, the 'rottenness' of the food which was very good actually – sausages and chips.

Prep now, maths, a crazy Arithmetic 'A' paper – full of unanswerable questions; still I'd better see it through. Gosh, I wish these papers were easier. This one's full of kilogrammes and tons. Ten minutes free time after cocoa, more watery than it used to be, pity, it was jolly nice. Free time, good, where's Hugh Pearson? We can get on with our book: – 'All that You Could Wish to Know About Latin', the fifth in a long line of comedy books about school subjects and occasionally other things – 'The Verb is a hairy thing with a lot of teeth, do not feed it'. A bell rings, hooray, rush to Martin Hall grab a seat in front row – now for TV and 'Blanding's

Castle', P. G. Wodehouse, what a super plot. Airguns going off at people, conspiracies, blackmail, and after this prayers and bed.

Rush to fold counterpanes, to get to the basins, wash, get pyjamas on and be in bed before the silence bell. I think routine is wrong there, silence bell I agree with but I don't see why all should be in bed by the silence bell, it means everything's hurried, but at last the lights go out. Saturday tomorrow, free time and films, and tuckshop. I wonder what my parents are doing now? . . . Not long to the end of term. Crumpets, I haven't written my diary, my ordinary diary, that is. Today's been a normal schoolday, packed full of work and play, all to a strict timetable. What will tomorrow bring?

Not all prep schools are like this. In sharpest contrast there follows a skeletal diary of a weekend of a boy at Tormouth, the prep school for Stanton, the progressive school. Life is less organized, less gregarious (everyone has a private room), there is no competition, little academic or other external pressures, few restrictions on movement or regulations, there are houseparents and housemothers, staff are called by Christian names, pets are prominent, the weekends are relaxed and informal and the school is coeducational. Typically this eleven-year-old boy does not reveal the latter fact.

Sometimes, we manage to get down to breakfast at 8.10. After breakfast, we all go to our own little jobs, if we have pets we feed them and clear them out. It always depends what useful work you do, bad useful work you either bunk or if you get one of the more severe housemothers or teachers you try to do as little work as you can (if you can). Easy useful work you still try to do as little as you can but don't mind not bunking. Me, I've got some easy useful work but I still bunk.

Bell goes five minutes before real work (writing etc.). There are two lessons then break, (about 40 minutes each). It always depends who is taking us, our English teacher, Sheila is too kind and we draw and don't work but she has got a little bit strikter. Maths with Alan is I suppose not strikt but we work and learn. Chemistry you usually doodle and look bored depending on the type of person, but that is usually the most boring classes . . . Drama with Gavin . . . it is hard to explain; he is a good person. We have him once a week (more would give him a nervous breakdown). We shout, run around, bunk and other things, if one manages to get anything done at all, he must have had to go through a great deal. At break if you are a boarder you go to your house and have a cup of tea and some toast by that time the bell goes and you trudge into classes for another two hours of three classes. Lunch is terrible (at 1.00) you have the usual bad grub, pudings are not so bad but you always get the nice English CUSTURD.

After lunch, I usually get my hamster out (if its a nice day) and laze on the terrace where quite a few people go. There are games acording to the term. The games are not compulsory. We have two more classes and we have high tea then and finish any time. Some people (boys) play football and some play in the gym etc., if the weather is warm enough we have a 7.00 swim and then go in to our houses at 7.30 bath, change and go to our tents, this sounds odd but when the weather is good enough we are allowed to camp out in summer, we are given three quarters of an hour to read etc., then we have to go to sleep . . . Sometimes people wake up at about 2.00 or 3.00 and go into other peoples tent and go on midnight walk and feasts etc. Then back to sleep.

Week ends are different to this (except the midnight things). Saturday, our House father David takes some people in his car to the nearest town and we go and buy things for about an hour then back to school. Saturdays you get up later in the mornings. We swim in the week-ends a good deal. Our house father takes people canoeing on good week-ends. On the middle of term we have camp for one week, the different groups go different places. The older group people can choose between going canoeing or sailing. The only thing I can say about this school is it is the BEST BOARDING SCHOOL IN THE WORLD.

After the white nineteen-thirties concrete modernity of Tormouth, we end this chapter with the attics of a mellow Georgian house in Wiltshire. Its lights are out; the hectic day is over. We eavesdrop as night and sleep falls over the prep-school dormitory:

Our lights are out. All should be silent. Morel throws his blankets off. 'Cor I'm hot Fox' (Fox is dorm leader). No reply. 'Fox?' hey Foxie! 'Whatdyer want now, Morel?' 'I'm hot'. 'So –?' 'Can you open the window please?' 'Ah, Dykes-Brown – Brown – open the window'. 'Cor that's jolly unfair! I was nearly asleep!' 'Sims?' Sims open the window'. 'No! I'm freezing!' 'Freezing! are you joking?' I turn over in bed at this point several times. 'Look shutup' I growl like a bear disturbed from hibernation. I groan: 'I've got those pyjamas on again'. 'They're about two sizes too small' 'Go on Fox!' 'Look here the next person, the next person to talk . . .' Fox's thick nasal voice droans through the dark bearing that all to familiar sentence 'and make unnecessary noises Sims'. 'That was necessary' says Sims 'I was just coughing!' 'Go to Sister then!' 'Morel I warned you to shut up'. 'Okay okay keep your hair on!' I yank the sheet over my head in a desperate attempt to shut out all sound. Eventually they'll stop I suppose. 'I'm sure the radiators on'. 'Look I'm trying to get some sleep!' Brown's always saying that, so am I for that matter but we never seem to get any. At last I think they've stopped. Perhaps now . . . 'Fox can I get a drink of water?' The tap runs, the mouth clicks, thump, thump, jangle crash now I can try to get to sleep it must be about half past nine now, never mind at last I can relax. Soon I'll be asleep. 'Fox can I tuck my bed in please?' Ah well!

Boy, twelve, prep school

3 Beginnings

'I shall never forget the house door slamming shut on me for the first time,' writes a public schoolboy, and for most boarders that moment can always be vividly recollected. As the parents wave good-bye, the child turns to enter a strange and often frightening society; he is probably really on his own for the first time in his life and uneasily aware that this is the first of many terms away from home.

Most children understand why they are at boarding school, parents having stressed the reasons; for some there is no alternative, some have chosen it themselves and for many it is the normal pattern of things, ordained at birth. They almost all share the belief that there is something to be gained from the experience, but the move from home to board, even the transfer from preparatory to senior school, is not easy. Most children are anxious, have little idea what to expect and are occasionally homesick.

The schools, with a few disturbing exceptions, make friendly efforts to assimilate the arrivals, although most stress the separation from parents to assist settling in. With cosy Quaker teas or a lordly address of welcome from the head of house, the integration of the new boy proceeds, while the other boys are indifferent rather than hostile. We will glance at fagging, an institution which, in the public schools if nowhere else, still ensures that the new boy swiftly, emphatically and sometimes painfully understands this new and complex society and his place in it. While the more barbaric initiation ceremonies have gone, now dimly and wistfully recollected with other folklore over endless Nescafé in the studies, exams in the rich slang of the schools still test and initiate the new boy. He must often learn an official and unofficial private language – an effort when the school may have a hundred words in the official slang book, and unofficially one part of the male anatomy might be graced with over a hundred terms all in current usage. 'Pass the test at the second go,' advises a boy. 'You mustn't be too keen at a public school.'

By thirteen most children will have arrived at their boarding schools, although some, we will see, experience a shorter residential life. Sometimes experiments in 'integration' will bring boys from day-school backgrounds to board at sixteen or later. Some comments from such boys conclude our chapter.

But, initially, why do children think they are boarding at all? Here are the answers given by some boys and girls at a state boarding school, a coeducational one where the pupils come for one year's stay in the middle of their secondary education. The *children*, not the parents, decide.

> I wanted to come because I have always wanted to live out in the country and to get away from being told what to do all the time. I wanted to see what it was like living with other people of my own age and to become a more independent person. I did ask mum if I could go and she talked it over with dad, and dad asked me if I wanted to go and I said yes.
> *Boy, fourteen*

> I decided to come when I was given the leaflet but at first wasn't too keen as none of my friends wanted to come. I told my mother and father and they said it was up to me, I could go if I wished. I then found out that Maureen Hayes, the girl who is in my class at the other school and lived five doors away, wanted to come. Also my uncle went to one and he seemed to enjoy it and ever since I was young I've wanted to come to a boarding school so I decided to come.
> *Girl, fourteen*

> I liked the sound of it, the opportunity was good. It gave me a chance of going away and living in a group. This decision was my own but I discussed it with my parents. I feel as an individual living in a community and helping others. About a week before I came I queried my decision but when I came I liked it.
> *Boy, thirteen*

Answers to the question 'why are you boarding?' at another state boarding school, a secondary modern one in a rural area, for boys aged eleven to sixteen, illustrate some of the variety in boarding 'need'. Not only home difficulties but isolation, parents abroad, health and similar problems may be eased by boarding. There is a substantial proportion of such children with 'need' in both independent and state boarding schools.

> I am a boarder because where I am living I'm cut off from friends, this is most garstly in the holidays, so I would have friends and try to live like humans, and to be used to being away from home.
>
> *Boy, fifteen*

> My father died and my mother thought that I should grow up with men. Not to have a woman around me all the time, and then we would have to move and I should settle in a school with out moving around schools.
>
> *Boy, fifteen*

> The reason for this is that my father is a farmer and if I went to a day school I would come home at night and have to help him milk and do odd jobs around the farm and I wouldn't be able to do much homework and studies.
>
> *Boy, fourteen*

> The reason why I am here is because of my mother or stepmother who has had some marriage problems. I came from my 1st mother therefore I don't like my city mother and she doesn't like me.
>
> *Boy, fourteen*

> Because my Father is in the army and we travelled so much that I needed a stable education, as I had been to 14 schools previously in all parts of the world. So my father thought that this particular school would be better for my education.
>
> *Boy, fourteen*

> I had to board here because my Mum is in hospital.
>
> *Boy, twelve*

Many parents send their children to progressive schools to escape the academic pressures and rigid external controls which they think

62 The Hothouse Society

apply in the more conventional schools, and because they favour coeducation. Children writing in two progressive schools indicate their reasons for boarding and suggest the distinctive nature and some of the character of such schools:

> I came to the school because I like this sort of school and so do most of my friends but it doesn't mean to say I'm a vegaterrean. I like meat and I am used to my mothers cooking and all the extras, and I dislike the food here. Also the school really believes in nature cure and I don't take pills but nearly all my friends do for one thing or another.
> *Girl, fifteen, progressive school*

> I came because it is an outdoor school, in the country and has boys, but just in case I cut myself or felt ill my mother told the doctor to bathe the wound in clear running stream water and I was never to be injected with anything. He didn't seem very pleased though.
> *Girl, fourteen, progressive school*

The public school boy usually boards earlier, at seven or eight, and has less influence on his parents' decision than children going to the state boarding schools. He may come from a family with a strong boarding tradition, or a social group that always sends its children to particular schools. They move through the preparatory schools with their friends and on to the public schools as a matter of course. They often show surprise at our question 'Why are you boarding?'

> I am here because it never dawned on my parents that they could send me anywhere else.
> *Boy, sixteen, public school*

> We all go, or have gone to boarding schools, its perfectly normal.
> *Boy, sixteen, public school*

> They have been coming here since the seventeenth century, I think, although what they did before that I can't imagine, had Tutors I suppose. You even used to be able to bring them here with you. Everyone I know at home is either here or has been here, Yorkshire is such a small place really.
> *Boy, eighteen, public school*

Everyone from my 'Prep' came on, it was rather nice, thats how I know people in other houses. All my friends came here, its a bit of a bore really, you just can't get away from them. Last holidays I went to Matins in Davos on Christmas Day – it was just like school chapel, all there, even John pulling the bell as I went in.

Boy, eighteen, public school

A boy describes his arrival at his non-conformist public school and glances at grandfather's study.

All of us then went to look round the school. We saw the new tennis-courts at the bottom of Hanson's. 'This used to be the vegetable garden,' said Dad. We then walked down and went into the Gym. It was a smashing Gym, with modern equipment. We then went into School House where Dad showed us his and his father's studies. *Boy, thirteen, non-conformist public school*

The public-school boy also has 'need' reasons for boarding:

One of the reasons for this was that at home I did not have any brothers to play with and here there were always boys around, with whom I could always have a game. *Boy, thirteen, public school*

I stay with my mother in the Summer holidays and my father at Christmas, at Easter I presume they fight over me.

Boy, thirteen, public school

But only a prep-school boy could have such a clear and unfashionable idea as to the reasons he is on his way to a public school:

If you don't, you go to a grammar school or something like that. I think that it is pretty well first class people that go to a public school, not the actual workers sons, but the bloke that is in charge, his sons. It is the sons of the important men really who come to a school like this and when your dumped into a third class school with all the village children it shows up a considerable amount because they all talk rotten, like 'urry up'. If you are talking

sophisticatedly like we do here then I think they would poke fun at us.
Boy, twelve, prep school

Now that we have some idea of why children find themselves in boarding schools, let us look at the hopes and fears they had at the moment of arrival. What did they *expect* boarding to be like? While the prospect excites some, most are uneasy. 'It is going to be living HELL!' writes a prep-school boy contemplating his move to the senior school. 'It's going to be horrible, every evening you will go to bed with a saw backside,' writes another. Even for the successful boy the prospect of boarding is not pleasant. 'I felt terrible when I won the scholarship, but my parents were delighted', writes another. Usually their fears and expectations are wildly misplaced. A boy from a state boarding school writes:

Before I came I thought it was going to be a very snobbish school, a big house with lots of teachers in gowns, and much more strict than this school. I thought more classrooms and children from public schools being not so friendly as they are here. When I first came, the first night was a long one thinking about parents at home.
Boy, fourteen

A girl at the same school, aged thirteen, recalls:

I wanted to come here because I had read so many books about these type of schools. You know, midnight feasts, and all that. Also because I hated my other school. All exams, stuffy teachers and old. Here the teachers are young, mod and funny. I have always wanted to come to a boarding school because they sound exciting. It is lonely at home without brothers or sisters. My dad wanted me to come, my mum didn't. I pleaded with her to let me come. On the very first night we had a midnight feast and since then we have had tons. This is good fun but none of the staff know. If we made a noise we would get 200 or even 500 lines. Nobody must split on anyone. If they do the dorm sends them to coventry. Lending clothes is being friendly. The girls like you doing this. Nearly all the girls have boyfriends. Tons of couples get caught holding hands or snogging, but they still carry on. We have a secret meeting place too. At about 8.30 the couples meet behind the (Toilets). Some have got caught so we are looking for another place now.

The expectations of children going away to school at eleven at another state (secondary modern) boarding school are similarly coloured by comics and old-fashioned school stories: the two main media by which boarding life is projected to the English public.

> When I knew I was coming to this school I said to myself I wonder what it will be like. I thought we could have pillow fights, have cubicles to our selves, midnight feasts and lots of other things.
>
> *Girl, eleven*

> I actually expected this school to be like the things we read about in a book such as 'Jennings' or 'Billy Bunter', with teachers going around with black cloaks and mortar boards, with canes hanging over their arms. But when I arrived here I was surprised, it is just like an ordinary school except we sleep here. *Boy, eleven*

A boy recollects his fears on arrival at a state boarding school for able children:

> I had a romantic 'Tom Brown' idea and expected to be tossed in a blanket and be instilled with school spirit, with harsh seniors pushing you around and making you fag for them all the time. I was scared of them, during my first meal I could hardly swallow and half way through lunch I rushed from the dining room retching up the back stairs, to be sick in the lavatories. I was thoroughly miserable.
>
> *Boy, sixteen*

Even the public school boy with his prep-school experience remembers some of the curious ideas he had on his school:

> I thought that Public School Life would be hard, and that the masters and seniors would be extremely strict. I also thought that it

would be a very posh place, and that everybody would be the son of a Lord or such like, in fact very much the same as Eton or Harrow. I had the idea that it would be a vast establishment where nobody knew anybody else and it would be every man for himself.

Boy, thirteen, public school

These then are the boarders' expectations. They are now going to face reality. Here are two prospective boarders in the process of arriving. A girl describes her arrival at an integrated school:

It was not hard to find the school, as it was such a small village. The drive way was very long, actually it seemed never ending. We no sooner got round one bend and there was another in front of us. My step-mother tried to cheer me up by cracking some witty jokes like 'I think we ought to thumb a lift' or, 'Look out for a bus stop'. To our great pleasure we finally saw a huge mansion in front of us. We began to wonder whether it was the school, – it was too good to be a school. Then we saw some girls which reassured us.

When I first heard I was going to a school I expected it to be like what you read in books. Well at first it was. we used to have midnight feasts and midnight walks or dances etc. But then the adventurous ones left and everything became *too* strict. There are only a few of us who still do these things left now! Worse luck!

Girl, fifteen, integrated school

Another sets out for a state boarding school:

When I received the information that I was going to boarding school, I was very excited. When the day came to go I went six miles by bus to get a coach surplide by the school. First the cases were put on and then the pupils. I felt very worried when I stepped on the coach. I will always remember the boy that sat next to me, and he did not stop crying all through the journey. When the coach left my mother standing there it made me think as though I would never see her again.

Boy, fourteen, state boarding school

Happiness in the school depends on one's reception by those already

Beginnings   67

there. Before we look more closely at the children's experiences over the first few days in their boarding schools we might glance at the welcome the other children extend. New friends and sympathetic authority are sought by the arrivals. Here a school house captain from a public school advises his successor on how to deal with the new boys and illustrates succinctly the ideals and structure of such schools. The extract is taken from one of those confidential books kept by successive house captains, with contributions by each house captain commenting on policy, the boys, the housemaster and so on. Rarely are they seen by anyone other than the house captain but many of them were given to us to use. Here the house captain tells his successor:

> Find out all you can about them before they come: – names, form, last school, and any notable past history. The last can be very helpful in attaching them to the right VIth, to give them a good start at their new school, for personal fagging. See them all together soon after they come and give them a short 'speech' telling them all they ought to know about house and school. They will be so entranced by their new surroundings, they won't remember a word you say, but there's no harm in trying! The following seems to be a generally accepted list of things to say:
> School Routine
> Corps
> Rules
> House Routine (games)
> Illness (notes of all kinds)
> Where places are
> Not to keep too much money on them
> Have games clothes marked
> A little about Senior Prefects, Deputy Prefects, their privileges and the internal organizations of the House
> Lots about fagging
> Ask for questions and tell them to come to you with any problems
> Stress at the end how many opportunities are open at this school, encourage them to take these right from the start, and to live as full a life as possible. *Head of house's private book, public school*

68 The Hothouse Society

At other schools the house captains advise:

> Individualism is alright for seniors but serious in the junior half of the house. House unity and spirit are of paramount importance in the junior half of the house. It is the secret of a happy house to be well occupied, and the efficiency and happiness of any house depends on how it moulds its juniors.
>
> *Head of house's book, public school*

> Look after the little boys if you do little else, it will make for a happy house over the years.   *Head of house's book, public school*

A special routine for the new boy may be posted on the notice board. He may be entrusted to a guardian slightly older than himself, and his duties and privileges made clear:

> *New boys are to note*
> i They are not allowed to talk in the corridors unless spoken to by a senior boy
> ii All money including Postal Orders are to be handed by boys to their Housemaster at the beginning of term or as received. He will issue pocket money
> iii New boys may not sit on the seats in front of the school block
> iv They may not leave the house after dark without their housemaster's permission or enter another house
> v They must not put their hands in pockets
>
> *House captain's notice, public school*

While most children seem indifferent to the new arrivals, not all share the house captain's innocent interest:

> I like the September term we buzz down and eye up the new 'talent', watch the cross country run and call out 'duckie' to those with nice knees as they go past.
>
> *Boy, sixteen, independent school*

> This place get me, I was just talking to a couple of new kids and

some of our mob leaned out of the window with a big wolf whistle.
I'm not a cradle snatcher. *Boy, seventeen, independent school*

You look forward to your second year then at least you can push the new boys about and duff them over.

Boy, twelve, state boarding school

What then actually happens to them as they board for the first time? We will see that most children writing of their first five weeks seem contented and even those boarding at the age of seven settle down happily. Not all are lucky however. Where staff or seniors are indifferent, bullying and homesickness can occur. In such schools children can be very miserable and protest in language that matches the schools' insensitivity. Unable to show the sympathy we instinctively felt, such schools put our objectivity and discretion under great strain. But first let us look at the majority, the satisfied new boarders. Here is one from Stanton:

I remember my first evening at school after my mother had dropped me off; I was wandering around the school by myself when I suddenly found myself behind a great tall boy and we were just about to pass through some swing doors. I didn't know whether to turn round and run in the opposite direction rather than risk having a great heavy door swing in my face. I made up my mind to be brave and have never been more surprised then when this boy stopped and held the door open for me. I have never been homesick since.

Girl, fifteen, progressive school

Another at a state boarding grammar school recollects:

My reactions were that I was a bit lost at first but I slowly found my way around every one was quite nice to me apart from a few 4th and 5th year boys making funny remarks something like this 'don't his ears stick out, hasn't he got a funny nose'. *Boy, eleven*

A girl at a short-term boarding school:

On the first night about six of us couldn't sleep and we started to whisper which grew into talking at 2 am. in the morning and the dorm mistress heard us and we got 200 lines, but now I've settled in very well and have got to know everyone and the routine of the school. Now I have been here for a few months, I find that the life at boarding school is far better than that of a day school.

The only thing I miss is my cat and budgie of course my parents and a hot cup of cocoa in front of the fire before bed.

Girl, fourteen

A boy begins boarding at a LEA secondary modern boarding school. Note the stress on homeliness in such state schools:

Before I came to this school I didn't realize what a wonderful life and *what a real home from home it was.*

The privileges are so good that you are happier doing work and learning things, knowing what wonderful things you can do in your spare time such as swimming, football, netball, rugby, table tennis, billiards, snooker, cricket, and many other things to do in your spare time.

I am proud of my school and I've longed to come to boarding school for years. The atmosphere is wonderful, the teachers are nice, the school is marvelous all together.

'Ben' our dormitory teacher is better than I thought even though he does punish severely. This schools is a real comforting home from home.

Boy, twelve

At another state boarding school for secondary modern children a boy recollects:

When I first came here I was very excited about all the things I would do at this school. The first day I was here I wasn't homesick. The second day when I was in the classroom I began to realize that I was away from home, and I began to feel very homesick but I soon got over it. The first week I was very shy indeed, but I was soon talking to everyone I came across. Saying hello, politly, to everyone. I soon found my way around the school, but first of all it was very strange. I must just say this. This is a very good school, and I am

sure that everyone here and anyone who is coming, they will love it here.
Boy, twelve

There are some surprises:

> I was disappointed that at 5.30 we had to stop what we were doing and wash our feet.
> *Boy, twelve, state boarding school*

> I didn't expect it to see any of the staff in their nighties. I didn't expect them to sit on the desks and talk to you unformerly.
> *Girl, eleven, state boarding school*

> I felt very funny sleeping with 21 other girls in the dormitory and have a shower every night.
> *Girl, twelve, same school*

and unexpected advantages:

> At home when I go to bed I am on my own and I am scared of the dark but here we are all together and I like it.
> *Girl, twelve, Quaker school*

> For a start I never used to hear from my real mum at my step-mum's house. If I did she used to censor the letter. But now I can hear from her in peace as our parents letters are not opened.
> *Boy, thirteen, integrated school*

Considerable differences in the approach to boarding are to be found even among the public schools. Boys writing of their first impressions suggest some of the variety of boarding style that exists in these schools. Here two boys describe their first moments at a leading public school:

> Everybody tries to be nice to you but that doesn't really help. In the Boys Dinner or breakfast the 1st evening or first morning it is frightful. Everybody takes sort of quick glances at you and you feel awful – you can almost here them say 'Look, thats the new boy, I wonder what he's like!'
> *Boy, thirteen*

My house seemed a maze of passages but they soon sort themselves out. During my first meal in the dining room I was very insecure knowing noone except my Dame. At first I could not get used to calling my Dame Ma'am. 'Yes, ma'am, no ma'am, why of course ma'am'. Calling my tutor Sir was considerably easier as I was used to that at my private school. Early school seems to me a frightful bore and having to wake up at 7.00 a.m. is the last straw. Luckily the senior boys are very understanding. Sculling in my whiff is great fun but to begin with pretty darned tricky.   *Boy, thirteen*

Arrivals at a non-traditional public school:

When I first arrived here, I was, naturally a little nervous, and empty. I stepped out of the car to be greeted by a prefect, who I later discovered to be John Fox. He helped me get my trunk and case out of the boot. When I entered the House room, I was hit by the queer atmosphere of a bar saloon, with the snooker table, the clanky old piano, and the table tennis table. The only thing lacking was the beer, and the men in a ring round the piano singing 'Auld lang Syne' or some other appropriate tune.   *Boy, thirteen*

The food, I thought, was surprisingly good. When one hears of 'Public School food', it immediately conjures up a vision of 'macaroni pudding' or some such stodge. But this certainly wasn't the Public School I had heard of. The school was too sparsely populated, the food too good, the beds too comfortable, the clothes too informal, the master to boy relationship too friendly, the number of bullies too low, to be the proper Public School (which one hears of so frequently, but seldom hears in praise). The meetings we had on the first two nights were chatty. Not the 'we expect every boy to do his duty for the Headmaster and myself' sort of attitude. But the 'How did your first day go?' sort of attitude. And I was also surprised at the number of papers we were given. The *Daily Mail*, *Punch*, the *Daily Telegraph*, the *Illustrated London News*, the *Observer* and the *Sunday Times*. I had expected, probably, something like *Education and the Flag Monthly* as our magazine and the *Daily Latin and Maths* as our Daily.

This school was all too friendly to be a 'Public School'.

Boy, thirteen

I was hustled into a small room behind the kitchen where I ate some baked beans on toast and some bread and butter; a friendly grey haired but nervous cook said 'Leave what you don't like, anything goes tonight'. Even by the first day I found how friendly and nice everybody was in the house especially the prefects who are always called by their christian names. *Boy, thirteen*

The contrast with life at some restricted prep schools is often noted. A boy at a public school writes:

After the terrible life in a prep school this school is like a palace and one of the greatest impressions I got was the sense of freedom. In the first week I saw boys coming back to the house with bottles of pop and food and I was amazed! I had never thought of it, actually going out of the school grounds and into shops! it was incredible yet it was true we were semi free to do what we wanted, and on Sundays being allowed to go on bike rides ten miles away. *Boy, thirteen*

Even life at a more traditional public school does not depress the new boys. One found the school pleasant from the start:

Everybody you met was very kind. Everybody helped you. The second day when the lessons started was a bit more frightening. The masters just took down your names and your house.

The first few days I didn't have any friends but then I found someone. Gradually I became acquainted with more and more boys. Because I didn't know anyone here at first I was very homesick. I was so bad that I wanted to run away. However, I said to myself 'Now that's a daft thing to do' and soon I was all right. I'd heard that this school was very traditional but I found that it was not really, not as much as it is made out to be. Anyway, I think its great here now. *Boy, thirteen*

Another gets used to its system:

When I first came here I found that the place was far larger than I thought and I felt very small. Everything seemed very confusing at first and I found it very difficult to do the right thing. The senior boys and monitors seemed to have been given their authority to make our lives a misery. However, if one avoided the monitors life seemed fabulous.

At first the staff seemed as though they would never shout at a boy or beat him. This idea, however, died almost at birth. The way one was treated by the second year boys was infuriating. It seemed impossible to do the things that one wanted to do. But it soon changed as I gained more confidence and I am now on a perfectly even keel.
Boy, thirteen

We now turn to those who are not so resilient. There are some boys who resent being away from home and whose arrivals are not so pleasant as those described above.

Here is a new boy responding characteristically at the Lady Margaret Foundation:

Lady Margaret is a shitty dump. Is bluddy fucking prison camp made to look like a palace out side and prison inside. I hate it and I have only been here 7 weeks. Its bloddy awful. The food is *SHIT*. I really hate it no kidding. We only allowed out three times a week and Mr Tomkins is a SEX omo!
Boy, eleven

At Beauchamp Manor, a seventeen-year-old boy remembers

opening the door. The first thing I saw was the list that forced you to stay in the Common Room with certain people, for good or for worst – usually for worst. I was then quite small, I couldn't even see over the tops of the wood to the window. Timidly and with a horrid feeling of dread I would creep in there and my eyes would rake the Common Room. 'All clear' or 'Danger'! Oh God – there they were, four of them, one sitting down, the others slouched over the tops of desks. My heart gave a jolt and dreaded what would come next.

They turned round and stared, God how they stared, up and down endlessly. Then they began to sing, slowly and surely, I had even liked that song once but now it was a most dreadful sound to me, a fearful noise that got louder. I walked across the room feeling their eyes on me. I didn't look, they laughed but I just kept on walking, I was near screaming point, the room seemed to shake with the laughter, I reached my locker and dived in the curtains flapped back hiding me, I was afraid and near crying. There was a long silence, I didn't run, I couldn't, then softly at first then louder they began to shout the letters of my name.

They would never leave us alone the first term, saying 'why the hell did I always have to be with my brother'. We were twins and two hundred miles from home stuck in a Public School. God only knows what brothers are for, they are always together. I can still remember having to write an essay on the school, what I thought of it, a week after my brother had run away. 'As I came over the rise of the drive I saw a nice building and felt this was the place for me', like hell, but the Headmaster was going to read it. Nobody gave a damn for you, even your guardian that's supposed to show you the ropes, look after you, just sat back and watch me get punished, he thought it bloody funny and said so.

Some parts of the *Tom Brown* myth can still come true. Bullying is a major sport at one secondary modern boarding school for boys run by a LEA. The rows of bare feet that welcomed us in a progressive school were replaced in this one by lines of little boys with black eyes. Here are a few typical comments by boys who had been in the school a month or so:

At first I did enjoy it but now you keep getting hit if you do not give a senior boy a sweet or anything like that or if you call them the wrong name they put you in the book or threaten you. Sometimes they even throw stones at you which is not really aloud.

Boy, eleven

Its really rather horrible being a new boy. For every other form can push us around. But I've found if I stand up to them they treat you with more respect. I've had three fights, lost one and won two. If you can fit in with a boarding school you have a smashing time and I think we are all slowly fitting in, I am anyway. You look forward to the second year, and then at least you can push the first year round. Some of the seniors are jolly decent and the head boy is very comforting if you feel homesick but some of them, if I was as big as them, I'd give them a real dandy black eye. *Boy, twelve*

I am being bashed around like every one else in the first year. But I have been told that I will get used to it after one year. Personely I don't know why people come to this school if they are going to waste one year in being sad. You come by black eyes esely here.
Boy, eleven

I miss home a terrible lot and I used to take for granted little privileges such as going and having a game with my sisters and my pet dog and going and doing something with a couple of nails and a hammer and tinkering about with old clocks and going and helping my uncle in his curio shop. *Boy, eleven*

I feel very, very small and pushed down. It feels as if you are being pushed out of the way. I led a good life till I came to this school.
Boy, twelve

When will I see my mum agian I have not enjoyed board school it is horrobul. All the big boys thump you and bash you.
Boy, eleven

I feel very lonly. I have mist my Mother and father and I feal as if I am Being Bullied. I have not enjoyed it because I feal as if everybody is against me. I got a Black eye for creeping. Creeping is to go and tell a teacher what another Boy has done. *Boy, twelve*

A boy at a grammar boarding school run by a LEA comes down to earth with a bump:

When I first came to the school I imagined that it would be rather like a holiday camp with games in the afternoon and a short spell of lessons in the morning and when that was over I would be free.

Unfortunately when I was here a short time I realized that I was not given much free time at all except during the weekends and even then I had to turn up to meals. Also for the first time in my life people, such as senior boys, were openly aggressive and I learnt to fear. I learnt at school how to put up with unpleasantness and pain especially on cross-country runs. The school has made me appreciate home and family.
Boy, fourteen

Neither do the public schools always escape criticism:

I felt very lost and very homesick. I was rather shocked by some of the language, dishonesty and the rather vicious way boys often settled arguments. As I haven't really been away from home for very long I didn't know what it would be like, and I was rather shocked. When I entered for the school I had to take two exams and I don't know whether I'd have taken them if I'd known it was like this.
Boy, fourteen, public school

Slowly the child finds his way into this bewildering society. He learns its slang, passes its tests, endures its initiations. In some schools the new boy becomes a fag after a few weeks. Personal fagging, whereby the new boy acts as a servant to a senior boy, is a system peculiar to the public school. It may exist unofficially elsewhere but only in the public schools is it an important official method of assimilation to the house for new boys. It provides for communication between junior and senior which the school's rigid hierarchy might otherwise make difficult. It strips the newcomer of past prep-school status, negates his outside social position and acts as an initiation rite. It is a custom criticized by some outside as a cruel anachronism, or supported by those who find the vision of a peer scraping clean someone else's burnt frying pan irresistible. We find even the fags themselves are divided on the merits of fagging.

A group from a leading public school think that

Fagging is a very good idea for in spite of moments when you deplore the whole system, it proves to junior boys like myself, that we are not anything special but one of fifteen or so. It is inevitable though that boys should detest fagging when they are sent down to get something when they have just come back from there. I am now entering my last term fagging and look forward to two years tranquility in the middle of the house before I appear again at the top.

Boy, thirteen

When you fag you have a fagmaster who is a prefect and every morning after breakfast you have to do some jobs in his room such as put his slippers away. After lunch there is a boy-queue where the last has to fag if there is any to do. Also you have to tea-fag when you cook the fagmaster's tea. After tea you have to do some more jobs like taking his slippers out. Also if there is a boy-call you have to run to the place where its coming from and if your last you have to fag. I think it is rather a bother sometimes.

Boy, thirteen

Sometimes the job has unexpected variety:

Yes, I am a fag. Being a fag can often be very amusing. I often tell jokes and stories to my fagmaster and vice-versa. Going to boy calls is often extremely irritating because I often have a lot of work for the next lesson. Fagging takes up a lot of time, for instance, one is often fagged down the high street to buy an article of some kind. Fagging before quiet hour is a bore and stops me from doing other things that are often very important. I have to make his bed and to tidy up his room. I have to remember to change his suit and take down his coal bucket in the winter term. Once I have even been fagged to write a love letter to my fagmaster's ex girlfriend. I was told to make it as disgusting and revolting as I could. *Boy, thirteen*

The fag may provide the only communication between the houses available to seniors organizing games etc.

Fagging is not too bad provided one has nothing to do. But if one is busy and is fagged one tends to think 'why should I do it when he can do it just as well as I can'. Boy queues after lunch are the worst thing, having to run flat out for long distances is very strenuous and gives one stitches (some houses are miles away) but fag masters are

usually considerate. Room fagging is not much fun in the mornings, but sometimes is worth it if the fagmaster listens to a pirate station on the wireless, or plays pop records on his gramophone. Fagging for a prefect is the worst of all.
Boy, thirteen

It gives a chance to gossip:

I look forward to talking to my fagmaster in the evening, when we arrange his bed, etc. because he reveals a lot about the upper class of school life (i.e. prefects, masters, etc.) which I find extremely amusing. Altogether I think fagging altogether is a good thing because I think the fagmaster gets more value out of being what he is than the fag gives when he is a fag.
Boy, thirteen

Not everyone is quite so keen:

I find fagging a bad idea, my fagmaster leaves his room like the blitz. A pile of corps kit here, a bundle of dirty clothes there. Tape-recorder on the floor and after I have tidied this mess I make his bed, get his water. Then a boy queue which could go on for an hour or more while boys are left outside. Potty requests and stupid footling jobs just to annoy me and my fellow fags. My fagmaster tells me I'm incompetent idiot and a most untidy fellow! Then a boy-call away stops you learning something. Last term I failed to reach a class 6 times, 3 of which I was put in the late book. Last term my work got worse and during the first days of the holiday my doctor told me to have 3 days rest, that was my first terms fagging's impact.
Boy, thirteen

Room fagging makes me feel rather like a 'daily'.
Boy, thirteen

For some there isn't much to do:

Usually in my house on an average, there are three boy calls a day of which perhaps you arrive last once every day. So it is not all that hard work.
Boy, thirteen

I personally do not mind fagging, but in some cases your fagmaster may be in the corps. This is alright but why he could make his fag put on the greenslime with his hands, and polish his badges until there is nothing left of them, I do not know. If your fagmaster wants to come top in the passing out test let him do so by polishing his own corps-kit, including his mess-kit. But I think fagging is good for discipline.
Boy, thirteen

It can have difficulties:

'Go off to the shops Jones min, there's a good fellow' they say. But usually one is not told which size of anything and you spend hours saying 'Is that the usual size?' or 'Which are the nicest?' or 'Which do you think I should have?'. You feel a frightful ass.
Boy, thirteen

At other public schools things are not so organized:

After 10 days the new boy has to fag and usually the older boy makes you do his fagging. If you say, no, they pick on you and make life miserable or annoy you.
Boy, thirteen, public school

The prefects picking on the new boys, and when I'm in the middle of doing something, they come in and get you to fag. A few days ago I was forced to take a dead mouse out of their room, which they caught in their trap I didn't enjoy that as it was covered in blood.
Boy, thirteen, public school

The good thing about fagging is you begin to know your prefects and after a time he will pick on you to go down to shops and odds and ends. If there is some money left the prefect usually gives some of the change, if the job is done quickly. The worst thing of fagging is washing dirty pots and pans with no washing rag and the prefects expect them clean.
Boy, thirteen, public school

A public schoolboy sees future advantages:

Fagging? Oh it's not too bad, gives us something to talk about – and

the good thing is that when you are a senior others will have to work for you!! Fabulous thought!!!!!!
Boy, thirteen

Not all boarders arrive at an early age. Some arrive at fifteen or sixteen, after 'O' level. Some come in from day-school backgrounds and different social classes. There follow the comments of four boys who arrived at a traditional public school from local grammar or comprehensive schools on an 'integration' scheme. This book cannot begin to explore the issue of 'integration' – though the extracts suggest some of its possibilities and problems.[1] It should be noted that all the boys were academically able and all volunteered to come.

The first, a favourable response, needs no further comment:

Let me start by saying how very much I enjoyed it and what a wonderful experience it was. Coming from a comprehensive school and a working class family I expected the transition to public school life to be a very difficult and undesirable one, in the first place, because I would be boarding and, secondly, because of the kind of boys I would have to meet. It proved neither difficult nor undesirable.

The idea of boarding was, then, at first repugnant to me. Strict discipline, no privacy, snobbish boys, such were the ghastly thoughts that pervaded my mind as I prepared for my stay. Yet if there is no home luxury or freedom prevalent, these sacrifices seem very worthwhile in comparison to the several advantages to be gained from boarding. When an old boy wrote in the House magazine, 'Whereas the material drawbacks are real and noticeable to a person accustomed to home luxury, they lose significance in the general friendliness and cheerfulness of a well-knit community', he pointed to the great thing which boarding does for a boy. During my stay I noticed how very true this was, how boarding created this atmosphere of a social community.

Having no home distractions is an advantage and the sacrifice of 'home luxury' is a worthwhile one. I feel, however, that to be

---

1. See Royston Lambert, John Hipkin and Susan Stagg, *New Wine in Old Bottles? Studies in Integration within the Public Schools*, 1968.

separated from home might be very dangerous, especially for a boy of thirteen. I felt in some way isolated from home, and though I enjoyed my stay very much I was still glad to get home.

Another thing I found irksome was the monotony which prevailed owing to the day to day routine. Every day seemed very much the same, terribly monotonous.

I said that the thing I feared most was having to meet the public school boy. Before I came I had never met one, and I had always imagined him to be a detestable snob, floating about in his own world and having no concern for the likes of me. On the contrary, I met some of the friendliest and nicest boys I could hope to meet, boys whose vocabulary did not include the word 'snobbery', it pleased me very much.

There is not much to say about the lessons for they are run in much the same way as at my school. I feel, however, that there is far too much sport, not because I dislike it – in fact, I like it very much – but I think that many boys might be more concerned with their games than their studies. At my own school we have only $2\frac{3}{4}$ hours in a fortnight, some only 1 hour and 20 minutes, compared to six afternoons at the public school.

The prefects have very much more authority than our prefects, obviously, because there is so much more to do at a boarding school. It was good to see the prefects thrashing out school problems at their regular 'pres' meetings, and good to see how efficiently the House Powers went about their work within the House.

Though I realise that rules and regulations are necessary, I nevertheless felt that some were tedious and harsh. One such tedious rule, for example, which was being discussed for revision while I was there, stated that no one other than the prefect must walk around the school with the middle button of his coat undone, another that only House Sixths can carry umbrellas. Also while recognising that a House Master cannot have his boys going all over the town at their will – this would be an impossible situation – I feel that there might be a little more freedom as to what places are out of bounds. The occasional visit to the cinema or the local concert hall (where 'pop' music is played) cannot do any damage, if permitted in moderation. Such requests are often refused.

The boys are, however, compensated in that there is so much going on within the school and the Houses themselves. An art appreciation society, a modern language society, a film society, a choral society, a gymnastics society, a drama society etc. – we have such things at the comprehensive too, but the boarder can give so much more time to them. How easy it is, for example, for the House to have play rehearsals or music practices!

Finally, a word on the House itself. It was strange to see that the emphasis lay on the House and not the School – or so it seemed – and that the Headmaster appeared to be nothing more than a figure-head. We have Houses at my comprehensive but they mean nothing compared to the Houses at the public school, which obviously mean more in a boarding school where a House is a House, in which boys actually live together.

And that, I think, is all, except to say that the food was well below standard in view of the sizeable fees the boys pay.

The second sixth-former was much less impressed though equally objective about his experience:

My first impression of the school was the notable lack of master supervision, with the prefects controlling the general discipline and running of the house. I thought the fag system, although not in this particular case, was very much open to abuse, with prefects able to cane younger pupils, an act which, if not totally abolished, should at least be reserved for the housemaster. However I certainly agree with the principle of prefects running the house, and organizing recreational activities etc. in the house, since it developed any qualities of leadership and responsibilities which the prefect may have. Discipline generally was excellent and I only wish that discipline at my comprehensive was as good.

Although pupils were not exactly 'caged in', I felt particularly restricted and life tended to get monotonous. Many of the pupils also felt restricted, especially because they were unable to go out on Saturday evenings, and this would perhaps account for their apparent extravert behaviour during their holidays.

The question of l'amour shocked and almost disgusted me. The boys obviously lacked female companionship and had tried to adapt themselves accordingly. Girls were not looked upon as friends, nor treated as such, but merely treated with contempt. Having been educated in mixed schools all my life I did not find the absence of females particularly noticeable, although I felt sorry that an occasional female voice could not rise high above the bass and tenors during chapel each morning.

The religious views of the pupils were not at all different to those of the pupils at my comprehensive. There were the usual sprinkling of atheistic, agnostic and general apathetic attitudes towards religion, but there appeared to be a certain dictatorial attitude by the school and religious views were occasionally thrust upon pupils.

The staff were generally older and adopted a more formal attitude towards pupils than found at my own school.

The pupils obviously received a first class academic education with excellent recreational facilities, but they appeared unprepared to meet the outside world – a world occupied mainly by the lower class, and some were accordingly narrow-minded. Social and class barriers exist but I felt that Public Schools do not assist in the minimization of these barriers.

Here are a few comments from another boy, this time from the local grammar school:

This concern with the individual is a refreshing change from the rather impersonal atmosphere of a large day-school, tho' I was not entirely happy with the way peoples 'souls' were pulled to pieces by a group of 17/18 year olds who would seem to have only a limited experience of humanity on which to draw when judging others.

Discipline: It was immediately noticeable that people of all ages accepted discipline far more readily than at my grammar school. Punishments were lenient – 25 or 50 lines compared with 4 or 6 sides of quarto, and yet were more feared because the climate of public opinion was against law-breaking. Some punishments however seemed rather unrealistic – for instance giving a 17 year old 25 lines for talking in chapel seems very petty. Laws regarding dress, and appearance were stricter and more strictly enforced and observed.

The libraries were very good, both general and departmental though the most impressive was the House library, containing more books I felt I wanted to read than the whole of my own school library.

At the risk of over generalizing I should say that while the people at the school are less well equipped to compete with the outside world, they are better equipped to be agreeable.

Finally another boy arrives at the school from a comprehensive school:

Throughout my stay a sense of restriction was hard felt – being confined to the same buildings (and people) out of normal school hours soon became a hardship. Most, if not all, of the boys greatly resented not being able to spend the odd evening in the town, and it was this continual feeling of restriction which – as so many of them so unashamedly professed – led to their running so wild in the holidays.

Apart from the occasional fleeting glimpse of womanhood as it speedily negotiated the Road, we enjoyed no contact whatsoever. The presence of the opposite sex having been taken for granted for so long made it's sudden absence all the more frustrating. Furthermore its presence had, over the years, furnished a natural and respectful relationship between us, a relationship which contrasted astoundingly with that shared by an uncomfortably large proportion of the senior boys; their general attitude towards sex, and their accomplishment in that field of which they often boasted, were most distasteful. I can only surmise that it was due to the perpetual sexual segregation and insufficient feminine company to which the boys had been forced to gear themselves.

The master–boy relationship at the school naturally varied with the master, but was perhaps less friendly than that at my comprehensive school. My expectations of a rather frigid teaching staff were thankfully disappointed, the average age of the teaching staff at my own school was apparently lower than that at the public school and this, at my school, undoubtedly facilitated communication between teacher and pupil.

An immense scope of extra-mural activities caters for all tastes and every boy is encouraged to take on active interest in the arts; this and vigorous seclusion from the lower classes tends to produce a far more individual and sophisticated type of boy than most state-schools can turn out. However, in an average comprehensive school, where most classes of the child population are educated together, it can be argued that a child receives a much broader education than in an ivory-tower institution such as the public school, and is thus more adequately prepared for the responsibilities of adult life.

Whether these verdicts, carefully selected for typicality, are as just as they attempt to be objective, we leave the reader to judge. Perhaps the rest of this book may provide more evidence on the matter.

The boys and girls have arrived and settled in. In subsequent chapters they unfold the rhythm, complexities, joys and frustrations of the life they lead.

4 The Pattern

Life is to a set timing and a clockwork setting.
Boy, thirteen, state boarding school

Everything, unless you have an extraordinarily active imagination is laid on for you. Your day is mapped out for you – so many minutes for work, so many for play. *Boy, seventeen, public school*

On this somewhat sour note, we can begin to explore the boarder's daily and termly life, the pattern which makes up normal existence. In this chapter, we illustrate the ordinary stuff of life: rising and sleeping, work, eating, religion, games, the weekend (an institution in itself in boarding schools) and special events. All schools have a routine, but in some it is more detailed, more all-embracing than others. Many public, some independent and a few state schools set out to use or guide most of their pupils' time, including 'free' time, to some approved purpose. Successive heads of house in an archetypal school advise their successors privately in their house books:

I feel if you keep boys occupied and busy, you are half way to winning the battle.

The key to good discipline is occupation, for 'the devil makes work for idle hands'. The more fully occupied – but not regimented – they are, the better.

I am all for moderate individualism, provided individualism does not go too far.

88   The Hothouse Society

A boy at another public school shrewdly assesses one possible effect of this all-pervasive, never-ending routine and organization into which the boy has to fit himself:

> We start off when Mr Saunders (my housemaster) comes in, switches on all the lights and says 'Good morning boys ready for showers – come on'. It is the same every morning and has been so for 2 or 3 years. Sometimes I wish he'd change it to something different, or lose his voice. But when he is ill and another master does it I hate it even more. I feel this new master is upsetting the routine which I have myself buried in and, strangely enough have come to rely on so much (this is why I think so many boys here join the services – or make a fool of themselves outside – because they have ceased to think for themselves, and when freedom is given them, they don't know what to do with it, so they fling it about). Myself I find I become more and more like the guinea pig kept in a cage for all its life, until one day the door is left open and it doesn't escape, why – I don't really know, in my case I think it is all laziness, with a fixed routine you don't have to think, you just go as you've done for years until you can do it in your sleep. *Boy, fifteen, public school*

Many schools are now moving towards greater freedom of activity. Even in fairly rigid schools, scope for individual and semi-approved activity can increasingly be found. Here is a member of an unofficial pop group in a public school in the commuter belt, near London:

> Then break, a piece of Bread to nibble, a quick of spin of the Beatles 'and your bird can sing' which always seems to make me happy.
>
> At one o'clock I was pleased as I thought I'd got a free afternoon. The rugger list was up before lunch.
>
> I was not on it, great! I met Dave and he said they were going to have a group practice about four and would I like to come to record them on my tape recorder. O.K. I said I'll be down at four. Then the bomb dropped. On my way in I met a Pre who said I had to play Rugger. 'Shit' said I. Rush indoors look on list, yes I have been put on it but the name has been crossed out again, so 'I don't turn up' says I.
>
> Got one or two microphones for this practice and at about

3 o'clock Alex, myself and Dave decide to wander out for a cigarette. When we get back Simon rushes in and says I should have played Rugger. 'Balls' says I 'my name was crossed off'. Simon then says 'well we played the whole game with only 14 men' 'Shit' says I.

At half-past four we start to practice. All goes well except one microphone gives up. So I have to try and balance five instruments and three voices into two microphones. Nigel Lennox (Pre) trys to pitch us out about five saying the Extra Work class is in there. Nigel Lennox overruled.

After tea at six I rush off to give a microphone back. Just as I get back Dave tells me the head of house was calling 'why haven't you put your name on the list to be out after six?'. God what a spastic! Another essay no doubt.

I am feeling a bit cheesed off as I write this, and I shall be glad of bed tonight. And oh my sainted fanny, Corps tomorrow!

Boy, seventeen, public school

But the staff like to know what the boys have been doing even when they are free. At a large public school the junior boys (aged thirteen to fourteen) record graphically and frankly in a book how they spend each afternoon out of class of the autumn term. Two pages from this book (reproduced overleaf) give a lively impression of their various activities. (Gridding = cycling; NHS = natural history society; CCF = cadet corps; Mem Lib = library; rem gym = remedial gym.)

Some schools deliberately allow more freedom of activity, time and movement in the hope – not always fulfilled – that the children will *choose* to use the education or cultural facilities of the school or neighbourhood. A few other schools give free time but provide nothing to do. We encountered under-provision rather than the over-provision described in our opening experiences. Here is a characteristic comment from a fifteen-year-old boy at Cromwell College:

After school this is our free time, but what can we do? Sweet Fuck all thats what. Between the hours of 4–6 this place dies. I looked around for the fellow from University but he was nowhere to be found. Most like eating toast and drinking coffee in some Senior Boy's study. Lucky bastard.

	Mon	Tue	Wed	Thu	Fri	Sat	""
Taylor	Gridding to Cynefin	went out	Gym	Gridded to West Wood	C.S.I.	Piano Practice	0
Cotterill	Hockey 5#	Hockey	CCF Rep ready Drill 1st	Went for a walk across the Downs to course	?Leave?	Out with parents	2
Saunders	Played Hockey	Went gridding in Savernak	Played Rugger	Did gym and went gridding in the Rain	Carpentry	Watched squash	2
Blackstar	Played Hockey	Hockey	Went to Rem Gym	Did Gym	Did Gym	Went out with Parents	2
Dean	Played Hockey	Gridded	Rugger	Fencing	Fencing	Fenced	2
Clark	Went gridding to Caraslot	Out with parents	Did gym	Went Gridding	Gridded	MHS	0
Robbins	Junior House Recce	Iced Hockey	C.C.F.	Rugger	Fives	Fives	3
Andrews	Hockey	Played shoe	Rem Gym Played	Had a Super Grid Ride in the Rain	Flat Feet Rem Gym	Squash	1
Lewis	Hockey Lat.	Hockey		Squash	? ball (lost)	Went Out with the car (lost money)	2

JHI

	SUN	MON	TUE	WED	THURS	FRI	SAT
Harris	Sanny	Sanny	Sanny	Sanny	Sanny	Scratched
Saunders	Played Rugger - LUT - on Pough. 0-0.	Watched XV v. St Mary's Hospital	Gym.	Played Rugger	Watched Basket-ball v. summer and Did gym.	Rugger watched Rugger
Blackstone	Played Rugger UVL	Watched Rugger	Practised Rugger	Went to London	Did Gym	Watched Rugger
Croxley	Played rugger	Went Painting. Went Painting and	Had Practice Rugger with Mr SIR	Played Rugger we won 30 -	Worked ! Yes !	Played squash
McDonald	Played Rugger on Intel UVL lost 6-18.	Watched XV v. Mary's May Played on Pitch pitch D.W. Repaired Rep all on as?	Rugger Coaching	Played XV Rugger	Went sitting	Watched Rugg off Wopps last 6 - M
Clark	Had Organ Lesson Say Elberton	Watched rugger. Say Elberton.	Played footer first time did gym	Played Rugger	Played fives watched gym	Watched rugger.
Andrews	RUGGER	Watch XV vs. St Mary's	Did XV gym	Played Rugger	Squash	Watched XV
Feather-stone	Rugger very boring	Gardening	gym pulled muscle	Played ruger VS. pulled our short badly	Gym	walked Rugger
Symons	Ruggers bored !!!	Watched XV Barry sick !!	Rugger	Rugger		Watched Rugger

We can now present some typical ingredients of the boarders' daily life.

FACING THE DAY

Nothing contrasts more with home and holiday life than the boarder's pattern of rising. Also no other moment reveals so perfectly the differing styles, atmospheres and even internal relations of schools. We drop in on a selection of dorms and studies as their occupants get up.

First, a public school boy faces the day with characteristic vocabulary, hierarchy, work, and chapel:

> 7.00 a.m. One of those annoyingly high-pitched little newboys comes in and shakes us to wake us up. Quarter of an hour to prep! A few tell him where to go, but this is just because it is the beginning, rather an early beginning, of another day: others just turn over. In a few minutes, after struggling to keep awake, I get up and go to the washrooms, where a number of younger boys are singing as they wash: incomprehensible, but just what we used to do a year ago.
>
> I go downstairs to the study I share with four others, turn on a tape-recorder and soon a newboy knocks on the door: 'Two minutes to prep!' One of my best friends now comes in and tidies his desk. 'Prep's started!' calls out someone, and we settle down, turn off the tape-recorder and begin to work. Our study-holder comes in: 'Am I late?' 'Yes'. 'Oh too bad', and begins his work. We all work in silence until 7.40. Then we go to breakfast, where everyone is fully awake but rather quiet. My meal at breakfast usually consists of a piece of toast and plenty of coffee. We go back to our house, and make beds, and then go down to our studies. Everything begins to liven up, and we chat, find out what our stars forecast for the day. Some people attempt to sing a few bars. 'Earthquake in Tashkent ... Chelsea alone in Europe ... How exciting ... Hey, look, live models in Carnaby Street ... who or what is that? ... etc. etc.' Someone fills in a passport form and I receive a letter from my brother in Devon, where he is teaching gym. The chapel bells ring for voluntary chapel, but few people stir.
>
> *Boy, seventeen, public school*

Over in East Anglia, at a coeducational school, a sixteen-year-old girl yawns:

> Feeble voice says 7 o'clock. Turn over. Feeble voice says ¼ past. If I'd been asleep I'd never had heard it. Wait till its my week to wake them up – they'll hear *me*!

Down in the south-west another girl:

> Nearly overslept but Philippa woke me in time for breakfast. I wish she wouldn't wear such heavy eye makeup, it spoils her eyes (she wakes up at 7.30 so she can do them in time for breakfast!)
> *Girl, seventeen, progressive school*

But boys are unresponsive to such elaborate feminine allurements at this hour:

> The obvious advantage is that of living with girls. Though this advantage is infinitely small when some of the slags in our room are viewed at the breakfast table. *Boy, fifteen, coeducational school*

In the far north a fourteen-year-old girl boarding in a comprehensive school rises in a bad mood:

> We are woken up by an unsympathetic matroon and the blankets are pulled off and I hate this hell they don't have any feeling do they? At 10 to 8 we have shoe inspection and if they are in a bad mood they say that our shoes are B awfull. I hate this and always think to myself 'I would love to be in there shoes and to be able to do what I like with them instead of it always being the other way round.'

Not only children have bad moods at this hour:

> Woke up to the sound of my housemasters voice. 'O gosh he is in a bad temper again as usual', he must have had another argument with his wife. *Boy, fourteen, integrated school*

Cromwell College arises characteristically, in hour, in method, in rituals, and in the quality of its personal relations:

06.45. That bloody bugle wakes us up the idiot down the end of the dorm who is meant to be in charge yells at us to get downstairs. Get my washing kit. Bugger! I have not got any toothpaste. 'Can anybody let me have some toothpaste?' Silence from everybody. I yelled 'you tight load of yids'. Somebody pinched my washbasin. 'Get out you bastard, seniors first'. 5 minutes till breakfast. Everybody out. We run from the dorm still putting our ties on clutching my coffee tin (I don't like tea).

07.00. Breakfast. Bloody fried bread again. I have been at this God forsaken hole for two years and always had fried bread every day for breakfast. Breakfast drags. I'm too asleep to think about it. Is there any mail for me? A dull voice yells my name. Oh great, but when I got it it was from my aunt wondering if I am cold at nights, and the old girl didn't send a postal order. Grace is said and we shuffle upstairs to make our beds. Pull them together and now we are to do work, in other words, make the place look tidy and can't be bothered. The Prefects can get knackered. I am going to read a book. Then when a bugle says so we cleaned up just so that a toff (a master) can inspect us and look important. After that everybody marches round in a circle and has a look at the Head. Pointless isn't it?

Other schools have early-morning runs. A state boarder observes:

The Head master is a big hypocrite I think, and I dont like him. He makes us do things that he wouldn't dream of doing them himself. Like a run. He couldn't run to save his life.
Boy, fourteen, secondary modern boarding school

Peter Nicholson, a seventeen-year-old boy at an independent school, describes in more detail what the morning run is like for him. We join him as he leaves the school:

... Then you turn right and an icy blast grasps you, drives out all the warmth out of your body. Suddenly a milk lorry comes hurtling in to the archway its horn pounding away like a banshi. Boys coming, dazed, stare in terror and hurl themselves against the wall. The horn echoes off the walls. I skip to one side my body missing the truck by inches and then I am out. Cutting the corners, I run on along the puddle laden track. A person is in front of me and he splashes and kicks back the mud I try to avoid him. Blast him, another bloody person is doing the same thing. By now I feel the weight of my trousers and I am getting down to the rhythm. I come to another corner this I cut to avoid a wedge of panting and puffing boys, really juniors. Why the hell can't they get out of the way? I run round the castle and then someone sprints past and gracefully peels off on to the left track. Lucky Bugger he has finished his run. Christ how much longer? I go faster now down the hill too tired to stop. I get ready for the long pull up the drive to the last crown of the hill. I pant. My feet won't obey me. I must go on. God I can't move. I see J. and I pass him for a moment I am elated when I slow again. My feet aching and feeling bloody heavy. My head whirls. Then I come to the tarmac. God O God. I stagger up that damn hill. Must go on. I force one leg up and then the other. I have no breath left. Swearing, cursing, I gratefully round the corner and let myself career down the drive. Faster and faster my legs fly everywhere. Then a last effort and across the square. Almost joyfully I splash myself in a puddle.

I grasp the black rails of the steps. Through to the changing room I throw my arms against the wall and try to regain my senses. Already I have automatically kicked off my shoes and chucked off my shorts. I stroll up to the checker and with an inhuman grunt call my name. Through the swing doors. I hit my arm on the door as someone barges through the other way. I step up onto the platform and walk under the showers. Thank god here is one hot. I straighten up still walking. Christ a blasted cold one, I turn at the end and come down the other side. I lurch forward and dash for the door. Thank God. No. Round again. Fuck it. I remember going round four times before some blasted prefect let me go. Must not stop though. Quickly I go out and pull on my shorts which have been kicked 3 feet away and struggle into my gym shoes.

This then is the morning run. Every boy has to go through the same experience. It seems strange. You are being taught to be a leader. All you are taught here is resentment and hatred for the people who try to rule your life.

One progressive school also has compulsory morning exercise, not a run but a walk:

> During breakfast House Mother has gone around with checklist catching people who didn't present themselves for Morning Walk – to post office and back in theory, just up and down access road.
> *Boy, eighteen, progressive school*

At another, an eighteen-year-old girl (atypically perhaps) arose thus:

> A boisterous boy of mild acquaintance woke me up half an hour before it was necessary and, as is his nature, tried to seduce me. Attempt failed because I was annoyed and very sleepy.

Much more typical is another girl in the same school:

> I didn't want to get up this morning, so I feigned a headache when my boy friend came to wake me at 8.20. 'Bring me some breakfast please' I pleaded. 'Oh, get up its a lovely day. I'll leave some toast on the table'. Grunt, roll over, doze until 8.28. Get up, immediately blinded by the bright sunlight. Kill five ants that are crawling over my lime juice bottle, and wash them down the plughole with scalding water . . . Sadist. By 8.35 I'm eating toast and reading letters, thank God, I got some this morning. 'Headache' gone. Make my bed, smoked my first cigarette of the day. Trundled off to chores.
> *Girl, seventeen, progressive school*

Many schools have housework or chores as part of the early morning routine; we have already encountered this. Here is one boy's description of his:

> 8.50 a.m. I swept down my landing stairs and began the painstaking task of scrubbing my stairs. I had scrubbed about two stairs when I began swearing to myself. Fuck this (why should I do this) they don't look any better than before. I continued in this manner till I had done about half my stairs and by this time was so fed up that I just wet mopped the remaining stairs (using the same scabby filthy

little mop). By this time I had reached the bottom Hedges came hopping down the stairs calling my nickname 'Aristotle' (I was given this name by another boy as I was interested in physics, and good at it up to a point; good enough to be first anyway; this name has stuck) – 'Ah – good fellow your the only person here that I can rely on to have a mop' to which I replied 'Thats because I always make a point of nackering (taking) it first'. I emptied my bucket of water and then mopped down my other stairs. By the time I had done this I was nackered (tired) and spent the remaining time skiving in the middle rooms. Fairweather, who is leaving on Saturday next, came in the middle rooms to get his trunk to pack. When he did this, Jenkins, a new boy who works in the middle rooms, began to cry. Naturally enough I suppose for a person of 14 who has become highly strung working on the sweep which everybody messes up. Fairweather kind at heart as he is tried his best to console him. I gave him a hand with his trunk, by which time work had ended.

Boy, fifteen, independent school

Finally, two prep school boys start their day in greatly contrasting styles. A conventional prep school:

I woke up rather late, to be greeted by the sound of the water running into the bath in Matron's bathroom next door. Presently it stopped, and Matron poked her head around the door and said good morning. Then she called the dormitories in turn, and we went along and washed our faces. We dressed slowly, and I had only just finished making my bed when the sixth form were called for reports. *Reports*! The very name strikes terror into the heart of many, at the thought of being alone in the headmaster's study with the headmaster: however I went downstairs and waited outside his study until my turn came. I went in, and Mr Casey said briefly what he thought of my report, and I went out feeling none the worse for wear, and had breakfast.

Boy, twelve, prep school

The prep department of a progressive school:

It was a bright sunny morning, when I woke up and rubbed the sleep from my eyes. I felt very warm in my bed. I lay there for about ten minutes, then the door opened and in came Betty to wake Paul and I up. (Betty is the House Mother). 'Time to get up' she said 'hurry up now, it's twenty to eight'. What a bore, I could not be bothered to get up yet so I sat up and read. I got dressed, the bell rang just as I was putting on my shoes. I ran downstairs and into the dining room. I eat a bit of breakfast and run outside into the sunshine. I had not gone far when the bell rang. I walked to the woodwork room. Where I did my chores. It was soon over and the next bell rang for classes. I went into Tormouth building and looked at the timetable, it read, Woodwork, pottery and painting. I had to run all the way back to the woodwork room. I am making a canoe in woodwork, I did that while talking to Jamie (the master).

Boy, twelve, 'Tormouth' prep school

WORK

Work at boarding school does not differ much in content from that at day school, though its range can be more varied and the conditions in which it is done are very different. This is not the place for us to examine the effect of boarding on the academic and other development of the child – our own assessment will appear in our companion report and the children's in this and the final chapters of this book.

Work is the focus of the daily round and so we give a few evaluations and criticisms and then slip into a few classes and tutorials: but very briefly – work does not inspire the most vivid writing by the boarders.

Some children in an integrated Catholic school in the north sum up what many think about the impact of boarding on their work. A fifteen-year-old lists the benefits:

> My work has been greatly helped: peace and quiet for study; regular study; proximity of library; staff present to help; not so many distractions as home.

Another agrees:

> It is absolutely true that you can study better here. I spent the last

5 years at a day school and subsequently I found it far easier to study here. Homework was a bore but now it is part of the curriculum. Everyone does it and I can spend more time on it. There are not so many distractions here.
Boy, sixteen

Two others stress another benefit to work which boarding brings at their school:

Very good attention from staff at all times.
Boy, fifteen

You get to know the staff better and so can discuss troubles, difficulties in work more easily and more often.
Boy, fifteen

A public school boy puts the same point in his own terms:

You see the housemaster regularly about work in general: every fortnight (order time) and my group tutor is always on tap.
Boy, fifteen, public school

Two sixth-formers in one public school have shared studies: a typical situation. Their contrasts fairly sum up the situation in a great academic school.

Conditions for studying have improved with studies, but whether a senior boy – and they are only ones who really have work – works conscientiously or not depends on his own integrity. Probably better than at home as no telly etc. What I hate is goddam unimaginative moronic housemasters who sneak up on the industrious, hard at it, student trying to cram the whole of English Literature for Oxford Scholarship in one term, and kick him up to bed at 10.30 p.m. on the dot. All night sessions only possible in some houses but practically impossible in mine, sod it!
Boy, eighteen

Work at school, with a study, can be relegated to various odd times, 'tomorrow' being the most common. However, once having taken the plunge, work is easier to get on with; interruptions are minimal and one's privacy is generally respected. Facilities, in terms of reference books, amenities (important for me as a musician) are generally very good and easily obtainable. Once you've decided to work, it is very easy to carry on, the decision is the hard part.

Boy, eighteen

Less exalted boys, even in the sixth form, do their prep in common rooms, or classrooms. Most find conditions better than at home:

> In the prep room you can really get on with it – the place looks and feels like work – and the prefects shut up talkers.
> *Boy, sixteen, direct grant school*

> At home there was TV and my sister playing and it was cold in the bedroom. Here we do prep in the classroom at night – no distractions, over and done with. *Girl, fourteen, state boarding school*

Occasionally, however, things are not so satisfactory:

> 7.00 p.m. Prep again now, same old background chatter. It depresses me really the way some people can't shut up for a little while living so close to the others. I often find myself hating them. Its not real hate and when I think about it I know its not based on anything genuine, just one incident. You hate them for about a day, and then it wears off. *Boy, sixteen, public school*

'No distractions', say the satisfied. By contrast, others find the schools provide too many distractions. One chief problem of boarding schools is the place of work in a society offering and encouraging many alternative activities. The multiple responsibilities of the senior boys can break up their work time and punctuality. A sixth-former in a thriving state boarding school in the Home Counties sums up this very common problem of priorities.

> ... I do not mean to imply that I think the choir, orchestra, 'Weekly Magazine' and play are unnecessary. The atmosphere is not intellectually sterile but for most seniors the planning, say, of junior rugby teams takes traditional and unquestioned precedence over a momen-

tary desire to read about Descartes. It seems to me that the balance is overweighted against work.

Our time-table is, as it were, forced upon us by that of the lower school. I am sure that some of our teachers must feel that forty minutes, often interupted by late arrivals for a multitude of legitimate reasons, are not sufficient to get to grips with anything. 'Study' periods alternate with lessons and contrive thoroughly to break up the time in which we could work unhindered.

The problem is our own, and ours to solve, but the system does not help. For when one becomes senior and the need to work hard is more real; the number of other things one has to do seems to grow. How often do the other things, because they seem more urgent and immediate, take precedence, and work is deferred?

Some other boarders echo this boy's dilemma:

I'm always just settling down to a bit of work when someone comes asking for something for me to do. 'Come and sing for the group', or 'Go and drive the motor club car'.

Boy, fifteen, integrated school

Being a Prefect's a bore – you don't have enough time for study. You have to stop every 20 minutes to check this, do that duty, give out a notice, collect such and such, stop so and so. Its responsibility v. work here! *Boy, seventeen, independent school*

Many children complain about their work or teaching. The narrowness of stress or of the curriculum recurs frequently:

The curriculum is designed with only one thing in mind – exams. There's no discussion, no variety.

Boy, seventeen, direct grant school

Nothing but A level, A level. There's nothing about everyday things, practical things, how to change a car wheel, first aid. We're exam robots. *Boy, sixteen, another direct grant school*

Its either science *or* Arts. If you're good at subjects like English *and* biology you have had it here. *Boy, seventeen, public school*

Of course many criticize the teaching. Here are a couple of the most typical:

> The best boys get the best masters, the worst boys get the worst. If your not bright here, you've had it. *Boy, sixteen, public school*

> Too much dead wood – doddering old retired Housemasters, or young staff who are merely good games players. We dim boys get these. *Boy, fourteen, public school*

> Brilliant – ought to be at college, really. He gets carried away by the subject and loses sight of one of the main reasons for doing A level – passing it. *Boy, fifteen, public school*

Most other criticisms of teachers are not specific to boarding schools except such as the following:

> I never see most of the staff after 4. They go into hibernation for the rest of the day. *Boy, seventeen, direct grant school*

> The teachers here aren't informal and helpful out of class, in the evenings. You go to Dodswell with a problem and you get your head bitten off. *Boy, sixteen, integrated school*

Let us leave the comment and enter a few classes through the pupils' experience. A very young girl first, an eleven-year-old, at a Quaker school:

> When we were having dinner I told the first form boy across the table that my nickname was Kit so he quickly told the other form boys to call me Kitty Cat.
> When I went to get the pudding Liz put salt in my water. when I came back I saw it looked a bit misty so I guessed and poured myself some more water. After dinner I tried to learn my french for a french test but I didn't succed in learning very much.
> Our first lesson in the afternoon was maths I was in a dim mood so when Mr Skyes asked me a thing I didn't have the fogyest what he was on about.

After Maths was music. Mr Olver showed us some musical instruments and he tried to make them play it was quite funny. After french the one lesson I hate, but we didn't have a test (thank goodness) we had to cover our french books, I did my own okay but then she told me to do a spare one. I did it all wrong so I just put it as right as I could and then gave it to her she then told me to do another one I also did that wrong. At four o'clock I went to feed the pigs. Then I went to ballroom dancing. Miss Dixon the ballroom teacher made me dance with Barnes, it was awful (I hate him) he kept on laughing it made me mad.

We then had tea it was awful fritters and tomatoes.

After tea we had prep. Batty (Mr Barker) took prep but I only had one and I finished that in five minutes so I just read my book.

A prep-school boy of similar age shows from a school in the countryside how different his curriculum and pattern are from the girl above: more organized, more traditional in subjects and exam-oriented, more secondary-school in style, with much use of the same staff for different subjects:

The History lessons are universally dreaded in our (the 6th) form. The Headmaster takes them, and when roused, has a most uncanny way of making me feel uncomfortable, and it seems to improve his throwing. He is the most accurate master with an exercise book or chalk-box. However this period was not the usual spine chilling forty minutes we expected. He quietly finished off the Hundred Years War ...

Then we had French with Mr Pumphrey. He set us a two hour Scholarship paper to do. At the start, he always tells us to do something (learn verbs, write out exercises or something) in French, and then for the benefit of those who didn't hear, repeats it in English.

The next lesson was latin, with Mr Easton. I like the Latin lessons generally, but in the last few periods we've been having a series of papers: he handed us a ghastly C.E. paper to do in that lesson and the one in the afternoon. About halfway through my translation I noticed that the form were rapidly evacuating, for the art period.

The art-room is a general mess, despite Mrs Wilmot's frantic efforts. When I got up there, Mrs Wilmot was busily telling the others to draw shapes and told me to draw the others, as she always does. There was one time when she thought as I was mad keen on drawing cartoons, my pride and joy was her art lessons, and she set me drawing all kinds of things. She even made me learn the biographies of various painters, until she realized little by little that my pride and joy was *not* her art lessons, and then she made me do drawings of the others, as she did that lesson. Anyway, I set to work and drew, and drew, and finally . . . the bell went . . .

The music lessons are generally forty minutes sitting still, and listening to music. However, for some people there are far more interesting things to look at than the piano. Harris was imitating Mr Webster, and it caused Franks to burst out giggling. This went on until the end of the lesson.

The next lesson was Latin again: finishing off the C.E. paper, I was having difficulty, when Mr Easton told us it was time, and claimed for marking. Every now and then he would utter a groan a red line would appear under half a sentence, and I would close my eyes, and try to ignore it. After break Mr Easton took us again, but this time for English.

A boy in a large public school started his lessons apprehensively:

Between chapel and periods everything is concentrated on getting there in time. Had Mr Palmer. Attitude of complete indifference to the thought of talking about Economics for $1\frac{1}{2}$ hours. When we got going though I became engrossed and actually thought economics to the exclusion of all else.
Boy, seventeen

Morning break follows:

Recess comes at last – a form room full of bodies, coffee and a haze of burnt toast smoke. Another large mug of coffee.
Boy, sixteen, public school

After French there is a little break, I buy a packet of crisps which are being sold in aid of something and I dash upstairs and put the kettle on, coffee time, Jenny brings some milk up and we make our drinks then we depart to a roof outside one of the windows which, as well as being a suntrap is invisible from most directions. We have a quick ciggy and by the end of break there are six girls out there, two day, the rest boarders. Then we dash into English leaving the science people who have an optional to wash up the mugs.

Girl, sixteen, progressive school

Form room empties slowly but only slightly. Get stamps from office for Amnesty. Have to write to a strange Greek as 'Dear Cousin' and make it convincing for the prison censors. Very difficult.

Boy, sixteen, coeducational school

Lessons, with the contrasts between schools they bring, resume. The researcher takes one:

3rd period. It is meant to be divinity. Oh joy, I can read Hammond Innes behind a Bible. The old padre shuffles in. Oh whats this. Behind him comes a rather dull looking creep with reams and reams of paper: a research chap from Cambridge. He plonked them on the desk and smiled. We had heard of this fellow. Lower V had him yesterday. He rambles on, I am sure this class will cooperate with him. I will, thats why I am writing this.

Boy, sixteen, Churchill College

Unexpected humour startles others:

The history master cracked a dirty joke during a test and we were all rather surprised as we did not think he knew such things.

Boy, fourteen, integrated school

Work to some can become oppressive, especially as exams draw close. At a well-known academic independent school, a day is haunted for a seventeen-year-old by a coming oral exam. We follow his fears:

I've now got to make a start on that bloody French translation. I'm slightly depressed by the thought of failing the exam yet again, thank god for the sciences.

11.30. Haven't got anywhere with French. I have just noticed my spots are getting worse around the neck.

12.50. Just finished a gym period with a very small group, did complicated boxwork, a good thing because was able to show my general superiority. It leaves me with a warm glow.

I'm a bit worried about French Oral practice. This afternoon, silly really buts its amazing how in this life of almost seclusion each event is magnified out of all proportion. Bloody annoyed that barber's coming this afternoon.

15.00. Have just been thrown out of French Oral practice for not preparing enough. Probably justified but Mr Hillier needn't have been so bloody sarky about it. I just can't understand French. I seem to be going backwards not forwards, forgetting more and more. Hillier does not exactly help; ever since the fourth form all he's ever done is sneer, sneer, sneer. Silly little ponce of a man.

22.15. Am now in bed, the best part of the day, Hillier who was duty master quite friendly when French mentioned. First time in four years.

Hope conversation at tomorrows breakfast with Lambert [the author] is sane and sensible. I hope also that he finishes breakfast a bit earlier, otherwise have to sit with him and miss most of eight o'clock news. Most unsettling as upsets regular routine built up over the years.

In some schools work seems not to oppress. At Stanton, the progressive school, the working pattern, the atmosphere and the size of class are quite different, but, for one girl, there are still problems posed by the very freedom and lack of pressure of the place and the burden of choice and effort which it passes back to her:

We were greeted by a door which would not open. Ha, Ha! when the inmates found it was us we were let in, to find that the barricade was to stop the teacher. A few minutes later the teacher tried to open the door, the barricade fell over and he yelled at us 'I'm not teaching you lot, teach yourselves' and slammed the door really hard. The 'big lads' who had thought up the plan, proceeded to tease and annoy everyone – and eventually go out feeling, I'm sure, pleased and very mighty.

After break, its music in Arthur's room. We all went up to his bedsitter and sat around in easy chairs listening to jazz – one boy – a pathetic one – makes a joke – no one laughs. At last for once, you feel the school has achieved something. We were all – 6 of us – sitting in this room, being quite civil, you felt that this was more like the happy family idea, which you are led to believe the school is.

After lunch, I talk to a friend, or do a prep. or go outside, according to the weather – in a way free time at Stanton is nice, 'cos you can do anything or NOTHING, as the mood takes you. Sometimes I wish we were *told* what to do as I worry a lot that I waste my time.

Others thrive in the same atmosphere. A sixth-former greets the tutor:

'Hello Susan'

'Hello Tom, here's your work today.' I look at it and see that it is inverse fractions. Must keep control of myself if I find that I can't do them. I manage quite well and go out of class feeling good . . .

After lunch I go over to Susan's house and do some more maths with her help. It's really nice there, so comfortable, quiet and we really got down to work. I do quite a lot and feel that I shall pass maths this time round. She gives us tea as we have missed break at school . . .
Boy, seventeen, Stanton

To end this brief review of work we turn to Brenda, our hockey girl diarist. We see the curriculum of a coeducational school for less academic children – and much else:

9.50. P.E. was a drag – volley ball and trampoline neither inspiring and my head feels worse. Just seen Butch, who hasn't made matters better by yanking me around in a passionate necking session.

11.0. Just came out of cookery to get my break and have a quick snog with Butch to restore him to good humour – I was a bit catty before. Miss Baines is a bum – her moaning and self contradictions are urging me to kick her up the backside but I'd better restrain myself. The coffee we had for break was nice, but the buns were horrible!!!

Just finished cookery – boy does she fag you out, I made two similar cakes, the better one to go to the san, she took it down there which was a pity, because I wanted to show it off a bit – got an attack and went down the san – they stuffed two disprin and a spoonful of Bismuth into me and told me to 'run on down to dinner' who are they kidding?

The bells just gone and we've got Zoo, Butch was very sweet just now and I feel miles better, he's just left the room cos Dozy (Mr Thomas) has just come in and yelled at him, didn't catch us snogging thou', so thats O.K., I don't really fancy being made a public example of, by being de-badged after only being a prefect for 4 days.

Zoo lesson looked as thou it could be boring so we side tracked her by reporting the thefts that had occured, my salmon, Linda's Marvel etc – that led her onto the discussion of the cleptomaniacs in the school, and how their physcos had told the head and her to deal with them – that took up the whole lesson, which was a relief as I'd not even started my prep let alone finished it!

After Zoology we had double English in the library we did 'Paradise Lost' and I was bored to screaming point. Still it was the last lessons till four – relief – After seeing Butch for a few minutes and having a 'sex up' that according to Pat, not me, – we went down and fixed up coffee for Spencer Millum (the researcher) ...

History – that was a morge of a lesson.

Just before the end of afternoon break Butch and I went to the other 6th form room. So he give me a pre-French boosting snog I need it I can tell you – those hateful hateful lessons – I loathe French more than Death, which is something! and I loathe Madeleine too – she's a bloody sadist and sadists in a close community like ours aren't the best people to have around.

Just had double French – as petrifying as usual – by some discreat cheating I managed $\frac{1}{2}$ marks in the test so I wasn't half decapitated this week – This brings the time to exactly 2 days from the time I started the diary – please excuse the spelling/writing.

FOOD

Of all the ingredients of daily life, there is none which arouses such fierce reactions as food. Many previous illustrations have shown what sort of reactions they are. In all but a few of the schools we have visited, children's reactions to food have been largely hostile. Unlike their responses to other aspects of school life, these have little necessary connection with objective reality. Food in any institution should be judged by its quality, quantity, variety, the amount of choice provided, the private supplementation allowed and by the care and quality of the way it is served and the environment in which it is eaten. Schools differ largely on all these criteria and to no particular pattern. There are some very expensive schools where the food, by all the above criteria, is excellent, and some equally expensive ones where it is bad. Small schools, large schools equally differ. In general, food is more uniformly adequate, according to the above criteria, in state and progressive schools than in other independent and public ones.

All this means little to the children. Their hostile comments are no objective reaction to food. The clue to their widespread repugnance is this. Food is one way in which institutional living violates the individual (he has to take the institution within him), limits his choice and self-expression and differs at least in imagination and setting from life outside. Complaints about food often canalize many other grievances about life in the school as well.

With these caveats in mind we drop in on a few characteristic meals and responses:

For lunch I had potatoes, cheese, salad and some tomatoes. It is a very good meal but when you have had the same thing every Tuesday for 4 terms you don't like it much anymore.

Boy, sixteen, progressive school

Contrasts with what 'they', the staff, are getting are frequent. Here is one from an independent, integrated school in the Midlands:

One of the cooks was putting the bacon on to the masters plate. Later she was taking the toast out of the grill. She took a sharp knife, and cut the crust off them. 'Why are you doing that?' one of us asked, waiting for the bell for taking the second course in. 'Because the crust is too hard for their poor little teeth' came the reply in a strong Irish accent, as she cut them into triangles. That was the

precise truth. Those high and mighty lords, had too much dignity to approach a crust even. We had to face worse things. I am not a hater of class distinction – I don't cry liberty and equality – for I accept it although in this type of society life cannot exist harmoniously with such a great gap between the staff and the boys. Everywhere they are supreme overlords, and have to be bowed and scraped to. They always have to have the red leather chairs; for if there are no upholstered chairs, they wouldn't dream of being present at anything.
Boy, fifteen

Some boarders feel very strongly about their food:

The dinners we have are apalling, we only get two slices of bread at teatime, and sometimes an apple or some sort of fruit. My mum said what about the starving people in Africa and I said 'We're in England not Africa'.
Boy, eleven, state boarding school

The worst features in this school are the haircuts which leave you bald, and food which makes you stand in the lavatories day in day out.
Boy, fifteen, independent integrated school

Not all children are complainers:

The food is very good in the House, but it's tea thats pleasantest – the fags get it for us – today we had tinned oranges, then scrambled eggs, tea and lovely chocolate cake that Nigel's mother sent down.
Boy, seventeen, public school

It's like a hotel! *3* courses for lunch *always*, serviettes, tablecloths at weekends, and lemonade with all meals.
Girl, fifteen, service school

At a progressive school in the Home Counties, the menu is characteristically more varied:

Dinner time, I hastily swallow a small amount of rather unimaginative salad and sickly watch the majority swallowing large quantities

of nutroast and beans. Anyway bad veg food is better than bad meat. After lunch I swallow a quick cup of coffee and with the remainder of the milk from break, then, with a couple of friends I wander out to the moderately sunny fields and join the large numbers of boys already out there. We sit and smoke and make daisy chains until its time for afternoon school.
Girl, sixteen

Two incidents from a famous public school about the social problems raised by meals conclude this section.

I regret to say that the Matron nearly drove me up the wall. sometimes. In particular, I couldn't stand it when she nattered at breakfast; anyone who speaks before 9 in the morning ought to be strung up. I told her so too, but as always, she didn't take me seriously. I sometimes wished that she had. Still, in spite of all her faults, and they are absolutely innumerable, most people including me are fond of her, because you can have her for such a sucker.
Head of house's private book

The Matron, outshines the Tutor by the fact that she watches every game played by the House. She is to be encouraged to speak to her budgerigar before breakfast so as to exhaust her conversation during the meal.
Same

RELIGION

Religion plays a more prominent part in boarding than in day schools: indeed for many schools their religious purposes are central to their aims and way of life. Even some secular progressive schools give religion, differently interpreted, prominence: a morning talk replacing the morning chapel or 'meeting' of other schools. The issue of the approach to and effectiveness of religion in the boarding school is too complex and important to be dealt with here. But religion – faith, problems and practice – concerns the children and their writings about their lives abound with it, as we have already seen and shall see in later chapters. In this section we present typical reactions to the religious life and challenge of schools.

Most prep schools present Christian faith and worship to their boys who respond warmly and positively. The following passage from a boy's diary beautifully expresses the simple, sincere acceptance of an eleven-year-old.

> Sister Mary came to speak to us on Sunday. None of us knew what she would be like and when she came into Cavendish Hall on that warm sunny evening she held the attention of us all.
>
> She was an old woman, wonderfully upright with a beautiful kind face. Her voice was soft and gentle and very clear. She had the ability to make her talk interesting and she never seemed to loose her vigour and vitality.
>
> So much for how she spoke; what she said was more important and, if it were possible, even more wonderful.
>
> She took as her text a verse from 1 Corinthians 13 – 'love never faileth' she spoke of her work in London among the sad homeless people, who had not something which we had – a happy home. I was impressed by her simplicity as she spoke of her courage in her work and God's guidance. She spoke of how people who had first struck her and been unkind to her had become reformed by her love and had ended complete friends and happy people. She finished by telling us how we ought to help boys at school with our love, and how it was possible to show our love by not letting anyone be beneath our care or unworthy of our love. Her talk also showed me what to do with boys who are in trouble who have gone wrong or unhappy with their life, how it is better to go up to another boy and treat him kindly even if he is being a nuisance or being disobedient or annoying.
>
> I was very moved by Sister Mary's talk, and I think it taught me a great deal about my dealings with other people.
>
> *Boy, eleven, prep school*

To many boys this early faith is matured, sensitized and strengthened by the religious life and discussion of their senior schools. A group of sixth-formers from one public school where religious life is given great stress sum up perceptively what that life has meant to them. They stand for many pupils in similar schools.

It has taught me to combine the religious and material life together: that we cannot live without the other and that it is useless to regard them separately: it is only if we join both together that we will find at least a purpose in life.
Boy, seventeen

Another responds to a more lively presentation of religion.

I have been able to discuss religion far more thoroughly than previously. A 'new approach to religion' has been attempted in which I have shared. I am extremely interested and involved and I can discuss religion far more freely than previously. My religious views have deepened and broadened due to the way of life here.
Boy, eighteen

Three other boys find in it the clue to their communal life:

It has had a profound effect on myself and my views. It has given purpose to my life at school and enabled me to realize the reasons for my actions. It has helped me to put my values in first perspective.
Boy, seventeen

It has made me realize that love and unselfishness are the most important things in life and that the Christian religion is right and should be lived as a code for all life.
Boy, eighteen

I can see something of what community spirit is about and I respect it.
Boy, seventeen

To others it has brought a more general challenge:

It has forced me to make a decision for or against religion.
Boy, seventeen

One is given a considerable feeling of dedication and seeking.
Boy, seventeen

It has made me realize the importance of religion in the modern

world and that it is not necessary to choose between God and
Science. They can be reconciled.
Boy, seventeen

To many other children who are questioning and hostile, the compulsory religious practices against which they react so strongly are sometimes recognized as of value:

After making my bed I did my weekly 'Small' washing talking to a dorm mate about our homes. Wrote part of my letter home, then the bell went to go to Meeting, I had a horrible tickle in my throat during Meeting so my thoughts were few, but I had a tune on my brain, a tune from 'sound of music' so I had to tap it out. But usually I enjoy meeting because it is peace and quiet and I can think of whatever I like, not necessaraly of God!
Girl, fifteen, Quaker school

Chapel: went with John, Pete and Garry talking inconsequentially and frivolously about the Commission (Thats YOU). Chapel is taken with resignation: organised religion makes me want to spew; but in some strange way Chapel is impressive.
Boy, sixteen, public school

Into Morning Talk. We wait. There is a general gossip – day people have arrived, boys and girls are no longer in their own areas at different ends of the school. Bell for silence. The Head and the person reading enter. Sometimes we have records, sometimes live music which we prefer. It is a time when I can think. Julian, a Housefather, reads excerpts from a book about young animals. It pops into my mind throughout the day.
Boy, seventeen, progressive school

Chapel, with all its faults, is definitely to me something in my life.
Boy, fourteen, public school

But to far more the compulsory religious rituals of schools lack meaning. One boy in a public school indicates the hostile feelings of many thousands who attend compulsory Sunday chapel:

I go into the minster not feeling at all holy. I walk in without bowing to the cross, I never do, and dejectedly sit down noticing to my surprise that a boy is sitting with his parents in the masters seat. People drift in all with a blank look on their faces. I look down and see a blue booklet in front of me. Damn that book, I hate it. I suppose the chaplins sermon will be shorter than usual. The chaplin is a normal chap, but by god does he talk. He annoys me and is the most hated master in the school. Where is he? Late as usual. He has just said some announcements. We stand up for the first hymn I always try to work out the dates of the composers on the hyms facing me. A sort of superstition I suppose. I am only superstitious because there might be some benefit in it. Later the chaplin gets up and says his sermon with practised skill and let my eyes go opaque and think of something else. Soon everyone stands up. I do as well. Collection a search my pockets for a penny. His sermon isn't worth much else. The plate comes nearer. I put my penny in with a dull lifeless thud. I pass it next to the chap by me, nice boy, he quickly passes it on. It is better than taking some out.

Boy, sixteen, independent school

A sixth-former at a state grammar school in the country gives his typical reaction to compulsory service in the local church:

I'm not a heathen or an atheist but if there's one thing I hate that's going to bloody church. The hymns are boring and morbid. The sermons are long and half the time even the vicar (if thats what the geezer in the flashy coat is called) doesn't know what he's on about. If there are no birds worth looking at I usually go to sleep, read a newspaper (News of the World) or play cards. I could think of a lot better ways to spend an hour on Sunday mornings . . .

Boy, eighteen

State boarding schools have assemblies in hall, not services in chapel on weekdays. Here is a fifth-form girl at one in the north:

The actual prayers in assembly mean to most people an interlude before lessons and the prayers are just rituals. The most interesting part of assembly is the notices afterwards.

Girl, fifteen

At a public school, a prefect describes house prayers and the religious situation in general. Many public schools have prayers in the separate houses every night.

> There are house prayers – a sort of minor chapel only a lot more ridiculous. Now though, we only have one a week – or reading and some prayers. I believe the chaplain met a lot of opposition when he suggested abolishing them, but the governors objected again: but after a lot of discussion they decided to leave it up to individual housemasters. We have one compulsory house prayers and one voluntary one a week. The voluntary one gets about 5 people (there are 45 people in the house). The 'religious' situation here is rather amusing: about 80% of the school get confirmed and after about 18 months 80% of them prefer to be agnostic and don't go to communion. It just shows how badly religion effects the boys here. It is taken as rather a bore, and we are supposed to be 'a religious, royal and ancient foundation'.
> *Boy, eighteen*

Even heads of houses privately confess that the nightly ritual of house prayers is a problem:

> I sometimes felt house prayers ought to mean more than they usually did; they are the only time when the House meets together properly. I thought they ought to be more than a mere formality during which fags and non-fags acquaint themselves with the names of those who have won university awards or XV's on the Honours Board and the fourths enjoy watching the Housemaster's face twitching. Whether the fact that we now have something different every day makes any real difference to this I do not know; but if all those who have anything to do with the conducting of house prayers are conscientious and plan what they are to do carefully, with some purpose, then the service may begin to mean something. If, on the other hand, a bible is to be picked up five minutes before they start and a passage chosen at random and read badly, we might as well give up.
> *Head of house's book, public school*

Divinity or R.I. periods occur once or twice in the boarders' week.

A girl in a state boarding grammar school in the far north sums up most adolescents' viewpoint:

> R.I.?
> Interesting: sex talks, discussion on problems.
> Uninteresting: fall of Samaria etc. *Girl, fifteen*

A boy confirms her typical viewpoint:

> The most interesting divinity lessons I have had were discussions on Christianity, its attitudes, morality etc. The most boring were those devoted to the 'O' level syllabus, the study of the Bible and the learning of a multitude of facts. *Boy, sixteen, public school*

Sometimes the R.I. lessons are frank:

> Made the Divinity master rather sad as most of the class told him that they hate going to church. *Boy, fourteen, integrated school*

The reasons for the widespread hostility to the religious efforts of boarding schools deserve some, if only a brief, illustration here.

Many pupils resent the dogmatic, narrow and above all compulsory aspect of religion in an institution which, in so many other respects, sets out to inculcate criticism, discrimination, breadth of view, self-direction and freedom of choice. This contradiction causes anger.

> The Christianity practised in this school is sheer ritual indoctrination put from the Anglican point of view – junior forms are given 'My Catechism Book' and taught only the New and Old Testament. There's no teaching about other religions or atheism. The whole thing is hypocritical. *Boy, eighteen, direct grant school*

> There is no religious toleration in the sense that if a person is an atheist he is very likely to be out of the school. A person has not been expelled for their religious views but people have been 'asked to leave'. *Boy, sixteen, Catholic school*

> Being at a Quaker school and indoctrinated with never-ending

Quaker principles makes one draw away from Quakerism and even God.
Girl, sixteen, Quaker school

Chapel to me is frustrating and we have to go every Sunday. I think that God gave us a brain and a mind to choose between good and evil, otherwise we would all be just like blocks of wood. We should be allowed the choice of whether or not to go to chapel. If we are forced, we take much less interest in it and it loses its meaning.
Boy, fifteen, public school

I have had a Housemaster continually trying to impress his remarkable faith on one who has none. *Boy, seventeen, public school*

In boarding schools religious occasions often have other functions – administrative ones – and chaplains often teach and exercise ordinary disciplinary roles. These mixtures often confuse children and, to their mind, degrade religious occasions or render chaplains hypocrites or baffling or unapproachable.

I don't mind going to church but the way they take the roll call during the service is a mockery of Christianity. If they can't trust people surely its *they* who need the church.
Boy, sixteen, independent school

The masters take roll-call in chapel, and the prefects check on your shoes and hair as you go in. Whats this got to do with religion?
Boy, fifteen, public school

One minute the chaplain is standing reverently in his church praying to God, and next minute he is barking at you – and giving you detentions. *Boy, fifteen, public school*

No, I wouldn't go to the chaplain with a problem. Tell *him* something private and the housemaster knows it next minute and the Head the minute after that. *Boy, sixteen, integrated school*

You are forced to tramp to church and if you arent keen, or don't turn up, the chaplain writes it on your report.
Boy, seventeen, Catholic school

Sometimes however, the clergy's day-to-day presence is an asset. Another Catholic boarder writes from his school:

I now know that monks are purely ordinary people, not saintly freaks.
Boy, sixteen

Or a boy at a public school:

John Wickham (the chaplain) is a friend really. His classes are good and he's always about. I've told him some things I would never tell anyone else here.
Boy, sixteen, public school

The final cause of the discontent with religion is the nature of the services. For large numbers of boys and girls the content is monotonous (this we heard many hundreds of times), or cold and remote, something lacking spontaneity or giving no opportunity of participation to the pupils themselves:

We have chapel every other day and 4 out of 5 people in our row read, write letters or draw and only one person listens – the reasons are (a) because we have to go every other day (b) because the chaplain bounces up and down and you can't hear what he's talking about and usually its a load of crap. Make it voluntary and brighten up the dirge any way.
Boy, seventeen, public school

When we don't sing we get cursed to hell, when we do sing good and loud we get cursed for that too.
Boy, sixteen, state boarding school

Chapel would be brighter if we had more reading from the New English Bible and other books, like the Pilgrim's Progress and less singing and praying which isnt any good at all to you.
Boy, fifteen, public school

Sunday services at church are boring – too repetitious and too formal. The only compensation is that there are new faces to look at.
Girl, eighteen, state boarding school

But the danger of being too 'with it' appears in the following:

> To improve the church they might give them a bit of life. The clergy are cold and distant, our chaplain is very stuck up, which isn't quite so bad as the old twits of 80 who make fools of themselves by dressing up in leather jackets – 'look God I'm with it'. If they sold the stone, the lead, the cassocks, stopped gassing to old women and gave to the poor then I might believe what they say. They might even convert someone.
> *Boy, seventeen, state boarding school*

To many, the only warmth and real participation comes, almost by accident, in the communion service:

> Chapel here is so boring except for communion which I enjoy because *we* take part in it.
> *Boy, fourteen, state secondary modern boarding school*

> I like communion most – the cup of tea afterwards, the friendliness of the chaplains, the girls there, singing the hymns.
> *Boy, seventeen, independent school*

Religion then is part of the stuff of boarding life: boys and girls have to come to terms with it. It is also a problem, and probably always will be. As the boarding school provides for areas of education and experience left elsewhere to the home, it will always have to present religious or moral issues and guidance and provide for religious expression. Certainly the difficult balance between the institution's aims and the individual's autonomy of conscience and behaviour is nowhere more difficult to achieve than here. Perhaps the children's comments suggest some ways of attaining it. Not a few schools are already moving in these directions now.

GAMES

Though less dominant in some schools than they were, games activities inevitably figure more in the boarding school than the day one: inevitably, because they fulfil so many functions. They help to fill in time – a major problem in a twenty-four-hour-day, seven-day-week community; they constructively use up energy and aggressive instincts which might otherwise be turned in harmful directions against the school or against other pupils; they harness loyalties to the school and to small primary groups like the house; they cultivate those collective virtues of give-and-take, working-with-a-team, which some schools value; they are one, and an important and very visible one, of the many channels of achieving status in the society which boarding schools provide; and, finally, they are enjoyed for their own sake by thousands of children: for the sense of excitement, disciplined competition and fellow-feeling which they provide, and as an exercise of skill, stamina and fitness.

In a very few schools, games still matter more than virtually anything else except work:

> A place on the rugger XV is more important than a place in the National Youth Orchestra. Sport is taken very seriously and it is wise to show keenness and enthusiasm in all sports. Apathy in games brands one as being a wet for a long time here.
>
> *Boy, seventeen, public school*

> I am no good at games, and this makes me an outcast.
> *Boy, eighteen, state boarding school*

A comment from the head of house's book in the same state boarding school, reviewing each individual boy's progress, shows how important games criteria are:

> Drysdale has had the great disadvantage of still only being a 'small boy'. He is not very old, but physically he has shown himself on the games field to be excelled by very few in his guts. In the rugger he fought on and on, frequently battered by a terrible strength of opposition. In the soccer and P.T. he was skilled and made use of it. He certainly throws himself into these sports.

Sometimes performance at games carries with it promotion in the hierarchy of power, and sudden loss of status in games can cause problems of adjustment:

I suppose I would have done a bit better in the prefect side of things had I not gone loopy when I smashed my ankle in gym. You know being fanatically fit, and suddenly being off all games (only for that one term) it went against the grain and I started chucking knives into doors and acting a little less sensibly. Still I at least made the grade in certain other fields.   *Boy, seventeen, public school*

Most boarders enjoy games for their own sake, irrespective of external pressures or status considerations. Here a fourteen-year-old boy describes his afternoon at a progressive school:

In the afternoon we had games. One of the games teachers were ill so the other one talked to us about cricket. I enjoy Games very much and it helps you later on in life, and it helps your limbs and muscels to strenghen. At 4.10 we finished school and I went to my house, and I was told that a person had backed out of sailing, and asked me if I would like to go and I accepted. There wasn't a very strong wind. I enjoyed myself very much, and I think these sorts of sports ought to be incouraged in other schools. I only got back just before 10 o'clock. I then had to go straight to bed, everyone else was just about asleep.

Another short extract from the head of house's book, this time from a distinguished public school, shows the very considerable autonomy left to the boys in organizing games at this school (*they* even decide which staff will coach):

It was a very uneventful term compared with the previous summer term. We started off with the Bumping Fours. Unfortunately our highly successful coach of the year before had left and therefore I had to find another. He did not seem to have the originality and energy of our former coach and therefore the four did not excell itself.

Not all share this enthusiasm for games. A sixth-form boy at a state boarding school poignantly describes his slow and painful conversion to one game, rugby:

I had never played rugby before I came here. Similarly cross-country, and though I hated cross-country, it was a most enjoyable recreation compared to the misery of being sat in a puddle of smelly, foul and cold watery mud, with a grey sky, drizzle, and a cold N. Westerly wind blowing down the pitch, only a thin cotton shirt on one's back to merely distinguish you by colour (blue or white) by teams, no earthly use in keeping warm. I remember returning from leave-outs (Sundays home) and returning with dread for another week of misery on the field. Now, though I still *dislike* playing rugby of all sports, I no longer hate it and dread it; cross country I have learnt to positively enjoy. *Boy, eighteen, state boarding school*

Like cross-country, rowing is primarily a boarding-school sport. At a public school situated on a river, a senior boy might spend his afternoon like this. Note the characteristic way the senior boys coach and help the juniors and the formality of staff–pupil relations (the use of christian names by the master on this occasion only):

After lunch I go back to see if there are any letters for me and then go across to the changing rooms. I cycle down to the boathouse and try to plan a German essay for tomorrow. At the boathouse I talk with a great friend, my rival cox, and cycle along the bank watching the 2nd VIII and then return, where I help some young coxes and oarsmen, and then have tea. Afterwards we have an outing on the river in the rain; the master calls everyone by their Christian names except me, which puts me in a bad mood for a few minutes.

Boy, seventeen

Games appeal for other reasons besides their intrinsic enjoyment. For instance, beagling occurs in some schools, mainly in public schools. Here, an eighteen-year-old, who runs and organizes the pack, explains what *he* gets out of the sport. His gains go far beyond the hunt itself: greater freedom, access to other social groups, domestic moments which the school's life cannot contain, the warm affection and dependence of animals (an expressive outlet which many progressive schools deliberately exploit) and the experience of organizing itself:

The beagles have given me some of my most enjoyable days here. Without them life would have been infinitely more boring and would have probably stagnated, with nothing more to do than football. They have really formed the centre of my life here.

Why? By nature I am basically a country person having been born and bred on a farm. One of the things which I dislike about this school is the atmosphere it has of a large town. I feel a sort of claustrophobia because there is noise, machinery and buildings on every side. There is no quiet open free expanse or space; there is the constant noise of traffic, aeroplanes, trains and people all around you and no escape from it at all at the school. But Beagling does do something to help satisfy a need to escape. One does get away to the country (such as it is) where you can enjoy freedom to move across an expanse unlimited by school bounds; where noise of civilization is relatively low and where the thrilling cry of the hounds is constantly ringing in your ears. Beagling is an escape from civilization and school.

Moreover Hunting is something from which I could never drag myself. The cry of the hounds is impossible to describe, but it produces a thrilling surge of excitement which throbbing in every nerve really makes you want to go. You realise the wild nature of the hunt and you learn of the wiles and ways of the hare. Knowing hunting is having learnt from experience about the weather, the scenting conditions, the country, the hounds, the hare and many other things. All this is something I enjoy learning. The infinite variety of knowledge required (including knowledge of how to deal with angry farmers) is something which no other school sport provides.

Beagling has brought me in touch with many new people – I have made a lot of friends outside the school, and as master of beagles, have had dealings with many different people. This has a very important effect. It helps to break out of the uniformity of school life, where you see the same faces in the same clothes in same places day in, day out, year in, year out. For it is nice to meet a 'civilian' during term. The Kennel huntsman, his wife and family are really wonderful people and make a sort of 'home' for me at school where I can go and watch the television, talk, drink tea away from school life and people. It is an escape to greater freedom. I do not however feel homesick in any way at all.

The beagles are in themselves great characters and to the master they have all to become well known. I really enjoy knowing each hound and realising that they know me and that they are *my* hounds. Finally being master of the beagles has meant that I have had to organise and run them for some time. This has been of immense value as an experience in organisation, administration and public relations. Although other posts give one practice in paperwork administration, school and organisation, the master of beagles has experience with the human element. He has to deal with people; for the hunt relies entirely for its existence on people outside the school and their goodwill. *Boy, eighteen, public school*

At many schools, public and independent ones subscribing to the same values and style, games dominate the boys' afternoons and are compulsory. At public and some other schools, the boys play three or four afternoons a week. The complex task of organizing House games belongs to a most important boy-official, the house games captain. On his shoulders falls the task of ensuring that boys play:

Anyone who is not taking official exercise must take 3/4hr. strenex (strenuous exercise). Names and activity to me. No skivers, I know your names. *Notice by games captain, public school*

Anyone off games with a cold (or cough etc.) must wear a mac whenever he leaves the house. The games prefects have a list of such sufferers from Matron and check up the individuals daily. This intended to make colds as an excuse for being off games less pleasant and in the winter it succeeded.

Also no-one with a cold may ride a bicycle.
Head of house's book, public school

At not a few schools it is compulsory to watch matches, especially for junior boys and in smaller schools. But even in major schools and for a house match compulsory attendance may be organized by the busy house games captain. The following notice from the games captain (public school) illustrates this.

> *Saturday*
>
> Those not in the Colts XV or taking exercise under School arrangements will give ♪ Vocal Support ♫ to the Colts team tomorrow, unless they have ~~enott~~ a reason for not doing so which will be communicated to me immediately.
>
> yH

Little so far in this section has given an indication of the loving care and concern, the deep commitment, the expertise, the dedication to transmit skills which games generate in schools. To savour this, we dip again into a head of house's book at a public school, this time more lengthily. Here the house captain is advising his successor on the various games played by the house, and how to get the best out of the boys. Only a few, typically public school, games are chosen here. Besides revealing a deeper concept of games-playing, these extracts illustrate certain other aspects of public-school life: the house unit, the mode of relations between senior and junior boys, the control exercised by the seniors.

First the major game of the autumn:

RUGGER

The basis of Rugger is fitness. Use the common at the end of the holidays, even if only four or five can turn up, some useful work can be done. Given fitness, then brain will beat brawn. Start their minds ticking over, Maltese crosses, scissors movements, the three p's (possession, position, pace). I learnt an awful lot listening to S.M. de J. (former master) commenting on 1st XV games from the touch-line when I was off with a broken arm. He has a fantastic brain. He is not only housemaster of Fennell's, but Master i/c Rugby, i/c Calendar, C.O. of R.A.F. section, and i/c sixth form economics – all in one! A try would be scored and everyone else would say 'superb run' but Joinville would just nod to the 25 line and say 'right centre up late again'. He always saw the cause while everyone else just watched the effect. As anyone in the first XXX knows, he can recount the whole course of a game he has watched or refereed, after the game is over. If you can get your players 'thinking' and 'seeing' like that, they will be much more intelligent players. Teach them the principles and give them the confidence of knowing what to do – then you can add the finesse and everyone will enjoy Rugby much more.

During the winter term one major sport is running. The house captain takes us to the heart of the sport and to the best side of senior-junior relations in the modern public school.

Our House now has a great tradition in running. It stems from new boys seeing the enthusiasm and enjoyment of the senior boys, so let this continue. Runners are made or lost in their first year. To anyone not used to running, and few are when they come, there is a physical barrier which they must overcome by hard and frequent running. If they merely go on runs because they have to and show no more interest – they are lost. Encourage them to go on runs on Wednesdays and Fridays, and, most important of all, be there yourself and give encouragement. If you run beside a younger boy, not only will he forget his aches and pains, as he tries to keep up with you, but he will also realise that you are enjoying your running, and that he can go almost as fast as you. This gives confidence and then the battle's won. I wrote that running is the best Easter Term Sport – it is the only sport in which personal ability does not matter. It is a mistake to do too much training at one time. I was laid up with pneumonia, not by any bug floating around, but because after going regularly on Pack Runs, I went out on a Sunday for 10 hard miles in cold, anticyclonic weather; it was a glorious sunny day but it tore up my lungs, so that when Tuesday came along with the Rywood Run, although feeling fine, my lungs were like bruised apples, and I suffered. *The Cup Run* is compulsory for all Colts (15 year olds). Too long notice of the day and there *may* be a flood of boys 'off-games'.

Someone should follow the race to pick up dead bodies.

Cricket is still the major summer game in most public schools, though its exclusive hold is diminishing. Our captain is imbued with the cult and eager to transmit its skills:

Hold nets at the end of the Easter holidays. I always think that efficiency in erecting nets is a sign of the real efficiency of a House. They should never, never fall down.

HOUSE MATCHES: The scorer wears the House boater. Attendance and behaviour at House Matches may merit some attention.

Coaching at nets and in games: All House Powers and members of the 1st XI should be told that they are expected to help coach at nets. If the individual thinks himself not good enough, remember that anyone can take a fielding practice. Half the battle in improvement is confidence, and that will come from the encouragement given by the presence of senior boys.

Bowling: It should be impressed on young bowlers that they are bowling badly if the batsman is continually playing back. They must pitch the ball up, and not bowl on the leg. Encourage them all the time. Set their field and *make them think*. There is very often no need for a slow bowler to have a slip, etc. Tell them not to be afraid to put all their fielders round the boundary Slow bowlers are meant to be hit. Practice is the key to good bowling and using your head. If you pitch a good length ball it may either be played quietly down the pitch, when you smile with satisfaction, or it may be driven hard along the ground, or lofted out of the ground or wide of your fielders. In the last cases you must teach the bowler to either bowl what looks like the same sort of ball but actually a little shorter causing the batsman to hit it in the air, or if he did this before higher in the air, or else to pitch the same ball a bit wider thereby giving the batsman a greater distance to go to hit the ball.

Batting: The main fault of the young players in the House is that they play forward rather than back. You must teach them that they do not play forward unless they can put their front foot next to the point where the ball is going to pitch.

Fielding: Watch the ball, if you are put in the deep stay right on the boundary don't wander in.

We end with two contrasts: schools where games are less compulsory and less central to the system. First, hockey and rugger in a coeducational school:

Just on my way up hill. Got changed for Hockey Match. Waited ages cos they were late. First half of game was okay, but 2nd half we had this awful umpire she was a hell of a fussy about fouls especially when it was us. So I did a lot of swearing in the end, its just as well no-one heard me. We won anyway which I was very pleased about, because we lost nearly all our 1st XI Hockey matches last term. After match I went and watched Rugby, great fun. Then I got changed and ran down the hill to wash my hair, then came over to Common Room and Sally did my hair. Then it was tea, that wasn't worth having. All very fattening and awful.

Girl, sixteen, coeducational school

Finally a cricket match with a visiting team at Stanton, the far-out progressive school. Though no games are compulsory here those who play take them seriously, though, as our description indicates, not *too* seriously. No greater contrast could be found to the majority of boarding schools.

The day was fine. A few billowing clouds, a sense of expectancy. The groundsman had done a good job.

It was decided that they should bat first. We took our positions, our captain, Dave, playing as wicket keeper with vice captain Peter doing some tricky bowling. The rest of the field was arranged and the two visiting batsmen came on. I suppose I could say that we had a chance, but I felt personally that we weren't in it. A partnership of fifty was knocked up before the first wicket fell. A hearty bowl by Sebastian Ford allowed that fine teammate Sebastian to catch it. The wickets fell after that at about twelve to twenty runs each, and they knocked up a score of one hundred and twenty for six.

Tea, and we clambered up the steps to a fortudinous tea prepared by Sally and Meg. They were impressed at least with our fielding. We chatted and talked of the various events in the first half.

We went out again and it was decided we should go in. It now becomes painful but amusing to tell you of the events which happened after that. Pow! a wicket fell, Hugh out for nothing. Wham! Sebastian out for nothing. Zonk! Eddie out for one. So the wickets fell until my dear old turn came, no need to tell you what happened, out for nothing.

Our hero turned out to be Nigel who by luck more than skill managed to stay in long enough to get the grand total of five. We were all out for nine, but we were in a good mood, what else can you do?

OTHER ACTIVITIES

So much of this chapter, and of others, illustrates the out-of-class activities of boarding schools – official and unofficial – that we need only pause and stress the fact that the range of official activities is often large and participation widespread. It is in the extent of facilities and involvement of the pupils made possible by residence that boarding schools sometimes score over day ones; though, as the previous reflections on priorities show, these activities may in themselves cause some dilemmas.

Two comments touch on the prominence of music as *the* arts activity in many schools – prominent not only because of its intrinsic value but because it can be both a team and an individual activity (unlike painting, which is solely individual) and because it can be used to support those collective values and occasions which are so important to the life of some boarding schools.

A head of house comments on the state of house music:

The House Orchestra tradition was started by Mr Ashworth in about 1951/2. He had the admirable procedure of press-ganging about half of each term's intake of new boys to learn some instrument. Many of course were utterly unmusical and gave it up after only a term or two, but it gave a great chance to those who were musical and who would otherwise probably never have taken up an instrument. I think that the orchestra reached its climax about two or perhaps three years ago, and since then has been steadily declining. However the House Orchestra is an excellent tradition which must certainly be kept up, even if, as the next couple of years may be rather lean, they don't partake in the competition. The very fact that there is an orchestra in the house keeps up the standard of music and the number of musicians, and, perhaps most important of all, means that the members have to practice.

Head of house's book, public school

A girl at a progressive school indulges in a little music-making and a characteristic interchange with one of the staff, Barry:

I went to orchestra which is a hellish bore. I'd like to give up the violin but I suppose I'd better support the orchestra. Orchestra is still very boring, and I don't like the bloke who takes orchestra very much.

Barry our languages teacher is in the orchestra, at the moment I hate him he is always telling me to shut up, if I twang a violin string once or twice. Today he said 'shut up' and I said 'Yes, *of course* Barry' rather sarcastically. After orchestra, I rushed away as quickly as I could and plonked my violin down and went upstairs. Nobody seemed to be anywhere so I went on making a pair of slippers for my mother's birthday. Lovely floppy warm dry ones which are very warm in the Winter. *Girl, fifteen, progressive school*

Societies often figure prominently in the prospectuses, long lists of them testifying to a flourishing society life. Behind the prospectus, however, things may be different, as this extract from the private minutes of the prefects' meeting at one public school indicates:

> Brown spoke of the appalling state of the societies. On Saturday, societies had failed in the following ways.
> Astronomical society – no meeting (bad weather conditions)
> Film society – closed membership (100) but only 50 came
> Modern Jazz society – only 25 patrons
> Modern Language Society – no meeting or announcement to its members
> Philately society – 8
> Literature society – full house (but this is only 15 or 20)
> Railway society – 20
> Tape-recording society – no meeting and no notice
> Motoring society – membership restricted. Many boys were told that they could go to the film; but this decision was reversed at the last moment.
>
> There was a singular lack of cohesion between the houses and the societies. Ingram (i/c societies) spoke of certain failures in the organisation of the societies: societies had been told to nominate a representative in each house, and this had not been done. A committee was set up to investigate the reasons and possible remedies for the present chaos of society organisation and attendance.

Others of the many extra-curricular activities in schools will recur throughout this book.

CCF AND SOCIAL SERVICE

Corps appears mainly in public and similar schools. In these schools it is usually compulsory in practice for one afternoon a week. In schools where it is genuinely voluntary, it is often popular and carries high prestige, but not so in those (the majority) where it is compulsory. CCF and its variants have multiple importance in the society of some boarding schools which the boys often do not grasp.

Here is a CCF expedition at a major public school which opened with typical indulgence and ended with less welcomed endurance:

> We got dropped off at 8.30 in the evening at a place called Shopton Green. We were in a group of 4 but we were soon joined by two other groups and then all 12 of us went into the pub at Shopton Green and stayed there for about 2 hrs. After leaving the pub at 10.30 pm we realised we had 10 miles to walk to the camp site, we were all in fairly high spirits so off we went. We got to the entrance of the park at about 1 am after walking the 10 miles, it was real hell, no don't laugh I'm being serious. It really was hell just keeping going on and on we were all O.K. for the first 5 miles, you know, singing and smoking, we must have woken up $\frac{1}{2}$ of Hampshire but the last 5 were the bad ones my feet were aching like hell and by the time we got to the park we were ready to drop. But we still had 2 miles to go, across muddy paths etc. of course by then all the check posts had packed up and consequently we didn't know where the hell we were going. We went into some old blokes back garden at about 1.30 am and woke him up and he came storming out bellowing about writing to his M.P. about us. And threatened to set the dogs on us, inconsiderate bastard. All he was worried about was his sleep, he didn't care a sod for the 17 of us (we had met up with some others) who were outside getting hellish cold and feeling tired. Eventually we found the place at 3 am and got some very cold and not very deep sleep. We only had 2 blankets each, in all we got about 2 hrs sleep and then had to get up and play bang bangs for the day. I ask you, how pointless can you get? I've never been so glad to see this place as that Friday night.
>
> *Boy, seventeen*

In many schools CCF is dwindling and is being replaced by social service and other activities. Though most boys dislike CCF, and some do not relish social service, they do see its point and some get a great deal from it:

> 10.15 p.m. Got back to the House late from the spastics school. I go up there twice a week now. It started on CCF afternoons as an escape. Now I enjoy it: its such a change from this place. I talk, play

indoor games, watch TV, help wash up, sometimes help them with their prep. It doesn't sound much really does it? But it helps me, at least. It puts this £530 p.a. place in a truer perspective.

Boy, eighteen, public school

After lunch, I went down to town to Mrs Springetts. Spent the afternoon weeding the garden and trying to mow the lawn with a Victorian mower. Tea followed in her little kitchen – she's a widow and hobbles about. I've been going for two terms once a week. It's meant to be service to her but, strangely, we both seem to benefit.

Boy, seventeen, public school

At one famous public school a set of imaginative social service schemes includes one for lowering the water levels of the neighbouring meadows, preserving the flora and restocking the fauna.

Funny isn't it? I hated Corps. I hated science – dropped every subject fast. I hated manual – what little we did of it. They put me on the water meadows scheme against my will – what *me* splashing around in that slime? Well, you live and learn. I'm out there now regularly in waders. I love the water, the mud oozing through my fingers, the sense of working with nature. I love watching the trout grow in the stew ponds, studying the force and direction of currents and the effect they will have on drainage, and the growth of the river plants, and insect life. This scheme has opened a new world, made me feel more organic.

Boy, seventeen

WEEKENDS

The weekend at the boarding school has its own unique flavour. The weekday routine ends, often around Saturday lunch-time, and there follows in some schools, public and independent, a sequence of compulsory events – games, films, chapel – of ritual cleanings and laundry changes, or prep, of cavernous moments of emptiness and others of frenzied organization. At some state boarding schools, the pupils go out for much of the time or spend afternoons or Saturday night at home. We shall illustrate their home-going in Chapter 7. At progressive schools they are often left to their own devices, as we shall see. In all, the weekend is marked by a curious unreality, a suspended quality – not many staff are about, dress is unusual, mealtimes different, above all the unending day-to-day routine is broken. For some, the result is boredom, for others a welcome moment to catch up with work, to read a book, to go outside to meet a girl, to renew home or local ties or – something which weekday routine in many schools scarcely permits – just to relax.

The Saturday afternoon games and the Sunday services we have already described. Let us fill in the rest of the weekend.

Saturday evenings are a bit of a problem – no prep is done in many schools, but equally many cannot or do not allow the pupils out of the school premises. Societies and activities absorb some. But in many schools in the autumn and winter terms entertainments have to be devised to stop the boys and girls, especially the younger ones, from getting restless. Evening films are common in many schools – with cheering, bottles of lemonade and sweets, and much bustling 'being excused' during the change of reels. Other schools try to use the time less passively.

Here at one public school in a town a house captain reminds his successor of how to handle the problem of Saturday evenings:

During Winter Terms most Sat. evenings have some form of entertainments. There will anyway be 2 school films and half term to allow for. Such things as fag's party, night-ops, debates, need not include the whole house, so everyone probably has 1 or 2 free evenings, even if there is something on every Sat. night. Don't hog the fags too much, they are not the most important part of the House, and the IVths for instance, get more value out of 'cultural' evenings than they will.

Debates: Appoint secretary for the occasion to read the rules, and to write the minutes. Invite Housemaster, etc.

Singing: IS enjoyed and IS popular, as long as there is not too much of it. Have $\frac{1}{2}$-singing, $\frac{1}{2}$-playing and listening. Mr Cartwright was very good with a quiz at the last sing-song. Other masters can also do a lot to give an 'atmosphere' to the proceedings.

Night Ops: (Expeditions and hunts in town). Must be well arranged. If you don't think you can do it well, don't try. Have only one section of the House involved in battles, there is no point in VIth v. Fag fights. Gramophone evenings, lectures, magicians, etc. have all been done.

Initiative Drives: During my last Easter Term had an initiative test on an afternoon. A couple of money prizes were offered and a time limit set. Then the House was let loose in the afternoon up till 5.30 pm. A report (written) had to be left in the House Hall by that time in a box, saying what had been done and by whom. One person played his violin half the afternoon in Mansfield Rd, another held a Gallup Poll in a road off the White Mill, some more enterprising (??) ones picked all the daisies on the school lawn. These are only examples of the sort of things which this entertainment involves. It does show of what sort of stuff the House is made.

At a state comprehensive school Saturday is symbolized by a change of style:

> I start thinking I'm sure my dads going to win the pools, its about time he did, and anyway *I* did it for him so he's bound to win! Get up think. What am I going to wear today. Its Saturday so I'll wear my jeans and blue jumper and a shirt today. Shall I wear my white socks or my black ones? I'll wear my black ones I don't want to ruin my white ones.
> *Boy, thirteen*

At another, a state coeducational school, an eleven-year-old spends his Saturday more like a boy at home, in his own clothes, out in the town, and in the evening watching a film and then attending the regular Saturday school dance:

> I get up at 8 o'clock. Half an hour later get my casual clothes on and then go to breakfast. After breakfast, prep. After prep we have dinner. In the afternoon sometimes go out to Elsworth and look round the shops, then we come back for tea and sometimes we have the film before supper and the dance after supper and sometimes it is the other way round, which means we go to bed late. Very good.

Meanwhile at Stanton, after an exhilarating afternoon watching ballet, a girl gets away for the Saturday evening:

Jane and I went into Stanbury and got a good lift right to the pub where we drank Alison's health and talked. Two male friends joined us, one an ex-Stantonian and the other a Stanbury bloke and an ex boyfriend of mine who is a good friend, and we had a great time talking about past and future. We left at 10.00 and got a lift, then walked up the hill. Our House mother gave us a funny look but said nothing. Bed by 11.00.
Girl, eighteen

In one of those many small, homely independent schools catering for less able or children with background 'need', a fifteen-year-old boy spends a relaxed, unorganized and freely ranging Saturday:

After lunch, everyone departs in his own direction, some go to Norwich, or the local market towns. My weekend usually consists of going down to the shop on a Sat. afternoon. Having come back from the shop with something different to eat I would sit down and scoff half of it before doing anything else. Myself and a friend usually go up to Littleport, I enjoy motor racing, but everything up there costs a fortune and most people are always short of cash. Tea is supposed to be at 4.15 but if you turn up on time there's nothing left – tea usually starts when Batman ends on TV – we all watch it.
Boy, fifteen, independent school

Down in the south a girl at a coeducational school, moderately progressive, gives an intimate sense of her Saturday in school – serious talks mixed up with girl-boy friendships, problems, warm companionships and sense of community:

Wanting breakfast, we dress hurriedly – I haven't washed the clearasil off my nails and my purple beatniks are showing – but I don't really care.

At break there's cocoa in the common room. Its warm and noisy and superb there. The gram plays incessantly. Someones tying Bill to a chair. A group of us huddle round the radiator. I do Nicky's Latin prep for him. The class below us sits in a circle. At least the 'in' crowd do. The others don't get a chance. Everyone's beatniks are showing. Nobody cares, except Martin, who doesn't like short skirts – or so he says.

138   The Hothouse Society

An alien from Form 3 comes in. He's hurriedly pushed out – he has another year until he can enjoy these tissue paper covered lights. We banter at each other, read our horoscopes and finish preps five minutes after the end of break – it's Saturday anyway and only gym next . . .

The gong for evening entertainments goes and we charge up the stairs with cushions from the reading room. It should be good – some Old Boys talking about their trip in India. We huddle up to the hot pipes. The school sits in its cliques and worships – probably wishing it were dancing we were having instead. It is a good talk. There's slides now and as the lights go down everyone peers to see who's sitting with who. I feel rather comfortable and secure where I am – even though Martin doesn't like short skirts. A groan as they go on again but now its easier to see. The school is laughing. It gives me a wonderful warm sense of security to be near to people I like, friends – and its always in entertainments that this feeling literally rushes up on me, and I think how I'd hate to be away from here – like last term when I was in Germany and missed the place like hell.

We meander over to dorm. Someone's crying in my room – we have to cheer her up and say how 'it'll all be different in the morning' and 'not to worry about it'. We talk and giggle for hours after lights out – and have a binge in the pool of moonlight on my bed. Carole and I have forgotten to write our diaries so we rush out to the bog and join Betty who is already writing hers in there.

'Superb day – not much happened . . .'   *Girl, fifteen*

Beauchamp Manor's weekend is unique – a combination of boredom and ritual, of frustration spilling over into violence, both physical and in feeling:

Some crank said that it did you good to be bored. I'll bet he never tried it. It is I suppose inevitable that one spends the whole week waiting for the weekend and when it does come it is a wash out. At weekend I think an awful lot about home . . .

At five o'clock I went to the library and read. I only go there when I have nothing else to do. It is a sort of punishment. Hell. I got up and went back to the study. Irritably and rather stupidly I lashed out at the chair. Fuck, I was bored and I knew it. Hell, was this the weekend that I had been waiting for? I rummaged around for an old *Playboy*. Well at least it was better than beating up some junior. Then a bell rang. My head throbbed and someone was thumping along the passage. Hell. I tore all over the place and finally got everything back into shape. Phew. The prefect walked in, one of these sadists, one who enjoys seeing people being kicked and then trodden on. I find that even when I have been with a group of boys bashing someone up I have always been afraid that they might turn on me. He went out followed by a couple of V signs. Bastard. Even at the top one has to fight and grasp and grab for what you haven't got . . .

Boy, seventeen

Sunday follows: getting up later, Sunday morning service, Sunday best (stiff collars, house ties), for some compulsory letter-writing, a roast lunch and the long never-ending freedom of Sunday afternoon, punctuated with parents' visits for some, and closed either by another service or prep.

Here is a public school Sunday in a country public school. Sophisticated, jaded, cynical as the eighteen-year-old house prefect is, he captures brilliantly much of the essence of this day; the chapels, the Victorian Gothic, the boredom and activity, the staff retreating into domesticity, sexual undertones, the isolation, worry at the future of the school, and even at 4 p.m. the ritual listening to 'Top of the Pops' – a programme heard in the studies and common rooms of almost every boarding school in England.

Filter into life slowly, crunch of communicant feet on the gravel outside my window, high fag chatter and endless pulling of bog chains push me into Sunday morning. I lie in bed and groan at the wreck of a study, cups, papers, clothes. 'Hello lazy' Peter shuffles in 'any sugar?', 'feel quite sick this morning. I'm reading the lesson'. The nit lets in the sunshine and I get up.

Breakfast is the same, but no letters, some read again those they've had in past weeks, most just sit and blink as the sun varnishes the honours board and shines the 'pots' (cups on the table), only the fags talk endlessly, crunching cornflakes, clashing plates. Oh sorry, we are in our grey suits, collars, house ties, ready to worship God in the school's image, a super Moss Bros advert straight from London's tube. Our chapel is hardly the place for scruffy sons of Jewish carpenters. I go off and start an essay.

The organ wheezes, Housemasters hang bat-like in their stalls, heads of houses lounge and up we get to eye the talent parade as it passes, unqualified in virginal white. The hymns are bellowed and I count the names on the war memorial, poor sods, and let the glass, bilious greens and asphyxiated blues, tell the bored, great moments in school history. Save a place for Saint Harold Wilson when thankfully this shrine becomes a chip shop. Christ, at home I would be still in bed!

Its now Sunday afternoon, God knows what I've done since chapel. Now off to the Art Room, no it will be full of little boys drawing aeroplanes, so I lie on my bed and read the 'Observer' get sick of its endless, earnest goodness, reminds me of the Chaplain, so I chuck it. My essay next. But they are limbering up for 'hippo' time next door, with those damn thumps and roars the rugby team will wreck the afternoon. No one will stop them. The housemaster is probably watching the TV Western with his hatchet-faced wife, 'how unsuitable for the boys darling'. The Head of House, sick with power, has gone off to drink Lapsang with the headmaster and to talk about us. So I rush out of this game reserve and walk across the school, past the pianists in the Music block, the tarts around the tuck shop and across the tired fields, some even now are practising. Do they ever stop? Curious clusters of grey suits going nowhere.

Along the river a four goes past paddling light, no coach, dazzling ripples and lovely sky, so I sit under a tree and think of my girlfriend back home getting ready for tea – with someone else. After a while I am cold so I walk back to school, the fields are deserted the pianos stopped, the permitted transistors heave their guts into the twilight. 'It's top of the Pops' and this great public school, guardian of our cultural heritage, twitches in grey. 'Darling I need yeew and I'm gonna have yew . . .' I go back to my study and lie on the bed. Underneath in the Junior Common Room piercing the clip-clop of ping pong, a fag yells over a broken model, and the kids sit on the pipes waiting for tea or a fag call from the hearties.

Tea, those on exeat come back, God knows where they have found to go, the untouched English countryside stretches for miles, a noose round this Gothic factory. 'Please God, send us a Motorway and an Airport'. And its chapel again, past Matron's window she's on her way into the Palm Court of Grand Hotel, then the Chaplain 'Are we pure are we loyal?' God Mark II recovered from the Lapsang gives a sermon on the car strike. We thank God for our day of rest, I pray for something to happen, now now NOW, thrombosis for the Senior Master? from the organ's totem pipes a gargantuan fart? can someone be sick? but nothing rescues us from Sunday. We wander out and sort our books for Prep . . .

At Stanton, where Sunday breakfast is in dressing gowns and people can come in between 8 and 9.30 a.m., a girl aged sixteen:

Dragged myself into breakfast. Sordid old rolls and foul coffee and no papers. Thought about bed and decided it was the best thing so I returned to sleep for another hour and a half.

At a small independent school, the day goes like this:

On Sunday we get a 1 hr lie in which is always looked forward to. Sunday morning is devoted to letter writing and going to church. The aspect to religion is – well it isn't. I don't mind going to church in the least, it's a chance to get out somewhere as well as worship God. Sunday dinner at 12.45 is usually the worst of the week, sometimes half the school don't turn up. The afternoon consists of either mending your bike from the previous day or going for a stroll somewhere, most people like to see some of the opposite sex and do anything which defies the school rules. Sunday evening is the same as Saturday basically. I usually retire to bed thinking of the horrors of another week of work.   *Boy, sixteen, integrated independent school*

In some coeducational schools the girls get very restless on Sundays: they like to get out far more than boys, as if suffering from some kind of claustrophobia. Their destinations are haphazard:

Two of us trying to decide where to hitch to by sticking my knife in a map. Result: Spalding! Heaven help us!

Girl, seventeen, coeducational school

Their journeys can be hazardous:

Decided couldn't hitch to Johnny's as went last weekend and his parents would begin to wonder. Therefore went to Mansted instead. Got a lift with lorry driver who was going to Ipswich, grrr. Reached the hub of the universe (Colchester), went to Jane's house and Jane stole $\frac{1}{2}$ bottle of port and made toast. Afterwards crept out to go and see her new house which is now rapidly growing and is fabulous. Felt slightly drunk going up steep ladder after 2 hastily gulped glasses of port. Wandered up to church, met Mrs J, then Mr gave us huge lunch, talked and hitched back in snow. Got lift with a vile lecherous man in a hideous van.

Girl, eighteen, coeducational school

At 7.15 I went hitching with Clarissa and Marty. We got easy lifts, (we usually do) and we got to Champton at 20 to 8. We brought some longed for fish and chips and started back. Got here about 8.30 and had a lovely hot bath.

Girl, eighteen, progressive school

Occasionally they meet boyfriends:

The dreaded moment comes, go and get changed, rush over to the house to steal someone's coat. TONY arrives, as creepy as usual and wearing that hideous college scarf. Had lunch at the White Hart, with champagne – started to like him a little more...

Girl, seventeen, coeducational school

OCCASIONS

Ceremonies and events in the boarding school are for the most part much like those in day schools. Speech days, for example, in summer or autumn terms do not differ much in content, though they may do in style – bands playing in the school court at 10 p.m., sherry parties for parents in the houses, family caravans parked on remote parts of the playing fields, lunches in country hotels for be-suited boys and their parents. We shall not describe events common to *all* English school experience – speech days, sports days and so on – but instead some of those with a boarding flavour to them.

Half-term in some few schools is held at school, the parents come for the weekend to events and take their boys out. A prep-school boy composed the following verse describing his half-term, the pattern of events, the desolation of a Sunday afternoon spent wandering about with no base in a small shuttered English town.

>Its Thursday
>Oh no
>Is my father coming to the concert?
>If he does will he come late?
>Will I make a bosh of playing
>My recorder when the others are
>Playing well?
>
>Its Friday
>Those sports
>Will I find myself
>Sitting in a deckchair
>In the middle of the running track?
>
>Oh no
>Not Saturday
>Not that boring masters match
>Not that ridiculous bring and buy sale
>With those stupid people
>Selling sticky cakes
>And gooey jam.
>
>Its Sunday
>Walking in the high street
>Of Queenstown
>Its deserted
>No people about

144 The Hothouse Society

> No shops open
> Just row upon row of houses
> Then he has to go
> And half term is over
> For me.
>
> *Boy, twelve, prep school*

Other boys respond to the parents' incursion in other ways. Some with apprehension:

> I bet Mum will look at my Latin book.   *Boy, twelve*

> I hope father doesn't lean backward against fire-doors in the concert. He did last year and they opened and he fell backwards right in the middle of a solo ...   *Boy, twelve*

Sometimes the apprehension is justified:

> Friday dawned bright and clear and I looked forward to enjoying myself. Suddenly the bottom fell out of my stomach as I remembered that I had to tell Mum the results of Quarterly Orders. I had come bottom in the form! I met my mum and as we were driving she asked:
>   'Where did you come in form dear?'
>   'Bottom mum.'
>   'Oh, please try harder. We're spending all this money on you'.
> Phew!   *Boy, twelve*

Others are gleeful:

> Yippeeeee!!!! half term: no work, no prep, no masters to bother me; ice cream, and mummy and daddy.   *Boy, ten*

Founders Day is in some schools an event to be organized:

> As is usual things get casual towards Founderstide. To ensure a successful Founders, all House Prefects must be on the ball to stop

people fooling around, especially seniors. Some Prefects may be going to the Founders Ball; make sure somebody is laid on to do the necessary duties. Also re Founders, make sure that you know about any prizes the House has won and you have to collect!

Head of house's book, public school

In many schools the end of term is celebrated with a supper or party (described in the next chapter), followed or preceded by a review. The review is a take-off of school life – a period of licence in which the boys reverse roles, and mock the staff, values, traditions and each other. They vary from the crude to the subtle, but the esoteric nature of the allusions make them difficult to illustrate. They sometimes have to be censored by the school authorities. Here a boy aged sixteen at a public school describes the sketch he is preparing. It is characteristic in its crude satire of head and housemasters, its caricature of working-class boys (they *always* appear), and its general slapstick.

My particular sketch starts with a motor bike revving up (on tape) reaching a crescendo, dying away and then crashing (the crash is a real long one). At this point I stagger on to the stage in rocker dress – black leather jacket with studs and chains, skin tight sky blue jeans and pointed black cuban heeled boots. In each shoulder a rugger shirt is stuffed under to fill out biceps and chest. On my head I wear a white crash helmet. The effect is something between an American soccer player and superman. Anyhow after spinning in and tripping so as to fall flat on my face I get up and start the rocker act.

'Roight! – who wants rockers, just come 'ere'. Then pointing to the housemaster in the front row who is then spotlit.

'Hey you! Yes you, come 'ere and I'll smash your face in ... Won't stand for that ... roight!' *Boy, sixteen, public school*

From the script of a house review at Christmas at another school, there comes this song, sung to a complicated beat rhythm and satirizing school chapel and the two chaplains (both of whom were present). The boys take off the 'with it' clerical approach, the tell-me-your-problem and sex-talk style of one chaplain, Dashwood, and the dominating rugger passion and the sermonizing style of the other chaplain, Duncan North.

> Chapel bell begins to toll
> Now a 'Top Rank Ten Pin' bowl
> Church of England up to date
> Off the rails and 10 years late.
> Dashwood's there at half-past nine
> Knocking back Communion wine
> Devils advocate is he
> Sex for Christianity
>
> Duncan North is very nice
> To religion will entice.
> 'I want you to listen to this last part of my verse as it is
> Very important. Please bear with me; I won't be long'
> Rugger is the shortest road
> Goalposts are the Gates to God.

Finally a brief extract from the script at yet another house review at another school: Lanchester College. Among the traditional Aunt Sallies (chapel, congregational singing practice and CCF) it takes off the new headmaster, who has recently arrived from a much greater school in the pecking order of public schools, and who has the nervous habit of blowing his nose when he speaks in public.

Curtain, lights out, except 4 spots.
  (SOUND OF CAR DRAWING UP)
M: And here to put you in the picture is the Headmaster ...
(ENTER HM) (CRASH OFF STAGE) and his wife.
  (HM GROANS) Oh dear! Another rise in the school fees. Oh! (Notices his audience and blows his nose.) I'm extremely happy to be able to talk to you tonight about Winchester ... er Lanchester. This as you may know was founded on the great traditions of *the* public school for the education of the sons of gentlemen. (Tape of fag call). I think it is true to say that such things as 19½" bottoms and ankle length navy blue macs are essential ingredients to the discipline

of the adolescent. THE school itself is undergoing some changes. By 1984 we hope to begin on a new dining hall.

THE END OF THE DAY

We started this account of the daily round with getting-up; we end with a few very typical bedtimes.

Brenda, our hockey girl, finally retires at her coeducational school, though her activities, gastronomic and illicit, never cease:

> Had some supper played the piano and came upstairs. Went round other Dorms talked to people in Bed and not in Bed. Came back to our dorm got undressed went and washed and did some washing. Got into bed at 8.55. Talked a bit and wrote my diary. Didn't curl my hair as it's greasy and it doesn't curl when it is. Had some of Anne's jelly in bed, strawberry (mmmmmmmmmm). Lights out at 9.15. Listened to my radio which is a terrible crime if copped. Went pegout (bog) it smelt before and after I went: washed hands and got back into bed. Listened to radio again. A play, some music and the news.

At Beauchamp Manor, yet another diarist, a prefect this time, ends his Saturday evening. Another boy: but the same tone and almost the same style of writing and life described.

> The film began, a cartoon about two dogs who fall in love. Sex, can't get away from it! M. in front was prancing around I snapped at him to shut up. He winced. Ah, I had got through. Then the main film came. 'Sammy Going South'. I think more people were interested in the boy than him going South. Films have as usual been awful this term except for one film. Christ can't these masters choose a decent selection of films? 'Sammy Going South'. Who the hell do they think we are? A bleeding prep school? We walked back to the school in the rain.
>
> I went upstairs and along to my dormitory. I went in. I undressed and slowly went to the windows. Slowly a question mark formed by a rift in the clouds showed itself. Good point, what sort of day had it

148   The Hothouse Society

been? Don't know. Hasn't finished yet. I went and washed and carried out the same routine. Flannel behind left tap and bag behind right tap and to hell with the rest. I grinned about something. I don't know what. Put everything back again and went to the lavatory. Then came back and went and read in bed. At a quarter to nine S-G came in and turned off the lights. Then I fell asleep and my day was over. God knows how many more of them I have here but the fewer the better. Complicated? No, just a bloody routine with no outlet.

At Stanton a game of hide-and-seek ensues between house-mother and her charges as bedtime approaches:

Pat came into my room and we talked for a while I was rather annoyed with her because she had told someone something I did not want them to know. But we ended up being friendly because she said she was sorry. Then Babs the housemother came up again. Pat got under the bed and I went out and said to Babs 'Can I go to the bog please?' She said 'yes'. She asked me where Gavin was (a boy who has his room near mine). I said I didn't know and went to the toilet. When I came back she had found Gavin talking in Celia's room. Somebody else was in there as well, but she didn't find him.
Luckily Babs hadn't gone into Pat's room so she didn't know she was missing. When Babs had gone Pat got up from under the bed and we talked about things for a bit longer. We looked out of the window, where we could see whether Babs was in her sitting room or not and as she wasn't there we waited to see whether we could hear anybody outside. We couldn't hear anybody so Pat went out and went into her own room. I played patience for a bit, ate an apple and then went to sleep.
Girl, fifteen

We leave the daily round, before turning to explore particular areas of the school and its pupils' existence, with a little nightlife in the dormitory:

Prep never gets done. Today I was in charge of the class because all the prefects are at dancing class. Hugging and kissing with ugly old tarts from Axmouth. Don't worry, it's sour grapes. But this prep we get talking as usual. It's sex.

And now its nine o'clock, up to bed, dive in, lights out, but that's not the end of the day, Oh, no, no, follows an hour of noise and torches for this that and another thing and finally at about 11 we drop off. I hope I dream that dream again. Next thing I know it's 12 o'clock and filing past me are three dark shapes off for a cigarette in the lavatories. What a bloody good idea! See you.

Boy, sixteen, independent school

5 'This Tiny Universe' — The House

Most people think of 'school'. Many boarders do not: they think of 'house'. 'It's house, house, house, nothing but the house sir, it bores me stiff,' writes a jaded fifth-former. 'What does this school mean to me as distinct from the house?' asks a prefect, 'nothing at all: I shall only think about the school rather than the house when I have left.' A sixth-form boy from a comprehensive school now at public school echoes him: 'The house system divides the boys enormously. It seems as if the boys go to a particular house, not to St Michael's College. It is the house which gives a boy character, not so much the school.'

To many children in boarding schools the house is the focus of their lives, the small primary unit on which their immediate loyalties, hatreds, activities and friendships are based. To the junior boy it is virtually his entire world; to the senior boy, whose friendships and activities may range more widely over the school, it is still his home, his base, the place where he learns to wield power and to organize, to manage and care for others, to come into hour-by-hour contact with the staff (housemaster, tutor, matron), to live in a close, indeed sometimes packed and tense community. Whatever the basic type of house — whether it is a little unit of forty-five in a separate building eating, sleeping, playing, doing prep, saying prayers as a body, recruited and presided over by a housemaster aided by his wife and a dame or matron; whether it is a larger body of 60–70, perhaps recruited and eating centrally, but still acting as a separate primary unit or segregated in part of a central block, the care, love, energy and worry which go into the upkeep of house form the basis of the life and effectiveness of many schools, and of the introverted myopia of some. There can be no understanding of boarding without experiencing this essential community within a community, this 'tiny universe', as one boy puts it.

But not all boarding schools have houses. Some state boarding schools and progressive schools do not believe in small, competitive, primary groups: they base their pastoral care or organization on the form unit, or age group (first year, fourth year, etc.), or on dormitories. Other schools which have 'houses' use them purely for administrative purposes – as labels to attach to teams, rooms or buildings, or ribbons to be attached to cups. These houses never generate the same deep response and identity as the house which lives, works, sleeps and plays together with its own rules under one housemaster. In some schools houses are horizontal in age structure: junior houses, middle houses and, increasingly nowadays, separate houses for sixth-formers. But the most common house pattern is all-age, thirteen to eighteen in one. This latter – the separate, all-age house – is the sort we are concerned with in this chapter. It is found mainly in public schools, and also in some independent ones. In describing it we shall draw close to the heart of public-school existence, and we shall draw heavily on some fascinating documents, the books kept by those important personages, the house captains – passing privately on to their successors their experience, the lore of the house, their ways of dealing with the housemaster and the boys.

The public-school house is not just a social convenience; it has become an ideal in itself. A head of house sums it up, and much of the public-school ideal, in impressing on his successor the importance of his new office:

> The system of Houses at a Public School is concerned with education outside the classroom – education in character, responsibility, self-discipline, leadership, etc. This is just the same purpose as that of the Boy Scout Movement. I mean of course the Movement which Baden-Powell founded, not Scouting as it is called in a lot of places today. If you have never looked at 'Scouting for Boys' may I suggest you take the next opportunity. Look at the introduction, look at B.-P's messages, and read the section headed 'Principles and Methods'. It is all there, isn't it? With Christianity behind it of course. And it has worked. The motto of Scouting is 'Be Prepared'.

Are you prepared? Are you confident that the system you will run is the best possible for the best purpose? Do you even have any idea what the purpose is? You will probably change your ideas, but it is essential to have such a view in front before you undertake any job like this. Above all, can you set the best example, the example of service, service not only to run the system but to make it and particularly the people in it fit to be the leaders of a civilisation which will not fall as that of the Romans did? There is so much more I could put: things like sincerity, cheerfulness, anti-conceit, anti-laziness, etc., and on a different level, delegation of authority, efficiency, which means plenty of sleep, exams, etc. I'll stop here, you go on thinking up little principles and ideas all day long, its great fun, enjoy being head of Smythe's.

Head of house's book, public school

Clearly the house captains, the most important and so often the most impressive boys in the public schools, take their job immensely seriously. Part of their job is to foster corporate loyalty, 'house spirit', that devotion to the community which is part of the aims of these schools and also one of their methods of control. The boys at the top should set the example:

The secret of success? A house which is united and happy within its walls will be doubly united in all spheres outside. Houses won't do well as long as senior men abuse their right. We must set a good example. *Head of house's book, public school*

The secret of good house spirit and a happy house is this: keep them occupied. The success of a house depends entirely on how it moulds its juniors. *Different head of house, same school*

The difficulty of maintaining this loyalty and spirit is sometimes manifest at the top. A head of house sums up his difficulties at a public school:

I was worried at the beginning of the term. It is a frightening prospect to run a house of 44 boys and more especially to try to keep the

'This Tiny Universe' – The House   153

prefects together. The most important thing in the running of the house is that the prefects do not split up into different factions. I cannot thank Piers Damarel enough for backing me up and acting as a go-between when I failed to fix my ideas on the other prefects.

During the last two terms the housemaster has excelled himself in the choice of new boys. A house is generally judged by its athletic standards and if this influx of promising newcomers continues, I can foresee a very successful house in the near future. Not only do the new boys show athletic promise but also some of the old tradition. There is bags of spirit at the bottom of the house and this is to be encouraged since the middle of the house lacks it completely. I doubt that one could find a more gormless, spineless bunch of flesh in the school. What a pity it is there because in a couple of years it will be at the top of the house. Piers, keep an eye on them because some of them have not been dealt harshly enough with. Once this core of bad ones either reform or leave, the house will be both better and healthier. I hope that I am not being too unkind on those concerned but that is what I feel about them.

One way of keeping up loyalty and spirit is by competition, especially at games. Success at games, even a collection of games trophies, can become a measure of the level of house spirit. Here are two public-school heads of house:

There still remains no cup on the dining room table and this is becoming a bit more than a joke. Not many members of the house enter in competitions and therefore must be encouraged if not virtually forced to have a go at as many competitions as possible.
Head of house's book, public school

Well that's about it – I'm very worried by the fact that we have no cups on the table, although we have a part share in two. But it looks as though we might lose one of those as well. It is terribly important that we get some back; I know this is easier said than done, but if you look at houses in general, it's the ones with a really rough constitution that do well. I would advise a really tough line for at least a year. It's no use pretending. If boys don't *have* to do some-

thing they won't do it. So the only way to get them to do it is to make them do it and this will have to be the policy for the next few terms.
Another head of house, same school

Others stress that it is not so much success but the unity and camaraderie created by team games which knit the house together.

When men become positively bolshy at soccer, this is very undesirable and ought to be stamped out.
Head of house's book, public school

I am in no doubt that good house sides – not necessarily successful ones but happy ones that take the game fairly seriously – are of paramount importance for the welfare of the house.
Different head of house, same school

Even one state boarding school which superficially follows the style and structure of the public-school house uses games as the generator of house spirit and example:

On looking back, I have enjoyed this year. It has been a hell of a sweat, but it has been worth it.

In the field of sport we have not been so successful as I would have liked, but we retained the rugger, the general P.T. and the Athletics, which to me are some of the most prized cups in the school. We have been handicapped by juniors lacking in talent and numbers. This showed particularly in the soccer, but it was not until the Athletics that they at last found their own and came romping home in one of the happiest afternoons of my time here. The Athletics was an epic I for one will never forget. The senior cross-country was really a walk-over, and it was this excessive strength in the talented and innumerable seniors that really has been the most unfortunate part of the year. This dominant factor has meant that the seniors have not been forced to set that vital example to the juniors, of going into a match where the chances of success were small, and where only a miracle could give us victory.
Head of house's book, state boarding school

'This Tiny Universe' – The House 155

We turn now from house ideals to their characters and structures. Schools differ: but so do the houses of which they are composed. 'Each house is different,' notes a boy from a comprehensive school, now at a public school, 'different characters, different policy, different rules, different reputation. It's baffling. It's a matter of luck if you end up in the house which suits *you*.' Here we set down the comments of three senior public school boys on their houses. Note the uniformity and disagreements of their verdicts, and also their view of the day-boy houses. Their judgements may not be accurate – but they do indicate the different communities co-existing in one school.

Headmaster's house
  (1) Good company – but noisy. The least law-abiding house in the school.
  (2) Rugger. Tough but reasonably cultured. Atmosphere of competition. Easy going rules for house powers. Very 'public schooly'.
  (3) Rather mediaeval. Great deal of house spirit. Think themselves the best house (they are) Plenty of character.

Broadwood's
  (1) Dirty and dim.
  (2) Have by far the worst atmosphere of any house. Provincial and dreary. Good at rugger.
  (3) Homosexuality. Good at games. Doesn't mix with rest of the school much.

Townley's
  (1) A goody-goody house where the rule-breaker is the exception. High standards in games and work. Great emphasis on serving the house. Friendly but not warm-hearted. Few lasting friendships made.
  (2) Probably the most 'civilized' and 'cultured' house. Nice boys.
  (3) Suspicious of others. Fair house spirit because the housemaster's love of learning and culture has provoked a healthy reaction.

Lloyd's
  (1) Good company, little prestige attached to office-holding.
  (2) Definitely the most liberal house and pleasant atmosphere.
  (3) Definitely the house to be in to have a good time. Easy going but perhaps the worst house to be in if you're a misfit. Good mixers, not very good at games.

Nicholson's
  (1) Suffer from the herd instinct and monopolize the tuck-shop.
  (2) Cultured. Tend to stick together and are isolated as a result.
  (3) Don't mix – our fault not their's. Wealthy, bad at games.

Dayboy house 1
  (1) Higher proportion of louts than any other house.
  (2) Full of yobs. Very social out of school.
  (3) Full of 'oiks'. Noisy and bad at everything. Not really this school at all.

Dayboy house 2
  (1) Spineless and featureless. Full of nonentities.
  (2) Phlegmatic attitude to everything – the few capable boys are unable to carry the rest of the house with them.
  (3) Pleasant and friendly.

From character to structure. Like the school itself, the house, particularly in the public school, falls into an elaborate hierarchy of status. Boys come as fags and move up the ladder to that of VIths or house prefects. A house book gives us a diagram of a very typical structure:

Masters	Housemaster House Tutor – resident Out House Tutors – non-resident
Boys	Head of House VIths Head Vth and Vths Head IVth and IVths Non-fags Head fag and fags

'This Tiny Universe' – The House 157

And a head of house in a traditional public school explains who and what these people are, and where they stand in the hierarchy. The staff first. Note the faint whiff of condescension of the boy to the junior house staff – a feature of the power system which we shall explore in the next chapter.

The Housemaster is appointed by the Headmaster, the House Tutors are chosen by the Housemaster. Here you can give invaluable advice, there are certainly no lack of good young masters in the school at present. In this connection, it is usual to have only one Out House Tutor but you can have 2, so if you think any unattached master is suitable, I expect the Housemaster would be pleased to have such a suggestion.

The house captain is head of the boy hierarchy and wields great influence. Here a head boy reflects on his role, that of the prefects (VIths) and their purpose in training leaders:

The H. of H. has the authority to rule as a dictator, but every successful leader knows that he must have his subjects with him. The acknowledged ideal is to have a happy house. For this, the leaders must understand what those under them want, just as much as the subjects must understand, respect, and obey the leaders. The leaders must also show no sign of violent argument among themselves. The first principle for VIths is therefore that they should know what they are working for, all should be in the picture, understand what is going on, and be prepared to back up decisions by others in authority. The more the H. of H. works with his VIths as their acknowledged leader, than as their master, the happier will be the VIth Study, and the better the House.

I have stated an ideal. The aim of this organization of VIths to Fags is to produce leaders, and should never be lost sight of. The H. of H. is *not* the only leader in the House. He has the far more difficult task of co-ordinating the ideas of all the other leaders into one effort.

In basic outline, the function of the VIths is to decide policy and organise the House.

158 The Hothouse Society

The rest of the house hierarchy have clearly defined functions too. Everyone knows where everyone stands: people above and people below in the chain of command – including the lowliest fags:

The Vths have responsibility over specific parts of the organisation, and it is also their duty to see that the House runs smoothly and that rules are kept. Vths are subject to all House Rules, and must be reprimanded and even punished by H. of H. But of course if it comes to it, demotion would probably be the only solution. All Vths' notices on the board have to be counter signed by H. of H., or, if not available, the senior VIth who is available. They have the sole use of the library during break. They must attend all call-overs, but their names are not called out (unless H. of H. makes a very embarrassing mistake!). They are responsible for keeping order at all times, enforcing tidiness, and maintaining a high standard of behaviour and manners. Vths may not use fags for their own personal convenience.

IVths have a number of privileges which non-fags do not have, and they still have no corresponding duties. *They are on probation for fifthdom*. Being a good IVth is the real test of any member of the House, and serves as a very clear indication of the person who would be a good wielder of authority (if you believe the adage about learning to obey in order to be able to command.) If they are KEEN, willing, and responsive to sensible discipline, the House will be in a good way and they will make good Vths. The PRIMARY duty of the IVths is EXAMPLE.

Non-fags come next and are subject to meal and net fagging, but are exempt from personal and regular House fagging.

Every boy fags for his first three terms.

Head Fag should, if numbers permit, be exempt from personal and regular House fagging.

There are two parts to fagging.

I: House fagging
   (*a*) Keeping the House Hall and Changing Rooms tidy.
   (*b*) Collecting and dealing with milk bottles.
   (*c*) Washing-up for VIths.

(d) Meal and net fagging.

II: Personal fagging.
Each VIth has a number of personal fags. The names and number are decided by H. of H.

Promotion up the house hierarchy, though it goes by and large by seniority, depends term by term on other factors; it is anxiously sought after by many boys because of the privileges it brings, earnestly and secretly discussed by the house prefects and the housemaster, and decisions are greeted with joy, apparent stoic indifference or crestfallen worry.

Promotions meeting:
All proceedings are for ever secret. The decisions are not made known until the next term. New Prefects are told of their promotion by H. of H., after the meeting, they must, of course, keep their knowledge in confidence.
The Housemaster and H. of H. should discuss any particular problems which may arise, before the meeting. They should always have clear together who they want as Prefects.

The problem of whom to promote, especially in the middling ranks of frequently disaffected adolescents, vexes the house prefects and staff.

Whatever you find to be the answer to these problems it is very important that the Prefects do think about these promotions at least a bit before they take place, even if this is only a few hours.
Head of house's book, public school

One house captain in difficulties wishes to use the promotion system as his solution:

The situation is serious but what can be done about it? People must be shown that promotion must be earned and in future will not be purely automatic. A precedent must be established whereby a V who openly breaks rules does not remain as a V and a IV who will

openly break rules will not become a V. It is very important that once a boy becomes a IV he realizes that his days of merely taking from the House are over. He will not benefit further without some give, and the more he gives the more he will gain from the House.
Head of house's book, public school

What other structural problems do houses face? One of the most common is a split between the various levels of hierarchy, or a split within each level. A house captain outlines his dilemma to his successor:

Dear Dodd,
As you must realise, the house is not in a very healthy state at the moment as far as internal affairs are concerned. The reasons for this are long, varied, and mostly uncertain, but the faults at the moment seem essentially to be as follows.

(*a*) The House V's are to a very large extent nonentities in the House without strong individual personalities (eg Bosking, Hawkings, Noble).

(*b*) The House IV's are mostly good and successful in at least one particular sphere, and thus are much more powerful than the V's.

(*c*) The V's are not united in policy. Some will support the VI's whatever, but others often side against them and even go so far as to slander them in front of IV's.

(*d*) This attitude which has grown up whereby those in authority are thought to be taking sides against the rest of the House and vice versa, is so obviously wrong. The reason for this coming about is not entirely the fault of the IV's, in fact the V's and VI's are much more to blame because it is they who set the whole tone of the House and should be able to stop this sort of thing happening.
Head of house's book, public school

The cure for some of the discontents which arise in the doldrums of the middle of the house can be discreet pastoral care by the head of house and, at all times, fair play:

I found that it was helpful to do a tour of the studies about once a week. This gave me a chance to talk to everybody in a social sort of way. I was very bucked to find them coming to me to sort out problems and arguments, and I firmly believe that this was because I was the first H. of H. that they had ever known as a person. This is of course up to you, but I strongly advise you to continue my policy, though it might be better to wait until you have established yourself fully first.

Above all, I want to give you one piece of advice. *Be just on all occasions.* It may mean that you will lose a friend, but in the long run you will gain many more. It is not easy, but it is essential to be just if you are going to get any real satisfaction from your job. Also remember when you don't feel like doing something that you have been chosen for this job from at least three candidates, and it is your DUTY to sort out problems, give advice, and lead.

Head of house's book, public school

Such popping in to the studies to keep the house together must not degenerate into familiarity, or an intimacy which cuts across the rigid hierarchy:

... it will help to make the House more of a unit in itself and break down these inter-house gangs which are springing up and are not healthy as you know. It will also make people more aware of the personal side of the Prefects rather than just the official side as they do at present and thus make the Prefects' job a bit easier I think. Don't let it develop into a Blake's House though where fags call Prefects by their Christian names, but I see little danger of this happening as things are at present. *Same book*

Another problem can be the sudden reversal of policy brought with a new house captain. It leaves one boy bewildered. He refers to the repressive and permissive contradictions of his two immediate predecessors, North and Stedman:

I for my part do not intend to give a list of some hideous vices that have been raging like forest fires in my term of office, and which I have, like the self-styled, chip-on-the-shoulder, latent – homosexual – sadist – self-deceived martyr that I am, tried to stamp out (North).

Nor do I intend to bore you with a success written from an entirely egocentric point of view (Stedman) by giving a list of boys for whom I have flamed with a pure homosexual passion and who are therefore the epitome of happiness. But the 'beat 'em, thrash 'em and they'll learn to enjoy pain' attitude of continued restraint and restriction as well as the 'spare the rod, spoil the child, then they will all go to bed with one another, how nice!' attitude are futile. We should face facts. In the last few years we have witnessed these opposed philosophies. Both are too extreme. Stedman failed utterly. There is a need for compromise. It is very difficult.

Head of house's book, public school

One other 'problem', as the senior boys see it, can be the housemaster or the house tutor: handling him is one of their major tasks on which they pass on advice to each other.

As you know, Martin (the housemaster) has his ideas, and it is as well to humour him by agreeing with him as far as possible. If his idea is not what you want, and it is not easy to just do what you want, it is quite possible to turn him slowly to your idea for a short time by repeating what he says and adding a 'but', gradually introducing your opinion. He will repeat his line, so do you and introduce more of your point with a bigger 'but'. Mr Singleton is a very conservative man, and it is necessary to break any new system to him gently. This method I have explained is one way of doing this; if you can find a better one, good luck! However, do remember this, he is a very shrewd man, and he has more experience than I, or this book, can hope to give you. More often than not, his way is the best.

With regard to the House Tutor, I can help you very little here, but I should see him as soon as possible, perhaps before the mob arrives, and establish yourself with him as a friend, explaining that you want to work with him. If you can get a drink out of him, so much the better. Try if you can to get him to take more personal interest in the house than Andrew did – he was so lofty and unapproachable – and be more hospitable than Martin.

What then should a *good* housemaster be like – what qualities should he have? Two contributions sum up the views of countless boarders:

'This Tiny Universe' – The House 163

1. Ability to judge character and act on that judgement for the good of the individual.
   Ability to make a house happy and progressive. There are houses which are happy but not progressive, and also houses which are progressive but not happy.
   Ability to make a sane dividing line between officiousness and efficiency.
   Ability not to pry into matters concerned with house too much.
   Ready to give advice but not impose it.
   Happy medium between sports and work.
   Ability to differentiate between boys of 14 and boys of 17.
   Boy, seventeen, public school

2. A good housemaster should have:
   Interest
   Attention
   Whatever line he takes, he should care about it, be it games or culture.
   Should he be a bachelor? Wives can be an incumbrance, a diversion, a nuisance and above all, a menace, ie the housemaster cannot be an ordinary mortal it isn't possible.
By some means, he must be in touch. It is ridiculous when a housemaster does not even know who is in the dorm in his house, or who has colours.
A balanced attitude that gives certain amount of prestige to games and a certain amount to work and a certain amount to music and a certain amount to House Art and a certain amount to drama is best.
   Boy, seventeen, public school

The hierarchy we have explored by no means covers all the jobs available in the average house. It is part of the policy of schools to give as many boys as possible the chance of acquiring initiative and responsibility, and status in the community. It is one way in which public schools in particular reconcile pupils to their systems and their aims. Other jobs are widely spread. In one house of sixty-five boys, for example, the house book lists no fewer than forty-two regular house appointments to be distributed among them. Most boys get one. We see again the extra-curricular range of one public school:

Games Captain	i/c Fagging	Instrumental
i/c Boxing	i/c Chess	Director
i/c Fives	Capt. Fives	Capt. Swimming
Librarian	Capt. Chess	Capt. Water Polo
i/c Changing Rooms	Capt. Running	Capt. Shooting
i/c Bicycles	i/c Rowing	i/c net fagging
i/c House Hall	Capt. Rowing	i/c Games
House Art Rep	*Either*:	Equipment
Sec. VI & V Reading Soc.	Sports Captain *Or*: i/c Sports	Electrician i/c Squash
Sec. IV Reading Soc.	+i/c Open sports	Capt. Racquets
Unison & Quartet Director	+i/c Under 16½ sports	Secretary of Gerontes
Capt. XV	+i/c Under 15 sports	Secretary of
i/c Meals	Producer of Play	Barnstormers
Corps Commander	Capt. Cricket	Secretary of
i/c Entertainments	i/c Tennis	Omega Club

One head of house lists the qualities necessary in various office holders; they tell us much about the office and the house captain's scale of values. The stress is on the 'good average' man and on the collectively rather than the individually oriented boy. Here are a few of his comments:

Games Captain: Outside H. of H. the most important job. A tough, exacting and interesting job which can be very rewarding. The G.C. in many ways represents the house to the rest of the school. Few efficient G.C.'s go through their term as such without a drop in form position. Calmness is a great asset. *Originality, enthusiasm, and enterprise make the great in this job.* The G.C. must be a Prefect. He must know what H. of H. and Housemaster think about 'problem boys' and how much exercise to give all sorts of ailing blokes, and must be able to be in contact with Housemaster over questions such as 'why Bloggs did not have a game yesterday'.

Capt. XV and XI: A captain rather than the best player, though these usually coincide.

Play: Must be appointed by half term in winter term. Personality, whether eccentric or not. Keep a careful eye on him as these people are in the happy position of being able to stir up internal trouble and easily to waste money.

Instrumental Director: A good ensemble often wins this, therefore, someone who could potentially form, hold together, and organise an ensemble would be suitable.

Net Fagging: Job for Deputy Prefect. Best done with 2 teams working Wed. and Fri. If he has original ideas be careful he does not overwork the fags or conscript them for extra jobs for himself.

Games Equipment: Vital. Give to a Deputy Prefect. If he shows no interest because it does not bring him into limelight, then the inference is obvious. If done well all Pres will be in debt to a very efficient chap.

Electrician: For the practical though not very bright chap. Give to a Deputy. May be called upon for Entertainments, Stage Set, Gilbert & Sullivan, running repairs around House and all sorts of queer things in all terms.

Librarian: Ordinary tastes, but wide reader. Prefect or Deputy.

Changing Rooms: Can be more than one in order to carry out checkups. A wretched job. One chap must be Pre, rest Deputies.

Art Rep: Prefect or Deputy. Interest and drive, rather than brilliance; above all, has to cope with BJK (the art master).

Song Director: Musician, preferably in choir, can be anyone, though if no authority, a Prefect should be delegated to help. Has to conduct at performance.

One way of knitting together and symbolizing house corporate spirit is by traditions and rituals. House gatherings usually take place to an ordained pattern in which the pupils' status is marked. The house books carefully lay them out (see page 166).

It is, however, the house supper, or dinner, held annually in many schools, which marks the high peak of house ritual, identity and self-consciousness. It is usually in the Christmas term. The house hall is decorated, the cups polished, the housemaster and guests, old boys and the prefects are all in dinner jackets. After dinner there are

The House in Call-Over Order

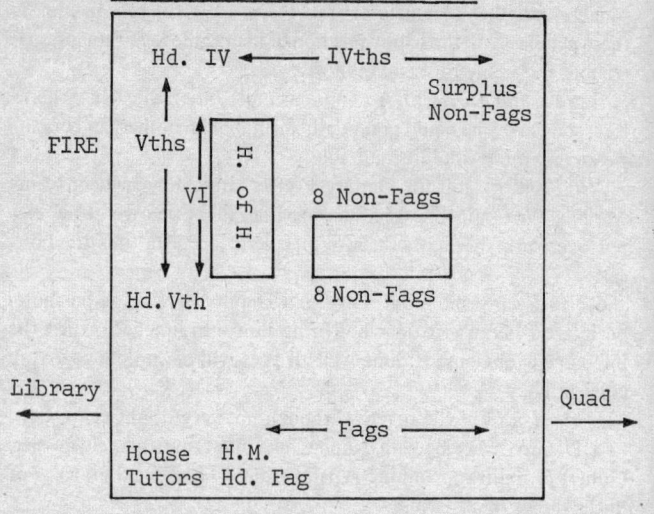

```
                Hd. IV  ←——  IVths  ——→
                   ↑                        Surplus
                   |                        Non-Fags
        FIRE     Vths    ┌──────┐
                         │ H.   │
                    VI   │ of   │   8 Non-Fags
                         │ H.   │
                   ↓     │      │
                Hd. Vth  └──────┘   8 Non-Fags

   Library ←                                        → Quad

                House     H.M.     ←—— Fags ——→
                Tutors    Hd. Fag
```

speeches and sometimes songs. The head of house's books again spell out the occasion:

The House Supper

This is probably the most important occasion in the House's year.

The first things is to decide which old boy or other celebrity is to be asked to speak. There are usually twenty to thirty old boys and about another fourteen on the High Table, plus sixty of the House giving a total of approximately 100. One word about the invitation to the speaker. The object should not be just to get a celebrity, but almost preferably a good after-dinner speaker. This is the sort of chap who did not rise awfully high in the school but inhabits the City and gets plenty of practice. Of course the difficulty is to find these people. It can be done by inquiring tactfully from old boys.

The following are usually invited as guests for the High Table by the Housemaster:

> The House Tutor and his wife
> The Out House Tutor (and his wife)
> The Parents of the H. of H.
> The Parents of other VIths.

The House drink orange and lemon squash and cider. The old boys cider and beer (I think that's the right word!)

The Hall is decorated in the morning. Put someone else i/c this. Put some of the 120 willing hands at your disposal on to the job – delegation of authority.

The idea is that the proceedings start (particularly when the guests arrive) with no electric light, just candles. However, ensure that the lights go on before the speeches if you intend to read yours.

The House should be called over in the corridor by one VIth after the concert. The House stand as you enter, and you go to your appointed places.

You should allow two hours for the whole proceedings. It would be best if you told the House exactly what happens and the order of events, and what they must and must not do, etc.

Procedure: The Housemaster will either say Grace himself or ask a clergyman, if there is one present, to do so. Then the meal proceeds. When it is drawing to a close the Housemaster will propose 'The Queen', and announce that guests may smoke. The next toast is proposed by the Housemaster, who then speaks. He gives away the cups first. Remember to leave slips of paper with the names of the winners in the cups so that the Housemaster doesn't go wrong. He proposes 'The House'. This is replied to by the H. of H. Your speech basically is a review of the past year in the life of the House. You may break away from this at times *but on no account must the speech contain any criticisms of the House or its members.* You must NOT wash dirty linen in public. This should be left to private occasions such as House meetings. Whether you agree with this or not, old boys and visitors will think it very poor if you do bring in criticism. It is something which is not done especially as the House Supper is meant to be a joyful occasion. This review is really for the old boys. I think it is also a good idea to say something to the house, although you do this regularly at House meetings, the House

Rough seating plan:

Guests	Housemaster	Guests
H. of H.		2nd H. of H.
VIth		VIth
		Fags
Non-Fags	Old boys	IVth
Vth		Vth
	House Tutor	

Supper is, if anything, more of a special occasion for them than for old boys. Certainly they will listen to what you say, and will expect to hear something of interest to them, particularly if you are leaving. You then say something nice about the Housemaster and his wife, and propose 'The Old Boys'. The chief guest responds, probably at length. After the last speech, the guests depart, followed by the old boys, followed by the House, who will, you hope, go straight to bed. The guests, old boys and VIths, at least for a few minutes, retire to the Housemaster's drawing room for another session . . .

So much then for the house, its ideals, its basic structure, and some of its problems. Other aspects of its operation and of the informal life which hums in its common rooms, dorms and studies appear in the following chapters. Few, in the traditional boarding schools, escape its impress, though some brave spirits try:

> I don't think the house matters all that much. My requirements are a single study and a House Captain who doesn't make me play rugger, with such rare luxuries as uninterfering Housemasters thrown in. *Boy, sixteen, public school*

'This Tiny Universe' – The House

Others who have reached the top and penned their letters to their successor sit back at home in the summer after leaving in a cloud of manly smoke and happy memories, the devoted old boys of future house suppers.

Well, thats the lot, and as I light my pipe and puff away at it now, I am thinking of you David and wish the best of luck. I am sure you will enjoy the job as much as I did and make an excellent captain. Floreat Wardell's! *Boy, eighteen, public school*

6 A Place in the Sun – Power

Power matters. One of the biggest differences between boarding and day schools lies in the scale, scope, nature and effects of power wielded by the pupils. Whether it is the traditional public school with prefects meeting in conclave within walls covered with fading group photographs and dusty and shrivelled tasselled caps of days long ago; or whether it is the state boarders grouped in the library – all white wood and polish – at a council in uneasy and unreal equality with the headmaster and staff; or whether it is the parliament of the progressive school, bare feet, long hair, head and staff being interrupted, animatedly discussing whether smoking should be banned – power matters to them all. Existence in a community for twenty-four hours a day, seven days a week inevitably means that – if the staff are not to be more numerous and overworked than they are – more responsibility and authority is passed over to the pupils than could possibly be the case in day education. In some schools it is delegated to a hierarchy of pupils headed by the prefects – this in the case of all public, most independent and some state boarding schools – in others, chiefly progressive schools, it is diffused, with everyone counting as equals, or is elective in character. In this chapter we shall explore mainly the power wielded by pupils.

That power matters, boarders of all sorts are well aware. On its use or misuse depends much of their happiness. One head of house reminds his successor of this:

> As you must know, as new boys they were subjected to such house prefects as I dread to mention. One must still hope that when these (who are now middle boys) reach higher positions in this school

they will not copy still the standards which their first prefects set.
Yet the fear is that irreparable harm has already been done: 'eternal
fate so deep has cast, her sure foundation of despair'. It is easy to
realise the immense power which prefects have in directing the
whole school career of the boys who respect them. I hope you will
believe me when I remind you of the words which I said at the first
prefects' meeting last term: 'that I wanted the prefects always to
treat the younger boys with civility and respect, and that although
punishment was the privilege of the prefects, it should not be regarded as their job' – and when I tell you now that this was not part
of a courtship of popularity, but an earnest desire to avoid the mutual
misery which existed last summer and to advance towards prosperity.
Head of house's book, public school

Another rubs in the moral more succinctly:

The prefects can by their authority and by their example, if they
are wise enough, do a very great deal of good, and if they are not
wise, create a hell on earth. *Head of house's book, public school*

Other boys recognize the importance of authority for another
reason – the fear of being left out in the cold without it:

A VI former who is not a deputy or a prefect is treated no better
than a new boy. *Boy, seventeen, state boarding school*

I'm nearing the top of the school but I have no authority and am
nobody – I want authority and to be someone.
Boy, seventeen, public school

Such sentiments are not just those of late adolescence. For the
majority of boarders – those who started in the prep schools – there
has already been a foretaste of power, a miniature version of what they
experience later at seventeen or eighteen. By the age of twelve, they
already know power and its burdens:

Thank you, Lord, thank you for giving me the leadership of Hawthorn House; thank you for my privileges and my prefect's tie; for the house cup that we so closely won and for the trust of the boys in my house, thank you, Lord, thank you.

Prayer of boy, twelve, prep school

Dear God, thank you for giving me this responsibility, and help me to carry out my duties loyally and faithfully. Amen.

Another boy, same school

From another prep school, a twelve-year-old house captain describes the difficulties and consolations of office: controlling others, living as an exemplar, discussing the characters of the other boys with the staff, enjoying privileges and learning 'responsibility' – being trained, in other words, already at this early age for the governing élite in society:

... The most important thing is to set an example. This is also the hardest thing to do. If a house captain does just a little thing wrong, it is immediately noticed. And so, *if* a house captain does something wrong, he must make sure not to be seen.

The next danger is hypocrisy. This is very heavily criticized when seen. For example, a house captain orders a boy to shut up, then, that same house captain starts talking to a boy. This gets boys in rebellious moods and should another house captain try to shut that boy up, he will say that 'So and so told me to shut up and just went on blabbing himself'.

House captains have many privileges which are often questioned by uncooperative boys. The main one is that a house captain is allowed to go straight to the front of *any* queue. This naturally causes moans and objections of all varieties.

Sunday evening is a house captain's PARADISE. After the story which is read by our headmaster, the house captains have a meeting and bring up any boy who is getting a nuisance or something that is not going right. After the meeting, the house captains go up to the headmaster's flat and watch television while eating peaches, crisps and cakes and other such things. This is indeed a privilege and treat because no boys are normally allowed to watch television or eat such delicious food, except the spoilt juniors who watch television twice for half an hour, but without food. The last house captain's privilege is that house captains are given a piece of toast each morning as part of their breakfast. This is a treat mainly because toast is not given to boys.

All in all, I think being a house captain is an honour and worthwhile because it gives one an idea of responsibility which is invaluable for one's future life.
Boy, twelve

In the few prep schools attached to progressive schools, things are different: no formal hierarchy or exemplars and more ostensibly democratic procedures.

No, we don't have prefects or monitors or those things – we all clear up ourselves. We do have a Council. It met last week up in the library – Paul (the Head) sat on a table and kept it going. He didn't need to – we went on for an hour discussing whether we should do prep in the evenings or not. The girls wanted to, the boys didn't – except for Jeremy, and he's a bit odd. I suppose Paul will decide.
Boy, twelve, Tormouth prep

But it is in the public schools and others like them that the officially ordained power of pupils reaches its greatest magnitude, most subtle ramifications, most complex difficulties and greatest impact on both the recipients and those over whom they wield authority: all as a means of training the pupils as responsible governors or managers of others. There is the *scale* of pupil's authority, its *nature* (the principles and practice of its exercise), the *privileges* which reward it and, finally, the *sanctions* which go with it.

In the public and similar schools, those pupils at the top, the house captains and senior prefects, exercise the same power as many members of staff, and often greater power than junior members of staff. 'Treat the prefects as masters,' advises a new boy at a northern school. Often much of house and school discipline, supervision and organization falls to them, and they often have a considerable influence on decision-making.

The house captains themselves have no doubt of the scale of their power:

174   The Hothouse Society

> The Head of House can do as much or little as he wants to do and can take as much authority as he wishes. His duty is nowhere defined and rests only upon himself and the tradition and precedents created by his predecessor.   *Head of house's book, public school*

> You have complete control all the way . . . it is you who make the final decisions on policy.   *Head of house's book, public school*

> It is very hard – indeed impossible – to say where the jobs of Housemaster, Housetutor and Head of House begin and end.
> *Head of house's book, public school*

Indeed, the key boy, the school captain, may have a role akin to that of the headmaster himself in his influence and his isolation. The school captain of a great and ancient public school describes it:

> The school captain is in an anomalous position. He is not a member of staff, yet must in many ways behave like one. He remains a boy, but is isolated from the rest by his position. Both masters and boys can be very resentful of this situation.
>
> Members of staff fully realise that the school captain is in very close contact with the headmaster. Some try to use this to their own advantage. One has to be very much on one's guard against such manipulation all the time. Usually it takes the form of pumping for inside information. I personally try to avoid discussions of controversial problems except with a very few trusted people. The danger of letting something slip (eg the headmaster's own viewpoint) is too great otherwise. Another point, is that of remaining loyal to the headmaster. This is the determining factor in many situations, and is usually the criterion which decides what information one disseminates. The headmaster is of the Arnold tradition that relies more on the senior boys than on the staff for some matters, and especially on the school captain. With him he will discuss criminals, housecaptains and staff indiscriminately. It is certainly a very maturing experience.   *Boy, eighteen*

Compare this stratospheric status with that of a school captain in an integrated boarding school who is not so influential or even privy to the Head's confidences, and even acts – how inconceivable in a public school! – as the glorified fag of another master:

8.10 pm.
Went up to deal with Dr Matthews, resident French master, for whom I act as orderly. Washed cups plates made coffee for him and sixth former who left last summer, and who returned for the evening (they can't keep away from it). Washed up cups again afterwards.
School captain's diary

But the average *house* captain deals not so much with the remote headmaster as with the nominal sovereign of the little kingdom of the house: the housemaster. How to manipulate the housemaster is a favourite theme of the heads of house in their confidential books – a theme very revealing of the actual or assumed power of these boys. Unfortunately it is beyond the scope of this book to illustrate how *they* are manipulated in return by the housemaster.

Some are loftily condescending:

It has become fashionable to regard the Housemaster as a fool, this is untrue.
Head of house's book, public school

The housemaster has many new and pretty odd ideas which, no doubt, he will try and spring on you. If you don't like them, don't have them. Just be politely firm and he will gently fade away. He does like to be kept in touch with the house and unless you do something about it, he will do this by wandering around it at all hours. It is worth ½ hour now and then just to keep him informed and thus curtail his wanderings. Don't let him interfere with the elections of deputies.

The housetutor: he has been with the house for a year or so now, and is still as retiring as ever. I despair of getting him into anything connected with the house other than rugger coaching. See if you can do better.
Head of house's book, public school

Boys who reach the top should not think that the housemaster is of

no importance. He must not be treated like a piece of dirt for any reason at all. Prod the House tutor along. He is very hesitant but very loyal.
Head of house's book, public school

Many, of course, establish a bond of complete working trust and harmony with their housemasters:

I found the housemaster a wise and broadminded man, for whom I have learnt to have the greatest respect and confidence. He is very sincerely interested in every member of the house's welfare and development. You may find that confronted with some serious immoral act, he will try to approach the case from a hopeful angle, and not condemn the person. When you go to speak to him, he will try to bring out your feelings before he states his own. I found this quite off-putting at first, but I realized that this was the best way of doing things, for by stating ones own feelings without them being tempered by the housemasters earlier statements, one manages to get ones own ideas straightened. Apart from anything else, if you went to see the housemaster and he told you exactly what to do before you got a say in, then you would merely be acting as a middle man between him and the house, and not a *Head* of House at all.
Head of house's book, public school

Others are brutally frank in the private analysis of the housemaster's weaknesses and how much they should tell and rely on him:

Next comes Cornford, the housemaster, whom I got more and more fed up with as the term progressed. He is a man who completely and utterly baffles me and I reckon that after sixteen terms I know him as well as any member of the house ever will. Like most things that baffle it is very hard to put your finger on what exactly it is so incomprehensible, but basically I think it is his inconsistency and unpredictability. On the one hand there is a man of extraordinary wit, heart-warming geniality, one who is a mine of knowledge on almost every subject and who has written a book which has been acclaimed widely by the learned press. And yet, on the other hand, there is this rather childish and petty man, inclined to several short-lived rages when he is rude to everybody in sight and refusing to take any major decisions for fear of criticism. On several occasions he was excessively and unnecessarily rude to the house prefects, notably one occasion when he asked me at 10.30 one evening to inform them of some development and then came crashing in to the prefects' study ten minutes later demanding why the bloody hell we weren't in our own dormitory. However, to be fair, I find that Cornford is always willing to give advice and almost always it turns out to be very sound advice too. This raises an important point: to what extent should a house captain seek the advice of his housemaster, and how much should he keep to himself? Perhaps this is a matter which is entirely up to the captain, but it is always worth mentioning that my personal decision on matters almost always coincided with Cornford's and when it didn't, it was because he shed an entirely new light on the matter with some new piece of information. Obviously there are a lot of things that *must* not be told, or are much better concealed from him.

Head of house's book, public school

One final boy writes with the assurance of one who has the house and the housemaster well and truly under his thumb. It has the tone of a school report on a difficult boy:

The housemaster behaved quite well throughout the term and was usually very pleasant. He was however staying out for nearly a week, and the prefects were left in complete charge of the house. During this period everything ran very smoothly which I think brings great credit on all boys in the building. So many things have already been written in this book about how to treat the housemaster, that I hesitate to say more. However he is very keen to help and will do so if he can, so trust him as much as you feel you can. He occasionally brings in petty schemes of his own. If these seem to be important one wants to tread warily, but if they are petty then one wants to get rid of them. It is necessary to distinguish between what is important and what isn't and to act accordingly. We only had one fracas in the term and that was when I made Smithson a prefect without asking him beforehand. It is very *important* for all captains to show him a short list before a prefect's selection.

If this is the way the most powerful members of the staff are seen by some senior boys, no wonder that lesser adult fry are sometimes conceived as of little account. By contrast, in state or progressive schools, where even the senior pupils do not assume staff roles or exercise large power, *all* adults carry greater weight. Two typical comments follow on public-school matrons.

> Mrs Darch did not go down too well. She has little to talk about and is apt to be stupid. However, I think she is tactful, considerate and quite pleasant so make the best of her. She does her best. She gave me a jolly good drink when I went to say Adios. Full marks.
>
> *Head of house's book, public school*

> Matron: All term long she will besiege you with complaints about dormitories, studies or the changing rooms. Usually these are not unfounded. Look into all of them and do something about them. Matron is a useful 'pal'.
>
> *Head of house's book, public school*

Other members of staff can also be put in their place. There follows an extract from the minutes of a school prefects' meeting in a large Victorian public school. At this school the prefectorial body has considerable influence: it can block changes and even discredit staff. Here we see the prefects voting (for guidance for the head) on the implementation of changes, setting up committees, administering rules, making appointments. In the latter connection the boy prefects again overrule the master in charge of soccer. The prefects do not want his nominee to be secretary, and despite his protests carry on looking for an alternative.

> A meeting was held in the prefects room at 7.30 pm.
>
> The head of school asked for considerable tightening up in the administration of punishments for petty offences. Lines *must* be given for a first offence.
>
> The head of school then read a letter from PNK (the master i/c soccer) on the subject of the election of a secretary of soccer. The letter expressed disappointment that the prefects had shown so little faith in his judgment and in the captain of soccer. The prefects

had deferred the election of M. T. Windham as the secretary of soccer pending further information about other candidates. After discussion the election was again deferred pending further information and investigations about Windham.

A. Redington was elected unanimously as the sub-editor of the school magazine.

The body considered the alternative suggestions as to when the proposed VIth form changes should come into effect: 7 were in favour of bringing the changes into force at half-term, on the grounds that the new lower sixth would have more time to mature. 6 were in favour of bringing in the changes in May to ease the problem of administration.

Prefects were asked to stay in chapel on weekdays, and to take note of those boys who sauntered out of chapel with their jackets undone.

Committees were set up on tea and societies.

Formal positions of power in progressive schools (counsellors, work bosses) seldom carry comparable weight. In many state boarding schools senior pupils do not usually *want* to be identified with the staff and staff roles and may refuse to be cut off from the other pupils by assuming staff power. Far from wanting to render the staff superfluous, and from relishing authority, it can be an unwelcome burden. A school captain comments on a forthright incident:

The old man (the head) asked me if we prefects would take prep in the evenings *and* take sole charge of the dorms at night. He said he had to push us to do everything: didn't we want responsibility etc.? I told him we had enough to do. Anyway, we're boys, they're staff. What are they being paid for – to pass off their dirty work on us? Not on your nelly, the lazy gits.

Boy, eighteen, state boarding school

Another state school captain comments on his job in a way inconceivable in his public-school counterpart:

I hate telling the other boys what to do and what not to do. I never asked for this bloody job anyway.

Boy, eighteen, state boarding school

180   The Hothouse Society

So much for the *scale* of power wielded by the pupils. What *sort* of power is it, how is it used, what are its aims and what problems does it bring? In the small boarding house or unit, there may be two house captains in a year, a change of personality bringing swift and sometimes drastic changes of regime.

> Each set of sixths and each H. of H. will have their own ideas, trying to establish a fair balance between harshness and freedom, remoteness and familiarity. One year, like, I think, this last one, will be a little too free and easy – another, like Bishop's, too inhuman and remote.
> *Head of house's book, public school*

In a few schools, as we shall see, the regime is perpetually brutal, older pupils taking out on others the physical horrors that once had been committed on themselves, without interference from the staff. These schools are seldom public schools, but independent or state parodies of them. One quote here illustrates the case:

> Everyone here lives in fear and dread of the prefects room, where boys about a year older than you bash hell out of you. I'm only a little chap and many times have to act hard in order to stop myself getting bashed in or picked on, and if you happen to tell someone who's hitting you to fuck off and a prefect hears you, god help you and I pity your arse when he's done with that cane.
> *Boy, sixteen, independent school*

Even in the public school a boy may rise to the top who, in an effort to raise standards, initiates a harsh regime. So great is the power of such a boy that the housemaster may be unable effectively to intervene. Here is such a boy, dismissing the housemaster, Shaw, as a prep-school milksop:

> In the bottom half of the house, the Bradley House tradition is extinct and unless the people who will be at the top of house in a year's time can inspire them with some guts, will and punch, this tradition will finally fade away and be replaced by the dominating prep school attitude of Shaw. This man Shaw must be resisted: as

long as you can, confront him with a sound logical argument; you are home and laughing. At the moment the house has got the most uninspiring, gutless slobs, Shaw and downwards, that it has ever had. Why this is, I just don't know, it may well be the fault of the prefects not kicking them around enough. I beat several people from the lower half of the house and there was only one who didn't scream blue murder. (Afterwards, we experimented on each other to see how soft the strokes really were. Bruce Kentwell seemed confident that he could take 100, not just five).

Head of house's book, public school

State boarders also often find the balance of power difficult to establish: they lack the long subtle training of the prep school, and can sometimes be hard, perfunctory, unimaginative, non-pastoral in their clumsy use of strange and wide authority.

The relationship between the house prefects and the house was not good, and at times, shocking. This is due to the prefects' lack of understanding, of tolerance, and for want of a better word, gentleness. It must be impressed upon them at the beginning of each term and especially to new prefects, that their job is not primarily that of discipline, but to guide and control the life of the house. To accomplish this, they must of course have certain authorative powers, but more important, must take an interest in all that is happening, and make the house feel that the prefects respect their views, even if they do not agree with them.

Head of house's book, state boarding school

These crude controls no longer dominate the majority of schools. In most schools, including public schools, those in authority nowadays genuinely seek influence by gentler personal means, their goal being communal happiness. Here is one of the immediate successors of the beating public-school house captain quoted above:

There are only about four or five undesirable boys in the house, and even they will no doubt improve given time. Tolerance and the art of living in a society are the two greatest things that one can learn in a House, and I'm sure that the air now is as clear as it has been for a very long time. Complete virtuousness I have no use for, as neither for excessive ill-temper and anti-socialness. The sign of a successful house is not how many cups it has got or how good at games its members are, but how the general atmosphere is, how cheerful the boys are, and how much ragging goes on – for without ragging a house is dead. *Head of house's book, public school*

Another public school prefect refuses to use the old harsh methods:

I have chosen the hard way. I detest the thought of having to impose punishment on to people younger than myself, and try to control them rationally, and with a 'No, we can't have this then, can we, please would you try in future . . .' *It works.*

Boy, eighteen, public school

Others modify or interpret the rules to suit their charges:

The old hierarchy is at last breaking down. Strict 'seniority segregation' is virtually non-existent. As a monitor in a senior house, I find that the whole social structure is far more cohesive than it used to be. People take each other for what they are and I try to let them live as comfortably and happily as they can within the *necessary* limits imposed. I'm afraid that I feel compelled to turn a blind eye on what I consider to be 'petty restrictions' and this is frowned upon by that notable and upright(?) character, the school captain. *Boy, eighteen, public school*

Another house prefect plays the same game but this time with a shrewd appreciation of the art of using apparently light but actually firm control.

The fact that they break the rules is only of importance when the rest of the house, especially the younger part, is aware of this. They are only likely to be aware of this when the people concerned start to brag about their various exploits. If you keep your ears open (as Dennis did last term and picked up the fact that Jenkins had a motor bike in the vicinity) you can hint quietly to them that you are absolutely aware of what they are doing. By acting in this manner you will be appreciated, a) for not having a blow up about the habit in question, b) respected, as they will see it, for your uncanny ability to be 'smarter' than the 'smart' ones.

Head of house's book, public schoo

In many schools the senior boys aim at a deeper pastoral oversight of those they control, based on a knowledge, concern and even action about the most intimate areas of a boy's existence. This 'expressive' control is something most commonly found in public schools. One boy outlines his modest welfare policy – expressive authority but with due 'awe and respect for seniors':

A house in which those in authority show intelligent interest in the activities and affairs of the more junior part of it will be a good one.

Chatting to the junior dormitories for a few moments when the lights are put out, sitting on other tables in Big School, and so on are very easy things to do. And Sixths do owe a little more to their fags than a daily pair of dirty shoes, or even a termly half crown.

Please do not think that I am advocating a 'kind uncle' policy for all House VIs; healthy awe and respect for senior boys is very right and proper, and it would be criminal to pamper one's juniors the whole time. But interest in and help for younger boys can be rewarding to both parties.   *Head of house's book, public school*

But some go further still and without qualification in their concern – as does this captain in a western public school, the *ne plus ultra* of the modern pastoral prefect:

Disrespect, frivolous behaviour, bad work, stealing, smoking, selfishness – one can always find a cause, lying beneath the surface. It may be an unhappy family life, fear about unpopularity or worry for a sexual trouble. Where six hundred healthy people of the same sex are living together, there are bound to arise bonds which mean more than the petty pretence of mere friendship, and there is nothing more rewarding, nothing more likely to endear you to a boy than to help him understand himself and to overcome a personal problem.

And the respect which he will bear for you goes far deeper and is more sincere than any ordinary respect.

If you want a phrase to paint over your desk, then write 'Take an interest', for where there is no interest there is no love; and where there is no love there is no understanding; and you cannot solve a question unless you understand the meaning.

Talk to them in privacy. *Head of house's book*

The pastoral and social problems such a boy has to face need not be minimized. Here a rather conventional and insensitive house captain analyses the problems he has had to face from another prefect in his house: problems which nearly came to suicide. Note that even in this extreme the house captain is defensive about telling the housemaster.

Maunsell was a problem of monumental proportions. Unfortunately far from being one of the stronger prefects, he must have been far and away the weakest that this house has ever been blessed with. I never did succeed in getting to the bottom of him, not that I ever had any burning desire to do so. But let me give my impression of him. He comes from an odd home. His father runs a clothes shop and is an actor at the National Theatre, and that must mean that he's bloody good. His mother is large and very foolish. Once you have met her, as I have, you can understand quite a lot. She is pleasant enough, and has good intentions, but her way of expressing herself is quite out of this world. For example, Maunsell and his parents, the housemaster and I had all been to a play in which Mr Maunsell was performing. After it was all over, Mrs Maunsell wished to say how thrilling the whole evening had been. She overcame her problem thus: 'Phew. I feel as though I've been tossed around on a rough sea and then been scrubbed down with a loofah'. She looked like it too.

Personally, I think that Maunsell suffered from an unconscious feeling of insecurity, and this led to emotional instability. Not that he went into fits or anything – his temper was much more controlled in his last terms than ever it was before. But I walked into his room one day before lunch and found him gazing out of his window in a contemplative mood. On his desk was a glass of orange squash with

30 Anadin dissolved in it. I threw it away and told him to pull himself together. Anyway, to cut a long story short, I had to tell the housemaster about it, and then a lot more besides came out which was a very good thing. I did not, however, make him look black, because I personally was not 100% certain whether his intentions were pure or otherwise. And one thing led to another, several people being rather upset by the whole affair (myself included).

Head of house's book, public school

Just how far-ranging the expressive control of the senior boys can be is seen in the following extracts. In some schools, at the end of his reign the house captain writes a confidential and frank report to his successor in the house book on every boy in the house. These comments tell us much about the values which senior boys hold, their methods of control, the hierarchy and relationships in the society, as well as revealing many other things about a boy's life in a public school. We publish two typical selections. The first, from a major school, has a distinctive style, a no-nonsense brusqueness. Fagging emerges as a major means by which the senior boys get to know and judge the juniors, 'familiarity' between seniors and juniors is frowned on, and contribution to the house appears as the chief criterion of approval.

Barratt is quite a pleasant person. He can be very charming but, can be obstinate, sly and difficult. He smokes, indulges in a spot of incense, and fills his room with women when he can. He once came back from a meeting of the Herbert Society completely drunk and provided us with some light entertainment. He admits he is a nasty type who likes nasty people. He knows exactly how to use people and on which side his bread is buttered. A cunning and amusing person. He is excellent value.

Dodsworth fagged for me and was rather incompetent. He is a nice person though he can go bolshy. He plays rugger rather well and I can but hope that he does not go 'crooked'. A cheerful and good person to have around.

De Moleyns. Rog as he is called also fagged for me, and after a couple of tickings off was rather more successful than Dodsworth. He is a good games player and is very cheerful; when accused of some crime he appears very hurt, but I think is more cunning than grieved. Perhaps a sheep, but a nice sheep. He is a very pleasant bloke.

Feverel mi. I do not like him since he has a mistakenly inflated opinion of himself. He has neither manner nor manners and makes no attempt to make himself pleasant. He is a pseud, and though a deputy prefect, he is no asset to the house. Watch him John, he is a selfish and misdirected character. Take no nonsense.

Groom-Halesworth. I used not to like this boy, but we made him a Deputy halfway through the term and he developed enormously and became a very good member of the society. He was competent and trustworthy. Though not very talented he is cheerful and pleasant and stocks a good trash library. You can use him profitably John.

Jenkins mi is a very wet boy. He was head fag and did his job moderately well. A good ticking-off put right any slacking. He is no great ball of fire and I can only hope that he will find his feet and develop some basic interest. A good shaking might get him moving. I hope he doesn't throw any more stink bombs into Atkinson's room. Such an act portrays a mean character.

Knapton mi. This boy is my brother. I have torn out my previous report on him since it was none too good. All I can say is that he caused me more trouble than anyone else. However, after half term he improved greatly and was a great support to me during the house play. He was made a Deputy at the end of the half and should do well. Take no nonsense from him John about anything, especially games playing. I hope he becomes C. of H. and I wish him the best of luck.

Lowesworth is another Deputy. He is the most ridiculed member and is called 'Bill' by lower boys and fags. This familiarity is his own fault and the prefects can do little to help him unless he also tries to rectify it. He is a ready games player and quite good, but he always thinks that he plays better in some other position. Thus, when playing forward he has to play back. This is infuriating especially as he is wrong. What part he desires to play in the sex game I hesitate to think. Bill is a crasher and a bit of an oil but nevertheless I quite like him and hope he does well. He is really quite a nice harmless person.

Palk is a clumsy and rather awkward individual. His behaviour last term left much to be desired and for that reason he was not even on the short list for deputyship. He tried playing the housemaster up over some illness and was selfish and troublesome. His offences were petty, irksome and numerous but nothing really concrete. A good thrashing could well sort him out.

Trease was another new boy who seemed to me to be cheerful, pleasant and respectful. I have however heard that he was rather rude to those well above him but without authority, so watch him John.

Vyvyan ma is a scruffy individual who is rather friendless. I do not believe that he makes any real effort to enjoy life. He fishes and is very clever but has no real *go* in him. After doing very well in the steeplechase last year as a new boy he hardly featured this year. No real guts! Get him moving on the track John it might give him an interest.

Vyvyan mi is little better than his brother. He is an incompetent fag with little commonsense or imagination. No great ball of fire.

Yarborough. He is the first music specialist that we have ever had and is a very good one. It is due to his effort and devotion that the house won the instrumental cup. He also won a strings cup. Well done!! Though inclined to be wet this boy is very nice and has the guts to stick up for an aggrieved party. I think he likes to take the losing side. I admired him and was amused by the way that he so successfully ragged Hughes.

In all not a bad bunch of boys. The new boys were a very good bunch and should all do well. There is one gutless and spineless section of the house. I should like to see the rules amended so that boys not as clever as them but with more drive can become Deputies before them.

A year later the succeeding house captain's comments are less brusque, more penetrating and still more frank. Note the undertones of homosexuality in the house, the off-hand comments on beatings by the house captain, his strong personal likes and dislikes as regards people, the way, in a small close community, qualities of cleanliness, order, sociability and action are at a premium, and those of wayward, scruffy or contemplative individualism are at a discount. The list of characters and their activities stress how exacting, responsible and adult must be the roles of the senior boys who organize, watch, punish and hold together such diverse and intense societies.

Ainsworth-Martin. He is one big joke although he does not intend to be. His room smells. He is a stupid boy, but he always tries to do the right thing, even if he doesn't manage to. Everybody takes the piss out of him but he doesn't seem to mind – he just puts on an insane grin, displaying plenty of gum. I enjoyed having him as a fag for two terms, because although he was not competent he always kept me amused.

Bartlett – now here's a born liar if ever I met one, and as far as I remember, I beat him for it – only once unfortunately, he needs beating along the whole time, he was always about three laps behind on everything – not particularly stupid – just slow.

Blackburn – some people say that he is up the wall, well he isn't. He has a most amusing laugh and is extremely keen on hunting; he always has something to talk about, even if it is bollocks. Not a great benefit to the house, but a nice character; one cannot help liking him.

Hales-Burnet. This is a boy with a great deal of character, who I am sure will go a long way in his career here. He is reasonably clever and good at most games and generally efficient, although scruffy at times. He started off his career by having rather a perverted mind, not entirely due to any fault of his own, but is now absolutely cured of it. He rags non-stop and is full of life. I liked him very much.

Carter – a member of the gang of raggers. I can't remember what I beat him for, but anyway I did. An uninteresting character, not so popular among his contemporaries as he used to be – also idle.

Chevringham. This boy is the perfect houseman – he is brilliantly clever (captain of the school one day I should think), he is outstanding at games and far ahead of his contemporaries. I think he is liked by everybody. He is a shy boy by nature, which is a pity in one who is blessed by so many gifts. He is not conceited, which is so often the case in boys like him. I have only one more thing to say about him and that is that if he regarded cleanliness with as much care as he regards everything else, I would like him even more than I do.

Curtis ma. I am sorry to say that I detest this boy. He is vile with uncleanliness and is without doubt far too intimate with those younger than himself. But to give him his due, he is some good to the house in that he is reasonably clever. He will argue to the bloody end only admitting defeat when there is no possible way out. I beat him about fudging the check-in and lying about it and I was not sorry to do so.

Derrick – is not really capable of looking after himself and was cruelly ragged by his contemporaries as a result. He is a very nice boy to talk to and will do well when he learns not to be afraid to speak his own views.

Ellsworth – a most unpleasant boy. He is a bully of the very worst type because he seldom uses physical force and prefers to employ his razor-sharp tongue with such skill that he is capable of reducing boys to tears. He is a very talented games player but made no effort whatsoever in the Junior unless the ball landed at his feet. He is also a fluent liar and yet when accused of any one of these crimes he was the picture of innocence. I beat him pretty hard at the end of term and I hope the memory lasts – if not, have no mercy, this is the sort of boy that must not be tolerated.

Fairweather mi. – is rather a hard worker. He acted the part of my wife in the House Play, which he did quite well (the acting, not the wifing) and was a pretty good back for the House Side.

Gould – a new boy who I'm sure peed in his pants on the occasion of his first ticking off, and then went and clobbered some unfortunate in the Junior match. That's all I really know about him and rather understandably, I don't really know what to make of him.

Gresham – another unimpressive new boy although I seem to remember him being a goodish fag.

de Harcourt – rather insignificant still, because he remains under Palk's shadow. But he does have a sense of humour and when on his own is likeable enough. I wish he'd stop his whining though, it's just like a frightened labrador begging for mercy.

Inskip – is a great wee character with a lot of guts and a completely disarming sense of humour; he'll get away with murder unless you've got enough self-control to keep a straight face. One of the more amusing problems of the house!

St Just – an extraordinary boy; from his mannerisms you'd think he was blatantly a queer, and I hope this isn't so; watch him nevertheless; a hopelessly incompetent fag, too.

Lancaster. This boy should not have come here – he is completely out of place. He should have gone to a girls' school; he is not good at all to this House. He is as effeminate as they come. I think he smokes – but not because he enjoys it but because he thought it the thing to do. He has now reached the age when he ought to become a Deputy but what is the good of having a person like Lancaster – he is totally irresponsible. No one holds any respect whatsoever for him. He had better pull his socks up. The fact is he does not belong to the House.

Martin. He is a junior boy and a weed. He would not dare put a foot wrong. I can't think of anything else to say about him except that I can't stand him.

Norton is an uncouth character. I don't dislike him in the same way as some others. He has no idea of tidiness and is always fly in that he says he has a bath at a most extraordinary time on Sunday mornings, although you can bet your bollocks that he hasn't. I don't think he knows what a razor is, and if he does he certainly doesn't know how to use it. But he has a great interest in painting and is very interesting on the subject. I myself don't actually like his style of art very much but he certainly knows what he is doing in this sphere. He is a mournful old fool, always up to something; he is totally irresponsible, and it becomes rather embarrassing to look at the house list and discover that he is among the group in the house but not of it.

Ormond. He is a very nice boy with plenty of character – a good oar – always cheerful. He is cunning in that he never gets caught ragging although I know that he never stops. He always sees the funny side of things – you always know when Ormond's around because of his particularly loud voice. I think this boy will go a long way.

Railton. I liked this boy very much indeed. He is tough, full of character and activity, and very sensible. He always has a lot to talk about and is very interesting on most subjects. He sets about everything he does with the utmost spirit and determination. We need more boys like Railton and I have a very high opinion of him.

Trensham is a farcical little boy, who likes to think that he is highly amusing. When he first came everybody laughed at him and he liked it and thought that he must be hellish amusing – in fact he is idiotic. When questioned, he always comes out with the most phenomenal reason for doing this and that, and then giggles stupidly. He is learning to play the bagpipes – I wish him luck but somehow I don't think that he is suited to this instrument.

Webster is a junior boy and very nice indeed. He is by far the best lower boy, competent, cheerful and amusing. He will go a long way. It is also time he grew a bit. An impossible person to beat as yet, as he is about the size of my thumbnail.

I have tried to state quite frankly my impressions of everyone and as you can see or at least I hope you can, they are a mixed bunch. But this is almost inevitable in any house – and anyway, if everyone in the House was absolutely perfect, I am sure that the whole setup would become rather stale. The main thing is that everybody should be happy.

Boys do not assume staff roles and attitudes so commonly outside the public schools and their imitators. In most state boarding schools the senior boys are reluctant to exercise that 'expressive' control, that minute oversight of the private lives of others which marks the public school prefect:

My job? To keep discipline in school, see they do their cleaning up of a morning, take detensions, etc. but its not my business what they do outside, whether they have girlfriends outside (or boyfriends inside for that matter) what they read or think.

Prefect, eighteen, state boarding school

In progressive schools, if they do have prefects, there may be more expressive concern and private reporting to staff about pupils than in the state school; but there is less than in the public school, and also less insistence on hierarchy and on the distance between seniors and others:

Nicky (a boss) caught us smoking. He looked severe and told us if he found us again he'd report us to our tutors, but he's nice really. Later than evening I took my maths prep to him and asked him to help me. I spent ½ hour and it was useful. He's 18 and I'm 15. And don't get me wrong – I'm not crazy about him ... Or am I?

Girl, fifteen, progressive school

A minute book in a public school demonstrates the attributes thought necessary in the more traditional school in prefects, this élite of élites. Here the heads of houses elect their own deputies and successors as school prefects. These elections are a solemn, fair and scrupulous business. The discussion of candidates reveals the devotion as well as the sophisticated maturity of the eighteen-year-olds. The following one started behind closed doors in the prefects' room at 7.30 p.m. and ended at about 11.30 p.m. The school captain summed up at the outset criteria by which a boy should be judged for office.

A candidate ought to conform to the following:
He should obey rules, there should be no secret rule-breaking and no likelihood of a 'final fling'.
He should be punctual.
He should have the respect of the school.
He should be a respected member of the House. (Worthy candidates may be 'drawn out' by election, and some may benefit considerably from election.)
He should have a sense of responsibility towards the school.
He should be interested in the school.
He should be able and willing to enforce rules, or take charge.
He should have a sense of the dignity of his position.
He should be helpful to masters and prefects.
If a candidate does not conform with one of these stipulations, then this should be stated.
Heads of houses should consider the following:
1. Why have you put up your candidate?
2. Will the election profit the school?
3. Might you consider the result of the election a personal triumph or defeat?

A Place in the Sun – Power

4. A deputy should serve the school.
5. The prefect must stand by the result of the election.
6. Do you deplore the past lack of scruples in running this election?

These ponderous assessments of the attributes necessary for power-holding are not shared by all of the senior boys. What qualities do *they* think necessary if a person is to become a prefect?

Sometimes promotion is automatic:

> You go up according to your position on the list. This is ridiculous but my housemaster believes it inevitable after the failure of one of his parvenues. *Boy, seventeen, public school*

Others suggest more positive qualities:

> He must be a leader, respected and capable of making his own decisions without being swayed by other people. He must be firm and resolute yet kind and generous. He must set a good example and be a good judge of others. *Boy, eighteen, public school*

Many stress one characteristic in particular:

> He must be a good games player: games carry you to the top here. *Boy, seventeen, public school*

> Get in the first XV: your chances of becoming a school prefect or house captain are quadrupled. *Boy, eighteen, public school*

Others are more sceptical:

> I suppose he has to be a fairly honest, upright and God-fearing member of the community in theory, yet in practice some of the biggest shags in the school have become school prefects, so it's difficult to say. Basically, your housemaster has to think you are someone who can command respect and obedience at the same time as being thought of as a 'good guy' by those under you. *Boy, sixteen, public school*

> Don't get caught. Four of my friends who are now prefects should really have been expelled for smoking, drinking and homosexuality.
> *Boy, seventeen, same school*

> A school prefect is often a religiously minded and unworldly character. Some are good at games. Most are insensitive to moral matters. Some are political intriguers running many committees and pad along the corridors of power. Most are reasonably affluent. Many are 'do gooders'. Those who seek promotion go about it efficiently; the rest drink and chase little boys or are nonentities.
> *Boy, seventeen, same school*

Many boys are downright cynical about the attributes necessary in a prefect:

> Someone willing to sacrifice his own ideals and thoughts. A prefect has just been demoted because he tried to live up to his own ideals and be fair. *Boy, sixteen, public school*

> Present a pseudo-image to a pseudo-perspicaceous headmaster of ability, responsibility, reliability. Say 'yes' always if you want to reach the real top. *Boy, seventeen, public school*

This discontented chorus reminds us that change is appearing even in this, the central pillar of the public school edifice, for there is a growing trend to diffuse authority more widely and democratically among senior boys – as in Quaker or progressive and some state schools. The voices remind us of other things too: that the solemn writers of house books may not be all they seem to the staff and that they too have problems.

What then are the problems of power in the boarding school? We shall briefly review them before turning to the consoling privileges and, at the end of this chapter, the sanctions of office.

Problems abound. Prep-school boys pray about them:

> Dear Lord, please help me to be able to control my house, and help them to realise how difficult my job really is, apart from all the privileges. Amen.

A Place in the Sun – Power

Please God give me strength to cope with my house. Make the boys realise what they owe to one another and help them not to be so selfish but let them do their best in aiding the house to come higher.
Two boys, twelve, prep school

One common difficulty is that of having to enforce rules in a system you don't believe in. This is a very real dilemma among many responsible boys, especially in the public schools, and can make them powerful advocates for change. Many innovations in the schools can be traced to them.

I ask myself, *why* should I send this boy to his housemaster for being in town at 3.30; *why* should we put 16 year olds to bed at 10 on Saturday nights; *why* should a boy be on time for every meal, every day; *why* should we force them to sing at compulsory house prayers? Why should we support this artificial state set up by the whims of old governors average age 93, whom you never see?
Prefect, eighteen, public school

Since I became house captain, I have refused to beat anyone – some of the other prefects and the housemaster (I suspect) think I'm soft. I find myself attacking rather than defending all the endless compulsory things – chapel, CCF, roll-calls, and so many petty rules and restrictions. It worries me no end.
Prefect, eighteen, public school

Many intelligent boys by the time they reach their last year at a place like this can't honestly justify to themselves every part of the system. They lose faith in their ideals.
Head of house's book, public school

Some resent bitterly the authoritarian rule which the traditional system forces upon them:

I hate having authority because I feel I am forced to be less a human being and more of a sergeant-major. *Boy, eighteen, public school*

I have a loathing for the institutions in the School which I am supposed to enforce: parades, roll call, etc. and thus find it extremely difficult to carry out some of these despicable duties whole-heartedly. I detest the high-handed hierarchical manner the other monitors in my house often assume even to my friends – their equals in age and superiors in intellect. There are frequent arguments. I have no liking for my housemaster who probably has the most insidious influence in a house in the school and yet I am supposed to connive with him and enforce his often idiotic rulings.

Boy, seventeen, public school

The dilemma is often resolved by partial enforcement of the rules – as long as the housemaster does not know. Sometimes the prefects break the rules consistently themselves:

We (the prefects) all slip down to 'The Crown' after supper. No one knows. The housemaster has no idea. I am scared that he will find out. Not because of punishment but because he's so decent and trusting and would be so hurt at the thought of all of us, day after day, deceiving him. I don't want to let him down – but we still go. I'm going to be ordained. *Boy, eighteen, public school*

At other times they connive in rule breaking by others, sometimes indiscriminately:

I am quite prepared to be quite two-faced about the question of my position, though I do have qualms about punishing people for offences which I have committed 100 times myself. Perhaps I was not born a leader, or perhaps I am too scared of losing a friend, but I just cannot bring myself to tell a person, a year my junior, with whom I am friendly that he is doing wrong. Most offences are not the crimes which they appear, anyway, and I would neither report a person for a serious crime against the establishment, nor deem it my duty to tell him he is morally wrong.

Boy, eighteen, public school

At other times latitude is given only to the seniors:

Smoking
    With older boys I took the line that they must remain incon-

spicuous to the younger ones. When this was not adhered to, I reported the matter to the headmaster and left it at that. I deliberately avoided jeopardising their positions in the house. I have never demoted and have always felt that house demotion is an unsatisfactory punishment.

With younger ones a much stricter line should be taken. I would make it abundantly clear that if they were caught smoking they would be seriously punished for their own good.

Head of house's book, public school

The house drinking and smoking society is going a bit too far. Everyone knows about its meetings at night and that prefects are involved. My position as house captain, knowing about this society and holding out on the housemaster is extremely difficult. My advice is to threaten the participants with being hauled up to the housemaster so that their activities become so clandestine as not to attract the all too vigilant attention of the rest of the house. The house captain himself should remain aloof.

Head of house's book, public school

Linked to this one is another problem of power – maintaining social distance. In many schools prefectdom inevitably involves giving up friends who are not prefects, or giving up 'over-familiar' contact with younger boys in the interest of being feared and respected, if not remote and Godlike:

If you are a Pre here you can't have friends who are not, so, as I do not get on well with the junior Pres and most of my friends are the so called 'bad lads', I am automatically a bad Pre and so am popular with the lads. *Boy, seventeen, Cromwell College*

When Sinclair and Lloyd joined the prefects halfway through the Michaelmas, they found a certain amount of difficulty in giving up their deputy spirit and loyalty, and in consequence, mixed with the deputies quite frequently! Thus they felt slightly resentful when told not to. Still, full marks to them for by the next term they had made the wrench and were very reliable indeed.

Head of house's book, public school

198 The Hothouse Society

In one school prefects are forbidden to visit or be visited by others outside the élite. A house captain describes how formal contact can be made with others, how useful it is, but how it should not undermine impartiality: the reason for the isolation of the prefects in the first place. Such detachment can be again an ingredient in the public school ideal of the good governor:

> It is a school rule that there is no visiting between pres and non pres. But it is often very useful to invite in boys to coffee occasionally with you. Let the housemaster know beforehand – it saves awkward questions from unexpected visitors. For in a mellow evening you are liable to learn a 101 interesting things about the boy – his room, the state of the house from his point of view, etc. which otherwise would never have come to your notice. You will find that a boy who is naturally friendly to you will tell you a lot more than one who comes in possibly with the idea 'I wonder what he wants?' But this is an important point. Whatever your relationship with certain boys in your house, you must be completely impartial when it comes to a question of duty. Whether to punish, etc. You must think of boys in this context as individuals and completely forget any personal likes and dislikes.
>
> *Head of house's book, public school*

It is no surprise that at the school above a minor 'blow-up' took place of which the isolated prefects had no inkling, except one. The house book explains:

> The one great crisis of the term was the 'blow-up' in the senior room. People were taken by surprise. A deputation to the housemaster took place – complaining of the lack of privileges and responsibilities. The alarm, though, was not so much the fact that there had been a deputation, but that there had been no forewarning and none of the prefects were aware of the forthcoming events, except for the possibility of one who has the tendency to be more one of 'them' than 'us' because he is despised by his fellow prefects.

Paramount to the power-holders is unity among themselves without it their authority and effect is lost. 'United we stand, divided we fall,' write many house captains in the true language of a governing group.

Sometimes this precious unity is attained:

> I have never been happier than I am with this lot. They have all worked very hard, our commonroom, for once, is really united. I feel not one was missing, all gave his best and was felt. Yes, I would thank them, for they have worked hard and I have worked them hard, I think. I think the most important thing about prefects is that they should be united. Rifts have occurred this year, I know, but as I write now, I have not met eight people more united in one cause than us lot.
> *Head of house's book, state boarding school*

Sometimes it is not ... A dissentient voice among the small band at the top can goad some to fury:

> For most of the time the prefects were happy but there was one element in it who seemed determined not to make it so. Ridgeway is the most tactless and one of the most personally ambitious people I have ever met. He is tactless and rude, argumentative because he believes he is always right – no one has ever been able to hammer it into that thick, obstinate skull of his, that he is very frequently WRONG. He believes completely in his own ability and relies entirely on himself, so when frustrated by someone else, as happened on so many occasions last term, he is inclined to go very nearly mad with anger. Lastly he has no idea – NO IDEA – how to deal with people, and if he achieves his ambition to get into the foreign office, and it seems this is very likely owing to some excellent strings, well World War III here we come! ...
> *Head of house's book, public school*

The other problems are more personal. For some conscientious boys, the burden of responsibility is too great; they desire less of an adult burden – like their counterparts in state and integrated schools. One boy explains in terms of promotion:

> I feel that we are not qualified to take decisions about promotion

which can make or break a boy's career here: we have not the experience and knowledge required to judge character sufficiently to make a sound decision. I feel this responsibility is too heavy – the housemaster relies too much on us.

Head of house's book, public school

For all there is the problem of duties conflicting with work. A head of house sums it up:

There is never the time to get all your work done – you have too many other things to do here when you're senior. If you ever feel disheartened about your work try to have comfort in knowing that you are bearing the same troubles that I and many other H. of H's must have. Anyway if your going to be emotionally balanced you must have your bellyful of misery from time to time.

Head of house's book, public school

From problems to the compensations of power. Many of these are intangible: developments in character, in self-respect perhaps. Many are deferred, such as the enhancement of career prospects. Some are quite unofficial – the freedom of action which powerholders can arrogate to themselves. But some freedoms are official and laid down. As the boy progresses up the hierarchy of power and, presumably, becomes more imbued with the school's values, so he is step by step released from the controls and restrictions of the school until, at the end, he almost has the freedom of action and movement of a boy in the society outside. This is the system of privileges. Progressive schools and many state schools have fewer privileges, either because they have less hierarchy or greater freedom anyway. In public schools and some independent schools they are carefully and jealously elaborated and laid down as a means of controlling pupils towards the official ends – though here also many of the more absurd symbolic privileges are now disappearing. To illustrate the system we quote a recent list of privileges from one typical public school. It is the material privileges in the *house* which count; those which come to the *school* prefects are partly symbolic. A house book describes the whole system from the lowest officials to the highest:

House Fourths:

House Fourths are those senior non fags who are 'on spec' for Fifthdom. They are expected to have reached a stage at which few punishments are necessary, and at which they are even able to set an example to the lower parts of the House. With these minor obligations are the following privileges.

1. Freedom from meal fagging (except in exceptions).
2. The use of VIths bath without permission. They must however give place to any VIth who may require the bath.
3. The right to queue barge ahead of fags and non-fags (for baths only).
4. The right to read the newspapers in the House Library before, as well as after 8.30, after making their beds.
5. Can have their coats open and hands in pockets around house.
6. House Fourths in charge of a table may exercise meal fagging power although it isn't to be encouraged. (It's a good way to judge a Fourth's character. A House Fourth worth his stuff probably won't do it).
7. Elbows on tables in meals.
8. In general House Vths do not ask IVths to fag.

They cannot wander about in prep, go out after lockup or stay up without permission.

House Fifths:

These are the minor House Prefects. They are responsible for keeping order in the house and for setting a good example. Though they have no right to punish miscreants, they may recommend them for punishment to a VIth. These duties carry the following privileges:

1. All privileges of the IVths.
2. Precedence in queues.
3. Movement in Prep without permission. (This privilege is liable to suspension if abused.)
4. The right to use VIths baths without permission.
5. Hands in pockets, coats undone as far as the House gate; can whistle and sing around house, etc.
6. May wear slippers at roll-call and house prayers.
7. Drink cider at the House Christmas supper.

House Sixths:

These are the House Prefects. They can set lines to any boy (in this house only) at any place (not in holidays) and recommend for beating. They keep discipline in house and school, read in prayers, take roll-calls, search studies when necessary, hold the more responsible house jobs (games, meals, library, changing rooms).

1. All privileges of IVs and Vs.
2. Stay up after lights out.
3. No attendance at roll-call.
4. Give out notices in prayers.
5. Wander around in prep.
6. Go out after lockup without permission.
7. Cook in own rooms.
8. Have personal fags.
9. Give fag calls when fags are needed.
10. Precedence in house queues.
11. Shouting for boys – can call a boy by shouting.
12. Free access to all dormitories and studies.

School Prefects:

Consist of house captains, games captains ex officio, editor of school magazine ex officio and others appointed by Headmaster. Have authority in school over *all* boys, not just those from own house. Duties consist of school discipline, patrolling bounds, reading in chapel, organise games, school meals, etc. They give lines, detentions, and can beat with permission.

1. Wear subdued jackets not school uniform in evenings and Saturdays.
2. Go home one extra weekend in Autumn and Summer term.
3. Have own common room and can cook.
4. Wear buttonholes on speech, sports days, etc.
5. Can use coffee bars and restaurants in town.

Many of the punishments used in boarding schools do not differ from those in day schools: conduct marks, star systems, lines and detentions, caning. In public and similar schools, the senior boys can usually cane the serious offenders. In most state boarding schools the prefects are not allowed to do so, while in progressive schools the senior pupils have few sanctions over the others and caning is unknown. This does not mean that state boarding prefects always use kid-glove methods – sometimes informal violence can take over (the reader may recollect the new boys' black eyes in Chapter 3), or other methods can be used, as at one state school where offenders were summoned before a prefects' court, and though never touched physically, were systematically bawled at and verbally degraded for ten or fifteen minutes and often reduced to tears. Even in progressive schools powerful moral, social and verbal pressures can be brought to bear both by the staff and the informal society of the pupils.

Residence and the inability of the pupils to retreat into the outside world inevitably enlarge the variety of punishments. Some schools make the food of offenders less attractive (bread, butter and tea, for example), others send them out on long and timed cross-country runs, or make them run up and down stairs to the dorm changing back and forth from school dress into complete Corps kit a certain number of times in a specified period; others impose early bedtimes, or early rising, cold showers, extra domestic chores, building, constructional work or weeding; a few give their delinquents pointless and heavy fatigues, and many more 'gate', confining the offenders to grounds, or to a central building.

It is not practical to illustrate all of these punishments. By the nature of the case, where punishments are neither severe nor obtrusive – in the majority of schools – they do not figure prominently in the children's writings. But in that minority of schools where they are both severe and frequent, the writings abound with references to them.

Whatever the official rules may say, boarding inevitably enlarges the power of the prefects over their charges. They can often search rooms, possessions and even – from whatever motive – search people.

There is a head boy, who has something like 15 'small boys'. He's a slimy person. He takes joy in seeing people caught with cigarettes. Earlier in the term, he stripped two boys, completely, to see if they had any cigarettes. This, I think, is going too far. Now, if you come into the school carrying a duffle bag, you are most certainly likely to be searched. The other day, someone came back from Highton and he was searched. By the head prefect of course, and he was found with 50 cigarettes. He got gated for two weeks. The reason he only got two weeks was because they weren't for him. I myself have only just finished four weeks gating for having cigarettes.

Boy, fifteen, integrated school

In a few schools they can – without the knowledge or with the tacit connivance of the staff and whatever the rules may say about corporal punishment – impose a regime of violence:

If somebody does something then I usually hit them instead of punishing them in the prefects room. I find this is better and they like you more so you get more co-operation.

Prefect, eighteen, Cromwell College

There are nice prefects who smash people faces in.

Boy, twelve, Lady Margaret Foundation

Well, they got me in the Prefects room. They made me put my hand out, fingers spread on an old desk, then T.H. (a prefect) got a compass and began to stab the gaps between my fingers with the compass point, back and forwards, faster and faster. Then when he was doing it fastest, he shut his eyes. I was terrified. Thank Christ he didn't miss. They sometimes do and boys go to Matron – they daren't split – 'My finger got hit by a nail' . . .

Boy, fifteen, independent school

Lesser officials can follow the example of the seniors:

The head of Common Room is the dirtiest bastard I have known. Every new boy who comes into the house has to go on the table. What is the point of putting a boy on a table and holding his arms and legs while the thugs like M and J-R and F beat him up? I can remember well being held against the bottom of a bed by the mattress and bloody well being pummelled with a pillow. Pointless. There is

one boy who is rather large and fat and even the F— prefects who are meant to set an example take delight in beating him up.
Boy, fifteen, independent school

These incidents have all been confirmed by our own research, and further examples of the power which pupils in some schools can informally arrogate to themselves will be found in later chapters.

But in a few schools even the *officially* approved punishments differ markedly from those of the majority:

He should not smoke: the punishment is 3 cuts (cuts are done with rope that is spliced and dipped in brine).
Boy, fourteen, independent school

Blast, so your put in the prefects room where you get two or three sadistic lashes with a primitive piece of rope. This cuts your arse and bloody hurts. *Boy, fifteen, same school*

The fatigues were always not less than an hour. Then when you did something wrong you were sworn at. God how can one be trained as a leader if he is cudgelled and degraded by the seniors? Must he always be bullied and pushed along to make him see discipline. Is public school discipline good for you. By being forced to sweep out floors and have your hands burnt for doing something wrong. *Boy, fifteen, independent school*

Such schools are a tiny minority, but in some schools more orthodox punishments may be used excessively by the boys with power:

Fines reached unexplored, almost stratospheric heights – round about £15 each term. One wonders whether too many people were allowed to get away with too little; I know for a fact that Chetwynd was fined at least 7 times and should by rights have been beaten long ago; but due to slackness he got away without. In my two terms I beat only three people *officially*. Perhaps there should have been more. On the other hand, the less it is used the more effective it is – to a certain extent as long as when you do use it you really let

fly. Wright tells his House Captain on the first occasion to 'do it really hard – so hard that you will regret it afterwards'. I agree; hard and many. Not a sadistic attitude: only when thoroughly deserved!
Head of house's book, public school

Beatings, well you can get beaten very easily here and you have to be a goody goody if you want to last the term, three blacks equal a beating and blacks are dealed out left right and centre by house prefects.
Boy, fourteen, public school

Statistics show that at the latter school each boy is on average beaten twice per year (this must mean, in practice, still more beatings for the junior boys). But in the majority of public schools beating is dying fast. In some it is dead already:

Here there is no corporal punishment and this I noticed quite soon after I got here. It is dying out in most public schools nowadays. If say one was caught smoking, instead of having the cane, one would be put on reporting for two weeks, and personally I think this is better and more effective than corporal punishment. Also another thing that I noticed was that there was no fagging.
Boy, thirteen, public school

In some schools it is the senior boys who are giving the lead in giving up the cane:

I don't think that automatic 'house beatings' for lines or lates are acceptable. And I see 'house beatings' as a retrograde step by a weak group of people.
Head of house's book, public school

Of course, they must be kept under control but there are better ways of doing this than by beating them. That is why only two boys were beaten in the last two terms.
Head of house's book, public school

When prefects beat in a public school, it is for a particularly severe piece of insubordination, or, sometimes, for an accumulation of other punishments. It is all codified into precise rules of conduct:

1. Punishments are set at the discretion of the prefect responsible, but there is a right of appeal to the Head of the House and, then, to the Housemaster.

    No boy should ever be prejudiced against because he exercises his right of appeal.
2. The extent of the punishment depends on the prefect although uniformity for certain offences is a good thing. Punishment may consist of lines, 2400 word essay for every 50 lines, or 30 lines of memorization. Setting of Latin lines is to be discouraged.

    The setting of essays which require some work on the part of the offender is to be encouraged.
3. Accumulations of 500 lines (or the equivalent in fatigues, essays, etc. etc.) or 3 lates are punishable by a house beating. The victim must, however, have received a warning when he passed the 450 lines or $2\frac{1}{2}$ lates mark.
4. No boy may be beaten without the consent of the housemaster. Maximum no. of strokes is 6.
5. Boys in the sixth are not beaten.

Head of house's book, public school

Even the solemn ritual of a prefects' beating in a hushed house is laid down in detail, It may go like this:

Having seen the Housemaster the Head of the House then calls the offender up before his prefects in the House Hall. He speaks to the boy and it shakes the boy up considerably if all the prefects put their spoke in, and if this is done sensibly without malice it can be very beneficial. He is then told to go to his study. There is then a 'studies' call given by the prefects. This means that no-one is to emerge from their studies or from anywhere else during the beating. It is the duty of the Junior Prefect to fetch the offender; if when asked whether he wishes to appeal to the Housemaster he says he doesn't, then he is beaten.

Head of house's book, public school

Or in some schools there are variants:

About beatings. Usually done in a dorm over the end of a bed. The canes are kept in the housemaster's room. You must have at least *two* house pres present to witness. When you have to beat a boy, send two pres up to the place to get it ready. Then, see the boy. Tell him to wait outside the place. On your way up, don't forget the cane. When he comes in, make him take his jacket off. As to how hard or how many strokes, that is up to you. At the end, don't forget to enter it in 'The Book'. *Head of house's book, public school*

Enough of the physical! We end with a diary from a seventeen-year-old girl at a progressive school. She recounts her escapade and her punishment. Note the prefects and the informal society of the children connive at the offence, and that instead of summary punishment (as in the cases above) the children are subject to moral pressure by delay, by letting their parents know (from the children's point of view one of the worst punishments of all), and then by exclusion:

It was Friday evening when Henry asked me whether I would like to come down to his house and have a drink there as his parents are away in America and he is boarding for the moment but still had access to the house. I was feeling in a crazy mood and I like drink so I accepted. Eventually there were five of us and we paid 3/6d. each and bought a bottle of sherry. This was Saturday afternoon. We then all went to Henry's house and drank the sherry, and then some rum was produced which I didn't like but I drank some of it with the others. We all got slightly drunk and stumbled back to school hanging onto each other and I went to bed, but the others went to activities.

The next morning it was the scandal of the school but none of the staff knew. Everyone was really super to us especially my dorm boss who had every right to report us but she just gave me a warning and that was all. I think everyone was amazed at me being mixed up in this thing because otherwise I have a good reputation and have never done anything wrong before. Sunday was misery but I went and told everything to Sam, a prefect. I had a sort of affair with him for about six months last year and I still go to him when I need help. He was sweet to me and promised not to report us.

Monday, Tuesday, Wednesday and Thursday went by and we

were all gradually forgetting it but knew at the same time that we would never do it again. Thursday night came and Patsy and I were having fun when Miss Murray called from the stairs and said she wanted to see me. I went down at once and she said she had heard about a drinking party with which I was involved and asked me about it. I told her the truth and then burst into tears. She was very nice to me but said that I should have realised earlier what I was doing.

Friday morning passed slowly and in agony, but by lunch we knew we were being sent home on Saturday morning not to return until the end of half term twelve days later. Sue and I travelled up to London together and that journey was awful because we were wondering what our parents would say. Mine were very upset to begin with which was dreadful.

Suspension like this is a severe punishment in all schools; expulsion is of course the most severe – a sanction not available to many neighbourhood day schools.

This then is power as pupils see and exercise it in boarding schools: hierarchical in some, enormous in scope and depth in others, limited in a certain group, abused in a few, diffused as barely to be perceptible in several, but important in one way or other in all of them. The ultimate sanction of authority is to banish the boy or girl from the closed society of the school back into the world outside from whence he came. It is surely time we explored, through the children's lives, the connection between the school and this wider world in which it is set.

7 The Outside World

'Its just like a prison, the gates are locked at five and you can't get out,' writes a disillusioned boy away at school for the first time. But in one important aspect schools are radically different from prisons: their aim often is to protect the child from the values of outside society rather than vice versa. Many schools, particularly those that set out to inculcate certain beliefs and values, are highly critical of teenage culture, feel threatened by outside mores and are sometimes suspicious about even the influence of the child's parents.

The schools therefore, with the exception of some state boarding schools, a few independent and most progressive schools, feel obliged to restrict their children's access to life outside. They exercise a careful control on who goes out and comes in, and what the children may do when they get out. Many schools place near-by areas out of bounds, forbid the use of public transport, visits to cinemas, shops and cafés. Even speaking to outsiders is dangerous: 'boys are not to associate with young village neighbours,' insists one rule book; 'girl friends in the locality are not allowed,' remarks another, or, 'boys are expected to introduce their girl friends to the Housemaster and ask for his approval.'

While the schools are worried by and frequently hostile to outside values, their pupils certainly are not: they seize every opportunity, however limited, to get out, and by letters – so important, as we have seen – and phone calls strive to keep in contact with friends outside and resist the isolation that boarding school imposes. There is a constant struggle in many schools between the desire of the pupils to feel part of wider teenage culture, reflected in long hair, casual clothes and pop music, and the authorities' hostility to that culture. It is a conflict which can damage the significant influence the school wishes to have in moral and academic areas. This chapter examines the relations between the school and the outside world, glancing at the control exercised over pupils' activities as they go out, their friendships outside, and the important contribution made by day pupils. It closes with the children commenting on the way boarding has affected their family relationships.

Let us first read the rather critical comments of children experiencing the restrictions placed on their outside interests and cultural pursuits by the school.

I sat in the schoolroom and by well-aimed kicks put ten years on the life of a desk, all the creeps came through on their way to some Shakespeare play. That's the only bloody thing you can get out for, if I asked to go to the 'Rolling Stones' or 'Kinks' the Old Man would throw a fit. I hate this bloody hole, he is always telling you what you *should* see or listen to, I'd like to tell him what to do with his cello!
Boy, sixteen, direct grant school

A senior boy from a public school happily accepts the school's cultural values but deftly bends the rules to make his evening out enjoyable, in his own way:

After the concert, a really delightful performance of the Brahms, I went off to a secluded pub. I had a sausage roll and two pints of bitter. The sausage roll is essential as the school rules say – Prefects are allowed a drink with a meal. We obey the letter if not the spirit of this curious law!
Boy, eighteen, public school

Sometimes the attempt to get round the school's rules can end in disaster. Here we see the school's values, the use of uniform and staff tolerance all neatly suggested by five boys aged between fourteen and sixteen. The incident was confirmed for us by the member of staff involved.

We decided to go to the football – City versus Wanderers, which promised to be good. Now football is forbidden 'cos its 'lower class'

212   The Hothouse Society

but you are allowed to stand all day and watch rugger which is a snob game. So we rush out of school and all cram into the nearest public bog to change out of our uniform into jeans (you can be seen a mile off in this clobber). Anyway while this is going on, in comes a policeman who wants to know what we were up to, said we had been soliciting and would inform the school! God, were we in a mess, so we rushed back to school and went to the master in charge, we were scared and it was embarrassing. But when we told him he roared with laughter and said we had made his afternoon. We didn't even get punished, but if we had been out with dirty shoes he would have given us hell. Aren't they difficult to understand?

Boy, fourteen, direct grant school

Many schools try to prevent their pupils from associating with local boys and girls, and some, public schools in particular, even have rules forbidding such contact. A shopping afternoon by some girls at a progressive school reveals the school's efforts to control their relationships outside:

We've just got back from town. Down there we bought some valentine cards. We went into this new paper shop. There's a man in there who I always talk to. I don't really like him, he flirts too much. Anyway, I think his wife was there because he pretended he didn't know us today. You could see he was pretending. We saw Bill Thomas. He's got a job in a shop now. I'll explain who he is. At the beginning of last summer term 5 of us met some yobs and we went out with them. They were quite nice and they used to buy us lots of things. We used to go out with them quite a lot. Well this crumby school didn't like it and one night we all got caught. Pru was really mad. They wrote to our parents and threatened to chuck us out. Bill was a friend of these boys and every time we see any of them now they give us queer looks. Sue and I were going to buy some rum but could not rise to it. Instead we bought some eggs to cook for supper.   *Girl, sixteen*

Similarly Churchill College views emotional display outside with distaste:

> While I was at the bus stop saying goodbye to my girl a master came past and said 'Now then, stop this softness, there is no need to hold hands, drop them, remember people can recognize your uniform.'
>
> *Boy, seventeen*

and at another school a boy bitterly comments:

> They even had a staff meeting because I was seeing a girl on the school estate. I was told not to see her again or they would kick me out. Now if I had been crackers on some boy, they wouldn't have even noticed. *Boy, eighteen, independent school*

Many schools restrict their children's entry to shops and cafés, as the following suggest:

> Because a boy went into a shop and bought a bottle of Tizer on our way to the swimming baths, we lost our swimming evening for good.
>
> *Boy, fourteen, direct grant school*

> As we were in Corps uniform we piled into the fish and chip shop without any risk. That's about the only advantage in it, you can get into shops pubs and cafes like anyone else when you are on an exercise. *Boy, seventeen, public school*

The prefects usually enforce the school's regulations concerning outside behaviour – they act as a police force outside as well as inside the school. At a large public school in a town the minutes of the prefects meeting reveal a planned operation and emphasize yet again those areas out of bounds to boarders:

> Each house in turn should provide two prefects to patrol the town on a Saturday evening. Route and clothes, etc. have been fixed. Checks are to be made on people leaving the cinema, the local pubs and all coffee bars. Particular attention should be given to the area around the Girls High School. Information gathered by prefects through their Houses should be passed on to those prefects on patrol. This will ensure the best possible results.
>
> *Minutes of prefects' meeting*

Many schools maintain that their children do not need to go out there are excellent leisure facilities inside the school and an official trip would be organized to anything of value outside. A glance at some of these trips is revealing. Here is a girl who goes out on a cultural expedition from her comprehensive school in the south. But what she gets from it is not at all what was intended:

Woke up feeling happy because we are going to Bournemouth to see the symphony orchestra. I do not actually want to see the orchestra but as Bournemouth has some decent shops I hope to be able to go out after the concert begins. Who wants to see a creaky lot of musicians playing classical music for hours. I will be bored to tears. At the orchestra found I couldn't go out because Musty Face was watching me and he would see me going out. Decided to pay 3d. and share a pair of opera glasses with Flo. DID NOT REGRET IT. Looked for some dishy boys in the audience. Saw a decent one with quite long hair. But close up discovered he was too young for me. My attention was diverted to the boys facing me each side of the stage. Flo pointed out a really dishy boy. Watched his every move. Soon he felt he was being watched and began to stare at me. Had a staring match. I won. Music was not bad but got a bit on the boring side. Boy, this bloke was dead dishy. Never seen such gorgeous hair. On second thoughts he was too good for Flo. Do better for me! Which school does he come from? End of the concert. Thank God! Ah, ah now I'll find out where Mr Fabulous comes from. Newton Grammar School! Well that's good. Lucky devil. He's not like us! Dishy goes out to his coach. Well, there are lots more decent boys in the world (I suppose). Hey, the opera glasses would be very useful to keep. Flo and I fight but we decide to shove 'em back. What if we get caught pinching them! *Girl, thirteen, comprehensive school*

The close staff-pupil relations which exist in many boarding schools enable cultural ends to be obtained much more subtly. Here a senior boy goes out informally with a member of staff and imbibes much as a result:

After making place look decent, School Governors are coming and the Head is in his usual flap, I rushed up to Peter's room (a master) he's invited me out for the afternoon. Changed into one of his suits because I couldn't go out in this gear and drank coffee.

Drive to Sherborne, look round the Abbey and ransack antique shops for Georgian silver which Peter collects. Visited Montacute, delightful garden, and then had a pleasant meal. Step on it coming back as we have a record evening every Thursday with day boys and even some that have left that return mainly to gossip. Listen to Elgar and Spanish guitar music and argue about school discipline. When I insist there isn't any and its mainly his fault, Peter just laughs.
Head of school, integrated independent school

Games take many children off to other schools. On the coach discipline is relaxed, and often permitted moments of unusual licence ensue. Here a fifteen-year-old writes of his return to school with the rugby team:

Departed in the coach after a good tea – much better than we have at our place. Started singing as usual, but when we got to the bit about the vicar and curate 'In Mobile', E came rushing down from the front of the coach and picked on T. Said he was going to make him repeat the verse in front of the old man next day. Miserable b ... Nobody else kicks up a fuss like that. He calmed down eventually and we started singing again. That's the best part of coach trips – the only other time we 'sing' together is in Assembly!!
Boy, fifteen, state boarding school

Schools face many difficulties in their attempts to regulate the lives of children outside their walls, and if they might sometimes seem over-zealous in their concern, we shall see that granting access to the outside world can bring very real problems to them. However, the schools can at least decide who shall visit the school and what outside influences it will officially allow to enter its precincts. These visits have a mixed reception from the children. First, a slightly condescending public schoolboy enjoys a lecture:

Really an excellent talk by Professor Lewis on coastlines, his il-

lustrations were just right, he handled his questions well. I thoroughly enjoyed it.
Boy, eighteen, public school

A girl at a Quaker school is captivated by a

> super man who climbs mountains, he has been up the north face of simply everything, he must be ever so brave, I forget his name for the moment; why don't I meet men like this when I am on holiday in Wales? They are always bald and horrid and leer ...
> *Girl, sixteen, Quaker school*

But not all find the visitors from outside stimulating:

> We had yet another missionary this evening. Oh, why do we *always* have to have good people; why can't we have a really wicked man for a change – a drug addict or a mercenary soldier? Suppose they are scared sin would be a bit too interesting.
> *Girl, sixteen, Quaker school*

Even the efforts of public schools to widen the experience and social conscience of their boys can have a chilly reception:

> This evening in chapel we had a fiery negro youth worker. He spoke endlessly about racial discrimination in the big cities. It was a frightful bore. What is this place coming to, last week the Public Schools Commission, and this week a provincial Malcolm X! Really the Establishment seems to have lost its nerve.
> *Boy, eighteen, public school*

Naturally our arrival at the school prompted many comments. Here a surprised boy warns us:

> God knows how you got in here. They must want to get boys into Cambridge really bad. And the school seems dead keen on you, little do they know what we are writing. It is the sort of truth they can't imagine. Not that it matters, nobody is going to believe what we say, they will pretend we took you for a ride. Still thanks for coming.
> *Boy, sixteen, independent school*

The Outside World   217

For outside lecturers it is sometimes difficult to get an audience:

> I had to round up some boys for a talk on the Common Market, then sat at the back and desperately thought of bright questions to ask and a vote of thanks because I knew the zombies I had roped in wouldn't say anything.
> *Boy, eighteen, public school*

And this notice appeared on the house board at a public school with an Evangelical bias:

> Boys on punishment will report to the lecture theatre at 4.15 for a talk on Scripture Union Summer Camps. The Headmaster will be present.

Some schools allow their pupils to bring in their own friends from outside; even girl friends come into some public schools on Saturday and Sunday afternoons. A careful eye is kept on the visitors. A public school boy meets his girl friend for tea:

> Jane arrived in her father's car, looking utterly fabulous, I hardly noticed anything else. I took her into the house and introduced her to the Tutor, even he looked rather dazzled. After a polite chat we went to my study and a fag whom Jane thought 'quite sweet' put the kettle on.
> *Boy, eighteen, public school*

In contrast, some boys semi-officially call on girls at a progressive school. Note how, even here, the attitude to youth outside is scarcely one of equality:

> Ahah!!! thrills thrills thrills we have a visitation from some town yobs, the four of us go and eye them carefully, there are six in a medium sized car, there are two revolting ones, one smashing one, and the rest are passable. We go over and demand who they want to see, they say two long haired blondes, my mind goes over the few hundred blondes in the school, we hail a passing pleb 'Go fetch Judy, Jane, Sue, Jenny . . .' soon the boys found the required girls and we departed, richer by a ciggy each. When you reach the

sixth your yobbing days are usually over, and the unwanted visits of eager 'town youth' have died down a bit. *Girl, seventeen*

Again rather unwelcome visitors at a coeducational school emphasize the anxiety, often not without cause, which we have seen the authorities have of the outside world. Note again how the local children are referred to:

Some yobs were whistling outside the windows so we had to pull the blinds down. This school has a sort of prejudice about yobs. They seem to think that you can't go out with a yob without getting pregnant. Quite mad! *Girl, sixteen*

By no means all boarding schools are exclusively boarding in character – many have day children, and in some they form the majority. This day element is important and schools with it have a routine which differs from those which are predominantly boarding. Day children give boarders a contact with the outside world, afford them envious glimpses of rapidly changing youth fashions and occasionally bring in contraband.

Those schools which hope to inculcate beliefs and a style of life in their charges as well as academic skills often view day boys with suspicion. As we have seen, outside values can threaten the internal ones and access to them even through TV and radio is carefully controlled; sometimes newspapers can be censored. In such schools day boarders must follow school routine even when at home. It is the housemaster not parents who sanctions cinema and theatre visits for them, bans motor bikes and car driving, while for them school bounds and prep times, grey suits and Sunday chapel, are obligatory.

In progressive schools there are similar pressures on day children to conform to boarding ways, not from the authorities, but from the boarders themselves. 'Grab a pair of jeans and wear them always, especially Sunday,' advises a day girl, and in such schools day children can feel left out, marginal to the real life of the society.

State boarding schools and some direct grant schools make fewer demands on their day pupils. Their manners and beliefs are viewed as largely the responsibility of parents, and, as we shall see, the stronger contacts that some of these schools have with the home and the flexibility of their boarding arrangements reduce the friction between boarders and day boys and give these schools a distinctive boarding style.

Let us now look at a few day children contrasting their lives with those of the boarders. Not all of them are delighted at escaping the restrictions which we have just described.

Here a girl at a progressive school suggests the difficulties day children face in having to live two lives, a clash of loyalties which, the schools maintain, can be damaging: to which world do they belong, outside or inside?

> Some people think that being a day pupil at a boarding school is getting the best of both worlds. You have all home comforts, yet at the same time you can share in the community life of the school. This is true to a certain extent but I think that the situation presents many problems. The most difficult problem which I found at first was that school and home were totally different. At school the atmosphere was free and the people were living in a world of their own with their own conventions, likes and dislikes, codes of behaviour. At home the atmosphere seemed dull and restricting and sometimes silly, compared with the way they did things at school. My parents were a little distrustful of the effect the school was having on me and tended to jib at the slightest sign of any deterioration in my behaviour and character. Also, spending so much time at school, I found I was being left out of the family, and yet because I was not at school all the time and did not sleep there, I did not feel accepted on the same level as a boarder. For a long time I felt torn between the two places. I had to go home to see my family and yet I wanted to stay at school to become more a part of it. However, now I have reached a sort of compromise my family has got used to the situation and are much more tolerant.
>
> *Girl, seventeen*

A day boy writes at another public school on the same theme of being an outsider:

The big disadvantage of being a dayboy is that it is difficult to fit in well with the boarders unless you are prepared to stay behind after school to join in their life, and since most dayboys have far better things to do at home, they go straight after school. In this way they miss most of the community life of the boarders. There are few activities for dayboys. The only advantages I can think of are the longer holidays we get due to this being a boarding school; also the feeling of one-upmanship of not being restricted.

Boy, seventeen, public school

Some day pupils integrate well and become indistinguishable from the boarders.

I am a day girl at this school. That is, I come every morning and go back at night because my father teaches here. I hate being a day person and I think that applies to nearly all the others. I always go to my friends' dorm at their house where I stay until they have their lights out. So apart from having breakfast and sleeping at home, we're much the same. I always come to school at the weekends and on free afternoons because I prefer my friends to my family. Much of the free time is spent in our common room. There are always lots of people there talking intellectually or telling dirty jokes, and the record player is always on (the HM always complains of the noise). Mealtimes are also a sociable time if you have a nice table that is. Places are changed once a week for lunch and every other week for supper, so one gets to know everyone, at home I know no-one.

Girl, sixteen, coeducational school

But not all day children feel they are missing things by being away from school at evenings and weekends. Many feel no clash of loyalties:

I'm a day boy, and would on no account want to be a boarder, I could not stick the discipline, early bedtime, reporting out in order to go outside the school gates, rising at 7.30, being watched by housemasters. I come here most weekday evenings to do prep and for the company, but I always have something to do outside school at weekends, and enjoy myself then. Being in 6-form is no different, except it is easier to relax and be unhampered by officials.

Boy, seventeen, public school

and a day boy at a direct-grant school in the west feels so sorry for the boarders that:

> Most Sundays we ask over one of the boarders, usually someone who comes from abroad. Otherwise they would never sit on a nice soft chair, watch TV or have a good feed.
> *Boy, fifteen*

However, for some day pupils their much-vaunted freedom is in practice somewhat illusory:

> All this seems very strange, for in having this extra freedom over the boarders, I do not use it; whereas the boarders fight constantly for more freedom, breaking rules and bounds. (This *is* confidential, isn't it?) I think that if one *feels* that one is free, one is 'happy', and it is for this *feeling* of freedom that they fight, not for the freedom itself. Similarly I can go to bed at whatever time I wish, but I find that 10.30 pm, is as late as I can leave it without 'suffering' the next day. If the boarders were given this freedom, I am sure that they would eventually find exactly the same thing and that the rules of bedtime are quite sensible – hope this is of some help.
> *Boy, seventeen, public school*

Actually the school day can be very long for the day pupil, as their diaries illustrate. A boy returning home after a day at a public school near London writes:

> Thank God I am home; it is 6.10. I make two thick sandwiches and switch on the television. The 'Flintstones' are on, really I'm too lethargic I am sitting here when I should be working. Supper is at 6.30 and goes on till 7.00. I think how most wasted evenings start with that initial half hour of 'the box' then go upstairs and do some prep. Nearly finished two sides of paper, good heavens! its 8.00. The 'Man from Uncle' is starting. At 8.55 I return upstairs because of my conscience. After another half hour I remember that at 9.25 there is a programme on called 'The Frost Report on Sin'. I watch that and then return at 9.50 to some prep. At 10.30 I quickly undress because my parents like me in bed by 10.30. I clean my

teeth and go downstairs thinking soon the end of another day and the best moment of the whole day is just as I fall asleep. As I go downstairs and get a mug of water for the night I remember this diary, that Cambridge fellow said I could put how I feel about small comforts like water; he must be bats! Scribble this and say goodnight to my parents and return to the bathroom. I have to have clean feet before I get into bed which involves another time wasting ritual. Now I have clean feet, Ah that moment of oblivion can't be far away now. It is quarter to twelve and I set the alarm clock for 6.30 again. Term is one long tired struggle but I can last till the holidays. Goodnight.
Boy, seventeen

A day girl at a progressive school makes a very perceptive point: how bad weather in the boarding school closes the society even more and produces destructive urges; day pupils are less confined:

Before I go home at 4.30 I happen to be sitting on the wall, a friend of mind comes and sits next to me. She has chosen me to confide in which is very interesting. She is going through a bad time, because some people are being very nasty to her at the moment. I realise how really terrible it must be. Boarders can't get away, when the weather is bad people go to their rooms and bored people come in and make a nuisance of theirselves. I find the weather has a lot to do with it, because when its hot people are outside and things are a lot better. Perhaps I have got a distorted view because I'm a day – or maybe I've got a better view because I'm not part of it. The boarders are left alone a lot. Most of this I found out when I shared a room with a boarder last year. I don't know what goes on in the evenings because I don't stay till then but one of the worst things about sharing a room with a boarder in the winter is the boredom of the little rooms. Its not surprising that people are destructive then.
Girl, sixteen

It is obvious that the day children keep the boarders in touch with what is happening outside, providing a taste of home for those whose parents live far away, even, as we have just seen, helping boarders at difficult times. However the boarders' own group of holiday friends might be expected to challenge more seriously the values of the school, and over these the authorities can have no control. Yet as we turn to explore their friendships outside and in the holidays we can see the school has little to fear.

Many boarders find it difficult to make and keep holiday friends. 'I have two lots of half-friends,' writes a public school boy, 'those at home and those at school.' The friends they have at home come from their own or similar schools, and some have no friends at home at all. Their friends outside are projections of the school society into the wider world, of the values and styles of the schools from which they come.

Finally in this section we will note the hectic, in some cases almost uncontrolled life of boarders during the holidays. In the first few days of leisure, the lack of routine and the difficulties of adjustment to the family raise problems for many of them.

First let us look at them commenting on their holiday friends and the problems of making and keeping them. Some of course have none:

> Friends? Now I have none because of this ruddy place, I spend my leave helping mum with the housework and do quite a lot of gardening, cycling and also a lot of swimming. I get quite bored on leave because I have no friends and then I think of coming back here and I feel like being sick and breaking my leg just to stop me from going back.
> *Boy, fourteen, independent school*

Even the state school's greater contact with home does not entirely solve the problem:

> I find that being here keeps me from being in touch with friends at home. I return home at the visiting weekends I feel odd because I have no idea of news of what is going on around me. When people sign for boarding school they think it will be like the story books, they don't realise you lose lots of friends.
> *Girl, fifteen, secondary modern boarding school*

Single-sex schools often isolate their pupils from the other sex, but if they are boarding, they may find themselves equally cut off in the holiday. One boy explains how:

> One feels a social outcast when one goes to a dance during the holidays period. You see all your mates with a bird and you have to 'hang' around trying to look useful. If one does happen to meet a bird she immediately doesn't want to know you, when she finds out that you go to a boarding school and that you cannot come out very often.
> *Boy, fifteen, state boarding school*

Sometimes the closed and powerful style of the school can make adjustment outside difficult:

> The school makes you a little self-conscious and you often get embarrassed because you are living away from the outside world. During term you become accustomed to the school language and ideas and these don't seem to go down very well in the holidays with your friends.
> *Girl, sixteen, progressive school*

A boy is suddenly overcome by his isolation from his friends as he returns from football at a boarding grammar school in the suburbs:

> After we won and got back changed I just went into the library and started to think about home and me girl, the things we might be doing now at this moment, or perhaps be out with me mates on their motor bikes or scooters or just watch the tele, oh I wish I was at home I wouldn't have to do half the things here if at home, have lots more freedom.
> *Boy, sixteen*

Often the friends of state boarders at home cannot understand why they have gone away to school:

> They think I'm O.K. They think my parents are touched.
> *Boy, thirteen, secondary modern school*

> They think I'm 'nuts'. They always mistake it for Borstal school.
> *Boy, fourteen, boarding grammar school*

They pity me, 'cause they think Boarding Schools are for snobs.
Boy, fourteen, technical boarding school

The reaction of my old school friends was one of horror at going away from home and also a slight feeling of my being 'snobby'. The reaction of most of the factory workers was either I went to Princess Anne's school or a Borstal! Friends going to segregated schools look on me with envy and are also a little shocked at the comparative freedom! *Girl, seventeen, Quaker school*

Some do have friends in the holidays. Who are they? Are they rootless boarders or long-tried local neighbours? Are they from different schools and social classes? Most holiday friends are similar in background to their friends back at school. First, a boy at a small independent school writes:

Most of them have left public school, are students or are at 'crammers'.
Boy, seventeen

and this comment is worth comparing with the school that follows:

We are very aristocratic and young. We shoot in Scotland, go on the yacht in summer and ski in winter. Always with the same people.
Boy, seventeen, public school

In contrast here are the friends of boys at an independent Catholic boarding school in the north:

Yes I have friends at home. My friend works on a building site as a labourer and I go and see him or my girlfriend. Second one most.
Boy, seventeen

About 10 must work at the shipyards but a few go to University. We normally go out drinking at a folk club, or football match. Very easy to keep up contact with them. All interested in girls.
Boy, seventeen

Progressive schools, because of their very distinctive style and philosophy, manners and the development they foster, often leave their pupils isolated outside: they therefore tend to mix, if at all, largely with friends from their own school or connected with it.

> I have a few friends during the holidays; most of them are in some way connected with school. I used to go lizard hunting with some village boys. I have working friends (middle aged labourers) who I have got to know during working round the school estate. Other friends are often relatives: cousins. Most of these are boys. Generally I am (or was) disliked by the local people of my age, not because I am a snob but because I have different interests and a different outlook. (The school does this to people, but it is generally a good outlook meaning that most outlooks of other people are bad).
> During the holidays I wander around the country (of which I am very fond) birdwatching, looking at flowers, watching animals. I walk on the hills. Make wine, tend my bees. Sometimes I take a job such as on the Gardens which supply the school with food, or with the School engineer or on the G.P.O. I read a lot, watch some TV.
> *Boy, fifteen, progressive school*

Again a similar comment from another progressive school:

> All my friends at home are from school and I work in most holidays. When I was young I had friends from the local housing estates, but now I spend so much time at school that I never see them, anyway they seem to think I am a 'Snob' from that place where the boys and girls sleep together. How wrong they are!
> *Girl, sixteen, progressive school*

At Cromwell College, an integrated school, the outside friends are amazingly diverse in composition but echo the tone of violence found, as we have so often seen, in the life of the school.

> None are yobos or scrubbers, but we are not really an asset to the public.
> *Boy, sixteen*

> We all live in Jamaica, well we have parents there, but we go to school in England. We all arrange our flights at the hols to fly out

together, they all go to Grammar Boarding in one part of England or another. We all go to beach parties together in cars or motorbikes. We like cutting up car tyres, destructive but a laugh, we are not old enough to drive or ride a motor bike but we don't give a damn. Also snogging, which we do all the time, cutting phones off police bikes, parties in general. Nicking car arials for the Hondas. Crashing parties. Make a noise at movies and of course, smoking.

Boy, sixteen

But the friends I gang up with are usually from 15 to 17. We all have girl friends. We are all at school. All mods! Our gang mostly have scooters go round doing no particular damage except the odd telephone kiosk.

Boy, sixteen

At an independent school in East Anglia certain aspects of the school's life are difficult to forget even in a normal outside atmosphere.

Friends, oh lots, unfortunately girls are the only people I have sexual relationships with in the holidays.

Boy, seventeen

Many public school boys seem to have a limited social experience in the holidays: boys from the same or similar schools are bound to a restless whirl of contrived activity.

Most of my friends come from school, as I live in London it is easy to keep in touch. We eat out, go to parties and watch rugger matches.

Boy, sixteen, public school

I go to stay with boys from home, or they come to my place or we meet at parties – there are always plenty of them: life would be lonely otherwise.

Boy, seventeen, public school

A few of these comments hint that the holidays can give an unreal, hectic contrast to the routine of term.

I just go wild for the first few days, even though you are shattered at the end of term, utterly flaked out, I find it difficult to sleep. You

start things and give them up, go out on your bike and for hours cycle round going nowhere special. In the evening if any friend turns up you do the coffee bars and pubs. Then you come back and row with the old man.
Boy, eighteen, independent school

A depressed public school boy near London notes how the small world of the school can prompt a wild reaction when outside:

Here you begin to realize that people get stuck in a rut of life. You just get a job, get married, get settled down and wait to die. Sometimes (eg the masters – or some of them) here you just give up and wish that the end of the world would come. In fact it can make you into a 'holiday rebel'.
Boy, seventeen

The girls are more passive. They don't turn into holiday rebels, they play tennis or sit in their rooms and daydream:

You know I seem to spend my time at the tennis club, then shopping, ages in front of the mirror, and about a week at the hairdressers; I never seem to get any work done at all.
Girl, seventeen, progressive school

I sit in my window seat and look at people going past and think how many nice boys there are outside and how I shall get to know them, and think of going away to places and the exciting things that might happen.
Girl, sixteen, Quaker school

Some girls immerse themselves in aspects of family life which do not reach into their schoolday experience:

In the holidays I look after my baby brothers, they are twins; always naughty, sticky, smelly and absolutely lovely! I miss them terribly when I come back here.
Girl, fifteen, Quaker school

Most of the holiday life is spent with the family and here we will look more closely at the return of the boarder to parents, brothers and sisters. Some schools, usually state boarding schools, for reasons already given, do not isolate children from home during term time. Their boarding styles can be more varied than those of the public schools, the contrast between day boy and boarder becomes less distinct and efforts are made to create a weekend pattern for all. As there is less attempt to instil cherished values and many boarders come from the locality, these schools are more open; boarders may spend Saturday night at the local dance and Sundays at home. The comments of such pupils show that local friendships are maintained, the formative give-and-take of family life is experienced and yet the cultural and spiritual values highly prized by more restrictive schools are not entirely jettisoned. There is more calling in at home for an hour, and in several cases parents help in the domestic and outside activities of the school.

For a boarder who has been away from home for a whole term the excitement of return is considerable. For many this is the first contact with the family for many weeks. There is little doubt that boarding changes the relationships a child has with parents, brothers and sisters – it may subsequently change the sort of relationships he has with everyone.

First let us look at the state-school boarder enjoying his contact with home.

A boy looks forward to Sunday:

After a moment of wild passion (I don't think!) at the school gates I left Sandra (my girl friend) and jacked back into school as it was gone ten. 'Rumble guts' was on duty with his nose glued to the telly so I was OK. Washed and went to bed and lay there thinking of home tomorrow, a good roast dinner, remember I am taking my bloody little brother swimming, he needs a good shove in the deep end – but then there might be some talent and I drop off to sleep thinking of splashing brown legs and twanging bikinis.

Boy, seventeen, state school

Less erotic and more industrious, another boy rises on Sunday. Note that the pace but not the quality of activity changes during his day off.

Got up early and did my exercises to keep fit and hold my place in first XV, took in John's tea (he's duty master for this weekend). Tidied his room and put on the fire, dozens of records out of their cases lying everywhere. After breakfast changed to Sunday shoes and socks, went back to John's room now full of boys, nice kid who does the washing up, he's a pez but very nice, my mission in school is to make him more cultivated. After chapel (read 'Pattern of Islands' in service its *so* dull) catch the bus home. Change into my own clothes, read 'Observer', have dinner and in afternoon go out with friends to look at interesting churches and the countryside. Had tea, watched 'Meeting Point' and international football. Did a little work and got a lift back to school from a boy in second form. Felt relaxed and read 'L'Enfant Prodigue' by Gide in library and after coffee with a couple of Masters and some Cambridge 'Don' studying boarding, went to bed.

Boy, fifteen, boarding grammar school

The proximity of home to the state boarding school means that visits can take place with or without permission. Here two boys decide to avoid the boredom of a Sunday afternoon:

It was about 1.30 when we changed from our Sunday best into our much more comfortable jeans and jackets. We borrowed two bikes from some second years who were dead scared of getting hammered, and cycled off down the drive. I had arranged to get someone to sit in my place as being one of the high and mighty bloody prefects I normally sit at the end of the table for tea. Before we were half a mile away from the school I stopped and lit my first fag for about three hours. We cycled up hills into a small village called Torton which is a right bloody hole.

Heads down we went belting past Fatty's house (Depty headmaster). With his house behind us I began to feel my freedom. We both stopped at the top of a hill, which had half taken the guts out of me, to have another fag. It was about 2.15 we done about 12 miles both of us were tired feeling rather depressed of the sight of another hill. Then a downhill run all the way into Frome. We went belting past the Traveller's Rest it was a great pity the dump was shut I could have just done with a pint of good old Somerset scrumpy.

Finally we got to my place where my old man laughed his head off and made us very welcome. He gave us a glass of light ale each which swilled my inside for me.

Soon after our arrival top of the pops started on the radio; our beat morale had been boosted to its highest limits.

My mate decided we had time to play darts so we did this at the price of sixpence a game, which was a bloody scandal. The radio blared all afternoon. For tea we had the frying pan special it was dead great! My thoughts drifted back to the poor bastards at school with the usual tea, watered down milk, last weeks corned beef and a bit of the cook's bloody old chutney, dead great!

My dad gave me the car keys and said one of my friends could drive us back to the prison. We cycled off down the road feeling very released after an afternoons bliss. I tied the two bikes in the back of the car and back to school we travelled, smoked most of the afternoon. When within a mile of the school I didn't feel too good. We unloaded our bikes and pushed our way back. Cautiously we progressed down the back drive and rode around the paths in order to avoid staff room windows. Our scive had not been noticed thanks to my fellow prefects and for the master on duty being so dense. He wouldn't know we had gone.
Boy, seventeen

Another boy at a state boarding school feels a little hungry and reminds us that Billy Bunter is not dead yet:

It rained so hard that rugger was cancelled, so I started to cycle back to school but I came over feeling peckish and remembering the large cake we had on Sunday I rode home, took the key from under the mat, went in and made myself a cuppa and finished off the cake. I made sure there was none left for my sister, she is a real guts, anyway she is slimming! Then I went back to school in time for tea.
Boy, sixteen, state boarding school

Another boy quite simply wants to see mum, and saves the school a pastoral problem.

It was my free afternoon and I felt fed up, the others went swimming,

232   The Hothouse Society

> but I went home to see my mum, she is always pleased to see me and sort of understands when things don't go right.
>
> *Boy, thirteen, secondary modern boarding school*

The next boy indicates that freedom is not automatically a threat to spiritual values. He also shows that strong contacts can be maintained with the locality and with the family, and that his friends are often from a much wider section of society than is common with boarders.

> Went to Communion and returned to make my bed, clean shoes and collected kit, etc. to take home, best way to keep it really clean. After morning chapel my mother fetched me in the car, as soon as I got home I changed, helps to forget school, then wash the car and do the usual checks on it, a friend I've known since Primary School comes round in his new mini-van, he's an apprentice electrician. After dinner to Crusader Bible Class, nice, as here I meet lots of people, know them quite well and some girls which makes a change. Go out afterwards and I drive the car with my mother and sisters to see an Uncle, have tea and watch TV football. After a long bath went back to school and had a chat with Dr F. and some boys about his new Art Appreciation club. Its chaotic but entertaining.
>
> *Boy, seventeen, boarding grammar school*

And as a final comment a small boy thinks of his weekend problem:

> If I was on janks (detention on the weekend) and I wanted to go home to see my mum, then I would tell one of the decent tempered teachers, and he would understand. He would let me go.
>
> *Boy, thirteen, technical boarding school*

Not only do children more frequently go home in some state boarding schools, but in some you need not go home at all to maintain contact with your family. The parents may come frequently to the school – sometimes a little too frequently, as the children indicate:

> My mother brought in my clean pinny on her way to the flower arrangement class, it was such a relief.
>
> *Girl, fourteen, comprehensive school*

Oh dear, my father was at it again, he is supposed to be here to help build the swimming baths with the other dads, but he tells funny stories to anyone that will listen. Most aren't funny and those that are, are usually rude. I die of embarrassment.

Girl, fifteen, secondary modern boarding school

State boarding schools with strong contacts with parents can be benefited at moments of crisis, as this girl illustrates:

I didn't mind the flu bug at all, it was even better when the staff got it, then all the parents came in, they have some sort of Association that gives money to the school, well they arranged it. Our mums looked after us and Dorothy's dad put on a white coat and looked just like Dr Kildare!

Girl, fifteen, secondary modern boarding school

But most boarders are not allowed these constant and routine contacts with home and family. Their holidays must compensate for the deprivations of term. As these boarders return there is a sense of relief and excitement, but it is sometimes clouded by curious anxieties and difficulties of adjustment. First we encounter some prep boys actually on the way home at the end of term:

Its a lovely feeling, when you're going home. A long holiday ahead, seeing your parents and brother. As the train draws out of the station, I look back, and watch the masters getting smaller and smaller, and as I see this I think of home, getting nearer, and I feel light, happy. I think, 'School isn't bad . . . but home's much better.'

Boy, thirteen, prep school

My last sight of the school was from one of the windows of the school train. As the train rounded a bend the school disappeared behind a clump of trees. An emense feeling of relief and happyness spread over me. I thought of all the enjoyable pleasures of home. When I arrived at Victoria I saw my mother waiting for my brother and I behind the barrier. It was a happy train journey. We chatted gaily of the events of the past term until we arrived home. When we arrived we had tea and then played football in the garden. Later on our friend Andy came round. *Boy, twelve, prep school*

Another prep-school boy writes:

> This train is so slow, why can't it hurry up? It's just wasting my holiday time. Why can't it just stop at High Wycombe?
> And now at last only five houses to go. Not far. I wonder if there's anything new. I wonder how my dog is. I wonder if my bedroom has changed. *Boy, twelve, prep school*

and with characteristic abandon a boy from Cromwell College returns:

> I belt down the platform and into the nearest bar. The next hour is spent in a haze of bitter and fags. You just want to smash things because you are free. *Boy, seventeen*

But others find the actual moment of return difficult:

> After school London is so noisy, the traffic seems to be tearing past, and everyone is rushing about. As you get off the train you feel almost lost. *Boy, fourteen, public school*

and for two young boys the school world seems more real and permanent than the home one:

> Each holiday I go straight to the back of the hall to put my things down, so that I am not seen by my father, because I always get embarrassed at seeing my Dad for the 1st time in six weeks.
> *Boy, thirteen, independent school*

> It was funny as the train pulled out of the station and the Master said 'goodbye'. I felt sort of *homesick*, it was funny I couldn't explain it, I just felt very unhappy probably because I am here at school more than at home. *Boy, thirteen, integrated school*

There is little doubt that for many boarders absence from home leads to a greater appreciation of the strengths of family life. Some feel home relationships have changed, leading to greater tolerance, objectivity and respect on both sides. First, a boy at an independent school thinks of home:

> Funny even here at school home is very important. I can remember people and situations much more vividly. Parents and pets are secretly pined for, and one is constantly seeking for 'homely' connections, eg the sight of a pair of slippers would bring a lump in the back of the throat!
>
> Things that are missed, are roller-skates, toast, cups of tea and things reminiscent of home life. One gets to the stage in the centre of the term where parents and home is forgotten completely (except when writing letters). Now, I have no feelings of homesickness but in the younger forms one could be miserable when thinking of home.
>
> *Boy, sixteen*

A girl at a Quaker school contrasts school and home; boarding has increased her appreciation of home:

> I never really appreciated my parents or home till I came here and then realised all the security and happiness I once had and never found here. Consequently, I now enjoy the holidays much more.
>
> I want to come back to school usually but I need to go home 'cause I have security there which isn't at school. I also feel that I could always be safe at home – and understood, which is more important.
>
> *Girl, seventeen*

At a state boarding school in the south, containing some children from broken homes, boys not so circumstanced emerge with renewed respect for their families:

> It has made me realise how grateful I should be having such a happy home and how lucky I am for having a mother and father.
>
> *Boy, seventeen*

> It has undoubtedly made me appreciate my parents more. Before,

while I was at day school, I definitely took them for granted. Living in a place without love, you learn what the love and care and worry of mum and dad really mean. Boarding has also taught me the value of helping them – home work and shopping. We respect each other more.
Boy, seventeen

For very many boarders, living away from home has another advantage: it has eased the transition to adulthood. They claim that distance has enabled their parents to recognize and adapt to their growing maturity and independence far more than if they had been living on top of each other during the process. They can handle their relationships more satisfactorily.

It has brought us closer together. I have grown up considerably and am far more independent – my parents realise this and I am treated more like a very close friend than a son.
Boy, seventeen, public school

You learn what home and parents really offer: love, 'roots', security. If you were there all the time, especially at my age, endless squabbles over silly things would spoil life. You wouldn't be so conscious of or able to enjoy the fundamental good things about your family. The same applies to them. You go away and come back a little older, more responsible, able to run your own affairs. They recognise this, it's easier for them to adapt to your growing up. Yes for me boarding has given distance and perspective but this has been gain not loss. We have learnt to realise what matters in our relationship, to see and accept the changes in each other. It has removed a lot of the friction and bitterness which day school friends have experienced. It has really helped.
Boy, eighteen, state boarding school

Public school boys sometimes take a more detached view of what home means to them. Many of the boys have been away from home since seven or eight and the loss of small comforts and constant affection is hardly mentioned. Here two boys from a public school give typical comments on home life:

One has a duty to be at home some of the time, fortunately I enjoy it. My father likes to sail and play golf, etc. I enjoy playing with him as much as playing with other friends. *Boy, eighteen*

When I am at home I like it very much indeed, but I also like to go to other places which I like and with people I like. My relations with my parents are so almost perfect that I don't *have* to be at home to help the relations prosper. Naturally they like me being at home and with them, as I do, but they quite understand if I stay with a friend etc. *Boy, seventeen*

Some children have parents abroad and their isolation causes concern:

I get on very well with them when I see them, but 1,000 miles is a long way, also one never knows quite what the situation is at home, whenever I see the word 'Congo' in the papers I am very interested but sometimes a little frightened. *Boy, sixteen, public school*

At a prep school a boy writes of his missionary parents:

I only see them once every three years, sometimes I forget what they look like or speak like and this worries me. I wish there were heathen people in Scotland, perhaps Jesus could call them there.
Boy, ten, prep school

and finally a prayer from another prep-school boy:

Jesus, my loving parents are far across the sea, send one of your army to guard them from animals which bite and men who kill, keep them well from disease.

Lord, bring their work home that they may come with it and be happy.

Lord try to make it soon I ask of you.

Amen.

Boy, twelve, prep school

But boarding does produce a gap between some boys and girls and their parents. 'A little bit of the parents goes a long way', writes one boy. These children have different interests from their parents, find home restricting and have not developed the capacity to avoid tension and clashes in family life. Naturally, many of these difficulties are common to all adolescents, and are not necessarily confined to boarders. Here a group of boarders point out how their relationships with home have deteriorated:

> I think that since I've been here, I've changed and my family has noticed it. They resent it I think; but at the same time they try and be very nice to me almost spoil me. I feel as if I were an outsider at times and I've found that I've developed two ways of speaking and two characters. One for home and one for school. At times I think my personality has been hindered by this relationship.
>
> *Girl, sixteen, progressive school*

Two boys comment at a public school in the home counties:

> The holidays at home can be a bit difficult – my parents are too curious about what I do with myself when I am on holiday or at school. If they did not ask, I would tell them. But as they question me it is difficult to tell them anything. *Boy, seventeen*

> I have a neurotic mother who hates me because I am exactly like my father – she hates him. *Boy, eighteen*

These problems could occur anywhere. For a significant minority of *boarders* the actual process of living away from home seems to have led to a real growing apart, a loss of understanding or even of affection:

> I have lost a lot of tolerance and affection for my parents and am impatient with them. *Boy, seventeen, state boarding school*

> It has removed me from my mother, especially as we are not together during the holidays much (she's out at work all day). My respect for her and sense of obligation has grown, but we have no time together, scarcely know each other any more. We have nothing to say. *Boy, seventeen, same school*

I am away from them for about two thirds of the year and it is impossible to remember everything they like you to do so when you get home you might do something which your parents don't like on the first day and a row will start and flare up throughout the holidays. I am drifting away from them.
Boy, seventeen, public school

Others, used to responsibility or independence at school, find their parents fail to recognize this:

I have been very independent and rely little on other people's help. If my parents offer help I resent it. I don't like being fussed over any more. *Boy, seventeen, independent school*

At school I have a great deal to do in the running of the place – 50 boys under me. At home, they treat me as if I was in reins with bells on. *Boy, eighteen, public school*

Another public school boy finds family interests differ from those he has developed at school:

I would find always being at home a strain. The holidays are quite enough because there is a general lack of people with any interests akin to my own (except my mother and she is very 'wholly!') A bourgeois and superficial society – shooting, drinking, conversationalists. I feel bored much of the time and a stranger with many of my family's 'friends'. *Boy, seventeen*

Some realize they are better educated than their parents and this isolates them:

It has affected me a great deal. When I went to school I was quite happy at home, but now I despise my parents and don't look forward to the vacation at all. *Boy, fifteen, vocational school*

I find sometimes that I want to get right away and go and have a good time. Mum bosses a bit. I know I am right in arguments

because I know I am better educated than her; this doesn't help
either.
Boy, seventeen, public school

Another public school boy voices the common complaint of teenagers against:

> Petty restrictions and lack of recognition of the adolescent desire for freedom. Parents regard me as thoroughly irresponsible. Atmosphere of considerable tension most of the time. Parents invariably overworked and tired.
> *Boy, seventeen, public school*

Sometimes the girls find the contrast between the excitement and gossip of school with dull family life is disappointing:

> Sometimes I get so bored I could scream. They wonder why I get ratty! All they do is watch TV and polish the car. They never go anywhere!
> *Girl, sixteen, Quaker school*

and even prep-school boys get a little disillusioned:

> When the holidays come it isn't all that wonderful. You trail everywhere behind your mother who is in a dreadful hat, and I'm in a hot gray suit with people saying 'Hasn't he grown', 'Isn't he like his father'.
> *Boy, twelve, prep school*

For younger children the effects of removal from home are much deeper and are greater than for seniors, but they are able only to hint at what they feel in telling images:

> When you live away from home you don't have your old mum saying put you coat on its cold outside you learn to live more by yourself, but you do miss your mum sometimes.
> *Boy, twelve, secondary modern boarding school*

and another boy:

> I miss my mum and dad and brother very much indeed. I also miss my big plate of dinner.
> *Boy, thirteen, state boarding school*

and here a little boy's tenuous link with home is his teddy bear. Its significance and removal receive consideration in a later book. He talks into a tape recorder because he cannot write very well yet.

> My Teddy helps me when I cry, it is from home, he's a bit old but I like him, Mummy always tucks us up and we say our prayers. I worry 'cause next year when I am in the big boys dormitories they take teddies away and I shall be by myself.
>
> *Boy, seven, prep school*

This chapter has tried to trace the contacts between boarder and the outside world. It should be realized that contact with outside society will always be a problem for schools, as much of the process of education depends on postponing immediate, transitory satisfactions for future, long-term benefits, and in this the schools and parents claim to know better than the children. In the boarding school this general situation is exacerbated by the division between the inside and outside society and the pupil's experience in shuttling back and forth between the two. The outside world is then a challenge. But what of the world, or worlds within?

8 The Inner World

So far we have dealt largely with the officially laid-down system of things, with children's descriptions of and reactions to the formal structure and pattern of boarding school existence. Now we delve beneath that formal world and into an inner world, one constructed and ruled by the children themselves. 'I am sitting on top of a volcano,' a headmaster said to us. 'I often don't know what's bubbling beneath the surface until something erupts.'

Groups living in institutions create little societies of their own – within the wider society of which they are all members. The staff in the boarding school is a world of its own – and one where the conventions of behaviour and attitude, the controls used and the system of status may differ markedly from that laid down by the official system and with considerable effect on it for good or ill. The children always have their own society too – with its own unwritten codes of conduct and values, handed down to each new generation and modified by each generation; its own system of controls for enforcing these codes; its own pecking-order of power and status (which may conflict strongly with that of the school – a boy with high power and status among his peers often never attains it in the official school hierarchy); its own élite groups, outcasts and divisions; its own culture, rituals, subterranean activities and private language; its own compensations and way of regarding and even using the staff and that other, official, world for its own purposes. Every child is involved in some way in this inner world and all schools have one. It need be neither lurid nor damaging to the official world.

What differs between schools is the way in which the formal world penetrates the informal one. In some schools staff–pupil relations or patterns of culture, or the hierarchy, or groupings of children, or channels of status coincide with or consciously exploit the children's own groupings or hierarchy, or culture and so on. The pupil world is thus broken up and diversified, one group is protected against another, and many are subtly directed to the school's own ends. In other schools the two worlds are separate, sometimes almost completely. In these schools the pupil society is autonomous, its codes, values, controls and practices can apply uniformly over the whole pupil society, counting much more than the school's official ones, and exercising an impact much more formative, inescapable and profound. If the values of the pupil society are directed towards those of the school then the school will be more effective in realizing its own, but if the pupil world is indifferent or hostile to the official values, these stand little chance of being effective when the inner world is so homogeneous. This relation between the official and unofficial worlds is the critical point in the effectiveness of all schools and particularly of boarding schools, where the aims are so often wide and varied and the pupil society is inevitably so much more powerful. In some schools the authorities have little inkling of what is going on underneath – not so much in the way of spicy vice, but in social controls or pupils' values. Occasionally an incident – a boy found drunk or in bed with another, a girl running away, an indiscreet new boy, a puzzled parent, an accidentally intercepted letter – brings the official world face to face with an aspect of the one underneath. There is an inquiry, punishments, vigilance, exhortations, changes, but then things settle down again, and the children's world continues as ever, much of it concealed, its more trivial aspects meshing day-to-day in tussles over discipline, attitudes and activity with the official world.

The boy or girl arriving at the school faces then not only the business of assimilation into the official system (described in chapter three) but also into the inner society of the pupils. This can be difficult and has its own procedures, varying drastically with the character of a school.

At a progressive school, an eighteen-year-old boy provides a recipe for acceptance – stressing the newcomer's need to make himself interesting, and adding a caution about mistakes which would cause social ruin in the progressive school:

244   The Hothouse Society

To be accepted this person should not be wearing grey flannel trousers; he should not impose himself on 'the old hands' as many people do in the glory of 'their new found progressive freedom'. It would be fatal for him to call a teacher 'Sir', this would retard his social entry by at least a year. But the most important thing is to be quiet, and make people think he has something that they don't have, eg. that he is a Junkie (a drug taker), or something. After this comes rapid social entry. Even when his new-found friends discover that he wasn't anything special, he has still made his basic 'entry' after that he can conform vaguely to his friends' opinions. Then when he is settled he can say exactly what he wants. Length of time? About two terms for the whole process. We live in a very conservative, socially discriminating society here.

By contrast the newcomer at a great public school discovers the niceties of the pupil hierarchy, of obeying the sacrosanct laws of status, of watchful but close relations with staff, of keeping in the background and repressing any displays of enthusiasm:

He should not walk on anything no one else of roughly his status in the school did not walk on.
Boy, seventeen

He should not talk of his prep school or ever wear its tie. He should listen rather than talk. He should try and make friends with the most junior men, and take an interest in as many sports as possible. This does not mean he should be particularly keen as this is a bad thing. He should attempt to learn and make friends with as many of the staff as possible who will give him advice.
Boy, fourteen

Scholars shouldn't sit at the end of the table at breakfast or you'll be sitting next to the Housemaster.
   Do what you're told to do, by staff and prefects, for the first few weeks. Be careful not to raise yourself to a higher level than you are at – there's plenty of things you're not meant to do till you're a 1 year, 2 year man, etc.
Boy, sixteen

He should know who the masters are, and thus to whom he should take off his hat, which avoids such embarrassing spectacles as taking off one's hat to the dustbin man who looks like a master and not to a master who looks like a dustbin man.

Boy, seventeen

At the Lady Margaret Foundation a new boy, entering at thirteen, should plunge straight into the underculture with its own activities, code of generosity and distinctive vocabulary. Typical advice is:

The first thing to do when you come here you go down the bogs (TOILETS) and have a fag and join in with faggers congregation and you will have a good muck-about with all of or most of the boys; you have a couple of HOMOs and you would be wise not to search boys for fags, because they hide near their prick; you should hand your fags round and not be a fucking Jew. Most of the prefects here are quite good blokes except for basteads who take your fags.

Boy, fourteen

Though less hardy spirits advise:

DON'T COME, it is horrible, you get beaten up every day.

Boy, thirteen

In a state boarding school, one where the underworld is more inclined to support of the official one, the recipe for an arrival of the same age is more complex: a mixture of work and achievement, distance from staff and cutting a dash, both sartorially and in behaviour.

In the first few weeks you must work fairly hard. Don't stick round the teachers. Do something that the other boys admire you for, but don't enter too much into the spirit of school life. Have a good set of casual clothes. Be daring and cheeky to the teachers and don't obey your House official. Try to be the best in your year at a certain thing. Have a girl friend and snog her. Be defiant to some of the teachers. Get on well with the elder boys. Don't mix with the Juniors.

Boy, thirteen, state boarding school

Some schools have initiation ceremonies into the children's society –

246   The Hothouse Society

not just the formal learning of school lore and language, to be tested later by the prefects at an exam, which still takes place in some public schools.

At one school a new boy

> was told that new Scholars had the tradition of doing it. But it was up to you. They dared me to – so I did. At midnight I ran round the quad in the nude wearing only (a must) a watch on the left wrist. Was it chilly! But its given me a reputation for guts.
>
> *Boy, thirteen, public school*

The ceremony is not always voluntary, as the encounter below reveals. The boys at this school all wore long narrow belts as part of their uniform.

> A bunch of them (the seniors) got us (the new boys) in the changing room and made us run 'the gauntlet' – run under a tunnel of arms while they whacked or pinged us with their belts. The bastards, did it sting! If you yelped or cried, they called you yellow and wet and they didn't let you forget it quick either. 'Here's yellow arse'. etc.
>
> *Boy, thirteen, direct grant school*

Not all newcomers are noticed. In some schools they are coldly reminded that they are outsiders, but are warned not to take the insiders at face value.

> Don't expect anybody to take any visible notice of you. They will notice you as soon as you walk out of a room they will all talk about you, but don't be upset if you are not regarded as a terrific novelty. Be friendly. If people talk to you, talk back and don't go out of your way not to talk to anyone. People tend to pretend to be something they are not here. They will seem to pretend being a king or a slavedriver or God but they are not, they are a person. You're going to have a hard time, if you sink you'll be unhappy, if you swim you'll be happy. And people like you much better if you're happy.
>
> *Girl, seventeen, progressive school*

Having entered, been tested and perhaps in the process gained an

The Inner World 247

initial reputation which it will be difficult to lose, the newcomer becomes a member of the inner society and comes to terms with its demands. In some schools, particularly those where there is a pronounced style of life, or where the formal structure is limited and the pupil society is therefore all the more dominant (as in some progressive schools), or where that society is strictly homogeneous, these demands may be strong. Somewhat cynically, but not inaccurately, a girl sums them up:

> Did you know that very few can survive the 'breaking in' of Roborough. After about one month or so the individual REALLY loses a lot of individuality – he is a Roburian – liked or unliked – he's a Roburian. Very few can remain like they were before they came here. Everyone has to gradually bow down and fit into their slot (and STAY there).
> *Girl, seventeen*

Some feel very strongly the pressures to conform, as in this minor public school:

> Never try to oppose the 'will' of the Common Room even though that 'will' may be against school or moral principles. The Common Room is like a closed Trade Union.
> *Boy, sixteen*

Or from another progressive school (here the very unconventionality of the school produces a pressure to conform, this time from the pupil society itself):

> Although this is a very unconventional school, everyone has the same type of unconventionalness and the social pressures to do what everyone else does are just as strong here as anywhere else its just that our 'convention' is different from everywhere else's.
> *Girl, sixteen, progressive school*

Pressures to conform to *what*? The children's society has its own codes of conduct and values: things that are approved of and things which are disapproved of or scarcely tolerated – and woe to him who transgresses the latter. One most obvious and universal 'rule' or norm –

it applies in all schools – is not to sneak on your fellows to the staff. Many children will undergo any rigour rather than violate this norm.

> They don't practice anything they preach. One thing here is you never grass on your mates but the head-master had me in his study for three hours trying to get me to tell him who was smoking with me. It was awful, I'd rather have had ten of the strap.
> *Boy, fourteen, state boarding school*

Some such norms apply only to particular kinds of school. In public schools and prep schools, for example, it is often the done thing among the pupils not to display too much of one's feelings, never to be over-enthusiastic or behave like a spontaneous child. This norm arises partly from the school's ideal of educating a governing élite in which emotional reactions might be out of place, partly from early training in 'adult' attributes and partly from the hurt which the pupil might suffer by exposing his inner self to the gaze and criticism of his contemporaries. Progressive and state boarding schools – where prep school training has been missed, the cultural background is different and the school does not aim at producing a governing élite – do not seem to produce this norm. Here are a few examples typical of many others.

> Never show your emotions here. *Boy, seventeen, public school*

> Never become too intense, it makes you vulnerable. Don't exhibit unbridled enthusiasm – it leaves you wide open to criticism. Be casual, easy going and don't let them see you're really deep. Above all, keep up a pose. *Boy, eighteen, public school*

> Keep your feelings to yourself – spare us the embarrassment.
> *Boy, sixteen, public school*

> Try not to speak with a treble voice. Do not cry at all as it is important that you should not seem childish. Never play conkers.
> *Boy, thirteen, public school*

The Inner World

We shall now examine a few typical codes which govern the inner world. First, let us look at codes which largely (but not entirely) express the pupil society's attitude to the official set-up, and then turn to those which regulate the inner world itself.

Here from one public school is a very representative list of things which a boy aged thirteen to sixteen should or should not do according to norms of most pupils. These show that the pupils' society supports the school's own official structure and ends – as they exist in most public schools: they permit achievement at work and play, close relations with staff, 'character' and fair play, obedience to authority, respect for hierarchy, control of feeling and convictions and manliness (not using Christian names).

Should do

Play games hard and 'go in' for as many peripheral activities as he can, but don't parade 'keenness'.

Always protest when he thinks a prefect has done him an injustice – tactfully of course. The prefect is just as keen to see fairness as the victim is.

Cultivate good relations with housemaster (outwardly), with subject and younger masters (really).

Should not do

Work but not too hard. Efficiency rather than quality. If you like it, don't be conspicuous.

Be fresh with those in authority in a way that is not tolerable.

Get a bad reputation. A good reputation is a cover for many vices (drinking, smoking, ragging etc.).

Lose temper when teased – it is bad for the character.

Shouldn't get out of bed to pray. Keep your piety to yourself.

Go to matron unless entirely necessarily.

Shouldn't talk about his home.

Shouldn't call anybody except his own immediate circle by their Christian names. *Boy, seventeen*

In other schools, the pupil society is ambivalent towards the official one – it will support some of its aspects and values but not others.

250 The Hothouse Society

This is particularly so in integrated schools, where the boys from LEA backgrounds support the academic ends of the school but not so much the wider moral, social or cultural ones. The following extract from a public school with a large number of able integrants is typical. Note the emphasis on work, the refusal to accept pastoral or overweening power figures among the boys, the non-conservative tendency, the stress on soccer (a game officially banned in the school), and the tone of 'mod' hardness and cynicism. These norms are for boys of fifteen and upwards:

> Don't be a homosexual, but do not boast about heterosexual achievement.
> Don't be an exhibitionist, but be in evidence.
> Be of a certain standard at rugger, hockey, and athletics but no enthusiasm!!
> Be very good at soccer and know something about it.
> Regard the school rules and such masters as make it their business to enforce them with mild contempt.
> Put officious prefects and those who pry in personal affairs in their place.
> Keep your distance from the staff – but get to know a few well and their wives.
> Work counts here, provided you don't narrow yourself as a result – don't display your brilliance.
> Cultivate hardness, but not fanatic. No chips. Mild neurosis, however, isn't frowned upon.
> Go for the esoteric in music (but anything classical).
> Read Penguin books. Wash. Don't be afraid of using after-shave, talc, etc.
> Don't be a militant Tory (but you can be a Nazi, or, of course, a Leftist).
> Be a Christian if you like, but not evangelical.
> Swear healthily, and don't mind excessive swearing.

In a group of schools containing a few public, and some state and some independent schools the pupil system was almost entirely alienated from the official aims. Here is a very typical comment from a state boarding school, where almost the whole official system – work, social ends, fair play and staff – were rejected by a dominant pupil culture (boys twelve to fifteen):

> Don't sneak, be cheeky to staff and don't worry about getting caned. Respect 5th formers, bully first formers. Look down your nose at 2nd and 3rd forms. Try and show the masters up, but never, never creep round them. Play football well – rugby's the school game. Don't swot. Hate this dump. *Boy, fourteen*

More sophisticated but no less alienated are the norms of the majority of middling and senior boys in an independent school. They express themselves in cynicism, conscious exploitation of the system and repression. The following set is typical:

> Keep in with your housemaster but try and maintain a neutral basis (i.e. don't speak to him unless he speaks to you and then no more than you have to). 'Creep' up some masters if you feel you can be sure of getting something out of it, otherwise do not fraternize with them. Don't complain to the head or the chaplain, its no use. Try and give an all round sense of balance to other people and if you have any peculiarities do not show them. This school doesn't want individuals.
> Always be impartial as far as possible when dealing with officials. If once show sides you will be marked down.
> Always be good at rugger or cricket preferably but if this is not possible do not try at any other game, it is a waste of time and you will not get anywhere in this school.
> Work reasonably hard: your success here is independent of the staff, you can even get your own back in a way they can't complain about. Prefects are either moronic yes-men, or (they have to be) hypocrites: learn to recognise the difference. Be ultra-careful, if you become one. Become a sacristan or any other official able to be appointed without official sanction. Its the only position you'll have without losing your integrity. *Prefect, eighteen*

Such is the range of responses of the pupil society to the official

252 The Hothouse Society

one. But the pupil society itself can be dominated by its own norms and style. How powerful the pupil culture can be is seen in this letter of a jaded girl at a progressive school to a prospective newcomer.

> Dear friend,
> Do you really want to come here? I don't advise you to because you used to go to prep school, you have a crew cut, you wear glasses, you feel more comfortable in baggy trousers. You are shy, aren't you? You want to be an atomic research scientist don't you? You are a sucker for bullies too if I remember rightly? Well, *don't* come your life will ruined, but if you are the sort of boy who doesn't notice other people, thats O.K. you will go along in your own way and be out of it. But if you care what people say and if you like things to be all in order you will be a quivering wreck by the time you leave. Do little things make you enthusiastic? Well if they don't your O.K. but if they do thats too bad. Dear friend, stay at your prep school and be made to run round the football pitch twice a day, it will do you good! (After all, you don't want to lose your energy by smoking and saunter around in bare feet and grow your hair like a girl and behave like a girl, except of course you will be sexy with the girls, that is expected of you – do you?)
>
> Love from —

In some schools, coeducational and progressive ones in particular, there are strict norms of dress and of appearance.

> The right clothes are a necessity: old jeans, thin large jumpers. Mod clothes for school. If she is a bitch she wouldn't get on at all.
> *Girl, eighteen, progressive school*

> Clothes should not be too loud, except in a few cases. No tie, and not proper trousers, except cordroys. Hair should be at least on the ears but not on to the shoulders. Bare feet aren't de rigueur.
> *Boy, seventeen, progressive school*

In other schools there are equally strict norms on social relationships. In public schools a very common pupil regulation keeps age groups distinct, partly to preserve the authority-obedience hierarchy by social distance, partly to control homosexuality:

> Not to associate with anyone more than a year older or a year younger than you.
> *Boy, fifteen, public school*

> Keep to your own age group and your safe.
> *Boy, sixteen, public school*

In some of the several schools where certain kinds of homosexuality are fashionable (see Chapter 11), the norm may be the exact reverse of the above – ordaining contact across the years. Here are two typical comments:

> If you want to be in with the crowd, grab a junior quick, and use him supposedly, as your 'bum-boy'.
> *Boy, sixteen, independent school*

> He should have a little boy. Don't have a lisp or stammer. Walk properly. Don't ask too many questions. Don't critisize other blokes with little boys. Learn the 'language'.
> *Boy, seventeen, independent school*

Contact with the other sex can equally be prescribed – even in a lonely public school, isolated in a fastness far from girls:

> You must say you have a girl friend and talk about her – even if you are pretending.
> *Boy, sixteen, public school*

In one or two coeducational schools it becomes the norm to pair off with a girl. Those who do not are considered misfits or 'queer', and even juniors are expected to follow the pattern:

> Julie's my girl friend – she's in 1B, I meet her at breaks. Everyone has a girl friend here.
> *Boy, twelve, coeducational school*

Later on there is a code regulating contact between sexes:

Not to get involved with one boy on their second day but on the other hand not flirt with all of them because they get embarrassed and start being nasty. If the boys get nasty and ask awkward questions ignore them. Don't be prudish about drinking or smoking but don't hop into bed with a bloke just because he's nice to you because being promiscuous will wreck the rest of your time here. You'll never live it down. *Girl, seventeen, progressive school*

In a very few schools, social relations are brutal, the pupil code keeps them so and society is ruled by gang morality and violence.

Be handy with your fists. Have a fight as soon as possible. Regard juniors as scum. Smoke and follow the form leaders. Mods are not acceptable. *Boy, fifteen, state boarding school*

Get your big friends to protect you.
Boy, thirteen, independent school

In the vast majority of schools tolerance – within limits – is the rule, how otherwise would boarders survive such close and public living where you

must not be bashful when seen naked.
Boy, fourteen, integrated school

Tolerance then is essential whether you are a prefect:

Do not use threats. Do not unnecessarily be rude to those below you. Their willing cooperation is essential. Friendly persuasion being much better than brute force in most cases at this school.
Prefect, eighteen, public school

or just a bright sixth-former:

There must be a lack of affectation.
Within that homosexuality, fraternisation with masters who are not considered 'good blokes', over-done exhibitionism are all

taboo: brutality and neo-passion are taboo. He who goes to any extreme will be rejected. It is better to be a hermit and a recluse than to impose oneself. It is wise to assume that one treats all with a certain amount of respect for their 'natural rights' although it will emerge that some are universally despised.

Boy, seventeen, public school

Toleration imposes some restraint on oneself:

> Let your moderation be known unto all men, ie don't be too reticent or they won't know about it, or too brash and self-centred so that it won't be moderation. *Boy, seventeen, public school*

In some schools, small ones or others where the level of intelligence is high, there may even be norms about cultural styles, not as regards pop music (the reign of which is universal) but in intellectual approaches or styles. At one progressive school it is essential to approximate to an eccentric existentialist:

> You shouldn't have too many fixed ideas, your mind ought to be free to circulate. I don't mean that you must be weak minded, but a person of fixed ideas, or a moralist, is not regarded as interesting. If you have long hair you are usually accepted easier, this is because people with long hair are usually rather eccentric existentialists already. I think that anyone who is different will get on here quite easily.
>
> If you are a loud mouthed talker then this is the place for you.
>
> *Boy, eighteen*

At another school sophisticated cynicism is the accepted mode:

> Thou shalt have a face for everybody.
>
> *Boy, eighteen, public school*

> 1st essential – thin veneer of cynicism – anything passes under this layer – provided you don't mind being labelled pejoratively for it. Hearty hetero is 'au fait' but easiest solution (my solution) is to

adopt God-the-father aloofness. School rules are of mainly academic interest.
Boy, seventeen, public school

In sharp contrast are the cruder norms of some integrated schools with working-class boys of less ability who are often alienated from the school: a mixture of sex, violence, pop and generosity.

be good at ball sports.
know some good sick and dirty jokes
hate the 'old bag' (the matron)
have some spirit ie break a window now and again or punch up someone
pretend to be a queer but not in fact to be one (as far as I am concerned)
like the Rolling Stones.
Boy, sixteen, integrated school

You shouldn't carve obscene words and pictures on the doors and walls, or smoke.
Boy, fifteen, integrated school

Should not hide food, fags, etc. from others. Should not masturbate in public. Should not believe in God or conscienscously go to church.
Boy, fourteen, integrated school

These then are some of the norms which govern the pupils' world. What happens if a pupil violates one of the more important ones? The other boys or girls then bring into force a whole battery of controls by which to bring the deviant back to the norm or to keep him as an outcast from their society. Force, which we shall illustrate in a moment, is one such control. But boarding, living in a closed community, with very little privacy and no escape, provides other and equally compelling controls, both verbal and social.

Reputation is one. One false mistake and the reputation you immediately gain can brand you for the rest of your time, day in, day out, perhaps for years of your life. A girl warns of this:

A decent new girl has to take it easy when she arrives. She must take a good look before choosing one out of the supposedly many ad-

miring boys. If she jumps STRAIGHT into someone she'll probably have to live with a 'scrubber' tag for a long time. She'll be dirt to all the nice boys.
Girl, seventeen, progressive school

A boy entering at fourteen a school where most pupils start at eleven violates the anti-piety norm of his contemporaries; he earns a nickname which will last and control his apparent eccentricity:

Some kid straight from a prep school kneels down beside his bed to pray to Jesus. So Fatty Foster shouts out 'Hey, wet pants, this isn't your old dump, you have to go downstairs, don't piss on the floor!' He didn't kneel down again, but we call him the 'Rev.' just in case.
Boy, fourteen, direct grant school

Sarcasm or cynicism or mimicry can also be used as a group control and repeatedly on offenders. Here the cruel streak in children invariably finds its target:

We have this boy, he's strange. He creeps round the masters like mad: hands up first, open doors for them and so on, asks 'what's for prep tonight?' when we all are hoping that the old bugger had forgotten it. This boy's got a hair lip – so we call him Tally (for Thalidomide) and now whenever he asks a question in class we all curl up our front lips and draw in our breath loudly.
Boy, fifteen, independent school

'Clarence' we call him, he's got a posh voice from some snob school and is a bit of a drip. Whenever he opens his mouth, one of us says something like 'Eowh, how frightfully spiffing, Clarence, old chap' – the stupid poncy nit.
Boy, sixteen, state boarding school

Ngomo's a nigger but we're not anti-black at all really, its just we didn't want him hanging round with us all the time, he wasn't wanted but wouldn't take a hint. So we waited in the corridor until a junior boy came along and then said loud enough to be heard in Ngomo's study 'Hey, nig-nog wants you!' 'What for?' says he. 'For dinner' we yelled. He's never bothered us since.
Boy, sixteen, independent school

Supplementing verbal controls come the social ones, again so much more powerful in the inescapable boarding-school society:

> We shun him – if he sits on the left of the form, we all sit on the right, if he sits in the middle, then the form sit round the edge. In the Common Room he's not allowed near the radiator.
> *Boy, sixteen, integrated school*

> Congreve's queer. *We* don't like them here. Whenever he comes down the corridor people stand aside and go 'Eeeuggh!' and say 'Backs to the wall chaps, here comes Congers!'
> *Boy, fifteen, public school*

> We knew Eileen had told Mr S. that we had missed music practice, so at all meals today no-one said anything or passed anything to her. Patsy came back from the farm with some hay, tied it into a small bundle and put it on Eileen's bed with a note 'From one cow to another'. That'll learn her. *Girl, fifteen, coeducational school*

Force however might be used in many schools for certain cases, irrespective of the existence of corporal punishment in the official system, or such elevated precepts as:

> NON-BRUTALITY in everyday relations with contemporaries
> *Boy, eighteen, public school*

Sometimes the controls are relatively mild:

> The bastard would – in a lower form – get punched, his ears flicked and pencil-box filched. *Boy, sixteen, public school*

Sometimes those in authority connive at the use of informal power as it helps their own more formal control:

> Lights out and we scragged Jones for what he'd done – the rotten spas. Bedclothes on floor and biffed him hard where it hurts. The dorm monitor pretended to be asleep as he knew what Jones had

done, but when Jones started to cry he told us to belt up, so we went to sleep.
Boy, eleven, prep school

Occasionally offenders against the pupils' code get more violent punishments:

We call ourselves the 'Samuri' after that old film at the club. Anyone who gets out of line in our year or a bit uppity, we fix. A note goes in his desk – 'Your next' – they're shit-scared, a duff over, heads in the wash basins four or 5 times. The prefects do fuck all – it helps keep the Middle School quiet.
Boy, sixteen, independent school

Nothing would be said to him unless it was intended to remind him of what he had done. He would generally be treated like dirt, ie his bed would probably be dismantled into about a dozen pieces and distributed through the house, he might get his hair cut, or have various other unpleasantries done, such as dubbining his balls and squeezing toothpaste up his arse.
Boy, seventeen, state boarding school

Girls prefer verbal or refined utilitarian controls:

Well, Jenny needed a lesson didn't she, so we all got busy and tied up all her shoelaces in hundreds of knots and sewed up her buttonholes on coats and dresses. They must have taken hours to undo. Serve her b— well right!
Girl, fifteen, coeducational school

From the codes of conduct and modes of control of the pupil world, we turn for the rest of this chapter to its structure, to the differing human constellations of which it is composed. The society of the pupils subdivides naturally into groups:

Closed cliques in definite age groups. Only those are admitted who fulfil the definite but unwritten entrance requirements for each group: the smokers, hearties, swots, intelligentsia and smart guys. Those not in a group are sorry pictures, true outcasts.
Boy, seventeen, public school

At the top of the informal world are the 'in-crowds', groups of senior pupils who think themselves, or are thought by the others, to be the setters of norms and fashions and conduct throughout the school, élites, in other words. Sometimes only the 'in-crowd' thinks itself 'in', but in some schools – small schools, progressive schools and some public schools in particular – true 'in-crowd' élites arise and wield considerable influence. Why this should occur in some societies and not in others we leave our companion volume to analyse. Here we can only describe. First a member of a powerful 'in' élite at a public school outlines its characteristics and sums up the other groups (a 'nonny' is a nonentity):

He should either be a 'crank', a 'non-entity' or a 'mod'. If he's a nonny then the school will go by him, he'll be alright for himself; he'll find other nonnies, and they'll all be happy together. If he's a crank then he (apparently or actually) tries to get as far up any master as possible. The main difference between this sort of fingering and that employed by the 'in crowd' is that the 'in crowd' are *in* very definitely. To be a real swinger and be a member of the elite 'with it lot', you have to be discreetly mod, either a nigger/cricket player or a literary genius (music is not really acceptable), you have to be 100% conversant with 'pop', but at the same time be 'secretly' fond of modern music (anything post c. Ravel). Have to have a 'good' Christian name, smoke, flaunt rules, but obey them, etc.

Boy, seventeen, public school

At two progressive schools the 'in-crowds', again very influential in practice, have similar ingredients. A hostile girl of sixteen at one school describes such groups:

Unfortunately, I find that there is rather a division between the so-called 'select' people and the 'unselect' ones. Especially in females, chosen by males on what you wear, say, look like, who you go around with, etc. eg if you have super clothes, are funny, pretty and have a boyfriend, you're more likely to be accepted into 'the bunch' than if you wear long skirts, are terribly good (never swear), ugly, and go around on your own, or with people like yourself. Often if people spend all their free time, working in the library they are looked down on (unfortunately).

A boy of seventeen at Stanton describes another:

> They should be in-crowd minded, only enthusiastic about obscure angles of the arts in a modern sense, ie some way out film one should admire, or some sort of pop art. Intelligence is greatly admired if used in the right way and hated if used in the wrong way. Intelligence should be applied to 'in' things and new weird ideas on 'in' subjects (the arts). PS definitely not too serious.

An 'in-crowd' of quite a different sort appears in a minor public school in a remote area:

> The group here which counts are the rugger players – they're nearly all house or school prefects anyway, tasselled caps in studies, read back page of papers first, think Saturday afternoons *the* climax of the week, and Twickenham *the* high spot of Michaelmas term, drink and swear a bit on the side, look tough (but can be kind), like to seem dim, finger in all pies. Come to think of it, this school is run from that ruddy pavilion.
>
> *Boy, seventeen*

Conspicuous in most schools – though they are very seldom 'in' in any sense except in their own estimations – are the self-styled intelligentsia. A sympathetic school captain of eighteen at a state boarding school urged us to see them:

> The intellectuals hover around Dawson – who runs the magazine and is filling in time before Cambridge. They write, drink coffee all day, are very smooth and intense – you should go down there they'd love you – they gather in the old barn – a beautiful place. They write to the newspapers, take all the in-magazines, run two competing ones of their own, visit everything in London thats 'with it'. On the fringe of these but still 'in' are the Artists, a bohemian group who never get up, who don't wash, won't play games, but paint frantically or make things out of old pianos and washing machines.

Musicians are a bit like that as well, they are all at the old barn or go down there to play tennis or bowls or croquet, to swoon over the roses, the lawns, the flowers and the little boys – Oh yes, they all pretend to be Queer as hell – Pettock must be he spends ages with the little kids, says he 'is interested in their problems', all got nice faces though – but that's his affair. They are good for the school, alive, a bit of a laugh. They get all the awards, they are rather nice in a harmless sort of way.

Not all boys regard them with sympathy:

There's that group which think they're a society unto themselves. I know them all fairly well – longish hair and longer talk. They are always talking about phases in their lives and starting a new one. Well, I'm not stupid but I can't see the 'phases' they talk about in *my* life, except child to adult – adult to grave. A load of PSEUDS,
Boy, seventeen, public school

The pseudo-intellectuals. They go around talking nonsense about Freud and obscure poets: they wear cheap perfume and flourish in the art studio, where they fall into the habit of doing no prep and become flabby effeminate things. *Boy, seventeen, public school*

Pseudos who claim to have seen everything in life and condescend to rules and routine, who moralise and are immoral, theorise and are mixed up. *Boy, seventeen, same school*

Towards the top of some public schools there emerge groups of 'smoothies', polished, exhibiting smartness and sometimes wealth:

You can tell them by their smell – brylcreem and Chanel, No. 5, by their dress, tapered trousers, 12 pairs of shoes, soigné hairstyles, by their talk, of the parties they went to at half term, the exquisite lunch they had last Sunday leave-out, the bright young thing, try-to-be-deb type girl friends who occasionally appear. They laugh very loudly so as to be noticed but aren't really very amused. They centre on Thomson-Burdett's study – his father's a baronet or something – pots of money. They don't do much harm, I suppose – or *do* anything else! *Boy, eighteen, public school*

Among other common groups of seniors are the professional 'antis' or 'bolshies', as they are still known in some schools – alienated and often clever. We shall meet them again in the last chapter.

Endless intense groaners, cynics, see good and use in nothing, break all rules, have to be *anti* everything, invite punishment, tend to hang about together but aren't close friends, hate the place yet obsessed by it – talk of nothing else. Professional pains in the neck.
Boy, seventeen, public school

But these boys in turn see some of their critics as

the 'yes' men. Those gutless, nauseating lifeless people who never stop sucking up to their 'superiors' and generally are good to an inhuman extent because they are afraid and haven't enough conviction to do anything else, or to disagree with all these stupid rules, puffed up prefects and smug little dictatorial housemasters. Our dead contemporaries old before their time, they gain power because they will do everything they're told.
Boy, seventeen, same school

Lower down in the school certain distinctive groups also emerge among the fourteen to fifteen year olds, gregarious adolescents who are in the doldrums, seeking to express identity, but without defined status in the community, neither eager fags or new boys, nor holders of responsibility, not even sobered by the imminence of public examinations. They appear, almost identically, in schools of many kinds.

Boys who go around in narrow trousers and cuban heeled elastic sided boots, they have loud mouths and do little except make fun of others and smoke. *Boy, seventeen, public school*

The yobs, usually IVth, gangs of 6 or 7 of them, they go around making life miserable for a minority of people. They play records of the Rolling Stones at full volume, wear cheap cologne, long hair, smoke (clandestinely), drink (likewise), love to be heard, drag their feet and seem incredibly tough. Individually they're spineless.

Boy, seventeen, public school

It is usually between this age group and younger boys that bullying occurs in some secondary schools, not, as is so often thought, between seventeen and eighteen year olds and the younger boys:

> Those gangs fairly junior in the school who hang together for their own protection, they feel big and inflated and are rowdy and bully any boys who are in any way weak or peculiar.
>
> *Boy, seventeen, public school*

One boy sums up their attitude:

> If theres one thing that makes me puke its juniors who think that they have got basic human rights. *Boy, fifteen, public school*

Outside all groups are some outcasts, or 'misfits', as they are frequently known. At one state boarding school they might be

> Very posh, big headed or very shy. *Boy, fourteen*

> A weakling, or bunker (absconder). Posh. *Boy, fourteen*

At another school dealing with cases of need, an outcast would be someone who:

> Hangs around masters,
> Gets big boys to protect him
> Wets his bed (or wets himself)
> A snob. *Boy, fourteen, integrated school*

At a public school an outcast would typically be

> someone distinguished at nothing, bad at games and work and

is not sociable or counts in the house. If he greases round a beak so much the worse for him. *Boy, seventeen, public school*

Some outcasts, however, retain their dignity:

I stand aloof. 'Odi profanum vulgus et arceo' – Horace Odes.
Boy, seventeen, public school

Ignored always by school inspectors, neglected by educationists and sometimes even by those in daily contact with the children, the values and structures of the pupil society profoundly condition the school's effectiveness in achieving its ends, whether academic, social, moral or physical, and they deeply affect each individual child's development, performance and well-being. They clearly deserve more systematic attention. But even so they do not exhaust the culture created by the pupil society, which generates modes of expression and a rich underlife of its own.

9 The Underworld

Of the many expressions of the under-society, we shall concentrate on three: language, illicit activity, and relationships both between staff and pupils and among the pupils themselves.

Boarding schools often generate their own language as part of the process of establishing their corporate identity and maintaining separateness from other organizations. In some, the private language is sanctioned by the official system, printed dictionaries are circulated and staff and boys and old boys all use the accepted terminology. But in many schools the children's society has its own language, expressing its own identity – a language which may change rapidly from generation to generation and may be largely unknown to the staff.

To the sociologist this private vocabulary, often ostensibly nonsensical or obscene, is of considerable importance, as it helps to establish the scale of values, the orientations and social relationships of the users. Basically, there are two forms. First there is the translation of ordinary vocabulary into the private one of the pupil society. A language system thus results. A girl at a progressive school explains how it is done (or was done – it changes rapidly as the 'in' crowds develop the language):

1. Adding – mble to all possible words: grimble = grim
   yemble = yes
   Variant + archikarna eg yemblearchikarna = yes
2. Consonants in middle of words changed to mm – smammer
   bimmer = bitter, now means unhappy
   Also end consonants to m: slim = slick
   breams = breaks (knickers)

3. Adding – mper to ends of words
   breampers = breasts
   lempters = legs
4. Proper names attached to things: =
   Oswald = the Orgy
   Peregrine = the loft
   Simon = the Salt

Girl, eighteen

More common is to bestow on an existing word a special meaning which, by and large, only the underworld fully comprehends and savours. In schools in which the pupil society is less dominant this private vocabulary (not to be confused with the formal private language recognized and used by the authorities) tends to be limited. Here, for example, at a public school is virtually the whole of the private language – about thirty words, of which some, 'flog', 'beak', 'Downtown' etc. are not peculiar to this school. Some of the language designates places of food, some is purely traditional ('brace', 'snare'), very little is concerned with sex or homosexuality (reflecting the unfashionability of homosexual practices at this school at the moment) and some reveal controlling norms of the pupil society especially its anti-extremism. At one extreme is the 'staunch' man, over-keen, and excessively establishment-oriented, at the other is the 'pseud' the excessively unorthodox. These epithets act as controls supporting the moderately pro-school and 'traditional' values favoured by the pupil norms. The word 'turf' shows us something of the hierarchy in such a school.

Basic – a derogatory term meaning simple or stupid (applied to people or things)
Lats – lavatories
Woods – lavatories
Tool – male sex organ
Randy – homosexual (perhaps rather rabidly or dangerously so)
Shag – either shaggy in appearance, or, more commonly, an adjective meaning just 'bad', with, as always, slightly derogatory overtones
Flog – to cane

Downtown – the High Street

To sack – to expel

Beak – a master

Sweat – cross country run

To kick up – make a fuss (especially applied to masters who complain about a boy's behaviour)

Brace – a snub

To brace up – to snub someone

Brace up! – telling the hearer he has been snubbed

Snare – exclamations expressing disappointment. Something has happened which the speaker did not take into account

To snare – to cheat or steal

Turf! – The speaker (senior) tells the hearer (junior) that he has been turfed off whatever he is doing, by virtue of the speaker's senior position, and in order that the speaker might enjoy what the hearer has previously been enjoying

Staunch – a person who is exceedingly keen on games and other house activities, and makes it unpleasant for those who do not wish to participate

Grid – a bicycle

Bushy – annoyed

Nip – cheeky

Oil – gravy

Spats – butter

Creasing – to make oneself pleasant to with the idea of getting somewhere oneself

Bugger – a type of rugger with no rules played in the water meadows

'Pseud' –
1. one who holds pretensions or unorthodox opinions
2. cynic
3. one who is insincere
4. someone who 'pretends' to be an 'intellectual' and has incomprehensible intellectual conversations
5. dry intellectual is always called a pseud
6. socialists (or any non-conservative)
   Usually used as a term of abuse – of brain versus brawn, almost the exact opposite of staunch

By contrast, schools with a pupil society which is not so much penetrated or controlled by the official one as this one above, or where the pupil world is dominant, often have an extensive and highly individual private language. Thus at one integrated school, only two thirds the size of the public school illustrated above, there are no less than 135 words in current usage, and they are known by all the boys, though by few of the staff. Of these, over thirty words refer to sexual practices or relationships, mainly homosexual ones, and this stress accurately reflects the intense and fashionable sexual underlife of the school. Some terms refer to the staff and again accurately sum up the antagonistic quality of pupil–staff relations. Here are some terms used for the matron for example: 'Old Girl', 'Fluie', 'Old Boot'. About seventeen words are purely terms of abuse and again tell us much about the harsh quality of relationships between various groups of pupils. Relatively few refer to formal status and hierarchy (except as regards new boys), which are relatively unimportant to the pupil world in this school. The only publishable ones refer to the food in the place (which, in the researchers' opinion, was well above average according to criteria outlined in Chapter 4):

Corny mash	dry hash
Gunge	muck
Durge water	tea
Sticking Jake	seed cake
Dead fly pie	currant pudding
Yellow Peril	haddock
Cow biscuits	malted milk biscuits
Flop	butter
Pea-do	thick pea soup
Roll your own	jam roly-poly
Seaweed	cabbage
Spewy	vegetables and mince stew
Typhoid steaks	corned beef
Moggy pie	meat pie

Our final illustration of language comes from a progressive school where the pupil society is inevitably important. Here the private language amounted to around ninety words, about a third of which is known by the staff. Only half a dozen terms, all heterosexual, refer to sex activities, and this again reflects the relatively a-sexual tone of this school (a later chapter mentions that some progressive co-educational schools produce this curiously a-sexual atmosphere). More terms concern status in the informal society, particularly the 'ins' and 'outs' which are so important in this kind of school, or reflect the faintly anti-games and secular norms of the pupils:

Keenite – likes games
Jaw – Sunday service (evening)
Proles, plebs, peasants – used by seniors about rest of school
Alien – outsider, doesn't belong to the common room
Select – the 'in' group, or pertaining thereto
A dreg – an 'un-select' person
Suave – trendy

It is significant of differences in the pupil ethos that at this school 'quickie' refers to a smoke but at the preceding one to masturbation.

That brings us to the activities of the underworld: illicit activities which, beside their own intrinsic satisfactions, knit the pupil society together in endless, immemorial skirmishes against the staff. We have found underlife which is really 'under' – as at the school where smokers and drinkers met in a baronial tomb in the near-by church, or at another in tunnels, or at a third in underground dugouts in the grounds, but sometimes the underlife is in reality 'over' – as at that school where a sophisticated set of drinkers met on the roof-tiles and solemnly scratched minutes of their orgies on the slates, or at that other school where a cache of whisky was jealously guarded in the roof vaults over the high altar of the chapel.

But before sampling the underlife of adolescent boarders, let us just glance, and take a deep breath of fresh air in so doing, at the more innocent underworld of the twelve-year-old. Here is a fragment of the diary of a boisterous little girl at a coeducational school:

Gong! A mad rush of girls towards the dining room doors. As soon as I got to my table, taken by Mother Goose (Miss Pearson), Johnson and I, as usual started a staring match.

The Underworld 271

After dinner we roller-skated. Pat and I had a game of hockey on skates. When the Child Killer (Mr Kersey) went past, we yelled Hansell. This was because we want him to kill Hansell next.

We are now going to play hockey, which most of us hate! I have just come in with an injured foot, and have no intention of going out again.

I have just met my brother. Now I am going to wash my hair. I am drying it now.

I am going upstairs to change. I am sending someone out to see if there are any boys around because I am in my dressing gown.

I have now come down to the dom.sc. rooms, to do some needlework. I am making a blouse.

I have just finished praccy. (Practice, music). I am waiting in the playroom for Pat.

Now six of us are sitting in the playroom window, playing around with the window cords, and watching the boys skate.

The gong has just gone for tea. We are talking about punishments. Johnson and I have just finished another staring match.

Tea is over. I have got detension. At least I think so, for chucking a piece of bread, soaked in tea, across the table.

I am now in the form-room. Pat and I are going to start swinging on the door in a moment.

Have just had a fight with Celia Wilkes, having just chucked her, Pat was cheering me on. But of course I won anyway.

It's maths and french prep, so here goes. Have just finished maths. Now for french. I have finished my prep with six minutes to go till the end of prep. We've already been told off about 20 times for talking.

After prep. Pat, Ruth, Hoppity and I going to jump on the beds upstairs. We jump from the top of the wardrobes. (Please don't show this to anyone here, especially not Mrs Hodgson, the matron!)

Instead of doing what we had planned, after prep, we went and did gymnastics in the junior common room. We made pyraminds. The boys came and opened the door and chucked some slippers at us.

Two girls were only in a suspender belt and knickers, but with full top!!

Last night we were caught talking 3 times.

Suky rattled the cupboard, and we thought that it was knocks coming from the cupboard. Suky pretended to be frightened. She got in bed with me, and Celia, who sleeps next to her got into bed with someone else. While she was in my bed, Suky told me that it had been her knocking, Celia felt sick with shock . . .

I am in the form room and about to start swinging on the door again . . .

Underlife proper often starts by the smuggling in of articles which children may freely wear or use in ordinary life outside but which certain schools prohibit. At one school such forbidden articles are known as contraband:

I haven't much contraband, except that I have a lovely pair of scarlet panties with lace on.
Girl, fourteen, integrated coeducational school

Such daring contraband (including books which staff have not authorized by signature) is carefully hidden:

We hide comics under the floor, making false bottoms for our lockers to hide toasters and heaters so we can have a nosh up.
Boy, fourteen, same school

We have books, cut the middle out and stick a transistor radio inside it. *Boy, fifteen, same school*

Contraband is kept under mattresses, under floor boards, in pillow cases, in chinks in walls, cigarettes in a chocolate box.
Boy, fourteen, same school

As children rise in the school their illicit activities increase in scale:

It is common knowledge that most of the boys from the 1st form up smoke and drink. Contraband, especially among girls, is present in vast quantities and in cunning hiding places. There was a time when we has our own private radio station; unfortunately it was picked up in Oldford and confiscated. There used to be lots of radios but now there is not much point as there are speakers in common rooms and house rooms. Sexual intercourse used to be carried on under the stage in the Hall; it is not certain if it still goes on, the VI form common room has actually come to the conclusion that none of the seniors now here would actually go that far. Most of the paperback books read here have not been signed. Much more money is spent than passes through house banks. Unofficial passes out, especially for those who live nearby, are common. Half the middle school who go to the sanatorium have nothing wrong with them. During exams people do most of their revising in the lavatories; occasionally the lights go on at 3 am. if everyone wants to revise. Lights go on after having been switched off by the duty-person nearly every night. Talking after lights out is the general practice.

Girl, sixteen, same school

Of the more common elements of the underlife which we shall now illustrate, none is more common than smoking. To many adolescents everywhere, the cigarette is the symbol of an adult identity to which they aspire, but in boarding schools it can have other functions as well. For some it is a way of injecting excitement into the dull never-ending routine of school life:

This is one reason people break laws, at least here. If you remained a goody goody you'd die from boredom and too much exercise (a nasty combination) so people break rules, usually they smoke, not because they are addicted, but because it adds spice and purpose to their lives. I smoked myself. Often I went with people going for a fag not for the fag itself, but for the thrill of doing something naughty, knowing you mustn't get caught knowing that any moment one could hear footsteps in the corridor and know the day of judgement was come. *Boy, seventeen, integrated school.*

Others enjoy the companionship it brings and express the psychological urge of adolescents to challenge authority, a challenge symbolized by a cloud of smoke:

In our particular group one common 'hobby' is (dare I say it?) smoking. One sure recipe for tolerance within this limited section

274   The Hothouse Society

of society would be to smoke (we gather together behind one big bush) for the common breaking of rules provides a symbolic common factor, a bond of friendship 'against' as opposed to 'for' something.   *Boy, seventeen, public school*

In some schools to be 'in' or to be fully part of social life involves smoking. A girl explains how at a progressive school:

A lot of the social life centres on 'going for a fag' and a boy askes a girl out by saying 'How about a fag?' so it is really a social necessity in the top three or four groups of the school.   *Girl, sixteen*

A fairly hardened smoker might indulge three times on an average morning, as this extract from a sixteen-year-old at the Lady Margaret Foundation illustrates – the rest of the activities described are more exclusive to that school:

6.00 Was woken up as usual but too tired to get up
7.20 Up! had my coffee. Then had a 'fag' in the bogs
9.15 Had a free period. Played snooker; lost by 5 points
10.40 Had a 'fag'. Played darts (won). Saw a fight between Shoesmith and Clayton (two of my mates). Shoesmith won. Smashed Clayton in the face a few times and that was the end.
1.15 Had a fag. Then had a game of darts. Loser had to take two items of clothing off after each round. (I ended up in the 'nude').

Some are connoisseurs:

Smoking is fairly widespread but I only smoke in town or on trains properly – Picador cigars, at school I only rarely cadge a drag – a system of tunnels under the school is best for this, better than the lavatories.   *Boy, seventeen*

For less discriminating addicts even rural remoteness does not cut off sources of supply, as a sixteen-year-old girl explains in a very isolated coed school in the midlands:

Smoking! Although the pavilion is often used for this purpose only about 1 in every 10 smokes. Cigarettes can be obtained from the fag machine at Durnford Garage. Boys can cycle there and back in ½ an hour with ease and it makes a nice ride between 4 and 5 p.m. Then you can smoke your heart out after prep.

Drinking, which has the same complex appeal as smoking to boys, is confined to seniors and, as we have seen already in earlier chapters, done largely off the premises, on occasional expeditions or sometimes regularly:

> Drinking. This goes on normally on Saturday evenings. If you use the off licence door of the 'Feathers' you will be served with your requirements. However one should not use the bar as it is frequented by Mr Fox. The seat half way down Shooters Hill is the most popular place for the consumption of these drinks.
> *Boy, sixteen, independent school*

When drinking does occur on any scale inside the school it is normally in celebration of some major success or tradition or leaving:

> Drinking is *not* rife, as access is so difficult. When friends or old boys visit the school, they may bring down a couple of crates (as happened last summer term) and mostly the leavers of that term would collect and have a big Baccanalian orgy on top of the boat shed roof or some such place and transport from the houses to the creek would be by matrons moped or the housemaster's son's tricycle! – On this occasion the receptacles of the liquor concerned were thrown in to the mud of the river and the next day two culprits were tracked down and had to retrieve them while the rest of the school broke up for the term. *Boy, seventeen, public school*

Bound-breaking, usually for drinking, meeting girls or boys, or to go to the cinema, or home is another favourite sport. Occasionally, in integrated schools children go out illicitly to keep up cultural patterns which the school does not recognize:

> We're not allowed to go out and watch football matches – but I get permission to go out for a walk and then hop on a bus to town.
> *Boy, fifteen, public school*

> I am very interested in engine spotting (steam) and I go quite often with my friend to town to see the many that are still there. I don't consider this bad, but as normal humans should live, instead of being stuck in the country.
>
> *Boy, thirteen, integrated school*

In some schools children respond to being 'locked up' in small units by breaking out. At one school aimless night-wandering expressed a need that some felt for more autonomy or perhaps a sense of claustrophobia created in the small tightly packed house and dormitory:

> Got out of bed about midnight – the Housemaster's lights were out, had a cigarette in the bog, climbed out of the library window and then crossed over to school, all dark Gothic and spooky – but quiet and empty and I was alone, alone, first time for how many days? I wandered round the field – empty and incredibly peaceful – strange sense of freedom – with 750 people lying asleep and oblivious around me. Got chilly, crept back in to House up to dorm, heavy breathing figures huddled together. Back to being another face in the crowd.
>
> *Boy, seventeen, public school*

In a few schools which provide no adequate and legitimate outlet for boys' sense of adventure, the night-life can prove extremely risky. Four boys cross a wide and dangerous estuary in two canoes at night and say why:

> Man, we were cheesed off with this little bunch of robots. So I bet Scouse and Nutter, two of my mates a packet of fags that they couldn't beat us across the estuary and back any time after midnight. Well it was bloody murder, first we had to pinch the canoes from the boat house, it was black as hell and blowing then paddled like fuck for the other side. Well after about an hour or so we made it but coming back we were caught by the tide and taken about three miles down it was so rough cause the wind was against the tide that we decided to keep together in case anyone got swamped. Then we had to lug the canoes back to the boat house along the sea wall. We got back into dorm at just gone five real shagged but somehow feeling great, and none of the lumps of meat in bed had even moved.
>
> *Boy, sixteen, independent school*

Climbing a monumental clock tower is a night activity at another independent school:

> When you get up to the clock which is about 150′ up you have to edge out along a ledge, it is only possible in dry weather as it slopes slightly down and rain plus bird shit is a good lubricant. From then on its easy until the very top, the tiles don't give you a foot hold and you have to edge about the wire that acts as a lightning conductor. At night it isn't too bad, but you mustn't look down, the lights along the main drive are so small and a car seems to crawl along. We usually climb between the hours as the chimes can give you a shock, the whole tower shakes and at a tricky place it might cause you to make a mistake.
> *Boy, seventeen*

Among the middle age group of boys certain mild forms of plundering are an exciting feature of the underlife:

> Rading the school's larder is another favouret sport which is carried on in the upper half of the school. This fete is easily performed when the aproprate time comes which is generally when the Headmaster and wife are having their supper. *Boy, fifteen, independent school*

> Some are brave enough to go with a gang of us down the kitchen at 3 'oclock in the morning and make toast and have a good nosh up.
> *Boy, fourteen, state boarding school*

In such adventures, and in similar raids, perhaps into cupboards where exercise books and stationery are kept, a vigilant watch may be kept for the keys:

> Keys! Now they present an interesting problem. If I want a set, all I do is hang around the music school. Mr Atkins often leaves his keys on the piano and admits he cannot remember where he keeps them. I just walk in and borrow them. However it is not worth being caught with them as it means expulsion. Another weak person with keys is Mr Chetwynd. Its possible to lift them from under his nose just by putting a book on top of them.
> *Boy, sixteen, public school*

Stealing from other individuals, as distinct from the institution in general, is never approved by the pupil society – though isolated cases occur in most schools. Occasionally, temporary approval might be given by the pupil society to stealing from outside but never for very long:

> Shop-lifting is a slightly more serious offence as it brings in people from the village but 'Jardines' the local shop is very popular. I have been in there when people have pushed and jolted yet never showing any sign of guilt and walked out with bars of chocolate etc. A more serious wave of this type broke out about two years ago when in one afternoon 2 boys went into Barton and lifted £3.0.0 or thereabouts of books and bike equipment. This went on regularly and we all got a bit fed up. It was a bit of a relief when they were caught as they tried to pass the stuff onto us.
> *Girl, sixteen, coeducational school*

Pilfering inside the school is detested by all pupils, though is mildly endemic in many schools:

> A lot of stealing goes on here. I know who by and so do I think several others. It is not safe to leave lockers unpadlocked or to leave wallets or loose cash or indeed anything of value in the changing rooms after 4 o'clock. Mr Lydiard checks boys wallets to see that they haven't got more than the 4/6d we are allowed to have. This rule is broken about 400 times a month. I break it regularly as I think we should have 10/– and in fact I would and do write home for more if I am short.
> *Same girl*

Confined more to seniors, and even then to only a few of them, is gambling. It is restricted to certain schools, but they may be of any kind. Sometimes it is purely an individual pursuit, though it can be an obsessive one, as this diary extract suggests:

> Wednesday, 2 p.m. Slipped down town and out of bounds. Changed school tie in the public bogs off Queen Street. Bus over to Eastgate. Then to Moore's Betting Shop. I'm a regular, been coming here for over six months, backed runners at Newbury – £2 gone.
> *Boy, eighteen, public school*

Before a major race or sporting event unofficial bookmakers sprout in many schools. Perhaps the most sophisticated and gentlemanly was this seventeen-year-old operating one day at a public school:

> I gathered the bets for the big race after chapel and as there were quite a few I decided to hedge them, sent them off to a friend of mine who left last year. He is at Merton and would put them on for me. Lovely morning, would like to be on my way to Ascot, still it is on the radio, a transistor with an earplug and a back seat will brighten the Headmaster's afternoon 'ethics' – better get there early though, as the back seats go quick!

Sporadic gambling is one of the unofficial 'extra-curricular activities' which relieves the boredom of weekends or dark evenings, though the players have to be prepared for unwanted visitors:

> Our little game of pontoon was doing well. Jervis was looking miserable because he was ten bob down and two '45' pop records. Then that big creep the Head of House decides to do a wander round so out came the Monopoly board to cover the cards and a set of faces to go with it. 'Oh goody I've got Park Lane' – big deal!
> *Boy, sixteen, independent school*

Gambling is an ancient ingredient of the underlife. One more recent innovation in schools, as in adolescent culture outside, is the advent of drugs. Their use is confined to a small circle of boys (less commonly girls) in the senior parts of schools and the pupil society as a whole rather uneasily condones the practice. We have come across these small drug circles in famous public schools, progressive and integrated schools. One boy is a 'pusher':

> This school has a small drug market, of about 10 people. I am a member of this. We got drugs from my brother who lives in Portsmouth. Most of these drugs are only pep pills but some of us smoke opium. We usually smoke most of the drugs. I make quite a profit at the end of the term. NO HYPERDERMIC NEEDLES ARE USED.
> *Boy, seventeen, integrated school*

Another describes a group in a famous public school:

> There is quite a bit of drug taking here. You remember that group you were talking to last night in Murisons study – about 8 of us were there, well, it's us and about 4 or 5 others. We smoke cannabis – it's the middle school who have purple hearts. When your young you've got to experiment – it's soothing and exhilarating, you get right away from these ancient stifling walls.   *Boy, eighteen*

A final glimpse is from the diary of an eighteen-year-old boy at a progressive school, where hashish was in vogue among a certain clique. His diary ends on this note:

> The day, to all intents and purposes, is finished. But mine is beginning: my daily joint: I live for this, my escape from reality, from the dull pressures of responsibility. Hash is used a bit in the school quite regularly amongst a certain group of people, from a good cross-section of the form. I have everything to say in favour of this drug as long as it is kept away from the real Junkies. If there can be no danger of getting into a social group where addictive drugs are used, hash ought to be fully legalized although I hope it isn't: it helps me feel 'entire of myself'.

We end this chapter by looking at another aspect of the underworld: the relationships which it permits between staff and pupils, and between the pupils themselves.

It is, of course, the possibility of closer, more informal relations between adults and youngsters that can give boarding communities an advantage over day schools. Some pupils experience the difference vividly:

> I went to a grammar school before I came here and the staff were entirely different – just distant old fogies, caring only about O levels, the staff car park was like Le Mans at 4 o'clock, there weren't many societies, the juvenile sods just gave lines. Here they're pretty mixed – but you get to know about them all and most seem to give up all their time to us – some seem never to go home, they live and die for this place.   *Boy, sixteen, public school*

Before going further, it should naturally be stressed that the pupils do not think of the staff as a whole, they group them according to characteristics which they might think are significant. Two seventeen-year-olds in one public school in the west illustrate this by summing up the characteristics of the masters as seen by a large sixth form. One is concerned with class-room characteristics:

Staff groups
The open air group
Those who threaten to beat in form, nearly all have at times
Those who dislike and like various people.
On a whole the staff are very friendly and can all be kind
The snuff taker and the weed-after-every-period type
The last-period-in-the-afternoon-annoyed type

The other ranges more widely:

Some are thicks
Some are sex bombs
Some just 'want to be one of the lads'
Some are weirds
Some have 'paternal instincts'
Some are great guys
A few are lousy
Some are bolshy
Some are effeminate

A state boarder summarizes what most pupils expect of the staff:

A good teacher should not have favourites, he should not be too unkind, should learn us in lessons, should understand each boy seperately. He should not go sneaking to the headmaster.
Boy, fourteen, state boarding school

How far then do pupil–staff relations measure up to this criterion and how far are opportunities which boarding provides for informal contact realized in practice? In most orthodox schools, where the informal system is not alienated, good relations flourish, particularly at the senior levels:

> Relationships with masters just now have never been better before. I find the housemasters very interested in me, my running of the house, and my hobbies and interests – most gratifying. I feel certain respect from others under whom I have authority, and this promotes friendliness, invites to coffee, etc. Last year, and in lower down the school in general, relationships are more formal – especially amongst older masters (of the old school of thought – not necessarily of age). These will not tolerate any disrespect or infringement of rules, whereas younger masters use their experience of life and of youth to judge their actions.
> *Boy, seventeen, public school*

In the public school, where the style of relationships is man-man and more formalized, sometimes the boy has to make the running:

> Relationships with masters are always pleasant for the boy who makes an effort to sponsor them. Masters react, as if by instinct, to a boy who genuinely wishes to make a personal contact, and I can say I have succeeded with at least four.
> *Boy, seventeen, public school*

In some, the informal society of the staff and of the boys interlock: thus at one school the staff wives had their little circles of adherents, virtually rival 'salons':

> Some of the relationships I most enjoy at this school are with masters' wives and the younger masters. Most of the masters' wives I come into contact with are very willing to interest themselves in the school and the boys. Mrs K's all music, Mrs D. games and T.V.; Mrs P. gets the do-gooders and Mrs F. the artists.
> *Boy, eighteen, public school*

In some public schools, however, relations with key figures can be strained or formalized, so that intimacy and a real dropping of barriers is not always possible:

With our housemasters, relations are usually strained – the prefects in my house are given to piling into studies and drinking, smoking, chanting, 'Sanders the pink', etc. and whenever we are taken before him (usually over some trivial matter), we all come out killing ourselves with laughter – he hasn't caught anyone doing anything really wrong yet.

We do get on better with one of the tutors ,– he is quite sane. The main trouble with the housemasters is they treat us like 13, 14 year olds (complain if 5 mins late for bed, etc.)

With our subject masters: some relations are friendly – but never very personal. With the head of the science department relations are terrible – he doesn't seem to be able to teach us a thing and consequently we are rather hostile towards him. The teaching approach is invariably formal, i.e. we sit down and are taught to from the blackboard – though of course we can comment, etc.

Boy, seventeen, public school

With the headmaster in most public schools relations are inevitably distant for most pupils:

Relationships master–boys: very distant really. I do not think I take them really seriously. I talk to those who I come across but in no depth. I certainly would not confide in any of them. The Headmaster, for instance, has only said 'good morning' to me in the six years I have been here. He is a distant 'God' who deals out justice and that's about all. I think it might be true to say that the only person who actually talks to the headmaster is the School Captain (if this year's model does at all). *Boy, eighteen, public school*

Sometimes when attempts are made to render relations more intimate a sort of formality only makes the pupils sense the falseness of the situation:

With my housemaster, I feel ungenuine – a facade, slightly hypocritical. When he calls me 'John' I long to turn round and say 'O.K. Pat, lets have it both ways then'. Some of the younger Masters are great fun – and really good guys. The sooner the old order completely disappears, the better. *Boy, seventeen, public school*

In progressive schools where christian names are always used, relations are always more informal superficially and often really close:

> Jamies' my tutor actually, I chose him myself, he's sweet, I drop round for tea or chocolate in the evening – its a nice change from school. Sarah (his wife) has got two babies and I help out a bit; I tell them most things, he never tells anyone else.
>
> *Girl, sixteen, progressive school*

Even in some state boarding schools this can be the case. Though in class and in school relations are formal, those of master-pupil, in the residential side the atmosphere and staff–pupil relations can change dramatically – more so than in some public schools where the roles which a member of staff plays in and out of school contrast less sharply. In the state boarding school, the residential staff can even drop being 'masters' at all and forget rules. The christian names in the extract from the next diary *all* refer to members of staff.

> 8.50 *p.m.* Left on pretext of imminent second prep and spent next hour with David re-writing scene of his play. Seemed fairly successful in the rosy haze of a bottle of Brown Ale but in cold light of morning illusions collapsed.
>
> 1.30 Lunch ended. Went up to David's room had coffee, argued with David and Hugh Richards (senior English master who had dropped in for coffee) about how their lessons ought to run.
>
> 3.30 *p.m.* Popped in to Len's room (senior residential master) for tea – he always has cream cakes – about six there 1st-6th form. Gorged ourselves. All attacked his idea for school holiday visit – we want Greece. He asked us for suggestions for a present for his fiancée, so we all packed into his car, drove to the record shop, squeezed into a booth and had a nice hour listening. Confused verdicts: he bought nothing. Back to school tea . . .
>
> *Boy, seventeen, direct grant school*

Even in the schools where relations are on the whole close and constructive, a few boys are alienated from many staff for various reasons:

There are too many socialists on the staff.

Boy, eighteen, public school

I hate the way some of the masters minds work. Some have one track minds and have no idea what the outside world is like. Some have spent all their lives here, this school is their life – if they left it, they would disintegrate, fizzle up. The few females here are mere machines, used by virile masters. Some of the masters are too fond of some of the boys. There should be a continual check on this – there isn't.

Boy, seventeen, public school

Generally too old and doddery lot – nice old gentlemen, but well past their days of teaching (such as my main master).

Boy, eighteen, public school

These, however, are isolated individuals. In some schools the potentiality of boarding is simply not realized because the pupil society as a whole is hostile to the staff and both sides maintain distance from each other. Far from an increasing intimacy as the boys grow older, their own world displays more and more hostility to the staff:

In the 1st-3rd form the housemaster is a God, and you may like him, but not really hate him, as any decisions he may make, in the way of punishments, seem to be inevitable and you don't blame him for it as a junior. As a senior, you learn to hate a housemaster or matron, and they cease to be parental figures. As a prefect we are not generally affected by any punishments but we get 'moans' over petty little trivialities. After these lectures one gets great satisfaction in returning to the prefect study and putting all the expression you can into 'Bastards' or 'Bloody 'ole Boot!' Our 'Old Bag' is fat, post-middle aged and rotund, she also walks with a waddle and nothing would give me more satisfaction than thwacking her over the rump with a broomhandle – the best practical way of handling her is to ignore her most of the time, and when it is unavoidable keep an air of superiority in your dealings with her. Our housemaster is particularly childish and has sulking moods but he is better than some.

Boy, seventeen, independent school

286   The Hothouse Society

In such schools hostile stereotypes develop and sour relations:

> The staff give up a lot of time but it's their *motives* that are wrong – all they want is to get boys for punishment or to enforce petty rules. Our housemaster doesn't understand us, he doesn't think we're mature human beings and have feelings: he thinks the strap hurts – it doesn't, he won't have a suggestions committee, he never acknowledges our ideas.
> *Boy, sixteen, state boarding school*

The memory of incidents, true or exaggerated, lingers and circulates in the underworld and serves to maintain alienation:

> One teacher, who's now left, caught a boy smoking and caned him, then took him for a drive in his car, and said, 'You think I'm a bastard don't you', the boy said 'Yes, you are', he drove him back and caned him again. Then he invited the boy out again and gave him a cigarette, when they got back he said, 'You've been smoking ... bend over'. We hate the staff here. Keep away from them as much as possible. The Shits.
> *Boy, seventeen, independent school*

> Once before I was yelled at so much I owned up to something I hadn't done to get it over with and shut the master up once he'd slippered me. They don't care about the truth, or you. We can't stand them.
> *Boy, fifteen, state boarding school*

Even with auxiliary staff relations vary widely. At a public school the prefects anxiously confer over one isolated case of swearing at a domestic:

> There had been a notable example of a boy swearing at a member of the kitchen staff. This was deplorable. Everything must be done to continue good relations with the kitchen staff.
> *Prefects' minutes*

By contrast, in the pupil cultures which are alienated gross insults are part of everyday life:

> I got one of the housematrons embarrassed by looking at her crude hairy legs.
> *Boy, seventeen, independent school*

I shouted out down the stairs (she couldn't waddle up them fast) 'Matron is a bloody old stinking, smelly rotten filthy bagful of...'
Boy, sixteen, same school

But, whatever the state of relations between the pupils and staff, good or bad, the pupil society always tries to exploit, to manipulate the staff towards its own purposes. One alienated boy points this out:

First, observe them – get to know the reasonable ones, and observe the rules, as it won't be long before the bastards show themselves, you won't have to go looking for them. Cultivate those you like – they might be useful. *Boy, fourteen, independent school*

Once 'they' have been observed and their weaknesses singled out, manipulation can begin. Sometimes a little gentle

... bribery. Unusual at school yes but Mr Masters a very decent bloke is susceptical towards it. I don't mean bribery with money, just little gifts or even asking to hear one of his violin records. This puts him in a good mood and if you want paper or exercise books he could get you one. *Girl, sixteen, Quaker school*

Another form exploits the master's known hostility to get an easy period:

We wanted to cut something off two periods of 'Paradise Lost' so we told old Fungus (he's got a beard like a worn bog brush) that the science sixth had already got their 'A' level timetable. He can't stand Marnton, the guy who runs all the science here, so out he rushes, saying no one ever tells him anything, to find out. We relax.
Boy, sixteen, public school

More subtle methods are used by seniors. One house captain simulates anger in order to curb the housemaster and gets his way:

Carruthers behaved fairly well both terms, but better in the Spring. I discovered in the Autumn that if he was delivering a salvo at you and you were almost rude back, or at any rate quaked with fury, he was so surprised that he calmed down and apologised. By this means, I stopped a great many minor restrictive innovations which he tried to introduce, such as having to take night-things upstairs by 7.0 p.m. and so on. I didn't have any major rows, but he did once tell me not to address him like a public meeting!

Head of house's book, public school

Occasionally the researcher, if not very careful, was used to flout the rules. A diary records:

9.30 *p.m.* Went up to Lambert's room (that's you). Had some coffee and long chat. It was interesting and pleasant – more so because by being up there I missed second prep, and a house meeting. I knew the housemaster couldn't object, though he scowled when I told him.

Boy, seventeen, public school

When the boys wish to express disapproval of a powerful master they resort to devious but pointed means. Here an unpopular housemaster is snubbed publicly. It is known that he dislikes the matron and has forced her to resign, so, to express their general dislike of him, the sixty-five boys collect a huge present of £100 for her.

The old — (the housemaster) had been rude to the matron, disliked her and sacked her. Now, we didn't like *her* all that much but as for him ... So we organized a collection of a present which raised £100. We got a gold watch engraved and gave the rest in premium bonds in front of him. You should have seen his face: he had got the message: anyone who dislikes him is a friend of ours.

Boy, seventeen, public school

We turn in conclusion to relationships among the pupils themselves, and to the most microscopic but the warmest and most important relationship of all, that of friend to friend. For most of them, when faced with the question 'what is it you value most in life in this school?', the answer is emphatically, 'relations with a few other boys or girls'. Boarders who are not eccentric either tend to be or are made extremely gregarious by their environment.

> I have a passionate hatred of being by myself.
> *Boy, eighteen, public school*

> A companion is needed by everyone.
> *Boy, seventeen, public school*

> Being alone for me is being lonely: you need never be alone here, but in the holidays...
> *Girl, seventeen, progressive school*

Sometimes those who do seek solitude or even privacy evoke informal social controls:

> In this school one is looked down on if one wants to be on one's own for any length of time – one is accused of being 'anti-social'.
> *Boy, seventeen, public school*

Even those who *can* be alone may prefer not to:

> Although a prefect is meant to be in a study of his own, I chose a double study (a) to keep going a perfect partnership in crime, (b) to avoid being lonely. P.S. it has not done my work any good though.
> *Prefect, eighteen, public school*

When senior pupils have the choice of several study mates or only one, certain norms usually come into operation:

> Two is company three is a crowd.
> *Boy, seventeen, public school*

> If you have more than 2 in a study, you can't really tell the others to keep quiet. Three in a study very often leads to a feud between two of the study mates against the other. Two in a study means that you really get to know your study mate and appreciate him in his bad and good qualities; you can confide in him.
> *Boy, eighteen, same school*

For a minority even two in a study is too much:

> We're cooped up together, with little in common, and tiny things

blow up into gigantic issues. Every time he picks his nose I want to scream, and he frequently can't stand the way I leave my things around – our sugar next to his filthy rugger socks. It's very tense.
Boy, sixteen, public school

The studies are too small. Everyone seems to talk while they are thinking. They *always* are telling you their troubles. Give me some privacy. *Boy, seventeen, public school*

In some cases a *modus vivendi* has to be worked out:

My study mate and I have an agreement whereby he never works in the study and I do. *Boy, seventeen, state boarding school*

His friends aren't mine (walking tailor's dummies they are – poncy smooth types), so we try to keep all our friends away – we go to *their* place. *Boy, seventeen, independent school*

Let us then drift round the studies in their variety, sumptuous contemporary bedsitters in some schools, scruffy wooden hutches in others, their walls covered with pop-group pin-ups (with a few choice nudes secreted behind the doors of cupboards and desks – away from the housemaster's eyes), or with sporting prints, or with large straw hats and guitars, or costly silks, or prim rows of school photos, or beer mats, or Marxist posters, or photos of past leavers – whatever the tastes or interests of the occupants may be; and, in drifting around, let us notice the basis of these friendships, the nuclear unit on which the whole informal world which we have explored in the last two chapters is founded.

Some companions are knit together by the common interests opposing 'the system':

I just think like my friend and he understands me – no one else does, even at home. He has a part share in my motor bike (for Christ's sake don't tell the housemaster we've got it near here) and we go drinking together. I do enjoy just walking and talking with him. *Boy, seventeen, public school*

The Underworld

Hugh and I see the amusing side of life and are vague exhibitionists. We have a feeling against the authority of the school and dislike 'yes men'. We just seem to suit one another. We are faithful to each other.
Boy, seventeen, public school

We are disenchanted with the school, we have risen together and feel that this school has not recognized us. We play games and work competently – but the school is incomplete. This feeling draws us together. We talk.
Boy, seventeen, independent school

In other studies or rooms – those perhaps with the beer mats, pop cut-outs or school photos – friendships have markedly different foundations.

We shoot, drink, go to dances, play darts.
Boy, seventeen, independent school

Boozing, birding and betting. This seems pretty rock-bottom but we're not as bad as all that really.
Boy, seventeen, public school

We like making a nuisance of ourselves, annoying the others. We're smooth, I suppose, smart dress etc., and *hate* hair cuts – we both live in the same county at home, same age, same background.
Boy, seventeen, public school

Those with reproductions, guitars or the Spanish craft weave on their walls are knit together by other things:

We are odd – We pragmatise, poematise and syncopate.
Boy, seventeen, Stanton

We are in the upper strata of intelligence – we're good at work and make talk interesting. We revile others rather too unashamedly. We profess soccer and Mozart.
Boy, seventeen, public school

We consider we have seen the light of truth concerning many things here, or at least to a greater extent than others.
Girl, seventeen, coeducational school

Some are brought together by deeper instincts which a later chapter will describe:

> John and I do archery and classics. He is attached to me closely, perhaps because he – no, I cannot be sure of that, he's never said and I couldn't prove it.
> *Boy, seventeen, public school*

> THRUSTING is what we do – looking and getting to know 'lushes' (handsome young boys) and generally talking about home and how stupid and creepy these people are.
> *Boy, sixteen, public school*

> Hilary and I are virtually married – well, almost, at least we are always together and are the oldest couple in the school – $2\frac{1}{2}$ terms now.
> *Boy, seventeen, coeducational school*

Some friends fall into no classifications:

> We seek.
> *Boy, seventeen, public school*

> One I'm academic with. One is more intelligent and pompous (an MP or General of the future) – I relax with him. The third I break rules with. None will stay close friends after I leave here.
> *Boy, seventeen, public school*

> We talk, discuss, laugh and live.
> *Boy, seventeen, public school*

But beneath the variety, amid the steam from the cups of Nescafé and the out-pourings of a battered portable radio or gramophone, these friendships perform one basic function, fundamental to the whole pyramid of the social order which towers around and upon them. However effective or not the official agencies of pastoral care (described in the next chapter), friends provide for the great majority of pupils the only outlet in the school for their deepest and most personal confidences:

> I need to discuss personal matters with one reliable, true friend and my study mate is the ideal person.
> *Boy, seventeen, public school*

The Underworld 293

Neil gives me someone I can really trust – the only one in this jungle. He keeps me company and he exists in a completely different sphere from my other friends. At times he's annoying but he is indispensable to my life. We depend on each other.

Boy, eighteen, state boarding school

There's only one person I can discuss my private problems with, frankly and freely and that's David my study mate. Everyone else – beak or boy – passes judgement on you. He doesn't. He cares.

Boy, seventeen, public school

On that positive note we leave this general description of the underworld – its structure, groupings, values, controls, activities and expressions and more intimate functions, including this vital pastoral care. Vital because boarding schools, like all human communities, generate many problems of a social and individual nature which need resolution. Those problems and means of resolution await our attention.

10 Problems

We have just seen how the children's informal society can create difficulties or provide support for the worried; we now turn to look at the wide variety of problems that can face boarders, and at some of their reactions. While none of these problems is exclusive to public schools or boarding schools generally, certain tensions are increased by communal living and responses to them are intensified in the small and often inward-looking boarding-school society.

This chapter first illustrates the difficulties imposed by isolation and life in single-sex communities. It then notes that different boarding structures, the ways schools organize themselves, can create problems for some children who cannot or will not accept the routine or conform to accepted goals. Not only does this formal world expect involvement from the children, their own world makes similar demands. In both there can be competition for status, expected attitudes and behaviour and we shall see the problems of the 'outsider' or misfit can be quite serious. Sometimes the difficulties seem trivial – 'I sleep next to a boy who has smelly feet,' writes one small boy. But the friction and pressures built up over time just by living in an enclosed community and sometimes accentuated by poor accommodation can be considerable. It explains why apparently small inconveniences often can become the focus of great discontents.

In boarding schools many problems become magnified and occasionally some children's responses are extreme. A few run away, some develop eccentricities, there can even be a few rare suicides, but it should be emphasized that residential education has one distinct advantage in that tensions can be readily discerned. Many boarding schools have an effective counselling system, staff and senior boys give pastoral care to those in trouble and our chapter gives many illustrations of their sympathetic attempts to meet the children's problems. In presenting the difficulties which children face we are not questioning the value of boarding or suggesting that all but a minority of pupils are not happy in residential schools. Any education involves some sort of discomfort and many day children may face greater stresses. Our companion report will deal with them.

First, the problems created by isolation from the outside world, which have already been suggested in preceding chapters. Homesickness affects almost all children occasionally and a few suffer deeply and persistently, which may prevent the full realization of academic and other potential. Here a prep-school boy describes what it is like:

> You aren't really sick but you have a funny, empty feeling inside, like when you go over a humpy bridge fast in a car, but it's there all the time. Anything can start it off, something on the radio, a dog that looks like yours, then you start to think about your family and this funny feeling creeps into your tummy. *Boy, ten, prep school*

And another two children at a secondary modern boarding school still have not got over it:

> The first day I was dying to come back, but the moment I said goodbye to my parents I felt homesick and I wished I was at home and I still feel I want to go home at this very moment but it comes and goes, so on the whole I like it here. *Girl, thirteen*

> I was very home sick but I said to my self 'I've got to lump it' but after a week it was gone. Some times I get home sick in spasams, bit by bit it goes off. *Boy, twelve*

While homesickness is usually transitory, isolation from the family can cause more abiding worries, as we said in Chapter 7. Often there is a feeling of being sheltered from grim reality, of not knowing the whole truth:

> I worry about my mother who, I suspect, is ill and my sister who is sixteen and never been kissed. *Boy, seventeen, public school*

My father died after I had been away at school for seven years. Would I had been home then to help my mother, I worry about her and how she is managing.
Boy, fifteen, public school

Some children in boarding schools are sent away to avoid the tensions of a broken home, but absence does not necessarily remove their anxiety. This comment also reveals how boarding can in time provide the security and trust that enables, as we shall see later, the discussion of personal problems:

The biggest personal problem which has arisen while here is that of my parents. I have in the past been very secretive over my mother and father being divorced. But during the last year I have got over the feeling of being ashamed about them and have started to talk about them which has taken a large load off my mind.
Boy, seventeen, public school

Parental expectations can worry children and there will be other comments elsewhere in this chapter that show absence from home does not lessen these pressures:

Even though they are miles away I worry about living up to what my mother wants, i.e. a dashing handsome man with plenty of money and giving her some. This is what I would like in order to please her. The other real worry is the fact that I do not, as yet, have a deep firm basis of understanding with anyone else but her.
Boy, seventeen, public school

Isolation is not only from the home. Most boarding schools are single-sex communities and this sort of isolation can provide many children with profound problems. Naturally the deprivation is more keenly felt by older children; boys often lose their girl friends, are isolated from the recipient of their confidences, the sympathizer with their problems. The sexual life of boarders is dealt with in the next two chapters. Here we just indicate a few worries caused by their enforced monasticism:

I worry often if my girl friend still likes me. When I don't hear from

her I feel depressed, imagine she has gone off with someone else. I worry about all my friends outside – are they in trouble, have they got a decent job, couped up in here you can't tell what is going on.
Boy, seventeen, direct grant school

and a boy at a technical boarding school states quite simply:

I miss my girl friend, she understands me and I love her dearly, I would do anything to protect her. She writes often but it isn't the same as the long talks we have when we are together.
Boy, sixteen

Another boy, re-emphasizing the problems posed by isolation from his girl friend, leads us to the next major area of worry, that of homosexuality:

I worry about keeping my girl friend, that she will find me dull with nothing to talk about except school. I worry because this school should be co-ed. Whenever I see the prefects chatting up the fags I know this system is at fault somewhere. Most of us just don't know any girls.
Boy, seventeen, public school

Homosexuality presents the children with many problems. By far the most frequent is concern over sexual identity – boys worry whether they are sufficiently masculine. It is a major anxiety. Others worry over their physical and emotional experiences, feel anxiety that they are the objects of affection or are disturbed by the approaches of boys and staff. As another boy comments, 'If you have got a pretty face, watch it there will be a queue in no time.' Some simply fear discovery, others are preoccupied with the moral implications of their attachments or battle with feelings of guilt. It is important to realize that these children are replying to our question 'What are the main problems that face you living in the school?' At no time did we ask children to write or discuss their private lives. However such hesitancies do not seem to affect the children once trust has been won. They write and talk with remarkable frankness about everything, and the difficulty is usually stopping them.

First a group of public school boys exhibit the very common worries about their sexual identity:

> I just worry about homosexual problems, the person I'm in love with. I'm queer, temporarily I hope, but permanently I fear, and because of this I am a rebel. *Boy, eighteen, public school*

> Well I've been in love now with another boy for about three years, that's something to keep one thinking about.
> *Boy, eighteen, public school*

and another boy worries and is reassured:

> I sometimes worry whether I am going queer but the next time I see a pretty girl I understand, I can reassure myself.
> *Boy, seventeen, public school*

Sometimes it is the younger boys who get worried:

> I get sick of the boys who are constantly making passes at me. It is highly embarrassing. *Boy, fourteen, independent school*

> I'm a bit worried about my fag master, he is getting a bit too friendly. It will be poems and holiday invitations soon, I'll play hard to get as we don't want a scandal. *Boy, fourteen, public school*

Seniors feel guilty and worried at the schools' sanctions:

> If you want to know what really worries me its the prospect of being caught. I am deeply involved with someone else in the house and people are beginning to talk. I try to keep away from him, I worry about being a bad influence – but I can't help it. If they find out they have your parents up and interview you in front of them. I would rather die than face that. *Boy, seventeen, public school*

But it would be wrong to imagine everyone worries deeply about their emotional life; many remain detached observers and in the school context most take their problems as a matter of course.

I don't worry about homosexuality, I just enjoy it.
Boy, sixteen, state boarding school

Another is amused:

It is surprising how little boys brag about their sexual exploits with girls, strange enough, they seem far more loquacious on the subject of their experiences with other boys.
Boy, seventeen, public school

Another is comforted by the thought of his parents:

If I ever get anxious about the surge of lust I feel as I take the junior colts, then I think of my father – at the moment he can't leave anything in a mini-skirt alone, – he too must have been as kinked as hell when he was locked up here. So I don't worry much.
Boy, eighteen, public school

and many liaisons seem scarcely romantic or significant:

I made a playful pass at young Randall, to my surprise he accepted, but I didn't really feel in the mood so I went off to read the papers.
Boy, sixteen, integrated school

But we reserve more illustrations of the sexual life of boarders until the following chapters.

Sexual deviation on the part of the staff however produces a less tolerant reaction. It seems to violate what all children regard as acceptable. It is probable that such situations are rare; in fact, the readiness of boys to comment suggests such activity does not remain undiscovered long. In each of the four schools concerned here (four out of sixty-six) it was mentioned by over three quarters of the boys in all age groups, often many times over even when it had no relevance to the questions asked. Such revelations put considerable pressures on the research worker and made places such as Lady Margaret's Foundation difficult places to work in. Here a group of young boys comment on the activities of Mr Tomkins, their housemaster. Their language is a symptom of their poor backgrounds, which the school was founded to counteract, and of their indignation.

> Mr Tomkins is a House master and I think he is a vulgar man, he is an actual 'OMO' and now I have met one. He does rude things to people, he has tried to malest me but he did not succeed on me as I have seen him on the spur of the moment with one of my mates, and every-body else hates him so please publish this to show every-body that a school master is not good at all. By the way he teaches French.
> *Boy, thirteen*

> ... there is a House master called Mr Tomkins he is an OMO, he comes round every night when he thinks we are asleep and shags us off. I know this for a fact because I have watched him do it and has a good fiddle with our things. He pulls down our pyjamas and once when I was sick he went right down below my belt.
> *Boy, thirteen*

> Mr Tomkins is a homo. He takes little First yr skunks into his room and fiddles about WITH THEIR Balls. *Boy, fourteen*

> What I do not like is my Housemaster, Mr Tomkins. He is very dirty in his mind and it affects his actions. He looks at you in the toilet and in the bath. When he canes somebody he hits you any where, on the arm, legs, back anywhere. He has had a warning from the headmaster about being sexy. Nobody likes him. *Boy, twelve*

These are only a fraction of their comments and by no means the most sensational – many more disturbing expressions are withheld in our research files. Again we have deliberately selected the children's own experience and not reported gossip which may be exaggerated. It is interesting that middle-class children faced with the same problem use language equally as vivid. From a state boarding school comes this advice for the research worker:

> Keep your legs crossed if you go to coffee with Oscar, he is as bent as a clockwork orange and a right queer. *Boy, seventeen*

> The Housemaster has been seen trying to bum a certain member of the house. He tries to get the Corps members to take off their uniforms – now enclose that in your book.
>
> *Boy, eighteen*

> When I was trying on a uniform, this bum bandit pressed his tool right up against me. Uggh! Get this homo banned.
>
> *Boy, sixteen*

In these schools the constant reiteration of this sort of comment and other supporting evidence forced one to accept them as plausible at least. At a couple of other schools we have many similar replies to our question 'what problems does life hold for you at school?'

We repeat that such comments about one master have been widespread in only four out of sixty-six schools.

Not all the schools are single-sex or isolated from the outside world, and the more open they are the less the problems just described manifest themselves. But all societies have their rules which limit individual freedom and present problems; it is as true of progressive schools as of others. We now turn to the problems created by the school's structure, by the way it organizes itself to achieve certain goals, and consider the children's reactions to these ends and means. Public schools not only expect high academic standards but also demand from their boys observance of a code of manners and values. Independent schools that are unable to share the intellectual goals of the public schools may place an even greater emphasis on acceptable behaviour patterns. 'We may not be clever but we are gentlemen,' one of their boys hastened to point out. Progressive and Quaker schools, while they have as clear a set of academic and cultural ideals as the public schools, employ different methods of achieving their goals, formal control is minimal, authority concealed, but some pupils find it hard to achieve the self-discipline implied in this freedom. State boarding schools and direct grant schools are more concerned with academic skills than a style of life and a set of beliefs, but the intellectual pressures of some of these schools pose problems for those who cannot keep up. Because they are more integrated with the state system than the public schools, we can find here boys from different backgrounds challenging the predominantly middle-class ethos of boarding schools.

With these differences in mind we can see how the pressures of routine and conformity build up resistance in the children. Lack of privacy, bad physical provision and questioned priorities can encourage apathy and rebellion. As one boy comments: 'What a dump this is, they have just spent pounds on the chapel roof while our dorm leaks like a sieve and the bogs won't work properly.' Competition in work, games and other avenues leading to status in the school can be unremitting; even hard-won success can be bitter, for approval by the school and responsibility can bring problems unknown to the nonentity. First the problems posed by routine are mentioned by a group of boarders:

> Sometimes you want to scream, you know exactly what you will be doing this time tomorrow, and next week, next month, next year. I'll be sitting down to prep, it gives me a sort of panic that I will never escape.
> *Boy, sixteen, public school*

But for some this provides security, as a boy comments:

> My real problems come when the routine changes, on Sundays, half holidays or when term is ending. I feel lost, almost insecure and get very moody.
> *Boy, seventeen, public school*

A girl at a mixed secondary modern school wonders:

> if all these bells and noises go on even when we are not here, like that creepy film the Ghost train, lots of spooky running feet and plates moving in the empty dining room.
> *Girl, sixteen*

At a progressive school the same problems are faced:

> Boredom is such a problem, meals are always at the same time and you know what you are going to get. Even though you don't have to do things, you usually do what the others are doing, they never change.
> *Girl, sixteen, progressive school*

Complex routines rely on the observance of rules many of which infuriate the inmates:

Some of the rules here are so petty, which is, I think, why so many people break them, it is as if they were especially put up for that purpose. With so many rules cramping ones every movement (you can't even go from one part of the school to the other without putting your name in the destination book), to say you are going for a walk is the same as admitting all the nefarious occupations possible.
Boy, seventeen, independent school

and another boy comments:

Rules are a problem there are so many of them, you can break them without realising – by the time I know the lot it will be time to leave.
Boy, thirteen, public school

Even the absence of rules doesn't make the progressive or Quaker schools very much different:

I would prefer a few rules you can break than the real difficulty of deciding to do what the majority disapproves of.
Girl, seventeen, progressive school

In most schools academic success is a major goal; it is a way of achieving status for the child with both the staff and contemporaries. It earns parental approval and for many children has more relevance to the outside world's criterion of values than anything else that the school offers. It gives them many problems, particularly the difficulty of relaxing while living in a school:

All your free time is available for work, any unfinished work can be done before breakfast. You always *can* work harder but the trouble is you never really relax. Sometimes everything gets on top of you and there is no way of escaping it. You get tired of the same faces, people moaning about the same things. Work seems completely overpowering. At the boarding school there is no escape, at home there is.
Boy, fifteen, public school

And at a direct grant school which shares the same intense pressures mentioned above, a boy tells us:

> He gave back the essays with some sarcy remark about mine I felt like belting him one, sat there pretending it was because this master hates my guts, but I know my work isn't really good enough. I try but – Christ knows what I shall do.
> *Boy, sixteen, direct grant school*

There is the additional problem of parental expectation:

> I worry about what happens if I fail my exams, am I doing justice to my parents spending so much sending me here, after all they have forked out £2000 on my education.
> *Boy, seventeen, public school*

and a prep-school boy (quite mistakenly!) comments:

> My work gives me the jitters – I bet you've never had to take home a rotten report. *Boy, eleven, prep school*

Work can cause worry at progressive schools just because they strive deliberately to diminish academic pressures. The scholars worry about under-achievement:

> Well one has to learn quickly that you are more or less on your own as far as work is concerned because it is against the principle of the place for the teachers to push you hard. It is difficult to rely on your own will power especially if you are only 15. *Boy, fifteen*

A boy who had moved from a progressive school to a Quaker school comments on his previous school:

> It was so free, people didn't worry about you all the time, but my brother left without any 'O' levels at all and my parents felt I would do the same. There I used to worry because I never did any work, here I worry because I don't seem to do anything else.
> *Boy, sixteen, Quaker school*

This prayer from a prep-school boy suggests that work worries begin early and the demands of the school are, for some, difficult to meet. He makes a very human plea:

> Dear Lord,
> You know that I have not worked as hard as I ought.
> I have shirked my work.
> And now, during this exam, I know I deserve to fail but forgive me and let me succeed. Amen.
>
> *Boy, twelve, prep school*

Competition is one method of control, of orientating children to the goals of the school. We have seen the anxieties it presents in the academic areas of school life but it exists in the athletic and social fields as well. Competition for positions of status and authority can be considerable in schools. It is perhaps more pronounced in the public schools, where the elaborate hierarchies have to be climbed and positions of responsibility carry great authority and privilege. Here are some pressures posed by competition, when encouraged by school policies. Two boys comment at a public school:

> I am very materialistic and ambitious, I always worry about doing better, promotion, getting into teams. I worry about getting into Oxbridge – how sincere am I in fact. *Boy, seventeen*

> I am worried by this endless rat race, tempted by power, snared by games success, flattered by scholarship, seduced by the approval of friends and authorities. *Boy, eighteen*

From a public school comes our title:

> I am always trying to push myself on in this hot house society. Perhaps I try too hard. *Boy, seventeen*

Failure to get on produces

> a terrible worry that I have not really an established place in school society. *Boy, seventeen, independent school*

Competition can produce bitterness and cynicism in some:

> No wonder politicians come from public schools; after the naked struggle for power here you are just right for Westminster.
>
> *Boy, eighteen, public school*

> Thou shalt not covet – they say in chapel but if we didn't this whole place would collapse overnight. Who will be next Head of House, will I make the first VIII, will I get better grades than him, am I more of a success than – we think about little else.
>
> *Boy, eighteen, public school*

But in the end it is difficult to decide whether success or failure provides the less anxious alternative. We have in an earlier chapter traced the problems of the successful, the authority holder, but there are worries connected to any status achieved, either official or unofficial, in this competitive society. As a prep-school boy learns early:

> 'If you become an officer you will have to face loosing lots of your friends' said the Headmaster when he asked me to be in charge of the senior dormitory. Well I didn't loose lots, I lost them all. The only friend I now have to fall back on is the school rule book.
>
> *Boy, thirteen, prep school*

Unofficial status can be equally as difficult, as this contribution shows:

> Because I am interested in archaeology I have been on several digs with my Housemaster. Now the seniors think I am ruthlessly ambitious and the juniors look on me as an enemy agent. It is very worrying.
>
> *Boy, sixteen, public school*

And a prep-school boy prays rather hopelessly:

> Please Lord,
>   Help other boys to realise that I can't help being a Favourite. do they pick on me to be kind to, just because I like games?

Make the masters treat me equally with the others, please Lord. I don't like being a Favourite. Amen. *Boy, twelve, prep school*

But to be ignored when one feels deserving, the depression of a boy who has been passed over, shows how intense the competition can become, how status really is important.

Once I felt a very direct responsibility towards the school, but now I am at the top, as Oxford is inevitable next year, I find I am not even a house prefect. Why? Because I am not old enough, promotion is done on age and if enough people do not leave your house its hard luck. The result is naturally discouraging, it is having a very bad effect on my state of mind. I tend to rebel. I cannot work my hardest at anything any more. I have been turned decadent directly by the school's organisation. *Boy, seventeen, public school*

The pressures of the official system do not cease with work, status and authority. Adherence to values is also expected, and while the authority holders we have just seen subscribe to them, at least outwardly, there are those rebels in the school who do not. Unorthodox opinions or behaviour can cause fresh difficulties.

I worry that the school like the Church appears to emphasise external conformity to the exclusion of individual freedom. How can I be free without cutting myself off or selling my soul?
Boy, seventeen, public school

In fact failure to accept and believe when everyone else is so involved can provoke its own anxieties:

It sounds silly but I really worry because I don't give a damn fundamentally about the school or the House, and everyone else seems to so much. *Boy, seventeen, public school*

Political and moral beliefs arouse considerable opposition and difficulty:

I really am most unpopular. I wore a C.N.D. badge into chapel, and

a prefect ran me before my housemaster who said 'I don't want any subversive activities here' then he took it from me.
Boy, sixteen, independent school

While a C.N.D. badge may be quite acceptable at a Quaker school other interests are not. We learn from a boy that

Miss Johnson is a right old cow. I was just settling down with the Kama Sutra hidden behind a book on Careers when she grabbed it, lets out a yell as if she'd been stung on the — and dashes off to the headmaster. *Boy, fourteen, Quaker school*

And a sophisticated rebel at a direct grant school groans:

I'm sick to death of the dreary lower middle class atmosphere of this place, its grey suits, Hillman cars and semi detached villas, all day long one listens to voices straight from Mrs Dale's Diary planning school coach trips to Belgium. Their idea of heaven would be Mr Heath conducting Nimrod at the school concert. *Boy, eighteen*

Girls are less concerned with these abstract problems but can find the school's notions of acceptable behaviour quite as irksome:

I want to wear my hair up but Miss Clifford insists we all have it down. 'It's quite unsuitable for nice young ladies' she maintains, stupid bitch, no one looked at them when they were our age, that's why they are schoolmistresses, and they are out to make sure no one looks at us. *Girl, sixteen, coeducational school*

Now we turn from problems caused by the demands of the official system to the various difficulties posed by life within a closed community. Happiness in a school depends more on how one is accepted by the other children than on school policies.

Many problems spring from continuously having to live a public life, for even in the most generously provisioned school, most teaching, sleeping, eating and leisure are spent in the company of other people. Many resent the lack of privacy, for some boarders are literally never alone. There might be a difficulty of changing friends in a society governed by numerous informal rules on association. Such societies break as we have seen into small groups, and amid all the gossip, busy routine, and cliques some find it difficult to make meaningful relationships with others and withdraw into themselves, while a few are misfits cast out by the others, bullied perhaps, scorned and lonely, with no one to talk to. The problems of the children's world are considerable and first we illustrate the pressure of living with many others.

A boy at a public school voices a frequent complaint that you can never get away from other people:

> You long for the moment you can get away from the noise and endless bickering of the others. The study is no good, someone always comes in, and the walls are like tissue paper you can hear everything. Sometimes I sit in the chapel or walk across the games field. In my prep school it was worse, the only place to read without interruption there was the lavatory. *Boy, seventeen*

In some schools the facilities are inadequate:

> There are far too many people here, not only do you have to queue to get a wash basin, you have to queue in the bogs as well. If you are mad enough to send your son to a boarding school don't give him a fiver because that will be pinched, press a wash hand basin plug into one hand and a toilet roll into the other. They're hard to find here.
> *Boy, sixteen, independent school*

Eating and sleeping again are moments when other people can rapidly get on one's nerves. A boy at an independent school asks us to imagine

> seven hundred sitting down to eat, you don't hold a conversation you shout your most intimate thoughts into the nearest lughole, and when the noise begins to shake the dust off the portraits, red lights flash over the doors and we all have to shut up. *Boy, seventeen*

Another boy comments on the unpleasant experiences of communal living:

I hate sleeping in dormitory and always have done. The sight of those bare bulbs and bare backsides just makes me sick. There is always a noise, grunts from passionate dreamers, snores from the hearties, the endless whispering of those who need no sleep at all. Then when you are just falling asleep the flashing torches of the housemasters vice squad.
Boy, sixteen, independent school

As the term goes on, nerves get frayed and there is much friction, jealousy and gossip:

The house pres quite drive me mad, they never stop gossiping, the masters, the domestics, the school love-life, anything everything is gone over with a fine tooth comb, and when things get a little dull they fabricate some scandal just to watch the effect on the people concerned. What it must be like in a girls' school I fear to think.
Boy, eighteen, head of house, public school

A girl at a mixed boarding school gives us some hint:

We had a lovely gossip about old Flo and Mr Wood, how far they had got, then how Marie looks a tart with her new hair style, she looked like one before really but we hadn't got round to her until now. Then we had to go off to the Meeting.
Girl, sixteen, Quaker school

Such gossip and jealousy can produce considerable unhappiness:

There are, however, many genuine good personal relationships between boy and boy, boy and master etc., and they tend to suffer because of the loud-mouth who will say all sorts of things about them, and tends to make the relationship become far less personal on the boy's side. Rumour and scandal are nasty things – many a good relationship has been spoilt and much worry has been caused to innocent people by nasty-minded louts, perverts, etc.
Boy, sixteen, public school

Gossip does not even stop at the school gates:

But you can never get away from this place, a boy in Johnson's spilled a cup of coffee at a party in London in the holidays everyone was there; so he's out and everyone calls him 'coffee' in the school. They won't let you forget even little things.

Boy, eighteen, public school

Jealousy is not confined to the mixed communities:

Johnson, the senior prefect, got into a frenzy because he imagined I was after one his little boys. Thomas, of all people, I wouldn't touch him with a barge pole, he's been touched by too many of those already. *Boy, seventeen, independent school*

And one very common and serious problem arises when friendships break up in confined communities:

One disturbing problem which does effect one very deeply during the years that you are here, is that you have to live with the same people for about 4 years. Now when you have a break up of friendship in this circle with a person you still have to go on living with, it can lead to a great deal of tension amongst the circle and can lead to a complete upheaval. *Boy, seventeen, independent school*

Although the gossip can be distressing, the cliques sometimes prevent harmony, and friendships can be for some difficult to manage, a worse fate is endured by those whom no one bothers to talk about, the outcasts, few as they are, of this society. Many children enjoy the endless scandal and intrigue, but the problems endured by the outsider are the most severe to be faced in the boarding school. Two boys comment on the fate of the misfit.

For a boy who is unhappy and does not mix well there is no escape at boarding school and life can be nightmareish. Victimisation can be carried further in such a close community.

Boy, seventeen, direct grant school

From a boy in a large academic public school who has a smattering of sociological jargon:

A boy with no friends within the House is usually able to make friends in his form, but those who fail in this also are very vulnerable, often displaying anti-social tendencies such as stealing or a complete withdrawal into themselves, or a reliance upon a larger boy for company and protection. These are ridiculed by one's age group, often bringing further withdrawal. *Boy, eighteen*

In an interview, a senior boy in the house describes what it is like to be 'out':

Of course everyone goes through a period here when they're 'out' with the group. Mine was worse, my greatest friend had got his examinations and cleared out, that's his photograph on my desk, we'd been together since we arrived he had the study next door. The first boy to go through hell absolute hell, was Brian, the state scholarship boy. How he survived I don't know. One feels rotten when one looks back at the things we did to him. We pinched his books, his clothes, broke up his study, that sort of thing and the senior boys didn't do anything. But he could at least play the piano which kept him sane but I couldn't escape into my stamp collection so I plucked up a lot of courage and went to the art room. You see here you feel you mustn't try in case you aren't very good, everyone will get at you, it's better not to have started. I got so lonely sometimes I didn't know what to do, sometimes I just wanted to jump out of the window and end it all. I used to come back to my study and sit and cry. It is one of the school's great advantages, most people love these studies but at times they're like little prisons, one didn't even have a radio to listen to. Some of them never show anything, Adrian has been 'out' at times but he never indicated that he even noticed people were being bloody to him. *Boy, eighteen, public school*

Attempts made to integrate the outsider into the house are not always successful, as a house captain points out:

There is very little you can do, they walk everywhere by themselves and even on the river they never seem to make an eight. I am against this tradition of boys arranging their own teas, someone always ends up having tea by himself, in his study while people are ragging about next door, its known as a 'dustbin' mess and must be quite grim to endure.

The following group of study chits, written requests by boys to the housemaster for study allocation as the new term opens at a public school, reveals again how the outsiders are clear to all and their companionship not sought after. In this house of sixty-five there were three such boys below the sixth-form level: Miller, Davies and Knight.

Study chit
C. G. Franklin and Sinclair J. P. would like to have a two study if possible next term.
If not possible *NOT* with Miller.

Miller's own study chit runs:

Since Andrew Finch is not going in a study with me next term, I do not know who to go with until I know what other people are doing.

Study chit
Davies and Knight would like to share a study as we are the only two left almost, we are hoping for a two study, but *not* with Miller.

Study chit
If possible I should like to go in a study with Oakman, Berril and Connington, but not particularly with (in fact, at all costs) Davies or Knight.

Study chit
Oakman, Berril and Connington would like, if possible to have a 3 study, but we do not get on well with Davies or Knight and please *not* Miller.

Those left outside can sometimes be bullied:

They get at you endlessly. Every lesson there is something. If you do answer a question you are a creep, if you don't your thick. They always take everything, your P.T. kit, your books, and when you finally break down they redouble the attack.

Boy, fourteen, public school

I got up to dormitory and found again they had tied my pyjamas into knots. They never leave you alone, so I got into bed without them, and everyone whistled. *Boy, fifteen, independent school*

And the bullied prep-school boy prays for help to make an Old Testament response to persecution:

O God, I'm awfully small and that bully always punches me. Make me strong and tall so I can reach his nose and punch it. Amen.

Boy, eleven, prep school

Sometimes of course the outsider can make a swift return to favour, as a boy of fourteen patronizingly points out:

Norwood is a swot really, and we gave him hell at first but he won a school scholarship after a couple of terms which meant he could move across to another house and get all his fees paid. But he refused to go and decided to stay with us, which we all felt was frightfully nice. So he is terribly 'in' now and can be really amusing.

Boy, fourteen, public school

Most outsiders pretend not to mind, and in many schools refusal to show the slightest signs of distress can command considerable respect:

One cannot help but admire Benson in a way, the others are really swinish, some days hardly anyone speaks to him, but he never shows he cares. I find him civil and helpful but the others just loathe him.

Boy, eighteen, head of house, public school

Refusal to show unhappiness in the face of persecution may be admirable, but in public schools and other single-sex communities where it is part of a certain clear ideal of behaviour, this sort of self-control can pose fresh problems. In such schools 'public living' has important consequences. From their earlier days in the prep schools these boys are carefully supervised and deliberately allowed no privacy. From the start the exhibition of any emotion is discouraged, sometimes by the school but more often by the informal society of the boys, as earlier chapters illustrate. Until recent decades, emotional display was not readily witnessed at home, for the upper-middle-class parent avoided the real chores of bringing up sticky babies and preserved a public self 'in front of the children'.

Single-sex boarding schools cannot officially provide their children with an emotional life; what there is must be hidden and furtive, and both the school and the boy world discourage the display of emotion and the revelation of deep feeling, as this makes people vulnerable. Instantly, one can become the target for gossip and in such societies the deeper the feeling the quicker and deeper the hurt. Hence some boys grow up with an inability to communicate real emotion, a fear of it in many forms, an acute sense of embarrassment at the sight of it in others, and a preparedness to accept relationships with others only within certain limits. Some have an inability to make deep affective relationships, and are keenly aware of this. It can cause them considerable distress, as does their ignorance of how to handle deep emotional situations. It is not only a question of deliberately imposed self-control, of the conscious stiff-upper-lip. A minority of public school boys find that they cannot act in any other way, they are affectively neutral and worry because of it.

First a boy describes his emotional difficulties:

I have enjoyed being here – it's mainly the people you meet, but I'm not sure that boarding is good over a long time. You don't see many girls and I feel awkward. Life with my girl friend has been difficult I was very fond of her for three years but never really said anything, you couldn't say that you loved her, in fact it took me ages to put my arms round her. I felt that I would die with embarrassment. In fact, we just used to sit and look at each other. It was the same with John here. The others used to hint at lots of things but as we were in the upper part of the house they didn't say much. I just don't seem to be able to talk to people. I went to bed with my girl friend but though

it all went all right I just couldn't talk to her and afterwards I just sat and looked out of the window in a daze, she burst into tears. We had a row in the end. She said I was too self sufficient and cleared out. I haven't heard from her for ages. I worry about this sort of thing a lot, there are sorts of high walls that separate parts of your life. I can be affectionate to my parents, they're both quite old and seem very sort of tired and you can be kind by just sitting and talking but with people of your own age it is much more difficult. I get in a bit of a panic at times and feel that there is something wrong with me.
Boy, eighteen, public school

and another boy comments:

Price-Cavendish is incredibly cool, he never really shows anything. Because the family is so famous people take it out on him but he never hints that he feels it. The only time he cried we were amazed, it was when one of his dogs died. His father died from cancer two years ago and he didn't react at all, he just apologised that he wouldn't be able to play cricket for the house.
Boy, seventeen, same school

Two boys from different independent schools again find themselves with similar problems:

What worries me most is that I can't be natural. How do you show you like someone, what sort of kindness do you give to parents and relations without seeming utterly soft and wet. Sometimes I feel I am empty and unable to feel things.
Boy, seventeen, independent school

Fundamentally I don't think I really give a damn about anyone except myself. You soon learn that its best not to be really interested too much in anyone or anything.
Boy, seventeen, independent school

The initiation into this world comes early and can be difficult, as some prep-school boys illustrate:

They take away your teddies and gonks, for no reason. To make us stand up for ourselves, but I cried when mine went, after all it is only a teddy to keep you company. *Boy, seven, prep school*

If a boy cries everyone laughs at him or goes away because he is a baby and very wet. *Boy, eight, prep school*

And others illustrate how the spontaneous affections of small children can be repressed and their emotional performances checked:

If you say 'Dad' to a master they get very cross, you don't mean it but you forget at first. You must not use christian names, but family names, or hold hands – that is soft. *Boy, eight, prep school*

English was not good. I was unhappy in the test as I got a black mark. Mr Jones got in a nark and said, there's no use crying, you are a baby, how will you get on at a public school, and the boys laughed at me.
Boy, eight, prep school

A great deal might be written on the use of christian names and surnames as a guide to affective behaviour:

They kept asking me my name and when I said John they all laughed and said not that one stupid, the real one, and then I said Ashton and they nick named me 'Ashcan'. *Boy, seven, prep school*

It was very difficult having to remember to call my elder brother by his surname when we spoke in school. He was really annoyed when I made a mistake. *Boy, thirteen, public school*

and the moment when the christian name is employed can have great significance:

He said you can call me Brian if you like, when the others are not about, and I felt very happy as he is quite senior to me and an excellent oarsman. *Boy, fourteen, public school*

Its use is learned early:

> If I am in a good mood with my friend then I use his first name but if I am niggled or he has gone too far then I use the second one. It's the same in school it lets boys know how they stand. You call every junior *always* by their surname. *Boy, twelve, prep school*

But even in the prep school self-control comes quickly, and with it some of the difficulties we have seen in their more senior brothers:

> We act more responsibly and are better mannered than children at the local school you should hear the noise as you go past and what they do in the playground. *Boy, twelve, prep school*

Demonstration of feeling can be out of the question:

> Lord,
> I ask you this,
> Why Lord,
> Why is it that I am left alone,
> Far from my parents, home and friend
> Far from those creatures I love and tend;
> I may not shed a tear,
> You know why Lord.
> Here I am, lone and friendless,
> I'm one of them
> Nobody in particular
> Just one of them,
> 'Smith' they call me;
> But I may not cry Lord,
> You know why.
>
> *Boy, eleven, prep school*

It is incidentally a pattern of behaviour set by the staff, a goal shared by most within the walls, as this example suggests:

> He told me my mother had just phoned to say that my father had

been badly hurt at work and may not recover. But I wasn't to worry
and must go off and play rugger as usual.

Boy, fifteen, independent school

If emotional display is difficult for oneself the sight of it in others
can produce intense embarrassment. At a groundsman's presentation
we learn that:

After giving him the cheque for being here umpteen years we had to
endure a speech. He was almost in tears and we were all quite dreadfully embarrassed. I can't remember when last I saw someone overcome with emotion, it must have been back at my prep school. I
have never seen a boy cry here.

House prefect, eighteen, public school

At a moment of triumph subdued behaviour is expected:

Johnson actually danced when he heard he had a Cambridge award.
He will never live that down. *Boy, eighteen, public school*

A prep-school boy voices the confusion felt by thousands of
boarders.

Parents can be so embarrassing even when you have cured them from
giving the farewell kiss. They fuss and put their arms around you, its
a relief to get on the train. *Boy, twelve, prep school*

Affectively neutral behaviour such as we have just illustrated may be
declining in public and prep schools but it is less common in other
boarding schools. State boarding schools, where pupils have lived at
home until eleven or twelve, exhibit far less of it; pupils are more
spontaneous, demonstrative, noisy and prepared to show what they
feel. Mixed boarding at any age prevents it, for in contrast to boys,
girls are expected to be emotional, tantrums are quite permissible and
the boys are not forced to behave very differently: adult behaviour is
not required. At senior levels girls make an emotional life possible, if in
some cases risky, for the boys. Neither do these schools have the goals

of 'responsibility' and self-control so high on their list of priorities as do the public schools. Just to point the contrast one wonders how some of the boys who contributed above would have responded to coffee time at this Quaker school:

> I was half way through my cuppa Nescafé when in burst Joanna in one of her Maria Callas acts, she burst into tears and said everyone was being quite unbearable to her. So John who is a bit gone on Jo made her sit on his lap and share his cup (I think that's why she did it). Then Peter accused Anne and me of being bitchy to her, he looks marvellous when his eyes flash and he's mad furious.
>
> *Girl, sixteen, Quaker school*

Let us now look at what exactly the children do when faced with the type of problems just illustrated. Some children seek advice, a few run away and the great majority just live through them. We find that over three quarters of the children in our boarding schools would not discuss a serious personal difficulty with anyone, and even fewer would take such a problem to an adult. (For day children the position may be worse.)

The boarding environment at once makes for ready and sympathetic adults to turn to, but discourages their use because of the disciplinary roles, the supervisory functions and constant presence of these members of staff. Occasionally it is the marginal members of the community, groundsmen, tuck-shop ladies, that are sought after by the children just because their positions are uncompromised by other school functions. In single-sex schools many senior boys may take up pastoral positions, and girls, enjoying a motherly role, are very important in the mixed boarding community.

Let us look at those seeking advice on a problem or hoping for some sympathetic response. First the younger children whose major problem is usually homesickness and then the older who have more varied difficulties. A small boy at a direct grant school in the midlands comments on the kindness of the staff:

> When he is on duty he comes round the dormitory and talks to each one of us, says funny things and makes jokes, he cheers up those that

are a bit homesick. The monitors get wild because they say it stirs up a lot of noise but they forget what it is like being at the bottom of the school with no one to talk to.
Boy, eleven

Another boy at a secondary modern boarding school recovers from a fright:

> I like it here very much and there is a lot of work to be done. Last night I was very scared because the dorm leader he was talking about ghosts. He said there was one up in the tower. He also said he was not joking, and I started to cry. I got taken to Mr Roberts room, I read a book, and 1 hr later I went back to bed. *Boy, twelve*

Another suggests a device for curing the unconsolable:

> I made a lot of fuss and said I wanted to go home, I didn't want his mouldy biscuits and lemonade. He wouldn't persuade me to stay for anything. So this master got out ten bob, gave it to me and said the last bus goes in half an hour. But I never caught it, I felt a bit silly and later gave him his money back.
>
> *Boy, eleven, state grammar school*

A prep-school boy suggests the great pastoral value of women in the school and a family circle.

> I felt very homesick so the Headmaster's wife was very nice. I played with their little boy and watched tele a bit, then I had a cup of milk and a chocolate biscuit. Afterwards I didn't feel so bad and as I had missed prep went straight to bed. *Boy, eight, prep school*

Senior children carry more specific problems to the staff:

> I had a long talk about my work with the senior master, he was quite comforting, even if the worst came to the worst and I didn't get to Oxbridge, somewhere is bound to take me. In ten years time it won't make the slightest difference he said.
>
> *Boy, seventeen, independent school*

Home problems can receive understanding as usually boarding staff, unlike day ones, know the parents. Many public school staff have very close contact with their boys' families, and the pupils turn to them often on family matters.

> I was utterly depressed and had a long talk with my Housemaster. He knows the whole business of my mother leaving my dad because he is going around with someone else. I am fond of both parents but they try to make me take sides, they talk about it incessantly and ruin any time I have with them. But my Housemaster was kindness itself over coffee and he said I must try to understand that they were both unhappy and didn't mean to upset me, there were many boys in school facing the same problems – and a lot more. He insisted that when I felt fed up I should go and sit in his study and wait for him to turn up. He's told me to come down to his cottage in Dorset in the Easter holidays to get away from it all. He's made a lot of difference.
> *Boy, sixteen, public school*

And on emotional (and other) matters the chaplain can be sought out:

> I had a long talk on my crushes for the middle school kids. He said everyone went through that sort of thing at my age even he did, in spite of the dog collar. He said you shouldn't be frightened of feeling strong affection for others, it is much better than feeling nothing.
> *Boy, seventeen, public school*

Even day boys can benefit in a good pastoral atmosphere:

> Though I am a day boy, I get to know some of the masters quite well. Our form master looks after the boarders and at lunch time we go off to his room to scrounge a cup of coffee. I've learned to talk about my parents being separated and lots of other embarrassing things which I wouldn't have done otherwise.
> *Boy, fifteen, state boarding school*

These two illustrations show the value of the schools' auxiliary staff:

Mrs Thomas who serves in the tuck shop is really kind, she always is interested in what you are doing. I often talk about all sorts of things when I am down there.

Boy, sixteen, public school

The maids here are very kind to everyone, they help lots of boys over a bad patch. You know it is said that during the war when old boys were in prison camps and hospitals they wrote many letters to the maids at school, more often than to their families.

Boy, eighteen, public school

Many find it easier to turn to other children rather than face the staff and much excellent pastoral care is done by the older members of a boarding school. A small boy remarks:

If I was in any trouble I would talk to one of the senior boys, they can be quite understanding and help you if things go badly. One of them is very kind, he lends you things and takes us on treasure hunts. He hasn't a father so he knows what it's like to be lonely. I would talk to him.

Boy, twelve, state boarding school

and the girls in the mixed boarding society have a busy time:

Peter sat and talked for hours about his university chances and how badly his work was going. I wanted to scream but tried desperately to say the right thing. Why are men so selfish. They want endless help and if we get in a state, they dismiss us as hysterical. Still he seemed much better when he finally left.

Girl, sixteen, progressive school

I think Peggy ought to run one of those problem columns in the school magazine, when I got over there who should be in her room but Susan in a mood and tearful. That great oaf Colin had gone off to play football without bothering to see her. Someone is always in there having a good weep or moan, it's like that silly programme about nuns on the telly.

Girl, seventeen, Quaker school

Yet in spite of these optimistic illustrations some children are inevitably critical of their school's pastoral provision and many will turn to no one:

> There is often a tremendous sense of loneliness since there is no 'in loco parentis' here whatever the prospectus says.
> *Girl, sixteen, coeducational school*

Another boy illustrates his need and the response to it:

> All the staff are against me, they make no effort to understand me. They're totally unsympathetic, they just hit you when you do wrong. Once I was upset because my father who I hadn't seen for years wrote and invited me to go to the pictures with him and when I got to the cinema he was with his latest woman. The staff made no effort to understand how I felt.
> *Boy, fifteen, state boarding school*

and another suggests his housemaster is preoccupied:

> My housemaster should really be a person who looks after the problems of each boy, however mine is only worried about his house band and nothing else.
> *Boy, sixteen, independent school*

or quite simply states:

> They don't worry about my needs, they dismiss me as a nut.
> *Boy, fifteen, state boarding school*

Even those people from whom sympathy might be expected and who have no disciplinary functions to complicate their pastoral care can be a disappointment:

> Went to Matron's surgery because had caught finger in car door yesterday evening; sympathy extended to telling me that nothing could be done to relieve the pain and that I needn't come down again

till the nail – now black – came off. Was given two aspirins in case of emergency! *Boy, sixteen, direct grant school*

Went to see Matron as usual on Sat. morning. Found her having a verbal go at one of the more defenceless juniors. I think she is a bitch at the best of times, but this called up a feeling of real hostility. Adopted attitude of *cold* civility. *Prefect, eighteen, public school.*

Some children stress the point that any member of staff, however sympathetic, is difficult to approach:

How can you go to talk about something that you know they should punish you for, or about private and personal things you never hear them mention. And if you did go how can you be sure they would forget it? *Boy, fifteen, public school*

and two girls realize the staff's real predicament:

You feel very isolated here, and it sometimes feels strange to think that the world ticks on outside without bothering about what happens here. It is very difficult for the staff who look upon you (sometimes) both as a friend and as a subordinate, sometimes indiciplined out-of-school. *Girl, sixteen, Quaker school*

People say 'When there is a lot of you, you can't have so many things as at home'. But blow it all a boarding house can never be a substitute for home. Who is there to tell your problems to no one, who is there to see your point of view no one. Oh they say come and see me if anything goes wrong, but its hopeless because the fact remains that you have to be careful what you say because they are still a member of staff so what chance have we?
Girl, sixteen, state boarding school

The problem of facing the person who is the recipient of confidences is emphasized by this boy:

If I had a real problem I would probably hitch a lift into the nearest

town and tell the lorry driver. Then I would slam the door and he
would drive away with it. I wouldn't have to face him again.

Boy, seventeen, state boarding school

As research workers independent of the school and its values we
were so often told

> its easy to tell you all about it because you don't matter, everything
> is confidential, and you will be gone at the end of the week.
>
> *Boy, sixteen, public school*

It would be wrong to move from this brief illustration of pastoral
care in schools without mentioning the very important function of
animals. To dismiss their pastoral value as sentimental would be to
underestimate it greatly. The reader will remember the beagles in an
earlier chapter; now we hear of some other animals:

> I have all these animals to look after and spend most of my time
> wondering if the calf has arrived, when the foal is due, the pigs are
> always getting their snouts caught in the wire. I forget all about
> school and its stupid worries. I forget about myself too.
>
> *Boy, fifteen, Quaker school*

Pets and animals can provide an affective outlet and make one feel
wanted in a hostile community:

> After tea I felt unhappy because the holidays seemed so far away, so
> I had a long chat with Pinky and Perky, my two pet mice. I will
> show them to you if you like. *Boy, eight, prep school*

> Just as I had decided to clear out of this dump for good, I remembered Gert and Daisy, these are two cows that need very careful
> handling. Nobody bothers to treat them right so I stayed put, I
> couldn't have left them to the tender mercies of this crowd of bums.
>
> *Boy, sixteen, farm training school*

and from a public school near London a boy informs us:

My horse arrives next week, he is staying on a field near the school, it will be nice to have someone to talk to.
Boy, sixteen

Those that do not seek some sort of help from outside usually put up with their problems. They survive happily enough. But a minority withdraw from the harsh realities of existence as they see it or protect themselves by eccentric behaviour. 'Kemsley hardly ever talks to anyone. He has been here four years and still pretends he doesn't know people's names. Still he is harmless and knows an immense amount about useless things like heraldry.' Very occasionally the escape from problems can be more extreme: running away from the school (not just the practice of small boys), drug-taking and even attempted suicide. These are by no means usual responses, but they are part of the boarding school experience and deserve a mention. The examples which follow are necessarily longer but they illustrate much else that this chapter has briefly described. First an outsider runs away from a state school.

It was Friday prep, I was sent to the Duty Master for laughing during time of work. I walked out of the prep room, but decided not to go as it would either mean seeing the Headmaster in the morning and having the cane or two hours extra prep indefinitely.

After prep I saw the duty master, as anybody who reads this can guess, I had to see the dreaded Headmaster in the morning.

As soon as I was clear I rushed up stairs gathered a few clothes, jeans, suede tie, greenish-brown coloured shirt, a jumper and torch stuffed these into a bag and hastily disappeared. I meant to go down to the changing room and get a donkey jacket, but I forgot. I ran down the back lane for 150 yards or so, turned off into a disused farm yard which had a convenient straw rick. I changed from my school clothes to the clothes I have just described, packed my school clothes in the haversack. I went down the lane and walked to the village. Here I met one of the dayboys who was going home after prep, he was waiting for the bus. I had no money on me. He asked where I was going. I replied that I had to go and see the doctor and I kept on walking. But it was no good after about five minutes he caught me up and held me by the arm. He was a lot bigger than I was and said he had rung the school and they were looking for me. So we waited and I just didn't care what happened. Then the headmaster drove up and I got in first we took home the dayboy as he had missed his bus. He talked with the H.M. about policemen etc. speeding and all that sort of thing.

The dayboy had now been dropped off. The H.M. started talking to me very kindly and being very understanding, saying that he realised something was wrong and asked why I did it; I explained that I needed a break for a while didn't really know what I was doing. I spent the next hour in the Head's House watching T.V. taking to him, and had some supper, which was heaven to the food we were getting at school. The Head left for about $\frac{1}{2}$ an hour to see the Duty Master and tell him where I was. Later I went over to the school to bed. I lay awake until half past twelve thinking things over. The Head Master said that I only had to see him if there was any trouble or anything bothering me again.

The next morning I had to see the Headmaster after assembly. I eventually saw him and was amazed that I was let off completely for this and was asked if everything was now all right. I replied that it was and left the study after this.

It seems a hard life for me at boarding school for I am always tormented and bullied, you can not do anything about it, as it would cause more trouble and make myself disliked even more than I am. Nobody likes a split not even myself. I want you to understand that I don't split but sometimes I get so tensed up and angry at these happenings that I don't know what to do. I've got to somehow let it out of my system. I don't know if all boys get in this situation but I always seem to be. It was really this that made me run-away or as it is so called here do a bunk. The being sent to the duty master only 'triggered' it off.

Boy, sixteen

Next a public school boy exemplifies many of the problems we have already described in this chapter. Like our previous fugitive he runs away because he finds his problems overwhelming and has no one to talk to. Again a trivial incident sparks off his absconsion.

It was on Tuesday evening, just before prep when I remembered a chance remark by one of the teaching staff. This had not been meant as a spiteful remark, but he had accused me of not having played rugger very hard that afternoon. This hurt, because I had played very hard. This sent me into a mood of depression which lasted throughout prep, and right up to when I went to sleep. Unfortunately my study companion had not been there that evening and he was the only one who could have cheered me up.

I woke up at about 1 a.m. and immediately the depression started again. I began to think of other things now. For a start, my housemaster. He and I did not get on well together. He had already beaten me twice, and was permanently being rude to me. This made me very annoyed, and I was often rude back. Then I thought of my parents, and 'O' levels. My mother, after promising implicitly not to be angry if I had not done well, spent the rest of the holidays making nasty comments about them and telling me how many other people had. This was becoming unbearable. I had in fact contemplated leaving home and joining the Merchant Navy. I was worried as well about the fact that I had only got two 'O' levels. I felt that I had let my parents down, which seem to be justified by the action of my mother. This weighed on my mind. I felt I just could not stand it any longer, I had to get out and live for myself, and not be pestered by these people, and especially by exams.

So I got up, flung a few very odd things into my case (e.g. packet of Daz, and my razor) and got out. I hitched a lift after $\frac{1}{2}$ an hour which took me through to London airport, where I slept for the night on one of the comfortable benches in the European departure place. Then I hitched a lift into Chelsea tried to get a job as a bar tender, couldn't get it. So I walked to Fulham and saw a film. Then I hitched my way back home. But I didn't go in immediately but waited behind in a field, trying to sleep. I think I was intending to steal some money off my parents, as by this time I had nothing.

But finally I was so tired and hungry, that I returned home, and finally to school. No disciplinary action was taken.

Since then everybody, including my housemaster, has been very kind to me. But why did it take such a shock action to do this? Why couldn't they have been more pleasant before? Why was there no body for me to talk to? *Boy, sixteen, public school*

But there is no need to run away to escape from problems, as a public school boy explains:

> About twenty must be on drugs although what they take I am not sure. I think it is very dangerous and its always the people who can't really cope with life here. The school have some idea who is involved but can't really get to the bottom of it. *Boy, eighteen*

Finally a tiny minority are tempted by suicide as these two contributions indicate. A boy returns from a football match to find:

> The place was buzzing with excitement when I got back because Walpole had taken a whole bottle of pills and gone off to sleep. They rushed him across the city in an ambulance with hooter going and flashing lights with Gran (the housemaster) inside holding his hand. That must have been a sight. Anyway they manned the stomach pumps and he's not coming back for a month. There was a big inquisition from which nothing emerged except that he was fed up – which goes for everyone I should imagine.
> *Boy, sixteen, independent school*

and another boy confesses:

> I feel I really rely on my friends too much. The few occasions that all three of them have been away, were spent in acute boredom and a feeling of absolute nothingness for me, leading me to contemplate suicide almost seriously, its a feeling I cannot possibly describe.
> *Boy, sixteen, public school*

Although schools may seek to shelter their children from the tensions and temptations of the outside world, the isolation and single-sex composition of many boarding schools, the pressures of their formal world and the demands of the pupils' own society obviously pose many problems that are unknown to the day child. We have seen the boarders' difficulties and some of their responses, but it must be emphasized that boarding schools are not usually unhappy places, that many children relish the scandal and enjoy the competition and the gregarious life of the boarder. 'It is more interesting than home, I think you worry more, little issues become big ones in this closed community, but you *do feel alive*. There is a lot of talk about even if it always inevitably comes back to sex.'

11 Sex in Single-sex Schools

Penny Curtis, one of our research staff, returned home from a stay at a state boarding school for boys. The next day there arrived with our mail a group of letters from the school, of which the following is a typical example. From a boy aged fifteen:

Dear Miss Curtis,
   Me and Tom were very sorry to see you go yesterday. Me and Tom are the best of friends, here we sit in the library writing a letter to you, my name is Michael Barnes. Me and Tom talk about you and we will never forget you. Me, Tom and a lot of other boys would like you to come back sometime. Miss Curtis I think you are the most beautiful girl I have ever seen in my life. Be expecting quite a few letters from this school, one from Me and one from Tom and from Trefer and one from Barry. Good bye for now.
                                        Yours loving
                                        Michael Barnes
   × × × × × × × × × × × × × × × × ×
PS   Please write to me and I have put my fortorgraf in the envelope. If you write could you please sent me a fortorgraf of you.

Wherever we went, as this letter shows, we could not avoid the question of sex. To the adolescents of thirteen and over who form the vast majority of boarders, the development, control and fulfilment of their sexual energies is a matter of overriding personal importance and a subject which pervades the talk, the imagery, the humour and the activity of the communal underlife as well as attracting the attention of the staff. The community of the school, with its own special deprivations and gratifications, with its protracted confinement to a society of adolescents, may possibly stimulate some aspects of the sexual consciousness, concern and complexity of boarders in a way less usual with dayschool children. Certainly sex is a major element of their personal and social existence: and that is why we are devoting space to it in this book.

We did not seek information on sex from the boarders, but it sought us in abundance, as the letter above suggests. Earnest, remorseless and omnivorous sociologists as we doubtless seem, we nevertheless felt we had no right to intrude and explore the more intimate and delicate areas of boys' and girls' lives. Our questionnaires, therefore, never asked them about their own sexual experience, though certain indirect psychological tests measured modes of sexual orientation and response, and other questions gathered their views on emotional and sexual life in the school in general. With headmasters, housemasters, other staff, school doctors and matrons our interviews systematically covered the subject, and our own notes of observation on day-to-day life in the schools and documents shown to us provide much else of relevance. But though we did not seek from the children, we found. In countless cases (sometimes ninety per cent of the sample in a school) replies to questionnaires on problems or satisfactions or friendships or pastoral care produced full and frank discussions of emotions and sexual life. The diaries, which children volunteered to write, of their thoughts, feelings, and doings, treated sex openly, and sometimes we were, as the reader may be, surprised, if not disturbed at their contents. As we got to know the boys and girls and they got to realize that we would not break the confidence of anyone in the community, many of them talked freely about their private lives and often produced writings, stacks of recent letters or poems. Several had never communicated to an adult before on such matters. A few still could not do so: their contributions came anonymous and pathetically authentic in brown envelopes slipped under the researcher's door or were left, minutely folded and heavily sealed with sticky tape – symbols of inhibition – on the researcher's desk.

The research reported in this book covered boys' and coeducational schools, not girls' schools. Only eight per cent of boarders of secondary age are in coeducational schools. The vast majority of secondary boarders are in single-sex schools, and most in boys' ones, of which we lived in fifty-five.

Earlier sections of this book have already illustrated the varying policies of the all-boys school towards the other sex. Some state boarding, some independent and a steadily growing number of public schools allow their boys to go out with girls or to bring them in: but these are still a minority of schools. Others allow boys to go out only with selected girls – one independent school has a list of approved girls in the town and any boy seen out with a girl not on the list is beaten; another, a public school, allows boys to meet the girls from the local grammar school, but not from the near-by secondary modern. But for the majority of boys in boarding schools girlfriends in the locality are either not allowed, or are severely discouraged, or are difficult to find. The schools content themselves with a few supervised formal meetings a term, dances and plays, with girls from schools of similar social standing near by (though often not *too* near by).

In a majority of schools, most boys over fifteen feel effectively isolated from the other sex by the official policy:

> The Head does not seem to realise what it is like being cooped up here for weeks on end without any real amenities for letting off steam. Dam it, what the hell does he think we are – sterile?
> *Boy, seventeen, public school*

> The staff seem to think that girls are 'the root of all evil' here, and if we see them we will be contaminated. I think they are delightful.
> *Boy, eighteen, public school*

Some feel constrained from any expression of their sexual natures:

> Sex is a disadvantage – no females and blokes resorting to little boys, even I who have tried to resist have found myself falling for a nice little chap – expulsion if I am caught. The point is that *no* sex is allowed, its as though we are not supposed to have it in our veins. Not allowed to see girls in town – let alone hold hands or kiss them. Not allowed either to go around with blokes younger than yourself. Even a quiet wank by yourself in bed (all thats left) is a sin.
> *Boy, seventeen, independent school*

Sex in Single-sex Schools 335

In schools where the official policy is more tolerant, the situation can still be difficult because of the geographical isolation of the school or because of difficulties inherent in residential communities:

Sexually you have four choices:
(1) Write or phone to a girl friend at home – if you have one and can keep one – very difficult.
(2) Find a girl friend downtown – impossible (too many boys and too few girls) and anyway the Housemaster will breathe down your neck and the decent girls don't want us birds of passage.
(3) Chase after little boys – a dangerous diversion.
(4) Ignore sex altogether – impossible.
Some choices!

Boy, seventeen, public school

Even when girl friends *are* allowed the watchful vigilance of the staff and its values can prove hurdles:

Oh yes, we're allowed girl friends alright – provided my parents write to the Old Man and say I can go out with her and provided her parents write to him and say she can go out with me. How do you ever bloody well *meet* a girl in the first place? I ask you!

Boy, seventeen, public school

Sunday 3 pm. Meet Sandra near church and took her for a walk on the common, sat by the river ... had a pleasant afternoon ... 9.0 pm. After prayers, called to Housemaster's study. Said he'd heard (who from?) that I'd been seen out with a girl not of the right kind, 'common', not the sort my parents would approve, they get 'boys into trouble', etc. Why couldn't I go out with someone from the High School? He might have to let my parents know – blackmail.

Boy, seventeen, public school

When outside girls are unobtainable a few hardy spirits may risk association with younger members of the school's own domestic staff – kitchen apprentices, assistant nurses or matrons or maids, who may not be so much older than the older boys:

336 The Hothouse Society

I think that the attitude towards women is very bad in this school. I am very fond of a member of the lady staff at this school and I hope and think she is fond of me. The idea that if the Head knew that I liked her and she liked me he would probably demote me and expel her proves to be a great buffer to our friendship during the term and emphasises the restrictions.

Prefect, eighteen, public school

In a large number of schools the main point of contact, officially at least, with girls is still the school or house dance. These occur usually once or twice a term, though in some schools there might be four – 'two home and two away sex matches' as one boy puts it. Fifteen-year-olds frequently find them satisfactory, but the older boys (and the staff) rarely do so.

Sometimes it is because of over-vigilance on the part of the authorities, which takes all the spontaneity out of them:

At dances the staff sit on a dais so they can see whats going on, all the lights are full on, people who sit out are asked why, the doors are locked so you can't slip out with your partner, and the route back to the coach for the girls is patrolled by one old bag from the girls school and Baldy. Just to make the evening 'go' a bit more, they only let us do ballroom or country dancing – modern dancing is too sexy, and we sip orange in the break. Coke is 'too common'.

Boy, seventeen, independent school

Sometimes, however the boys find a little variety:

We have dances with convents but the girls are terrified of the nuns, who prowl around, and these are a washout. Non-religious girls schools are more fun, though one must admit that the general tone of the proceedings becomes somewhat coarse . . .

Boy, eighteen, public school

It is this latter feature which makes dances so problematic for the schools and distasteful to many boys:

I think it is ridiculous having 2 or 3 orgies with some girls schools each term – it makes sex like salty water to a thirsty man.

Boy, seventeen, public school

Sex-starved boy and girl boarders meet for three hours of artificial behaviour in an atmosphere of excitement: the lights go out (if possible), the staff are ignored, 'snogging' frequently takes place as if the individuals concerned needed to publish their sexual prowess or identity to the world. The manifold comments of pupils are again confirmed by our own observations at many such occasions:

The dances we have with girls are one night stands – everyone rushes in to grab a piece of flesh.

Boy, eighteen, independent school

No wonder then the staff frequently feel they have to step in and punish or admonish after dances or ban them for a time:

I hadn't kissed a girl for 10 long weeks, and I had been dancing with this girl for 2 hours. I couldn't get out of the school hall with her, I felt I had to, I couldn't stop, so we smooched around in the last waltz – one long dreamy kiss – it was great. I could see the Head (all done up in DJ) watching me. Balls to him, I didn't care. Next morning he gated me for a week and told me I wasn't to be allowed to the next dance.   *Boy, seventeen, public school*

9.10 am. 'Bug' (the Head) said after prayers that the end of term dance was off – because last Saturday the party that went off to Cardington Girls place had 'disgraced the school', they'd kissed in the dance, taken girls out into the grounds, everyone was late and cheeked the mistresses. Christ, if you've seen those hard faced frumps, you'd realise how hard up for sex our lot are . . .

Boy, eighteen, integrated school

But even the boys who feel the urge to indulge at dances stress how inadequate they find them as they do not enable the sexes to get to know or understand each other at all.

> Dances – 3 hours or so 6 to 9 pm., one meets a strange girl, fails to get to know much about her, yet kisses more deeply than a man does his wife. Its grotesque and doesn't help one to get to know any one girl or girls in general.
> *Boy, eighteen, public school*

> Dances are just excuses for necking – you don't get to know any girls properly. They're no help really.
> *Boy, seventeen, same school*

The boys call for more regular contact than these contrived encounters:

> Dances aren't enough – we want more regular contact, lessons together, evenings together, discussions and plays. Then we could learn to appreciate girls for what they are and not look at them through frustrated and lustful eyes.
> *Boy, seventeen, public school*

Some schools are moving towards more regular contact, allowing local girl friends:

> The head said he didn't mind us bringing in girls to watch the 1st XV on Sats. – but not to walk with arms round each other, and not to go in studies without Housemaster's permission.
> *Boy, sixteen, public school*

or having shared play readings and societies. A tiny few have gone further and have regular contact with work.

> The girls come here for sculpture, and we go to the Quaker language lab, and the other girls school for 'Renaissance studies'. A year ago it only needed a pretty girl to walk in here and the whole school stopped, panting, tongues out. Now no-one notices.
> *Boy, seventeen, public school*

But schools which are either large or geographically isolated find such solutions difficult: some are now allowing their boys home more often so that they can see girl friends more often there.

Does this segregation from the other sex have any effect on the boys?

Sex in Single-sex Schools

It should be remembered that the vast majority of boy boarders have since the age of seven or eight been educated in all-boys' schools. The question of the effects of such protracted segregation, short-term ones and long-term ones, is complex. The pupils, whose views we report here, are emphatic, overwhelming in claiming that it *does* have effects, though how long-term they cannot discern. The uniformities in their answers and writings, between widely different schools and different kinds of pupil, are most notable.

It should be said at once that many boys recognize and are grateful for the strengths of the one-sex school. Some think they can work or concentrate better.

> It is better at this stage of one's education to be with one's own sex, so that the average male mind may not be hampered by the average female one.
> *Boy, seventeen, public school*

For some it provides a toughening experience and certain masculine kinds of freedom.

> No squeaky voices or hens pecking. No time wasted in amorous pursuits. Boys are free in manners and behaviour – for the only time in their life.
> *Boy, seventeen, public school*

> This school could not develop the same spirit, courage and guts if we had girls about.
> *Boy, eighteen, independent school*

A few descry material advantages in later life:

> Male friends are often more useful in later life than girls. 'Connections' which get you on in your job are nearly always male friends whom you have met at school or via other school friends.
> *Boy, eighteen, public school*

And some perceptive ones point to the differing rates of development between boys and girls:

> Boys are given time to mature in peace without worrying about the

all-seeing and all-demanding women who mature earlier and prey on the boys.

Boy, seventeen, state boarding school

The majority however stress the closeness and warmth of an all-male community where deep and lasting friendships are made (with no homosexual connotations) and society is not divided by sexual competitiveness.

Society is warm and close knit – not ridden by jealousies. Boys aren't catty like girls. Girls couldn't create this sense of community and comradeship – real affection and loyalty to each other. A marvellous sense of togetherness and teamwork.

Boy, seventeen, independent school

One boy acutely sums up the less articulate feelings of many. In his suggestion that the presence of girls may weaken ties and divide the boy society he accurately indicates one of the problems that some kinds of coeducation can in fact produce.

It gives you a chance to thoroughly understand the male makeup and nature, the reasons behind most people's reactions and ways of life. You can have really close friendships which might be difficult if girls were present. There's no need to show off your virility and it doesn't matter if you're ugly or good-looking. An all-male community gives the chance of deep and enduring friendship and for people to judge each other on what they are rather than what they look like or affect.

Boy, seventeen, public school

Some, however, positively exult in the emphasis on the masculine identity which they think is the effect of single-sex education:

It makes us more masculine. If we are to be males, for god's sake let's go the whole hog. Let's learn to understand, command, live with males. We MUST understand our own sex fully and cannot if females are tripping and flirting around.

Boy, seventeen, public school

So much then for the most frequently claimed strengths of the single-sex school. What then of its effects on boys' relations with the other sex? The great majority of older boys, as we shall see, think the negative effects outweigh the positive advantages above and have a sense of loss:

One longs for the smell of a nice perfume.
Boy, eighteen, public school

The female sex may as well be living on the moon.
Boy, seventeen, public school

When I was little many of my friends were girls. I now feel I belong to another species. *Boy, eighteen, independent school*

A minority claim no particular ill-effects at all:

For me, there is only one girl and she writes every week.
Boy, seventeen, public school

After the first week of the holidays girls become as much part of everyday life as motor bikes and washing up.
Boy, seventeen, state boarding school

I haven't become a rabid homo nor do I avidly collect pictures of nude women. I find a game of darts and a drink at the pub with your friends releases most tensions.
Boy, eighteen, public school

A smaller but interesting minority think it is a positive gain not to have contact with women. In some cases here it seems that long segregation has caused or reinforced the psychological forces and fears which prompt such reactions to the other sex. How deep and enduring these sentiments will be we cannot say:

One comes to view women as an optional extra – in my view the right attitude. *Boy, seventeen, public school*

> I really get fed up with girls who compared with very close boy friends are completely empty intellectually.
>
> *Boy, eighteen, independent school*

> It has accentuated my contempt for them – school dances make me feel they are just sex-machines. I realise this is not true but I feel convinced that not seeing them has shown me quite well that one can do without them. The only girl friend I had gave me up while I was away in term – 'frailty thy name is woman'.
>
> *Boy, eighteen, public school*

> Most mature boys with sufficient intelligence should not be interested in such dull creatures. Those who *are* infected in this way are obviously only those incapable of controlling their physical and carnal desires.
>
> *Boy, eighteen, public school*

The first main negative effect of single-sex boarding which large numbers of boys feel is that they are deeply and damagingly ignorant of feminine nature, outlook and reactions. 'Girls are a lifetime study', one boy says, and 'I am off to a late start, shall I ever catch up?' His fears are echoed by many:

> They remain a mystery. You can't understand their personalities and characters, their neuroses and complexes, and their finer points. It becomes difficult to meet them socially, to tell the attitude behind their actions and words. This leads to (a) fascination, (b) mystery, (c) timidity for fear of touching what you do not know.
>
> *Boy, seventeen, public school*

This ignorance has its own side effects, they claim – a tendency to be overwhelmed:

> One is slow in learning the 'feminine mentality' which is necessary in life, I feel. When one *is* distracted by a girl, the distraction is complete. You've developed no defences.
>
> *Boy, seventeen, public school*

Sex in Single-sex Schools

or to underestimate them:

> I tend to treat them as inferior. This is probably due to my close scrutiny of middle-aged women in the holidays and of the idiotic way that many of the fair sex dress and behave. I am often very insensitive towards them and do not regard them as persons.
> *Boy, eighteen, public school*

So much for ignorance. The second effect which many report is the crudity which an all-male atmosphere engenders.

> All-male society tends to make one more vulgar and ill-mannered – leads to lack of gentleness which is often quite noticeable. Also dirty jokes about women are the order of the day.
> *Boy, seventeen, public school*

> Its a good way of producing bad language which would not normally come out in mixed company. My language has slowly got worse and worse. It picks up in the holidays but goes back again within 2 weeks of the start of term.
> *Boy, seventeen, public school*

Of much greater, and perhaps long-term, importance are the alleged effects which we now illustrate. That an all-male society can lead to the inhibition of emotion, the 'stiff-upper-lip' reaction we have already noted. It can also lead – at least according to the testimony of a substantial proportion of boys – to a deep shyness, a sense of unease, an inability to communicate with girls. Here are some typical shy boys:

> I am far more cautious and embarrassed with them than are my friends at day school.
> *Boy, eighteen, independent school*

> I am shy, I don't know how to become acquainted and I easily become embarrassed. I think I tend to go after girls who are too good for me and prefer boys better looking than me – who can dance – and have more money and more interesting conversation. The tendency to seek other boys company can easily be forced on you here.
> *Boy, seventeen, state boarding school*

344 The Hothouse Society

Some who find it difficult to communicate:

> It has made me become estranged to them so that I become embarrassed in their company and cannot talk to them properly – one is flippant endlessly.
> *Boy, eighteen, public school*

> In the washroom this evening immediately after writing the previous piece, started thinking of Susan as I usually do at this time of day. Belongs to same Sailing Club and is regular member, unfortunately belongs to horsey-shooting set. I've known her since I was eight and we've more or less grown up together. Feel awkward talking to her (or any adolescent female) on land, however when sailing together feel can and do talk about anything. Unfortunately no place for love play, impossible to control boat at same time. She's not particularly good to look at and not very intelligent or witty, however is only girl who have had chance to know for any length of time. Tends to become an obsession with me here.
>
> This is the first time I've tried writing anything like this down and somehow it makes me feel happy and yet worried at same time. Thanks.
> *Boy, seventeen, independent school*

And some who simply cannot make relationships with girls, for which, they think, their segregation may be partly to blame:

> My emotions have rarely been stimulated by a girl as I have not known any for any length of time. My life is sheltered here.
> *Boy, seventeen, public school*

> I have a girl-proof screen around myself. I can't break out of it and life at school reinforces it.
> *Boy, seventeen, same school*

> By the end of term, they mean very little to me and I feel indifferent to them. I feel an acute awareness of femininity when they are present. I have never had a girl as a friend.
> *Boy, eighteen, public school*

A few seem to be able to make stable relations only with older women – with whom, of course, they have had more experience in their lives than with contemporaries of the other sex:

> I don't know them intimately enough to really talk to them. I get a kick out of embarrassing them. I prefer older and even married women – they are predictable and you have had experience of them.
> *Boy, seventeen, public school*

> I find that when I am in the presence of a girl my conversation seems to me to be very false. This is only due to being cut off from them and therefore not being able to treat them as my equal. I find I am very much at ease with women of twenty-five and above.
> *Boy, eighteen, public school*

This inner unease, or fear or feeling of inadequacy can produce a response the opposite of shyness: a compensatory eagerness or sexual display or superficial interchange, something which comes out for some in hectic, restless boarding school holidays. Some boys stress the sex side:

> Because I don't really know them, I put on an act, pretend I am an expert, the Casanova of Surrey! Holidays are a time for as much kissing as possible. I screw the first few girls I go out with.
> *Boy, eighteen, public school*

> One has to make a startling impression in a short time and this must be consolidated quickly owing to the short length of the holidays. One's attitude therefore becomes hasty and exhibitionistic and the opposite effect to that desired is often achieved. It also becomes desirable to squeeze as much sex into the relationship as possible.
> *Boy, seventeen, public school*

> I get a little like a sex maniac in their company – if I could get a regular girl friend I don't think this would happen, but it's impossible here. I find myself getting off with as many girls as I can in the holidays.
> *Boy, seventeen, state boarding school*

Behind these modes of behaviour lie deeper sexual attitudes which are being formed by experience. A substantial and significant number of boy boarders, we find, do not think of girls as 'real', rounded, everyday people. Their conceptions of the other sex polarize markedly, some 'thinking of them as something sacred', approaching them 'with a kind of reverence' (boys, eighteen, public school), others thinking of them as physical objects only, for use. In either case, girls are not being conceived as whole people. (In these attitudes it is likely that many boy boarders differ markedly from day pupils or boys in coeducational boarding schools and that, though many may adjust to more realistic attitudes later in life, some never do and carry the impress of these reactions into their most intimate sexual and personal lives. What evidence there is on the later sexual adjustment of this group of boarders supports this view.) Of these two common reactions to the opposite sex, we illustrate, first, idealization:

> They are an unknown quantity – one imagines them as too perfect, idealises them, they seem goddesses far away. Girls are human beings: segregation for long periods warps the mind.
> *Boy, seventeen, public school*

Another, typical of this group, but at another school, describes the same feeling:

> I have developed idealist notions of what they are like. At a school like this one cannot take them for granted as one rarely sees them. I am over-romantic. *Boy, seventeen, public school*

Others retreat from the physical:

> I appreciate women: compiling in my mind the ideal qualities to make a real woman. I do not think of physical relations with women, only mental ones. *Boy, eighteen, public school*

Sometimes this approach produces a bitter fruit:

> Failure to grow up with girls has made me far too romantic about

them. They appear as a different kind of being. I don't understand them. I have been jilted by a girl and feel I haven't the understanding or experience to cope with another.
Boy, seventeen, public school

The other (larger) group is of boys whose interest is purely physical, or mechanistic:

My interest is girls (undressed). *Boy, sixteen, independent school*

This may have been a joke. But many boys are only too conscious that their physical conception of girls is at the expense of human ones.

One tends to look at a girl and say 'Oh, she's good enough to go to bed with . . .' and that's that. Sexual experience is the ultimate goal. Knowing a girl for the sake of knowing a girl is practically never the case with me or my friends. *Boy, eighteen, public school*

They become pure means of physical satisfaction before you return to this compound. *Boy, seventeen, public school*

Some are disturbed and perceptive about their reactions and those of their contemporaries. One boy claims that he has learnt lust but not love:

For eight months of the year I see little of them, and I am sure that the novelty of them is to many of us too overwhelming and we attempt to go too far in love. If we became more used to girls we wouldn't lust after them. We might learn the difference between lust and love. We *can't* learn it here. *Boy, seventeen, same school*

Another is guilty at his physical absorption:

I enjoy their company enormously, tend to be a little lusty (in a real sense) and a little ill at ease. I am much too much concerned with their bodies than with their characters or intelligence both of which will count more in the long run. When I emerge from here I wonder if I shall find difficulty in making any real and deep contact with women – except physically. *Boy, seventeen, public school*

We are not contending that a majority of boy boarders react to girls in this way, but a fair proportion do and probably more than comparable day boys. We do not contend that those who do react thus are permanently affected or damaged, but some will be. How powerful is the impetus to react in this way can be seen in the following extract from a boy who was at a Quaker coeducational school and then transferred to an all-boy independent school:

> There just isn't any social life and sex drives one just mad. One must get rid of it. Whenever you can get out you find the nearest bit of stuff you can find and one gets as far as one can as quick as one can and jack back here to safety. It makes one an animal. At the Quaker school you got used to them. They weren't bits of machinery, you didn't talk about them all the time, but they did make you aware of sex in a way you're not here. They do put bromide stuff in your tea to calm you down but it doesn't work over well but you don't seem to enjoy it so much. The boys get very het up but they're not as queer as I expected they would be. *Boy, seventeen*

Isolation inevitably produces, as in other male institutions, substitute erotic stimulants. Most schools have (legally or otherwise) pin-ups and in some circles there is a market in erotica. A boy at an integrated school describes it in his own way:

> You get so sex starved being away from home that one brings back thousands of nude books to keep up the morale and to remember what they look like. *Boy, sixteen*

A seventeen-year-old public schoolboy in his:

> I have a pornographic outlook on girls. Not having much to do with them, I am physically attracted by their bodies, and this is all I usually see in a girl. I enjoy reading pornography, and I'm sure I wouldn't if there were any girls here.

For many masturbation follows up to the end of their school career:

> I became very conscious of women in general, excitable by nude pictures, exquisite form of the opposite sex. This interest tends to become one-track, especially at night, whether the interest develops towards bodily contact with a member of the opposite sex or a strip club. This leads to masturbation. *Boy, seventeen, public school*

Whether these masturbatory habits occur more permanently and over a longer period of life among boy boarders in single-sex schools than among boys elsewhere, we cannot of course, even guess. Some boys however note that it happens more during school term than the holidays:

> 10.30 *pm*. Lights went out ½ hour ago. The others were too tired to talk, they went off to sleep one by one. I lay there thinking and (well you asked for the truth didn't you, and you're b— well getting it), then I had a long 'flog'. My mind dwelt on a sort of ideal girl – bits of all the pin ups behind the study cupboard door! I do it twice a week here, sometimes more, but scarcely ever in the holidays. You don't seem to need it then. *Boy, seventeen, independent school*

The last word on this topic and on relations with girls in the single-sex school we leave to a mature, sensitive and worried head of school and head of house in a distinguished public school:

> ... this repression produces the lonely adulation of masturbation – having your weekly flog. Inevitable, I suppose, but the endless absorption with sex (10 of us, all sixth formers, talking after lights out in the dorm, constructing collective fantasies) is exhausting, monotonous, and I feel, corrupting to my sexual nature. Will I recover? *Boy, eighteen*

The single-sex school does not only, according to the boys, affect their attitudes to the other sex, but also to their own. 'One begins to treat boys as girls'; 'one is apt to turn and appreciate the beauty in one's own sex and as a result becomes sexually interested', note two public-school boys. The subject of homosexuality has been contentious, delicate, and up till recently, devoid of factual foundation. None of the material we are now presenting should be interpreted as supporting the common and crudely stated notion that boys' boarding schools produce more adult homosexuals, passive or active, than non-boarding schools. The complete evidence suggests a situation much more complex and varied than that. In this book it must be stressed we are not dealing with the long-term homosexual effects of boarding.

The short-term effects, however, are clear throughout the children's writings, and are supported by our other evidence. Single-sex (as opposed to coeducational) boarding definitely stimulates the pupils' homosexual instincts, and their perception of it as a sexual response and an 'ethos'. Large numbers of boys in many schools of all kinds claim this effect. Here are a few comments typical of thousands:

> We get too fond of each other. We start thinking *only* of boys.
> *Boys, sixteen and seventeen, state boarding schools*

> One gets drawn to 'lush' (pretty) boys.

> We turn our attention to our own sex – we've got to give vent to our instincts and make the best of what we've got here – thats what we think.

> A lot of us are attracted to other boys.

> One tends to develop an unwilling love for other boys.

> You find yourself lusting after handsome small boys.
> *Boys, seventeen and eighteen, public schools*

Of course, many day pupils discover their sexual nature through homosexual experience, though this is more often of a mechanical-physical nature than the emotional kind which boarders experience. That most boy-boarders claim increased homosexual awareness does not mean that their schools are hotbeds of homosexual activity: their perceptions or instincts may be controlled by the self or by external pressures, as we shall see. Many stress that their feelings are so controlled:

> It encourages homosexual feelings, which I keep in check.
> *Boy, seventeen, state boarding school*

> You get sex starved and look twice at younger boys and have to keep yourself in hand. *Boy, seventeen, public school*

> You have to exert strong will power not to be a practising queer here.
> *Boy, seventeen, public school*

Such control is sometimes aided by the release of conversation. In many schools there is much homosexual talk, whether or not there is much actual activity. The boy community in some aspects becomes homosexually orientated. The following extract from a diary enables us to hear a snatch of this sort of conversation – typical of much in the boys' diaries:

> Immediately Mr Davis left the room everyone stops work and starts talking. Discussion came round to 'little boys' – very interesting. Smith talked of Cooper, Peters of Markson (jokingly discussing his figure). Then we spoke of Aston (a prefect) and Travers (a junior). Aston asked me to send Travers along to him in Prep. so I sent someone else. When he came back he told me Aston wanted to see Travers, so T. went. There was uproar from the form that Aston takes when he walked in: they know about the affair. Half the school heard it. Everyone in VI2 was most amused. The 'Puritans' in the Common Room were discussed by Aston and me. Discussion lasted all period. Also discussed Mr Simon's homosexual tendencies when he takes showers, and how he went down to fetch his glasses so that he could see more clearly. Mr Wallace's keen interest in Fenton was also mentioned and Mr Gower's favours to Martin.
> Discussion turned to politics and the state of the country. I said that we were a second rate power . . .
> *Boy, seventeen, independent school*

The boys unanimously point to one main cause of their homosexual awareness or tendencies, whether it is a working-class boy at an integrated school:

> We go up to bed at night and sit on Peoples Bed and then your hands starts to wander. Now (Just use your imagination). This is because the school is all male.
> *Boy, fifteen*

A head boy of a secondary modern boarding school:

> Most of us are very sex starved. The local tallent isn't much to talk about and we get homosexuality if you dont mind me saying so Dr Lambert, but this is true, believe me or not.
> *Boy, fifteen*

A sixteen-year-old in a public school:

> Its back to house to make our beds and a free ½ hour. There is no letter for me which puts me back even worse why can't the silly bitch write to me – a girlfriend I ask you, letters from a girl are about all the sex that you get here – except if you are like most people and talk and glare about somebody who is a treble or alto in the choir. This is what Public School does to anyone.

Or an eighteen-year-old prefect in a public school:

> With no females around everyone seems to be talking about lush boys and heterosexuality is frowned on while homosexuality is approved. Pictures of girls are equalled by pictures of boys in the school and photographs of nude boys from the film 'The Lord of the Flies', etc.

In pointing to the absence of girls as the cause, these boys stress the obvious conditioning factor. It is certainly true that homosexuality plays nothing like the same part in the experience of boarders in coeducational schools – though, we have found, some juvenile forms of it are not unknown in them. Nevertheless, though the most pronounced and widespread homosexual reactions occur always in single-sex schools, it by no means follows that they occur uniformly in such schools. On the contrary we have found the greatest contrasts between schools in all other respects similar. Thus in one school the indices (tests, interviews, children's writings, observations) will register a high homosexual orientation, but in another school similar in catchment, composition, siting, staffing, structure and policy and where the research was of the same duration and met the same frank response, all the evidence points to a negligible homosexual orientation – though this may still be higher than that of a day or coeducational school. This diversity is pronounced: boys in single-sex boarding schools are always individually sensitized to and more aware of homosexuality than others, but the collective behaviour and the life of their schools may show little discernible trace of it. The causes of the homosexual behaviour and life of schools are therefore much more subtle and complex than most boarders themselves think: it is subtle compounds of social structure, tradition, and even the alchemy of individual personalities which work on the conditioning single-sex situation of some schools and activate the homosexuality latent in them. The whole matter of why homosexuality occurs in one form in one school and in another form or not at all in a very similar school is extremely complex. It will be analysed in our companion volume.

Two forces powerfully shape the incidence and kind of homosexuality in schools: the official policy towards it and that of the children's society – this latter being immeasurably the more important. Official attitudes in schools can vary: they are repressive, or tolerant, or manipulative, sometimes all three in one, as at this public school:

> It is not very often that boys spend nights with others, but this does happen occasionally. Attitudes range from one housemaster who says 'This has got to stop' and 'they must both go' to a chaplain who said 'I think homosexuality in a public school is a damn good thing'.
> *Boy, seventeen*

But some schools are unanimous in repression and offenders are punished severely if their questionable affairs are too obvious and expelled if actual sexual acts occur:

A slightly unhealthy preoccupation with homosexuality intensifies this situation. In the cases of relationships between boys of widely differing seniorities, and in one house, it has even been enforced, I cannot say how effectively, that boys of more than two years difference in seniority, may not converse with each other. There was a scandal last year and two boys chucked out.

Boy, seventeen, public school

Driver was seen a lot with Roberts and after a time the Head saw D and told him not to go with R again; he didn't want any 'dirt' like that in this school, or he'd be out! *Boy, sixteen, independent school*

In more schools the policy is more tolerant. Though physical sex is disapproved and punished (not automatically with expulsion though, as in some of the more repressive schools) emotional relationships are not immediately suppressed. The staff recognize that these are an inevitable occurence given the single-sex nature of the schools, that the feelings engendered may be valuable in themselves, that suppression might do damage, and, instead, they vigilantly and sympathetically urge restraint on the pupils. One boy describes how a tolerant headmaster contradicted a repressive housemaster when his love affair (non-physical) was discovered:

The hostility came from our housemaster, as we have the same one. He came in one Sunday morning and T. was sitting on my bed. Mr Higgs (housemaster) sent him out and saw him later in the morning. He bluntly said 'I think it is about time you stopped being friends with Jenkins'. T. came and told me this and he seemed quite satisfied with this state of affairs. I was very upset and so I went and saw the headmaster after church. He got quite upset himself and obviously saw that I felt guilty of being friends with T. He said he would see Mr Higgs.

From then on until the end of term T. saw very little of me. He refused to speak. He felt guilty and accepted all that Mr H had said on the matter. He was too young to be discriminate. He did, at last, come back to me in probably a much stronger way.

Boy, sixteen, independent school

Another is advised by a sympathetic housemaster:

> I've felt this way for over 2 terms about Simon but he's like stone. I can't help it – I contrive to be near him. At times I can't stand it – this place is so close I couldn't avoid him if I *could* try. Sometimes I don't want to go on living. Someone whispered it in Geoff's ear (the housemaster), he called me in and asked me about it. I've told him all and he seems to understand, he's even seen Simon and told him not to be too callous, he's told me I've no right to injure S's development. He's right, but something's still burning my guts.
>
> *Boy, seventeen, public school*

Very rarely the staff can be manipulative. For the sake of actually knowing what goes on, of closer control over the boys or good relationships with them or to keep the boys on their side or just to be 'with it', the staff can go beyond tolerance and become cooperative up to a point:

> I'm new here, and I noticed at breakfast in the House that the places sometimes changed, X would come and sit next to Y, or B go off to another table away from A. It was a bit puzzling – but then I realised they were 'friends' – starting or parting! Old Francis, the Housemaster, let them, it gives him some sort of kick to be in the know – perhaps it *let* him be in the know anyway.
>
> *Boy, seventeen, public school*

> Needless to say, Mark, the House tutor, noticed my behaviour and put two and two together, but wasn't worried in the least, even encouraging the relationship in quite extraordinary ways. He said the friendship might do us good providing we didn't go too far. He even 'lent' us his room by going out and leaving us two together alone. He knew it was the only place in the school we could be private.
>
> *Boy, sixteen, integrated school*

The tolerant or manipulative approach means that the staff may have a better chance of knowing what is going on, though seldom to the full extent. Sometimes they exhibit their knowledge as a means of control:

It is spoken of a lot in this school, but it very rarely comes to the surface, and hardly ever gets back to our parents. The staff are forever making sarcastic comments about the relationships, but this can be ignored. They are not innocent themselves.

Boy, fourteen, independent school

But in all schools, and in repressive ones in particular, the staff, until awoken by an incident, often have no idea of what goes on.

There is no doubt in the houses a surprisingly large amount of homosexual behaviour. My house certainly seems to have got rather out of hand, anyway. The housemaster was obviously quite out of touch with the situation and a great scandal arose when he walked in on a fairly minor incident. *Boy, sixteen, public school*

It is the pupils' own society rather than the staff which effectively determines how much and what kind of homosexuality prevails in the school. The pupil society too can be repressive or tolerant or actively supportive, and its approach can change from one to the other in a cyclical pattern.

In some schools any homosexuality is taboo and checked by the pupil system. At one school, remote, restrictive and brutal, the very place where one might have expected it to flourish, a boy accurately describes the position:

As far as 'queers' goes, I think the school must be quite exceptional, people who are *known* to have association with other people are branded, they live under an umbrella of shame, they can never really take part in a conversation with other people, because these other people feel uncomfortable in their presence.

Boy, seventeen, independent school

The culprits suffer severely in such places:

There is a boy who attempted a junior in the music room. He got a sock in the right place. He's called 'B.O.' by everyone and treated as if he had the pox. We don't want that filth here.

Boy, seventeen, independent school

Sex in Single-sex Schools 357

At more schools – a majority – the pupil society is tolerant always of emotional relationships, often of sex between contemporaries, less often of sex between older boys and juniors if accompanied by emotion, but never of sex between an older and junior boy in which the older one enforces his desire on the younger – this latter kind has almost disappeared from boarding schools. There are, however, degrees of tolerance. Scandal at the following public school attempts to control homosexuality:

> Most boys by the time they have left have committed some sort of sexual offence with another boy. Most boys are interested in other boys in the termtime and girls in the holidays. Of course there are 'lushmen' who live an artificial life and are permanently chased. Anyone seen talking with them is immediately condemned and scandal is spread between those two. The noted Marston Wood is a favourite notorious haunt of these boys.
> *Boy, seventeen*

An extract from a boy's diary at another public school describes how tolerance works in practice; 'affairs' are watched and not condemned, but displays of emotion are not encouraged:

> ... Still, assuming I have attended chapel – which is the rule rather than the exception – I shall slip out and the first thing on my mind is when I will see my little friend who I've had a crush on for about a year or so. Incidentally that is all it ever has been, just a mutual thing for each other, on and off. Just about the Christmas term I suppose it was beginning to wear off but towards the end of last term (1966/67) I have felt far more strongly for him than before. It's hard to describe exactly what it is which makes me like him. I think fruity, playful good humour is fairly apt. He is also quite pretty, although in saying that I might say that this is just in my view – for no-one else really likes him also, and the stunningly good lookers tend to be liked by lots.
>
> It can sometimes be a bit embarrassing, as I remember once walking across the quad and hearing from right across the other end someone yelling out what sounded like my *Christian* name. Not being too sure I didn't turn round; but when I heard it again a gaze

over my shoulder revealed this chap gaily waving both arms at me. Of course, no one said anything but some people must have seen and thought 'Funny, funny!' However, I think he is a bit more sophisticated now than to make it so publicly obvious! By the way, our ages are 14½ and 18 nearly.
Boy, eighteen

At a group of schools, the pupils go beyond tolerance. Homosexual relationships are positively encouraged, become fashionable, the done thing. The deviant is he who does *not* engage rather than he who does. In some schools the staff have no inkling of this pervasive feature of the underlife. As at the following independent school where:

For some unknown reason it seems to be the done thing to pretend to have a crush on some small boy and even if you don't have your name will soon be linked by your friends with some small boy who you say you have glanced at once.
Boy, seventeen

or at this public school where:

It is 'big' to talk about lusting after the smaller boys, ie fags.
Boy, seventeen

and where the 'with it' élites

mostly at the top of the school, congregate in the Hall after supper and stand there talking about 'crushes' and 'queers' and all the 'lushes' and 'thrushes' of the school. I think this is shocking because they are the people who the younger member of the school look up to and everyone follows suit.
Boy, seventeen, same school

At another school emotional affairs bring prestige:

There is here –
1. Sex life proper (or improper)
2. Emotional love life.
1 is usually kept secret and would not generally be disclosed even between friends. This sort of scandal rarely comes on the open market, and even then is discussed in corners.

2 the emotional attachment is a far more common variety of derangement and is definitely in contrast to 1. discussed among friends. It generally occurs between, or rather from, an elder boy and one rather younger (in contrast to 1. which is almost indeed as far as I know, completely restricted to relationships between two exact contemporaries). 2. is generally regarded with tolerant amusement by onlookers (even when associated with 1.) and a number of such affairs will bring a reputation, always favourable to either of the two concerned.

Housemasters are understandably terrified of 1. and 2. and are very hard on both, doubtless because they feel that this is beyond their immediate control. *Boy, eighteen, public school*

It should be stressed that the pupil norms can vary, that within two or three years homosexuality can change from being fashionable to being barely tolerated or the reverse. A sixteen-year-old boy at an integrated school describes such a change for which there is much other evidence from his school.

When I first came here homosexuality was in full swing. The bigger boys would openly wait around by the dormitory until the juniors had gone in and then they went in too. Prefects generally took no notice because they also used to do exactly the same. I was 12 and had no experience of this before. I was fair haired and blue eyed and so I soon had plenty of experience! More recently a master has stopped these journeys to the bedside and a certain air of primness has come and altered most boys. Whereas before 'affairs' attracted no comment – it was so widespread – now when two boys are seen about together, there's nothing but nasty remarks. Of course it still goes on (even in the dorm) but not so openly as before or perhaps so widespread.

So much for attitudes. But what does this 'homosexuality', in schools where it exists on any scale, consist of? What basic kinds appear, what sort of relationships or systems of them, and what might the average boarder in such schools experience?

The children's writings tell us in full. And, as they were written with no fear of retribution, they use frank and uneuphemistic language. One boy sums up the basic pattern of relationships:

> There is not much homosexual relationship between the senior boys themselves. Either senior-junior, junior-junior, middle-middle.
> *Boy, seventeen, public school*

At the junior and middle stages (eleven to fourteen-plus) it is usually mere physical experimentation, self-discovery, or horseplay unaccompanied by much mutual emotion.

> They fiddle about with each others penis at nights, True.
> *Boy, twelve, independent school*

> Nearly everyone is a homme and a bum banilit except me. They fiddle about with each others penis at nights.
> *Boy, thirteen, secondary modern boarding school*

> We get into others beds and have some fun.
> *Boy, thirteen, public school*

It is at the middle stage that collective activities, such as dormitory fantasy activities, can sometimes occur. A boy at an integrated school in the south describes them:

> Dormitory orgies have included, in those in which I have participated in
> 1. Doing naked war dances by torch light.
> 2. Projecting erect penises onto the ceiling and walls by torch.
> 3. Wearing scanty swimming trunks in dormitories and dancing in them.
> 4. Getting as many into one bed as possible.
> 5. Each getting into each others beds, and feeling erections, and lustful pantings, etc. Nothing serious.
> *Boy, eighteen*

Most boys experience some physical activity with others at some stage of their school career, usually at the junior stage. Rather than

Sex in Single-sex Schools 361

quote randomly from the mass of evidence on this, we give one boy's account of his sexual life history at school. He was a prefect at a state boarding school and this account was presented to us out of the blue, certainly not asked for. It is however typical in the sense that many boarders in all schools will have shared some very similar experiences, though many will have stopped *before* his stages (3) and (4) and only a minority go on, as he did, with mechanistic sex in the sixth form.

Speaking from my own observation and experience, during the five or six years of our stay in boarding school, one goes through the following phases:

(1) *First year* (11–12). Almost complete innocence in the first few months at the school during which time masturbation as a hobby and daily exercise is discovered. Little or no attempt is made in the lines of mutual masturbation.

In my Easter term, first year, I first discovered true masturbation, completely by myself in the showers, one Sunday morning. I had experienced erections before, but this was my first real experience. From then on it became an enjoyable occupation at night in bed, and later still, the field was widened to include lavatories and quiet corners. This is common to all, I think.

(2) *End of first – Second year* (12–13). Towards the end of the first year, some slightly older boys (2nd year) might start introducing a deeper interest in the bodies of your surrounding fellows, either by those senior boys finding an attraction in the 'blue-eyed boy' or the boy with fair hair, though this does not necessarily make the boy attractive to others.

It is under these conditions that some boys make overtures to others, and some 'fiddling' goes on.

My first engagement in fiddling was with the boy next to me in the dormitory.

(3) *Third year* (13–14). Serious homosexuality does not usually begin until the end of the second year and into the third, from what I have gathered.

But now many boys begin to have an absolute lust for mutual engagement, if they have not permanently been repulsed by their early investigations, and investigations by older boys towards the attractive juniors. My first real 'pants down' was in the summer of my second year, on the last Sunday of term, when I was trying to revise for the end of term exams. We went into the woods together, got bitten by flies, and I thought it was awful – my partner had obviously done it before; he was in the same year as me then.

I did not do any more until the summer of my third year, that is my 'O' level year. Then my interests were not often, usually in the woods.

(4) *Fourth and fifth year* (14–15). This lustful, but not too frequent activity is continued in the lower part of the school, i.e. those not vice prefects or prefects, and it does not always take the form of a sordid two-in-a-dark-hole, but often (when I was in junior status anyway) as a dormitory muck about.

Most of my activity was done in the 4th year, and up to now.

My fellow associates have always been in my own year, the year above or below. In the 4th various other experiments are found congenial between a few partners.

(5) *Sixth year* (15–18). When one becomes of VI form status, of about 16–17 years of age, the pressure is greatest towards homosexuality. Some respond physically, others passively.

Physical contact between a few becomes even more passionate, and fairly frequent. Boys tend to get more of a relationship than the mechanical 'Wank me off' type of relationship that particularly prevailed amongst them earlier. Now when boys become seniors, then much more care has to be taken to avoid scandal, and it becomes a finer more intimate relationship.

The physical engagement becomes more limited, and new friends (I find) are not usually found: more limited because of one's seniority and that some of your old associates have given up, or are trying to do so, or else have left.

In the passive line which most boys take, boys talk more freely, joke about, admire so and so's lovely botty, and so on, which though it may appear superficial cynicism, and those boys will usually deny that they are really attracted to the object of conversation, I personally feel that these people joke to cover their deep seated passions – the insistence that they 'get a bit of finger' off some low moralled girl on some occasion is more a cover up for their guilt that they do

still find themselves attracted to male members of the community.
Prefect, eighteen

This is the physical side of homosexuality in the boarding school. For many boys aged fifteen or more it is, however, the emotional side which dominates, frequently unaccompanied by the mutual physical sexual activities catalogued above. They experience intense attraction towards a contemporary or, perhaps more often, a somewhat younger boy: this is the classic 'crush' relationship of the school.

The first-term boys in houses are inspected (in the showers or elsewhere) and by the end of the 1st month, whenever you say hello or something to the attractive 'little men' people snicker. Relations of an intimate nature between boys whose ages differ by 4 years aren't so common as those between boys of 14 and those of aged $15\frac{1}{2}$.
Boy, seventeen, public school

The junior boy at the receiving end may react by

hating his position. He resents a deep love, he feels falsely secure among a group of people his own age and any deep sentiment forces him to question his own position in his society. A situation is forced upon him. Used to being in a crowd, he is unused to individual attention, anything deeper than cars or football. He has to escape his pursuer, he is driven further into himself, into his clique. They, the other members of the group, resent outside interference and gather around him and he spurns the older boy.

Boy, seventeen, public school

Others turn their attractions to good purpose and become the school 'tarts':

Some boys flaunt their charms, lushes who are especially attractive. They attract friendships with older boys – it gives them a protector, or saves them from punishments, or they get access to studies (coffee, etc) or just like being run after. They get a bit shop-soiled and are known as 'tarts'. *Boy, seventeen, public school*

Other juniors are so overwhelmed by the senior's attentions that – for a time – they react with ardour:

> The 'crush' sees his admirer as the Messiah. He's been delivered from the day-room and cliques, of course the older boy is more intelligent, he's quoting Plato, thinks the crush. He follows blindly, sometimes really believing everything he's doing is right, never having had a deep relationship before.
>
> *Boy, seventeen, public school*

At this stage, many senior boys give vent to their feelings in writings (poetry, diaries or accounts) which often have more sociological than literary interest. We quote only two examples from many. One tells us something of the physical and 'innocent' qualities desirable in a 'crush':

> Cute,
> little boy,
> soft legs and long hair.
> Unaware.
> That's the sin, he's unaware.
> He talks; a style he's known for years,
> He was there before, I love it.
>   laughing eyes I wish he had
>   so small and soft is.
> I wish for many things as well,
>   It's natural, is it wrong?
>
> *Boy, sixteen, public school*

A second 'poem' written by a thirteen-year-old to his senior admirer during prep tells us more: how the junior imitates the style, and emotional tone of his friend, how conscious he is of having power over that friend, the sexual undertones, and the genuine tenderness which suffuses that relationship, however brittle it may prove:

To John:
Joyful, courageous, a man in yourself,

Exerting any power to do what is right,
You admit, you submit
To anything I want.
Those pimples so manly,
That voice so heavenly,
Those arms so strong,
Those feet so smelly (well it rhymes)
The whole of that body so John-like
I admit, I'll have to submit to your gentle touch, one day,
Even though it may be a Sunday.
I admire you
You're handsome
So lovely, so mansome
You poor old thing
Soon's coming the dreaded 'O' level mock
You've got brains, I can tell that you have,
You're generous, holy
And want matrimony (it rhymes again!)
I adore you
You talk so comfortingly
That anyone could be won around
To your way of living and thinking
If you want something and I do not
Then *you* are the one to give in not I.
To end this little piece I will say this
I think you are so good and nice and gentle
That no poetry of mine can describe you.

Boy, thirteen

In some schools this individual 'crush' relationship which is found widely elsewhere is taken out of an individual context and becomes part of a social one. A *system* of big-boy–little-boy connections operates by which many seniors have recognized small-boys, one or several, and their small-boys may have their own smaller-boys as well. Chains of these relationships weave through the community and are recognized by all the other pupils. In some schools to be in one confers definite tatus. They are seldom accompanied by physical sex but in some cases do generate stylized codes of conduct and rituals reminiscent of medieval courtly love. Two boys in one school and in one particular chain explain their positions. First the fifteen-year-old in a big-boy–small-boy chain which runs: Thompson (17) – Miles (15) – Collins (13) – Smith (12). It is Miles writing:

> It started on a Sunday morning when I asked Thompson if I could inspect his study between four and five on the same afternoon. This was because I wanted to listen to the radio 'Top of the Pops'. He said 'Yes' and so I went up to his study. We talked about everything and he gave me a mug of coffee. I started it, as you can see, for material benefits.
>
> What happened after this I am not quite sure, but all I knew was that I was in his study more than I was in my own common-room. We used to speak for hours about nothing very much, and I felt proud that a prefect should take notice of me, and treat me as an equal. I had never been treated like this before. We used to do loads of things together.
>
> At this time I became attracted to Collins. I saw him about and he was a very voluptuous child. I used to plan his whereabouts, so as they would coincide with mine. Thompson and I were making out the dinner table-list on a Sunday afternoon, once and he asked me who I wanted to sit next to. I said, as innocently as I could, 'Oh, shove me next to Collins or someone'. He saw through this immediately and said that he would help me as much as he could.
>
> I went out for walks with Collins and we talked about each other. At that time I did not have a study so he could not come in and I could not entertain him. He came into our common room to see me, but I felt I was imposing on the other boys.
>
> He has an aversion to being called a 'small-boy'. He thinks that it suggests an indistinct person, and that the big-boy is the important one. He wants to be a big-boy himself and has tried to capture a boy, called Smith, with much difficulty. Smith is, as it were, a much sought after small-boy. There is great jealousy between the elder parties. The amusing part is that Smith thinks that everyone is just being nice to him, and doesn't get the message.
>
> One of my study mates says 'I couldn't care less whether Collins

is your small-boy, or not. It is just aggravating at times for him to be in here. I don't consider it immoral, unless you do immoral things with him.'

Scandal plays a great part. Everyone accuses everyone of homosexuality, but very few mean it. There is often a great amount of jealousy between Big boys over a S-B. This can get very fierce, particularly if the S-B is hesitant anyway.

I, now, do not feel guilty of being emotionally provoked by other boys. I accept it as natural, but am quite easily made to make myself feel guilty if a person, who should know, calls me a queer.

I have never done anything sexual with either Collins or Thompson, although I have had my arm around him and he has put his head on my shoulder in an affectionate way, while alone, underneath the trees in the games field.

Now Collins, the thirteen-year-old in the chain, has a word on *his* situation. He indicates, what everyone else knows in this school (and in a few others), that the small-boy system extends to a few of the staff too:

There isn't a lot of homosexuality in the school, of course, there is some. But there are some very close friendships. The senior boys see someone in the junior forms, who they like, so they 'adopt them', these people who are 'adopted' are called small boys.

There is a lot of this in the school, and it is perfectly natural. Nothing sexual goes on, and I think that it is all right. Some people, who aren't the nicest of people, spread untrue rumours, about these friendships, just because they don't benefit from it, whereas the small boy does. I myself, am a small boy, and I know for certain, that nothing goes on.

Even the masters have small-boys. Some masters have them closer than others. One master has a small boy, and in the Greek period (the master teaches Greek) he talks to him all the time, and he is also giving him friendly little jobs to do. The ultimate is the headmaster, even he has a small boy, Simpson.

Such close friendships lead to manipulation:

... give my 'friend' a second helping of jam.

Boy, seventeen, public school

Another tries to get his 'friend' out of a disciplinary prefects' meeting by getting the complaining prefect's 'friend' into trouble, so that, by blackmail, the charges against both will be dropped:

At the moment I'm in the middle of a complex scheme to get Peter let off going up to the Prefects meeting. The prefect who sent them up has got a crush on Tridgell – so I've got to get him up there before the others get punished – what a life!! I've only got tomorrow to do it! I've got people to talk to him in the corridor, chase him, everything!

Boy, seventeen, independent school

In schools where 'little boys' or other kinds of homosexuality are fashionable, the topic becomes a major preoccupation, individually and collectively. To illustrate this we quote the diary of one day in the life of a head of house at an independent school. We did not ask for diaries like this – they arrived, to our surprise. This one is typical of others from this school and elsewhere. It is slightly abbreviated. Note the close association with one friend, the collective homosexual orientation (looking for 'talent', giving boys marks for good looks, semi-serious banter), the endless homosexual awareness – yet, despite all this, the boy has a girl friend outside whom he longs to see, with whom he corresponds, and whom he discusses in school. This sums up the paradoxical state of boys like himself in boarding schools.

Woken up 6.45 and think I haven't done my bloody English essay. Watch all the plebs making their beds, no bloody talent in this house except for old prosy Symes, who gives me a smile. Still he can get stuffed I'll stick to Dick (my 'friend' in Forde's House). Time to go into showers and feel that my pyjamas are still wet then I remember that I had a wet dream about Nicholson of Westons – a school tart. I dreamt I had a snog with him – funny that as I've never spoken to him before. Housemaster makes sarcastic comment on way into showers – bastard. Get dressed same old routine. Supervise jobs making sure they are good today as the Matron won't spare me. Am on duty today, clean my shoes which are caked with mud.

Go up to Dining Hall and try to arrange it so I meet up with my 'friends'. Saw Dick in D.H. and he gives me a smile, and walked halfway back house with him which cheered me up. Get back house – no letter – got books for school. Have to go to Chapel. Saw Dick on way to Chapel. Walk down corridor with friends keeping eyes open for talent. Johnson told Paul (a pal of mine) to keep away from him – reason J asked P how much he wanted for his fur hat – P said 'half an hour'. Double French first two periods – buggar – can't stand it although I am doing it for 'A' level . . . French is over – couldn't stick that any more. Got maths next and see Nicholson walking in front of me (corr he ain't half got nice legs – we the group gave him 8+ out of 10 for them – wish that dream came true) . . . 11.00 break usually see Dick but he is having exam so stay in VI form and had usual sex conversation with the boys. We have Mr Jones for English next – always a laugh – never do any work. Paul comes in late as usual – saved him a seat and tells him about my dream – he thought it was funny and also that he had been chatting N. up the night before. Didn't do any work that period – late for the next period as saw Dick and had little chat with him. The master taking us didn't do anything though – meant to hand in essay but hardly any of us had done it so he set us another one – bastard. Five minutes after I had come in had to go for my haircut. Wondered if I could get a good one off him – wasn't too bad.

End of morning school soon came after haircut. Back to house – good meal today – punished 'prosy' Symes – he shouldn't take the mick out of Dick – he's jealous. Great day outside, sun shining. Got trial for 2nd rugby team. No talent in the rugby teams except for Pratt – but he is too fast for me – never catch up with him – pity. Bloody Richards swings his fist straight into my nose in a loose scrum gives me a nose-bleed . . . thank Christ that match over – never thought it would end. Saw Symes going back house – don't know how I control myself still only another 5 weeks to go – 5 weeks! I'll never last. Took my shirt off and walked into the bootroom where I saw Eldon Jr. playing around – get everybody upstairs except him – have a scrap with him – the sex maniac. Back into showers – wish

I was in Forde's with Dick – it would be a right old sex orgy. After got dressed noticed Symes has a clean pair of very tight trousers – give him a wolf-whistle – just gives me a dirty look. Comb my hair and has a chat with the boys who want a look at these notes – tell them to get stuffed.

I don't mind Tuesday afternoon lessons – only music and a free period. Free period with Paul. We read each other's girl friends' letters – can't wait to get home. D.H. again – not a bad tea – see Dick afterwards. After that walk down corridor with Paul and others and see the three junior tarts standing outside their class as we do every bloody night of the term except Sundays. All of them are very nice – make a number of comments about them whereupon they turn round and smile at us – funny. Take prep – never do any work as they are always making some sort of noise or else annoying you. Saw Dick after prep had great chat with him.

Went up to his dorm to see him at 9.15. Great talking to him. The lights went out – still talking. Another prefect came in. Said jokingly he had 'caught me'. Made feeble excuse 'listening to records'. He went to see a 'friend' of his. Then yet another prefect came in. He had me worried for he still had his uniform on and the master on duty had a dark uniform. He had come to see a 'friend'. The trouble with Dick is that he's so sensual in bed. He writhes and wriggles fantastically.

Went back to House and had a cup of coffee.

Conversation as usual ended on 'little boys'.

Looking back on the day I seem to have no work and talked and thought about 'little boys' all day. You'll find this is typical of this place.

Boy, seventeen

These then are some of the ways in which homosexuality occurs in the boarding school. To understand some of the apparent paradoxes (the boy above with the girl friend and yet his school 'friend' as well), and the persistence of 'crush' relationships and 'little boy' systems and some of the underlying compensations to the pupils, we should consider what they say. All children wish to be wanted and cared for for their own sake. Boarding schools seldom gratify this feeling. However dedicated and concerned the staff may be, their care is diffused

Sex in Single-sex Schools 371

impartially over many children and to concentrate their affection on *one* child is not permissible. The pupil is continually judged by objective or collective criteria: his behaviour, his contribution to this or that, his performance, his social acceptability. The sense of being wanted for one's self irrespective of performance, behaviour or contribution is often lacking. This is what the 'crush' or 'little-boy' relationship provides: to be cared for or to care for someone individually, irrespective of their school's 'objective' standards. For many pupils, this warmth and intimacy, rather than anything overtly sexual, is what really gives value to such relationships.

> I got out of being a small-boy a feeling that someone cared for me and would be there to spill out all my troubles to. Of course, I liked the extra privileges too, but this was just incidental to the affair.
>
> To be a big-boy, I feel, is an honour. You feel responsible for your small-boy and will do almost anything for him. At the moment, C owes me money and has eaten all the food I possess. I wouldn't say that I love him but it is a word that is very near to the 'love' meaning, which isn't in the dictionary. He has brought emotion to me in a world which, otherwise, could be cold and bleak.
>
> *Boy, sixteen, independent school*

> Lots of people have little boys – if you can call them that, but mostly they don't do anything – just talk, I think it gives them a feeling of wanting someone, wanting someone to want them, a better association with someone who will rely on them and not conflict with them, not be in opposition to them.
>
> *Boy, seventeen, independent school*

> Its not bad here really. But we're all the same, same routine, same food, same clothes – we even have numbers stitched on everything. I'm No. 79. The masters are helpful – but they don't really care about *me* and what's going on inside – how can they, they've got 424 others on their plate. With Peter its different – we just like what each other is – the differences and the similarities, and our point of contact is somehow deeper than most others in the school which are,

marks, rugger, the House, etc. etc. Sounds smug, I can't explain, except that he makes me feel all warm and very close to another human being.
Boy, seventeen, integrated school

These are the compensations. What of the present effects, the short-term ones? We can only briefly indicate the range of them here. Only the minutest fraction of boys feel that they have become truly homosexual through their experience, though far more worry, as the last chapter explained, about their sexual identity. Even so, many say they adapt to ambivalent sexual roles:

I tend to get homosexual gravitations towards the end of the term and begin to forget about girls, but I soon rearrange myself when the holidays come. *Boy, seventeen, state boarding school*

I tend to have sexual feelings towards other boys later in the term, when we return home this is forgotten – I am not worried on the whole. *Boy, seventeen, public school*

Some feel guilty – at least for a time:

We have all been called queers. Things like this make one wonder whether one's a queer or not. I feel very guilty that I had lead astray a young boy that I was emotionally attached to, and was very glad to find that I still liked girls when I went home.
Boy, sixteen, independent school

Others, 'lushmen', can become spoilt:

Such boys can themselves be led astray in this way, and start smoking and otherwise breaking school rules. They can in certain cases develop a feeling of self importance – a result of too much attention – and this has done harm to several boys who I know here.
Boy, eighteen, public school

Some, either because of personal make-up or the anti-emotional tone of the school, suppress their feelings and powerful urges. Here is one such boy. So strong is his repression and sense of guilt that he writes in the third person – the 'subject' is himself, the 'victim' is the person he is attracted to. This is an extract from a longer piece, delivered in a sealed brown envelope. The boy, aged seventeen, in a public school, had never communicated his homosexual leanings to any adult before. Like many other withdrawn or isolated boys, he is mainly interested in railways.

'Affairs' began at an early stage in prep school life, roughly each summer, as a sort of hero-worship based on looks, and these matured into genuine feelings of sexual attraction for colleagues.

In growing up, affairs increased in duration of time. Longest to date about short of 2 years.

The relationship (i) with someone the subject does not actually know to speak to is one of a background wish that he did know him – this, due to personal modesty and reticency is seldom accomplished – and a thrill of delight on setting eyes on him in the street; (ii) with a *friend* lasts rather longer, includes 'thrilling' factor in (i) and generally manifests itself by a simple wish to be with the person just because he is nice to know, (if he is not, this serves to break the relationship). Again strong will, or rather more personal modesty and reticency, prevent these feelings coming out (in, for instance, bids to make contacts) so that the victim knows nothing of subject's feelings, and on the whole the relationship is a perfectly normal one of two friends.

Feelings let themselves out in a sort of minor neurosis, especially in Summer. No poetry produced, but sometimes a musical composition with affair in the *back* of the mind, which is soon burnt. (Those compositions influenced by something of wholesome, permanent interest like railways generally survive or are *even* revised!)

Activities such as masturbation *not* resulted in at night. Thoughts and imagination suffice, and will-power stops any 'fiddling'.

Finally, we touch on the scale of homosexual activity. On this the children are the best judges. In schools where the pupil society tolerates or makes it fashionable, a majority of the pupils might express homosexual inclinations (as distinct from indulge in homosexual behaviour):

> 60% of the school are inclined homosexually to varying degrees, I would say.
> *Boy, eighteen, public school*

> According to one authority, 80% of boys here are that way inclined during term – a little bit high I think.
> *Boy, eighteen, public school*

> You can't get away from it – even over half the senior school are actively interested.
> *Boy, seventeen, independent school*

However much this may be the case in these kinds of schools, more serious activity is difficult to estimate in any school. It is deeply concealed or buried:

> When I arrived at Tim's went inside and was immediately presented with a House Roll and asked 'How many have you had?'
> I was surprised – so was every one else. Some of the things which came out seemed incredible at first.
> The thing that really appalled me was the fact that some people had forgotten some of the people that they'd slept with. It seems to me that there is very little wrong with the act itself as long as its part of something bigger and deeper. Every time it happens – just as with a girl – it should be part of yourself: it should really mean something. It should not be the sort of thing one forgets completely and can only recall with great difficulty.
> *Boy, seventeen, public school*

At one of the schools where homosexuality is fashionable an expert pronounces:

> I am a statistician and the practising homosexual percentage in this school is quite low – 5%.

At a famous public school where the pupil society was mildly tolerant, a comment in the head of house's book gives *his* knowledge of the scale of activity in the dormitory. There are forty-five boys in the house.

> I cannot conclude without saying a little about something that I have always striven to stamp out. No one however has ever believed my theories. I hope that in years to come when the criminals may read these words they will blush with shame for doubtless they will all be very distinguished. I refer to homosexuality. I know of 10 people in the last two years who have been to bed with someone else. Evidence is always slim and not enough to satisfy the housemaster. The culprits who remain in the House may consider themselves very lucky. My theories will die with me and they will go on being lecherous little boys.

Perhaps the most accurate estimate comes from this prefect at a state boarding school where homosexuality was tolerated but not fashionable. He produces other evidence to support this:

> I reckon that 90% of the boys who pass through here engage with one another at least once in their life here. I also say that about 10%–5% of these continue actively until they leave school, about 30% as passive 'admirers' until they leave.

Whatever the pupil fashions may be, this evidence indicates that serious sexual activity in the upper reaches of the schools is confined to a small minority. There may be more of it than the school authorities know, but much less of it than is commonly imagined outside.

On that down-to-earth note, we end this chapter. Some qualifications should be borne in mind. Though it is true that most senior boys are hostile to complete sexual segregation, this does not mean that they favour full coeducation, or that single-sex education may not have merits which they do not perceive. Though most boys become aware of and may share some of the various experiences of homosexuality we have outlined, the individual responses and the situations in schools vary enormously from place to place and year to year. How this experience differs for children in other environments, what its effects, if any, are, and other analytical questions, it is beyond the scope of this descriptive book to answer.[1]

[1]. The subject will be treated analytically, with evidence and discussion of the factors producing different situations in schools, in our companion volume: *Boarding Education: a Sociological Study*.

12 Sex in Coeducational Schools

'Someone asked me where I went to school and I said here, and they replied "Oh, that's that breeding centre isn't it?"' This reminiscence by an eighteen-year-old girl at a progressive school accurately sums up the attitude of many people to coeducational boarding. Though a small particle of our boarding system (there are twenty-six mainly boarding schools which are coeducational and their share of the secondary boarding population is only eight per cent), the influence of these schools is considerable and growing – all the more so as the problems raised by single-sex education are turning the minds of many authorities in such schools towards variants of coeducation. We lived and researched in fifteen of the twenty-six schools.[1]

Like single-sex schools, coeducational schools vary in the contact permitted between boys and girls, who now live in the same precincts. In some schools, though the pupils do lessons and activities together, their lives are otherwise kept apart (for example, no mixed common rooms), and the staff are vigilant in maintaining distance between them. Girl or boy friends are not allowed. These schools are virtually two separate schools in one – just the reverse of the 'breeding centre' conception, as this state boarder explains:

Yes all my mates at home think I'm having a marvellous time here – shagging off the birds no end. Well, its nothing like it, believe you me. The girls live in separate houses which *we're* never allowed near, they sit on different sides of the form, in break we have to keep to

1. For a fuller description of styles of coeducational boarding, see an article by a member of my research staff: R. Bullock, 'Coeducational Boarding', *Where* (September 1967).

different sides of the playground, at dances the staff (especially the old mistresses) sit like hawks (no snogging, no makeup, etc.), and at weekends on walks we go into Wicksted but the girls have to go to Laverham. We're not supposed to meet, but ...   *Boy, seventeen*

At a few other schools the policy of separation is only a little less extreme:

Boys and girls have just been granted mixed walks on Sundays! But we're only allowed out if 3 pairs go together.
Girl, sixteen, state boarding school

We're not allowed out at weekends together. They expect us to have 'platonic relationships' with boys and if we talk with a group of boys in the corridor they split us all up.
Girl, sixteen, independent school

When I had a girlfriend here about 3 terms ago, she was two years older than myself, however, ever since then I have been, what you might say, put down by all the staff, which I think is unfair.
Boy, sixteen, same school

Sometimes the children are encouraged to behave like brothers and sisters, which provides a typical reaction:

Brother and sister! – thats all we're supposed to be. Bloody big family if you ask me. And I don't like snogging with my real sister (whose here) but I do with some of these chicks here. Brothers and bleeding sisters – its not natural.
Boy, fifteen, state boarding school

Occasionally the family fiction is supported by very unfamilial regulations:

They try to create a 'family atmosphere', yet they even have a rule saying that couples must be six inches apart. In this atmosphere it doesn't seem like home at all.   *Girl, fifteen, independent school*

And one or two feel aggrieved for other reasons:

> The Head is against boy and girl friends, but I do not think this is fair for I know what some of the teachers get up to at night.
> *Boy, fifteen, state boarding school*

Most coeducational schools are in a second category: the 'moderately mixed' type. Lessons and activities are shared, so are common rooms and playtimes, and boys and girls mix freely during most of the day, but if serious emotional friendships develop they are, gently or otherwise, discouraged.

> We're mixed here alright. We're with the girls all day (not PE or games or washing or sleeping). Still we hear the girls singing in their dorms and sometimes see them ready for bed – done up in coats like eiderdowns and faces covered with selotape to stick their hair down ready to be glamorous for us, some hope. Seeing them all the time, they don't seem glamorous anyway. Its OK, till you get fixed on one and want to be alone together (they've planned this place to stop you *ever* being private), or stick around together. You then get sarky comments from the staff, and if that doesn't work, everything you do wrong (bad marks, miss a goal, cheek the teachers) is blamed on the affair – 'its making you anti-social' they say. Then follow talks and so on till they think they've stopped it.
> *Boy, fifteen, state boarding school*

Sometimes in such schools sanctions are severe:

> Once Miss Samuels (the senior mistress) had a lovers parade – all the pairs had to walk up and down in front of the whole school in assembly: 'to shame us out of it'. What's wrong with having a girl friend?
> *Boy, fifteen, state boarding school*

> If a boy is seen walking around the school with a girl, he's immediately picked on by the staff. Any love (I don't mean going too far either – but kissing, holding hands, hugging, you know) is banned. Any real love between a boy and a girl has to be hidden from the

teachers. Several expulsions have occurred through love (not going too far either) in this school. Your only chance of a nice snog is when you're in the 5th and you've got the school store key.

Boy, seventeen, state boarding school

The final group of schools go further: *they* permit emotional affairs between senior pupils, regarding boy-girl friendships as inevitable and natural. Such friendships are, however, discreetly and closely watched, physical sex, beyond mild petting, is prohibited and punished as in the other schools.

Staff do not encourage these relationships which is understandable as there are always, as anywhere, the minority who will take things too far. However, the staff seem to turn a blind eye to the seniors of the school, where, it seems they think it is only natural for these relationships to exist. Therefore it does not seem to be at all odd that more than one couple have left the school only to be married in later life.

Girl, seventeen, independent school

There's nothing against boy and girl friends here! We sit next to each other in class, visit each other's rooms, go out for walks or to town together – spend most of the day with each other if we like. My tutor always invites us out *together* to his house – nice isn't he? Mind you, they've got their eyes open. If they think someone's going too far, they interfere, long talks in the study, anxious eyes following you about. Its irritating, but then, my parents would do the same I suppose. Some very nice relationships are built up here, you learn what point you can go up to in sex. They don't like you going round with boys from outside though – 'we've got no control over *them*'.

Girl, seventeen, progressive school

These, in summary, are the three varieties of official policy. But beneath the official there is the unofficial world. How does coeducation operate unofficially? What sort of relationships and atmosphere does the pupil society create, whatever the official attitude may be?

First, a girl outlines the way the sexes respond to each other over time, a description true of most schools:

Sex in Coeducational Schools 381

When the school year commences there are once more a large group of new girls. As the term continues they learn each others names and make friends. Generally, however, except for a few, there seems to develop almost a kind of feud between the two sexes. They walk round in their own groups and seldom seem to speak to each other without some sarcastic or irritating remark passing between them. This manner often continues into the second year but as the year goes on their attitude changes and they tend to try to show off to each other; – boys mainly by showing how strong and tough they are, the girls by their dress and general giggliness.

Sometimes in the lower forms they try to imitate the seniors in their attitudes to each other, but this does not usually last long. Third form tend to stay in mixed gangs rather than making friends with any particular member of the opposite sex – however there are a few exceptions to this and sometimes boy–girl relationships do develop.

Fourth to sixth form, couples tend to become more frequent as they grow older and are much the same as if outside the school.

Girl, seventeen, independent school

In the middle forms in a school of the moderately mixed type, a girl of fourteen to fifteen might spend an afternoon boy-spotting like this one:

3.30. We saw the boys coming from their matches and ran up the hill to see if there were any decent ones. There weren't except for a few of ours. Went to the Pavilion to the team teas and had a drink of water and whipped 2 biscuits from the team teas. Went down the hill but stopped and talked to some boys telling each other jokes, etc.

Had tea and went into the kitchen to get some more tea and see a bloke who seemed quite nice.

Just before tea went to the bogs washed my hands and went to the dorm. Talked to a boy out of the window and he was told off (typical) saw him downstairs and talked to him for a few mins. until Miss Rider came when we both went our own ways quickly.

Girl, fourteen, independent school

382   The Hothouse Society

Coeducational schools have their own rituals, which, apart from so much else, create an atmosphere utterly unlike the single-sex one. February 14th becomes a day of special activity for some:

> I'm going to send Bob a Valentine (He's an old scholar who left a year ago. He's two years older then me. I used to go out with him before he left and I still write and occasionally see him). Well anyway, I'm going to send him a box of confetti for Valentines Day and say 'Darling, Valentine, keep this till we're married!!'
>
> *Girl, seventeen, independent school*

and an occasion for sensitivity for others:

> Sorted Valentines and concocted a hasty one to Judy (my girl) after that, then wrote this scribe. The bedroom was happier, as all the prefects had received at least one Valentine. (One hadn't, but I told Judy to send him one: he's quite happy, he thinks its from some little first form fan, and has boosted his ego no end.)
>
> *Boy, seventeen, independent school*

Even the weekend, so often boring or similar to the weekday, can be transformed in a coeducational setting, as at this state secondary modern boarding school:

> *Saturday:* Miss Harris said 'Let's have a Hallowe'en special!'. So while half the school (*you* as well) went off to that old concert in London in the morning, me and lots of others got down to work. We scrounged some turnips and cut them out and put candles in, all spooky-like, decorated the hall, made lanterns and covered the lights with soft pink paper (we like soft, soft lights for a dance). The 4ths cooked lots of sausage rolls and did sandwiches, and the Scouts sold hot dogs, coke, lemonade – they did a roaring trade. We all wore fancy dress. (Sandra was judged by you the ugliest witch). The dancing was mainly country dancing at first – because of the juniors but it warmed up after they went to bed (late). We danced to records and the school dance band – with Joyce (5th) at the piano dressed up as a slave girl (who'd buy her? She'd find it difficult to *give* herself

away – still she plays nice). They weren't at all bad really. The Spanish cooks and the boilerman came in and the staff was there. Miss Kater did a special demonstration stomp for us, and then you and Miss H. did a jive. After the juniors went to bed we did a lot of mod dancing – I danced a lot with Richard, he's ever so nice ... We stayed up ever so late as it never got boring. At midnight we all rushed off to 'haunt' the junior dorms, but Mr T. (The Head) stopped us just in time. I enjoyed it, it wasn't like being in school at all on a Saturday night.
Girl, fifteen

Conversation and banter takes on a different tone too:

After prep I went up to the common room. They've got a wireless back in there now. You know, someone else asked me to marry him. The sixth person this week. Its funny – a real coincidence. Johnny and Paul want me to go hitch-hiking with them in the holidays to Loch Ness. They say ...
Girl, seventeen, independent school

In schools where emotional friendships are allowed there are often only very few recognized, regular and intense couples among the senior pupils; the rest of the pupils tend to be less deeply involved, or less continuously involved with each other. Here the boy partner in a long-standing couple (two terms make a couple veterans) describes how they meet in a school with little privacy and what their relationship means to them: warmth and affection in deep communication (the same as the crush set-up we have illustrated in the single-sex school):

Then we went down town with Sally, my couple (girlfriend) and bought various foodstuffs. More about couples later. Back in the Prefect's Room we consumed ('noshed') soup and chips, and sat talking until 5.20. No-one else in the room, they were all out working. When the room became populated at 5.30, we moved. The reason for this requires explanation.

Sally and I are one of the few 'steady' couples in the school, and have been for 6 months. During the winter, when its too cold to meander outside, sex has to be obtained indoors (this may sound crude, but it isn't) or frustration builds up to an unbearable pitch.

Officially the school objects to our holding hands in public but is unofficially hazily tolerant. Unfortunately, kissing indoors (no more than that) means kissing in public, which causes embarrassment to a few prefects and frustration to the rest. One develops a hard skin about this – we are not embarrassed in the least – but naturally prefer privacy ...

Looking back it seems that I spend all my free time with Sally. This is true because we like each other so much and because there is nothing else to do. When you have a girl, weekends are OK; when you haven't they are the purest form of torture imaginable. Boredom, frustration and anti-authority feelings build up until by Sunday night depression is inevitable. The main reason for couples in this school is simply a need for affection and comfort: I worry about staff a lot less and feel more secure knowing that I can say exactly what I feel to someone and have her on my side. With girls this applies to an even greater extent.

Boy, seventeen, independent school

Sex in the coeducational school seldom goes much beyond this. Contrary to the torrid 'breeding-centre' conception, there seems from all our evidence no indication that sexual intercourse occurs more than rarely in most schools, however progressive, more rarely probably in this protected environment than among groups of adolescents of similar age and class in the outside world. Most schools have isolated or group cases of it which become public knowledge of course, but these are rare enough to cause a sensation.

Tuesday: Scandal! rich, juicy, scrumptious scandal – yum, yum, we'll live off *this* for weeks. Grand Inquisition day – the Head's been locked in the study with the senior mistress (don't get me wrong!) and interrogating the 3 girls in dorm 11, apparently Jeremy Biggs spent the night there on Sunday and it just got out!

(Later) Jeremy B. left this evening.

Girl, seventeen, independent school

Lack of privacy, moral qualms, fear of 'going too far', fear of severe punishment or odious reputation – all these factors tend to confine physical sex even in progressive schools largely to various forms of petting. There is another reason. Though the children mock the 'brother-sister-lets-all-be-a-family' conception of the staff, in some schools, growing up day to day with the other sex does produce a familiarity which can lower the sexual temperature and reduce the desire to go 'too far', as one girl explains:

> Not many of the boys and girls who've been here since 10 go out together because you know each other too well, you regard each other as close friends not people to get crazy and romantic over. *New* girls who are attractive get pounced on and have to be careful.
>
> *Girl, seventeen, progressive school*

In such an atmosphere when sex does occur it can be strangely sexless. Sometimes this has been accounted for by a sort of incest taboo which is created by the brother–sister atmosphere in a close friendly group, at others by the explanations we have listed above. A girl gives personal testimony, borne out by others:

> Everyone talks about sex a great deal but people seem to hate promiscuousness as if it were the plague. Some couples have extremely intense relationships so that one couldn't go up to the swimming pool without letting the other know but others have a relationship which consists of hopping in and out of bed and not much else, though they don't go too far there. Although opportunities for love-making abound, little advantage is taken. Girls here pride their virginity more than anywhere that I have come across! People sleep together but very few have sexual intercourse. I don't think anyone can give a really good reason for this but I think it is marvellous. I was going around with a boy for almost a year on a very casual and lovely based relationship and we slept together frequently but never had sexual intercourse. We were 17. *Girl, eighteen*

In the schools of our two latter categories, where emotional affairs are accepted, many pupils happily exist outside the couple relationship; they have experienced it and claim the self-control and detachment of experience as a consequence. As in this snatch from a diary:

Bikkies in the quad, shivering with the bareness of it and back again into the snug cosiness of the Common Room. I sit on the windowsill – there's a group of us watching the couples outside. Mick goes by with Lindy – she's got him at last, been after him for terms; there's Joe and Treza, never apart – seem to be *one* person; Pam and Nigel talk – not too good there, it won't last much longer . . . Some boys hang around our window, waiting hopefully. I feel past that now – though probably I'm not – I enjoy the company of everyone. I don't want to go back to a private world of two: nice as that was.

Suddenly the lights go out and the gram glissandes to a standstill . . . *Girl, seventeen, progressive school*

Not all coeducational schools allow such open relationships; in many it has to be concealed, go underground, and a running warfare between staff and pupils ensues. A girl bemoans it:

I have a boyfriend and we usually go to the drying room or bootrooms when I'm taken over, to enjoy ourselves for as long as possible, then he goes back and tries to get in without being seen. If he's seen coming in late too often, he might have extra work or something. There are quite a lot of couples – say about twenty, I think people are quite sensible about sex, and rarely go too far (the housemistress doesn't think so tho'). At weekends, especially in the summer, people often go to a far away field to sex or smoke or occasionally drink. (They try and stop us but they can't).

Girl, sixteen, independent school

Others elude it:

There are several places we can go to, but none of them secure from sudden untimely interruption by outsiders. The Gym is avoided because you can lie down, and staff consider lying down three feet apart worse then passionate embraces standing up. This guilt complex is bad on the nerves. *Boy, seventeen, independent school*

Country schools afford many places for illicit emotional activities:

People try to restrict the sex life here but they can try as hard as they like for they are never in the right place at the right time.

One favourite place is the music school where the cubicles are very handy. It is possible to use the one farthest from the main door completely undetected by putting the door at a certain angle.

Another place is the new hen house. I have used it frequently and its only disadvantage is that you have to have a key for it. But these are easily obtained.

The library is a place in the eye of masters where a lot of love-making goes on. Just opposite the door is a kind of cubicle affair with a radiator. If you are, like myself fairly tall then you can see over the top of the bookcase whilst sitting on the radiator or standing near it.

So far I have just covered everyday sex but on Sundays is completely different. Firstly it is compulsory to go for a walk on a Sunday: in either pairs of your own sex or 4 mixed. The latter is often on not too cold days the most popular. There are to my knowledge 6 barns within ½ an hours walking distance but I have only known 4 to be used regularly.

So much for sex. *Girl, seventeen, independent school*

Coeducation is not however all idylls in a henhouse. It produces problems as well as advantages of its own. Some of the more important disadvantages lie on the staffing side, in turnover, conflicts over policy and power, none of which can be illustrated from the children's material. Here we recount the disadvantages which the children directly experience.

In the less-permissive schools, it is the policy to render the girls less sexually alluring by restrictions which many adolescent girls experience deeply as deprivations and assaults on their identity:

We're not allowed to have hair touching our collars – or its shorn off, and we have to wear it tied up like six year olds. *Never* any make-up and only once in a blue moon one's own dress and then 'sober'. Nuns look prettier than we do. *Girl, sixteen, independent school*

The constant vigilance of the staff in some schools can lead to a diminution still further in what privacy or autonomy the boarders are allowed, especially again the girls.

> They search our lockers when we're not there – creams, perfume, lipstick, coloured undies, eyeshadow – they confiscate the lot. Miss X sends the good coloured undies to Oxfam! We're not allowed in the town by ourselves. Sometimes they read our letters. There's no free time – we're pushed off to clubs and games every minute of the day. They're frightened of us being free.
> *Girl, fifteen, state boarding school*

In some schools the girls resent the freedom which the boys are given, even in small things:

> Why should the boys be able to watch TV while we're packed off to bed?
> *Girl, sixteen, independent school*

or:

> The boys can roam about outside as they please, we're cooped up in here – to keep us pure.
> *Girl, sixteen, independent school*

Junior girls at times find the boys a bit overwhelming.

> Some boys are too filthy. Boys often use dirty signs. They often try to get the upper hand with us. Like throwing weight around we don't get a chance to say yes or no they just take the answers for granted.
> *Girl, thirteen, state boarding school*

Or their presence can hinder as well as promote female flirtation:

> As you see a boy every day (night) one cannot go with him and then drop him without seeing him every day again. If you were at home, it wouldn't matter how many boys you went 'out' with (within reason) but here you cannot, because you would either be teased or called a flirt.
> *Girl, seventeen, same school*

Sex in Coeducational Schools

More seriously, and irrespective of the policy of the school this time, some of the senior girls are conscious of a strain and hidden competitiveness which creeps into their work and which results from the differing rates of development of the sexes. An extract from a diary pinpoints the feeling:

> 7.30. Back to library, work, work, work. Funny, come to think of it when it was 'O' level, I didn't seem to work so much, and more of the girls got better results than the boys. Now its different, we work harder, the girls that is, but don't seem to get so far. The boys seem to spend so much less time on their work, we slave away for hours and *they* do just as well. That's how I find it anyway. But back to that French exercise . . . *Girl, seventeen, independent school*

Some of the boys find the girls distract them from what they might otherwise be doing:

> If you go off circuit training, or do a bit of running practice, or just want to be alone with a book, they complain – especially after supper. They want us in all our free time, I sometimes think they *run* us. *Boy, seventeen, independent school*

More serious social problems arise in those schools where the coupling process gets caught up with the status system, where it becomes prestigious, the done thing, to have a boy/girl friend. Boys tend to go out with girls a year or two younger or more. The result is that the community becomes fragmented and soured. At the top are a group of girls whom no one seems to want. They are frustrated and bitter and their energies can be disruptive:

> I hate this place. I feel all shut up. The boys don't want us, they say they've seen enough of us for six years – they go off with the leggy tarts of the Vth and 4ths. So who've we got left? We're not allowed the yobbo boys outside, though some of us do go out with them. Some go for the younger men staff. After all, Mr P. is only 23 or so, he's nice looking and kind, Miranda's keen on him, they've played tennis together . . . *Girl, eighteen, independent school*

Equally problematic is the fragmentation which such a set-up brings to the boy society, where the close friendships, solidarity and security which often exists among boys can be broken up by jealousies. As the coupling relationship itself is so brittle (it seldom survives two terms), some boys find themselves without deep permanent relationships:

> I've had several girl friends and my latest, Frances, is much sought after. There's always been a lot of jealousy here. Some of them get quite bitter at me. I don't trust them and wouldn't tell them what I really thought. *Boy, seventeen, independent school*

Another boy develops the theme and notes how the girls can control male friendships:

> No-one's really friends here – we've all (except B and S the wets) have all got birds you see. The boys don't need each other – sometimes we get in each other's way. You don't really get close relationships among the boys here. If you do, the girls get quite catty – 'Hello queenie, how's hubby and wifey?', they say.
> *Boy, seventeen, independent school*

Indeed, in such schools, boys who do not go around with girls are frequently condemned as homosexuals – an epithet which carries far greater odium than in many, even the most prim, single-sex schools. In the following diary, the accusation comes immediately to the boy's mind:

> They sometimes get at me. But I see quite a lot about these boys. They're insecure and unstable and as they are all four of them over 16 and all of one sex and hang together, we (the rest) suspect a little homosexuality – not physical – there's none of that perversion here – but a certain element of 'indecision' shall we say, about what they are. The girls let them know it too.
> *Boy, eighteen, independent school*

To be such a boy (the situation does not arise so much with girls it seems) is perhaps to endure the loneliest experience which any boarding school provides. One speaks:

> I don't dislike them, but I don't go around with the girls like the others. I'm *not* queer either. They all think I am funny (peculiar not ha-ha). Since 4A I've been called, wet, sexless, homo ('Oscar'), etc. I'm used to it now. They're (the others in this Common Room) all out on the field now with the girls. I just keep to myself. I'll be really glad to leave.
> *Boy, seventeen, independent school*

We end with the advantages of coeducation. We shall be brief, for there is little of the diversity of view which exists concerning the disadvantages: the chorus from the children is unanimous, one of satisfaction with the principle, if not with the practice, in their particular school.

For some, coeducation has tangible benefits, in keeping brother and sister together, as for this youngster, typical of many:

> I haven't got a dad and mum's out at work. So we've come here – Jill first, she's older she's in 3B. I like this school cos my sister's here, she keeps an eye on me like home and when I first came it really did help. You don't feel cut off from home like with your sister here.
> *Boy, twelve, state boarding school*

or this one:

> Mummy and Daddy are out in Singapore still, before that in Aden. Nan's up in Yorkshire. When the others talk of home, I feel funny – we haven't got one really. Still, Dennis is here, my brother in the 3rd year. We don't have all that much to do with each other – except when letters come. But its comforting somehow – you feel there's someone really close who knows about your life outside school, you feel you have roots, you belong to someone.
> *Girl, seventeen, independent school*

Some other advantages are only prospectively beneficial:

> There's nothing left to learn about women. I feel I know the lot and what to do later.
> *Boy, eighteen, state boarding school*

392 The Hothouse Society

Even younger ones feel it has sharpened their discrimination:

> You get used to talking with them. It prepares you for later life when you come to get married you know what to look for in a girl. You know how they feel about things when you are living with them. You are not shy any more. *Boy, thirteen, state boarding school*

For most the haze of unreal romanticism or the purely physical attraction of women, which loom so largely in the single-sex school, cease to be significant:

> I treat the girls here as equals, not coveted specimens of niceness or passionate lumps of flesh as they are in imagination. Many of the girls here are foul. *Boy, seventeen, progressive school*

A girl reciprocates:

> Living so close, you soon stop going all gooey over them. They're not heroes or pop stars: you see them bite their nails, the dandruff, or being ticked off. It doesn't prevent you liking them though – for their real selves. *Girl, seventeen, progressive school*

Others claim they have learnt self-control – not through repression but through experience:

> The best thing about it (ie living with girls from the age of 11) is that the considerable emotional disturbances which often accompany going out with girls, being refused, or fancying one, occur lower down in the school (say 3rd, 4th, 5th form) and by the time I reach the sixth form, though these feelings still occur from time to time, I am able to control them and not make a fool of myself.
> *Boy, sixteen, independent school*

Some boys sense a civilizing air, like this one who transferred from a single-sex to a coeducational school in the sixth form:

> Christ, I thought, what's this for a lark: it seemed right cissy at first:

all giggles, gossip, flirting and the smell of scent in the evenings, the boys ponced up too. Still, the legs were nice. But I've changed! I don't swear so much, I'm not so scruffy. I don't pant after legs so much either now. I've got a steady – she's got me in the choir (blackmail) – not that we don't play a good game of football here.
Boy, seventeen, independent school

Many state boarders in coeducational schools find it hard to think of themselves as peculiar, as an extraordinary minority in an educational system. They have been used to girls and boys being at school together since they were day children at state primary schools:

Them, nothing special about them – I've been to school with them since I started, you take the boys for granted like desks and chalk and things. *Girl, fourteen, state boarding school*

I first went to school – I can remember now – with Mum and John the boy up the road, and his mum. I've been at school with boys ever since – I don't really think about it.
Girl, fifteen, state boarding school

Whatever the complaints, the problems and disadvantages of coeducation, which are greater than we have been able to illustrate here from the children's writings, the vast majority think it is worth while and would have no other kind, for one simple but fundamental reason, summed up by a thirteen-year-old-boy at a state boarding school:

Boys and girls together: its natural, its life, isn't it?

13 Adaptations and Verdicts

In the preceding chapters we have explored various aspects of the life in boarding schools as the children experience and express them. In this final one we turn to the children themselves and consider their reactions to their own experience. Given the differing structures in which the boys and girls find themselves, what basic kinds of adaptations do they make to them? Going beyond the particular structures to the nature of this relatively unusual experience they have had – that of boarding – how do they assess it all, what have *they* found to be its benefits and its disadvantages, what, in sum, are their verdicts?

First, we concentrate on how they adapt themselves. The many different attitudes boys or girls can adopt towards school can be reduced to five basic ones, according to the children's attitude to the school's aims and the means it adopts to attain them. At one extreme are the children who on the whole accept what the school is trying to do, and also the methods it adopts to realize these ends: we call these children (with no derogatory overtones) *conformists*, because they accept both the ends and means of their society. A second group are not interested, do not understand or particularly accept what the school is trying to do, but do accept or contentedly go along with the system: we call these children *ritualists*. A third group of children neither accept nor reject the ends of the methods of the school – they are uncommitted but also unopposed to them: we call this group the *retreatists*. The fourth group, though it generally accepts what the school is trying to do, disapproves of its current means and practices: we call this group the *innovators*. Our fifth group brings us to the opposite end of the dimension, the reverse of the conformists, for these

Adaptations and Verdicts 395

children do not accept what the school is trying to do or its present means and structures: we call this group the *rebels*.

Conformity, ritualism, withdrawal, innovation and rebellion; these then are the basic adaptations among boarders which we shall examine now. They do not occur in similar patterns among different age groups. Also different types of school produce reactions different in scale and in depth. We may find conformity, for example, more widespread in one kind of school and ritualism in another. But the commitment of children who are predominantly conformist may differ in degree from a mild to a really deep commitment to the society. Reactions may differ also according to the nature of the school's ends. Schools pursue *instrumental* ends – those concerned with the imparting of academic, social, creative and physical *skills* – and also *expressive* ones – those concerned with the fostering of *values*, whether cultural, religious or social. Boarding schools differ markedly in their emphasis on these two kinds of end – public schools, for example, placing great emphasis on both, state boarding schools tending less to stress the expressive goals. Pupils too react differently to the different kinds of goals: some may conform to the instrumental ones but rebel against the expressive ones. We shall illustrate this in a moment. Finally, children's reactions differ according to their age. Juniors are usually wholly accepting or ritualistic; around thirteen to fifteen they go through shifting phases of adolescent rebellion; and thereafter their reactions crystallize more completely. In this chapter we are concerned mainly with the adaptations and the verdicts of senior boys and girls, those of sixteen and over, those in the sixth forms.

Conformity – acceptance of both ends and means – is the response of most seniors in many schools. At more junior levels, especially among girls in charitable or state schools, it consists of a total and parrot-like acceptance of the staff's viewpoint – as in the case of this fourteen-year-old girl who solemnly reiterates the very phrases of the staff:

You must be prepared to let people alone or in other cases to try and understand. You must try to enjoy and make use of everything put before you, it is not good to be snobbish as you are hated. You must share out all food from home and you must not tell tales as even the teachers hate that. You should never hold anything against the teachers when you are caned or given lines as you cannot live together peacefully. Always try to add humour to life, as crying makes everyone else miserable. Stealing is wrong and even a paper handkerchief is not to be borrowed without permission.

Girl, fourteen, state boarding school

Among seniors in different schools, however, conformity has quite different elements. Conformists in state schools, where the stress on expressive value-fostering ends is relatively less pronounced, tend to emphasize their acceptance of the instrumental ends and means only – academic skills and qualifications. They see the school as a means to a good job or training, less as an end in itself as do other boarders. A boy in a state boarding school exhibits this: full acceptance of the school's methods, but in an instrumental sense only, and seeing the school as a means to a good job.

I like the school in itself but I hate a lot of the boys in it. I want to work hard because I want a good job, but it is hard to work with these kind of boys around you. I was chucked out of another school because I slipped a disc and had to stay in hospital for months and I missed exams. I want to work and I will. I won't take any notice of the trouble makers.

I am new here and I have not really been accepted here. I am always being called grammar dog and other names. You get called brown nose if you want to get on with work. I have found out it is best to be low and quiet here. Never stick your nose into anything. I do not take any notice of them, they bully me but I can stick that. I promised my mother that I would work when I came, and I will keep my promise and get on in life. I think the school is great, and the masters. *Boy, fifteen, state boarding school*

Another state boarder, an eighteen-year-old girl at a comprehensive school, again accepts both ends and means. Her commitment is broader and warmer than the boy's but again it is the instrumental aspects which take pride of place – in this case, school certificates.

> When I first came here three years ago I was told I may be able to take 2 or 3 'O' levels – I now have 10 'O' levels and am taking 3 'A' levels. This would have been impossible had I stayed with my parents. Being a new modern school with a tremendous drive there is a never ending series of things one can do. The opportunities are tremendous – due primarily to the size of the school. Yet the boarding houses are not large and institutional but small and friendly. There is a distinctly friendly atmosphere. One is respected as a person and as such gets a certain amount of freedom. If this were not the case I would have left by now. I also have a room to myself and therefore privacy. I like this place.

In sharp contrast are the conformists among public school boys. Not only are there relatively more of them, for a greater proportion of the senior pupils accept the school's aims and methods in public schools than in state or integrated or direct grant schools, but the quality of their acceptance is strikingly different. Though, like state boarders, they accept the instrumental aims, they also accept the various expressive ones on which the schools put such great emphasis. A few snatches illustrate the sort of expressive ends and means which they accept.

> I am conscious that it is the best school in England and will give me an excellent academic and religious education.
> *Boy, seventeen, public school*

> I am proud to be part of an institution as well-founded and successful as X. I like the freedom to develop my own philosophy and to think and discuss my religion, which I would be unable to do in Anglican schools of this sort.
> *Boy, seventeen, public school*

> I have made some very good friends. I feel I am part of a community here. I enjoy many of the games and activities here. I enjoy

acting very much and have many opportunities. I am getting a splendid education spiritually and academically.

Boy, seventeen, public school

This is not to say that the purely instrumental aims are less cared for:

I love Russian like a woman or I would love to love it like.

Boy, eighteen, public school

But for some pupils the expressive ends and life of these schools are all-important. It is not 'A' levels or such that some wish to make their mark in but in such things as

Ability to get on with all from the masters to the humblest fag, without losing any respect which my position might entail.

Boy, eighteen, public school

1. Being fair and rational in running the house – when a VIth or above.
2. Having a good and lively sense of humour.
3. Keeping largely to the rules of the 'establishment'.
4. Having achieved something positive in work or play or both.

Boy, eighteen, public school

A head of house, describing to his successor the aims for which the school and he strive, completely ignores the instrumental ones – to him the expressive ones are paramount:

A public schoolboy should at all times behave as a gentleman. This does not only consist of 'capping' ladies and passing through doorways after your seniors, though these things are not unimportant. The words 'behave as a gentleman' go further. They include, the ideals of decency, cleanliness and good manners, abating one's personal nuisance value not only to other individuals, but also the well being and the reputation of the House, and finally in behaving in such a way as to assist others and so to promote the welfare and good name of the House and of the School.

Head of house's book, public school

Adaptations and Verdicts 399

Other seniors find in the pronounced religious aims of these schools its and their own *raison d'être*, like this boy who believes that the school and he are working together to

> find myself and what they call God. Then I can be settled and lead a life. But I know that I cannot find God as such; to quote St Augustine 'if you think you have found God then you have not'. The thing I want is contentment of mind. *Boy, eighteen, public school*

or like this one who zestfully accepts so much else that his community is trying to do and its methods:

> I like the company on a whole because most of the boys are intelligent, genuine, co-operative and come from roughly the same type of background. This last reason could be called snobbish, but even so I do think it is a very important one and perhaps even an unfortunate one. I like the wide range of activities offered because this really does help to produce interests in people, and this in turn helps to keep them on the right road and channel off any excess energies in legitimate activities. I also like the atmosphere in the school – it is an atmosphere in which one can both work and play very easily – one feels that the masters, especially the headmaster, are really interested both in the boys and in the school. Also the fact that the whole school, and all its activities, are fitted into a religious shell, however thin that may be at times, and however many times that that is criticised, does very definitely help. *Boy, seventeen, public school*

Public schools not only generate relatively more conformity, wider acceptance of their purposes and basic means among their senior pupils, and to a wider range of ends than other schools, but the *quality* of that acceptance is, as the previous examples indicate, deeper. Conforming pupils do not simply accept, they are deeply committed to the school's aims, values and structure. We saw how state pupils, even conforming ones, tended to view the school with some detachment, as a means to their own ends, as a mechanism for jobs or qualifications, however broad or enjoyable in itself. Public-school conformists, however, adapt more deeply; to them, the school and its values can become identified as ends in themselves, to which a warm loyalty and a sense of belonging are generated, which feelings may endure perhaps for the rest of life. Indeed, for some it generates (as very rarely happens in state schools) the fundamental affection of home: superseding or rivalling perhaps that of the boy's own home. Here is one boy who is committed deeply all round:

> I love its rather traditional public school architecture, its uniform, its near vicinity to the Abbey which unconsciously adds to the atmosphere. Its faith which makes us at least have *one* thing in common though not all of us. Its rooms, its reasonable food, its film days, and sleep days, its games, compulsory Masses and 'Unofficials' and coffee parties. *Boy, seventeen, public school*

Another illustrates how closely identified with the school some can become, even to the point of a deep personal dependency:

> This school has given me some very close friends which is perhaps the most important thing of all. It provides a sense of belonging. I don't *belong* like this anywhere else. *Boy, eighteen, public school*

A third boy, deeply committed again, shows both the school acting as a focus of loyalty over generations of one family, and the way it kindles the same kind of response as the family itself:

> It is a school that's secure; it allows me to educate myself and be educated. I like its traditions and I've had relations as well as a brother and father here. You're always part of the school, even when you've left you're still welcomed back any time at free expense for any length. The masters live in and one can always come and see them – its really a second home. *Boy, eighteen, public school*

Finally, a hint of the long-term nature of the public school's impact on its accepting pupils:

> It teaches you to live in a community. I like that because it makes it easier for everybody else outside school. The life in general, because

it is an experience. Belonging to X – I feel I belong to something great and which will always help me if I need help. You never really leave.
Boy, seventeen, public school

On this fundamentally committed note, the *nec plus ultra* of conformism as we define it, we leave the first on our scale of responses.

The next adaptation is ritualism – non-acceptance of the aims of the school but indifferent or cynical preparedness to go along with the means. It is common in all schools, and especially in state or integrated schools where it is a common response to any expressive ends in the school, religious or cultural inculcation for example:

Course I go to church, even mumble those old prayers, I go to those concerts (it helps to be seen there), go off to highbrow plays (well it gets you out of the hole doesn't it) and I enjoy some of the sport, but its all like water off a duck's back as far as I am concerned. Those prayers, the Mozart go in one ear and out of the other. I'm here to enjoy myself any way, get good grades, get out and get on. Unlike Smith, Cohen and those in the lower fifth I'm not going to fight the place – float along with it, but to where *I* want to go, that's what I say.
Boy, seventeen, state boarding school

To others who react by conformity or rebellion, the ritualists can seem

hypocrites – they're numerous, you can talk to them and they will agree, but even though they're clever they won't *do* anything or change anything. They're cabbages.
Girl, seventeen, coeducational school

Whereas state-school ritualism is calculative and frequently cynical, public-school ritualism is often different: not so much a refusal to accept the school's values as total unconcern about them and willingness to accept the whole apparatus of the school without bothering about the purpose it is all serving. One boy puts it this way:

I am naturally lazy. I walk into the school and lie down on a conveyor belt. I am carried along, stamped, have pieces cut off me, bits stuck on, am encased in exam certificates and emerge at the other end capable of becoming top of any profession I go into. The temptation to just be carried along is great, and the fewer questions you ask, the further you get. *Boy, seventeen, public school*

Another expresses it this way:

> Yes, I'm a prefect, I'm in the House rugger XV, I'm a monitor in chapel and a group leader in social service. I enjoy these things, I like it here. But when they talk about 'learning responsibility', 'service to others', 'team spirit', and that never ending Christianity I'm left stone cold. I don't bloody well care about these things – I like my activities for their own sake and *my* sake.
>
> *Boy, eighteen, public school*

Finally – the ritualistic response, though very common, is not very varied or vivid, and lends itself to only brief illustration – a girl at a coeducational school, whose response is a sort of passionate ritualism:

> I have no respect for the people who run this place and my behaviour is ruled by a respect for references and parents and not for these belching hypocrites. *Girl, eighteen, coeducational school*

Less widespread, but much more arresting and colourful, is the third of our adaptations: retreatism or withdrawal. All societies have their outsiders, those who, for inner reasons or defence against external pressures, opt out of the general run of society: neither accepting nor rejecting its ends or means, apparently indifferent to both. Boarding schools have their share of retreatists – among both staff and pupils. As they are not many and do not challenge the system but drift aimlessly along with it, they are tolerated and sometimes even flourish behind a defence apparatus of picturesque eccentricity. Withdrawn children are found in all schools, but the ripest eccentricity tends to be found (in staff as well as in pupils) mainly in public and progressive schools, as the homogeneous and rigid norms of pupils in state boarding schools are less tolerant towards such deviation.

Here an extract from the diary of one mildly withdrawn boy at a public school in central England introduces us to his thoughts and his private world within a world:

> After this we are free – it is now the afternoon. Off goes the whole school on to the playing fields to hit a little red ball about and run between wickets.
>
> I go off for a 'fag'. It is my only pleasure at school. I go down to the river where I can sit down and think. I enjoy thinking but at school all I can think about is school. The typical Public School boy – one who wants to chat – the pathetic type who doesn't do anything – the hero at sport who thinks that he is the bloody top man – the bastard who always thinks that he is the best, the best girlfriends, has the best car, has the most money – they all make me puke. I'm not anti-social but there is hardly anybody who I can call really a friend. I often spend all afternoon down by the river, watching it, the birds, maybe a water-rat. It is very peaceful, and I can be on my own. Life is another topic I think about – I wonder what will happen to me in the next 20 years; will I end a failure, or will I be a big success and make a fortune. The former – I think.
>
> *Boy, seventeen, public school*

To understand more fully the inner world of the really withdrawn sixth-former, we present two longer extracts from diaries. The first boy, aged seventeen, at a state boarding school, at first seemed socially integrated but, as this extract from his moving diary shows, lived in a deep world of private withdrawal from the school – its aims and methods – a world of hard 'mod' language and imagery, of blues, pop and folk music, and a deep sensitivity and loneliness:

> I've got the 'Stones' music pounding through my drums. I'm feeling low and depressed, and I'm missin my bird. I'm hating my mates cause they're just gone for a fag, and left me behind. Man! I wish I wish I was out of this ole. You asked us to write a bit of a diary about the place, well this is what I'll try to do, you want the truth I'll try to give it to you . . .
>
> Of course I realise I'm not the only kid that feels like I am now, so I'm not feeling sorry for myself.

I try to dream all though breakfast and usually succeed with little disterbance. Things such as sex, cigs, drink, drugs, flash across my sub conscious brain. Then this is broken by the ringing of a little breaky bell by the master, we rise and say, ta to God. I walk half float out to the prefects room hopin unciously that I've got a line from my bird, or my mate, its usually 'Oh bugger it from Mum' (Don't get the impression I don't get on with my mum, she's great). I feel loanlines creeping up on me again. I drift to the dorm, and get some kid to make my bed. D'you know I don't know many kids names and theres only 176. I don't want to know them, I hate them; you think I'm mad, I'm not, you see I class meself 5 million times higher than them, there turds, there minds still love playing with toy cars, and they still get great satisfaction in lifting girls dresses, they hate poetry and they hate blues and rock. I hate them because I was like it not so long ago. From watching this naked minded lamb make my bed, it's my normal practice to go to the bog, I must mention this as it is all in my days work. The prefects room comes quickly, as I call there I sit and listen to Huddie Leadbelly or the blues of T bone Walker, or praps some Dylan. Time goes quick like, I think the expression is; 'flys'. Assembly faces me now I hate it, man does Dave (the old man) carry on. I go back to my coma in that half hour. My girl keeps appearing to me, then a photo of what she wrote in her letter, about her going back to school before I get home. That means I shan't see her for 12 weeks. There's a sudden look at me, stop starin, I say, then I realise its all over. The days work digs by its no problem. I sit an read, usually science fiction, I dig it, I think of the writers and what there brains must be like I envey them, to me there like there books 'out of this world'. To me they convey what could happen to us all, if it wasn't for the plan. Oh yes I believe in a great plan, every thing that happens to the last person. Take me, you might say 'you; you sound a bit gone', but I've got big ideas on lots of things, anyhow thats getting of the subject.

About 5.15. we have tea, I've woken up a bit by then and I'm realising what I'm doing. I become more aware of what going on in big brother world, as I read the days paper, taking imediate noce of the pin ups especially the ones with least on. We aquire a board of them, and gaze at them and wish they could be here, and no they

they never could be. I'm back feelin in a different mood altogether and I don't feel like caring on that subject. I've just read a letter from my mates mate, man what a letter, its from London and he's having a hip time. I'm feeling free don't know why, wishing I was smokin, drinkin or having sex but no deal I'm just sat in the prefects room meditating. I've just come back from the park had 5000 fags and I'm full of joy and insanity and I want to jump out of this hole I'm in oh I've gotta get out and meet and mix with the people who live life. I mean live not exist. My heads spinning wild and my thoughts are mixing and building bricks. I'm really trying to think how I'm going to last another year if it wasn't for my exams I'd jump right out of this rut. Why can't they let me live, you don't know how changed I am, and loanly. Every bloody thing I do its compulsion if you don't wash your called a Gipo, so you wash; if you don't dig 'Pop' much your called a square, no I don't dig it and never could. I'm rebelling no I don't wash I don't dig 'pop'. I don't follow fashion, I hate dances and theres plenty more about boredom would surround you if I continued. As soon as I'm out of here I shall rebel against society so much the world will go back to the stone age. Oh why do we have to have exams I wish I could go and live with nature and reality. Oh I'm blue I'm boring you so I'll finish. I wish I could go on for years writing on nothing.

Carrying on. I thought I'd better finish properly so I'll just carry on with days routine – go to bed and think, I think of everything. I sometimes think I'm mad and then I convince myself I'm not. I dream of my bird and good times and my mates and good times and my family and good times and my dog and car and scooter and the world, Vietnam ban bomb 'Death or grass' 1984 'Midwich cuckoos', 'Brave new world', 'Birth pills' and every bloody thing in existence and gradually melt into relaxing memorandum of life.

Hey you, hope your O.K., your great to have around come back some time. I'll come and see you some time hope you still want to no me.

I'm *stoned*.

The final extract illustrating withdrawal is from a true eccentric, a boy of seventeen, a bearded isolate, handicapped by speech difficulties and a painter of strange works of art. In his progressive school, he was tolerated by all and flourished personally and artistically. This diary was delivered heavily sealed with large personal seals in red wax, and written in bold medieval black-letter script – reminiscent of a papal bull. People in it are identified by letters of the Greek alphabet. The few fragments below stand for eccentrics of one kind or another in many boarding schools, not all as sensitive and supportive as the one where this one was.

A June Day

This is an account, as it might be of a song, but is not based on any particular day in the week but is more or less a combination of several.

Awake! Awake! I open my eyes before my alarm rings, so I stop it from doing so, I who being first to appear in this account am Alpha. A light breeze blows outside and I arise to see if any people have yet gone to the post it now being in the eighth hour. On seeing that none have gone to the post, I remove to the room of Beta, knock, and on entering say 'Are you ready to go for a swim?' 'Nearly' says Beta 'Gamma and myself will see you down there.' We spoke quietly, as all was quiet . . .

. . . There is a break during the morning, during which the wise drink milk and others drink tea. After this I venture to the art rooms again to commence with a picture I am painting. To strange eyes it is incomprehensive (except in physical appearance which is more than can be said for many works today!)

In my imagination I dream up pictures of the Millenia prior to the Titanic cataclysm which dispersed the noble dreams from their land of spring and the 'dawn of thirty days', away into Europe and Asia and Africa. Their land is being flooded and frozen.

'The woman is breast feeding a baby' said Zeta 'What a lovely idea!' Also in the picture are two masculine figures, one silhouetted and the other with his back to us, seated. Also there is a large bird on a rock.

After this I go to the Common room for a few minutes before lunch. I glance at the headlines of a paper, and then read between the lines this:—'The English peoples are become decadent and like other once great nations withers and declines, until it shall become a mere humane scum, leached by wars, plagues of her cream' ...

... Having had a restless night of celestial brainstorms I have a sleep before supper, and after the latter I write, or read. If my reading is that which is not connected with my academics, it will be the Bible or the Koran or an historical novel or a modern one.

While reading a glorified account of a black mass, in which 'The Great Ram' (or arch priest) causes an abortion in a woman by means of a black 'imp', Omicron announces through the 'speaker link' that he and his dear friend Mu are going to swim again so I came as a third person ...

Innovation, the fourth kind of reaction, produces less colour than the previous kind but has more impact. Innovators are those who do not question the school's aims and position in society but do question its current means and practices. Found in all schools, they are more numerous, more vociferous and perhaps most effective in public schools, where they have been a major source of change in recent years. Sixth-form innovators of this kind accept both the instrumental and expressive ends of the school but frequently wish to bring its system closer into touch with that of the outside society. Here are a few such voices:

We must change the rules – they have become an entity in themselves divorced from their original intention. They allow for no original thinking – in their pride they assume themselves equal to any situation. *Boy, seventeen, public school*

There is too much emphasis on religion, which tends to become a habit without much meaning. Too great an emphasis on 'house spirit' regardless of one's nature. Too many rules most of which are only applicable to an irresponsible fringe of the school. Not allowed to have a bicycle even though I am a study boy, and have possessed a full driving licence for $\frac{1}{2}$ a year. *Boy, seventeen, public school*

Innovators are frequently found at the topmost positions in their schools, as they are dedicated to its ends and simply seek a more effective and realistic way of achieving them. This head of house sums up some of the changes such boys in public schools seek:

1. Abolish call-over. Used to detect those who run away. Does not prevent it, and their absence would be found out at bedtime any way.
2. Change Corps. The new system of being allowed to retire after a period of service has resulted in an air of apathy which can only be changed by abolishing it all together or going back to the old way.
3. Abolish Privilege. No one benefits from it in the long run, and it certainly does not increase ones respect for authority. Why should we have our hands in pockets and coats undone and not others – its silly and divides.
4. Abolish Compulsory Chapel on Sundays. It would make the day a more pleasant break if one could have the day off without having to come back for a service. If one does not go regularly at home, why should one go here? Chapel on Sundays certainly does not encourage people to go when at home.
5. Abolish Compulsory Games. Though some games are desirable and people should do another activity instead. Too great a compulsion for games can breed 'bolshiness' not only for that hated trek out to the field, but also for other school activities for which a person might even have some talent.
6. Less insistence on 'petty conformity' – ie not driving cars if one wants to (even if one can't bring one to school), or having to get permission just to shop down town. Such irritating things only breed discontent and frustration at school life.
7. Greater opportunities for contact with the opposite sex within the framework of school itself – often not enough advantage is taken of fact that this school is in a town. Reason for this change: obvious.

Boy, eighteen, public school

Occasionally, however, the innovators feel defeated by the system, particularly by the apparently unchangeable structures and traditions of some schools. Here is one such boy profoundly committed to the public school, but frustrated by the fundamental immobility of the one he finds himself in:

But I must say, in defence of the system that, even if it has not influenced me directly in any positive way, which I don't feel it has, it has allowed me to meet, in the other boys, people who have brought out a lot more in me than I'm sure a state education would have done. This is mainly, I suppose, because contact with very intelligent people with similar attitudes and those who are not inhibited has allowed me to rise with them. Of course, once standards are set by authority, it is inevitable that the net result will be a 'sausage-machine', for there is virtually no scope for true individuality inside these standards. And if someone does try to break away he is immediately sat on and threatened with expulsion. The merit of this form of public school, though certainly no merit in my present way of thinking, is that one is made to behave and think in a so-called responsible and conservative manner. But the sacrifice to individuality is, I feel, too great. However, I would not hesitate to defend X on a comparative basis, against state schools, with many clichés. But what I do say is that X could improve itself enormously – though to do this would need more than a radical headmaster. It would need a complete resetting, almost impossible with a school of X's tradition and conservative outlook. That is why, unless the present unseen advantages of conformity reveal themselves to me as I grow older, I would not send a son of mine here, but rather to a freer thinking new public school, which is not bound by tradition. I hope that does not seem too scorning of a system to which I must be very grateful in many respects. It is just that I feel I could have been much more grateful. *Boy, seventeen, public school*

Innovators, in their way, contribute. Rebels, our final category of reactions, do not. They reject everything: what the school stands for as well as its system. Boarding schools produce deeper and more extreme adaptations than day ones. Just as the closed hothouse society of the boarding school generates a much deeper conformity among its children than do day schools, so in a minority of children it provokes a much deeper-seated hostility – a profound repugnance. Boarding schools with pronounced expressive ends, public schools in particular, arouse a more acute hostility (just as they arouse among others a deeper dependence) than those schools where expressive ends and controls are fewer, notably state boarding schools. There is nothing quite so negative, so uncompromisingly iconoclastic, so consumed with self-destructive hate, as the ripe public school 'bolsh'. Rebels are found in all schools, but why some are so markedly more intense than others, we shall soon illustrate.

In a few schools rebellion may be fostered by poor conditions or poor relationships and starts early. At one school poor physical provision produces this typical reaction:

> This school is a rotten old dump. You get rotten old bloody food. You get maggots in your spuds. The boys swipe all your stuff. Windows get smashed. The bog rolls are all down in the bogs and in the slash oles. The beds come from the junk yards. They can't even afford two bog rolls. Our House Master is a fat gutted rotter.
> *Boy, fifteen, integrated school*

At another school, poor staff–pupil relations prompt this typical reaction:

> I hate the staff. I could kill them for all the misery and cruelty they inflicted on me in the early years when this place was very strict. Teachers snoop – they crawl on all fours to the back of the bunkers to pounce on smokers. They're always at people, enforcing petty rules and inspections and they hit you without questioning. You should see how they smile before they cane you. They ask questions afterwards but most don't ask any. They delight in making life a 'physical hell' for the offenders of the pettiest rules.
> *Boy, fifteen, state boarding school*

And at a third, the relations among the pupils themselves produce a similar alienation:

> Many boys in their first and second term get homesick, the seniors make it even harder for them by sending them on errands and punishing them for petty things like having dust on ones shoulders. If you want my real opinion 'I hate this bloody hole' and I'd give anything to get out. I do hope you read this and do something about it.
> *Boy, fifteen, Cromwell College*

But the most intense rebellion among the seniors is not so simply induced. It arises because of the ill-matching of the pupil's personality with the total society of the school.

For some it is aroused by the intellectual limitations and oppressive norms of their schools:

> Boys and masters alike are so Conservative in outlook and politics as to be forever breathing Conservatism down the necks of those who do not conform. It seems to be almost a crime to have thought a bit about politics and not to be forever making unqualified statements against anything not conforming to their tastes.
>
> *Boy, seventeen, public school*

This can induce a conscious intellectual revolt, the public-school bolsh:

> Be cynical about all the most precious held traditions of the school. Hate all manifestations of rigid authority – treat the headmaster irreverently, behind his back. Get in with the 'in' crowd – mostly intellectuals – who sport various defects of dress. Ridicule the set-up of the school. Try and be as devil-may-care individually as possible as the school seems to attempt to stifle all individuality. Don't work too hard academically. Radical attitudes towards important topics – Vietnam etc. Revolt against the school.
>
> *Boy, seventeen, public school*

At a much deeper level some feel the restrictions, necessary or unnecessary, of residential life, the inescapable nature of the society and its pressures as stifling, destructive of their own identity, as erosions of the self. The only way to preserve themselves is by revolt. One boy at a Direct Grant HMC school puts it this way:

> It attempts to stereotype the 'individual' into an artificial character who will merely be a reputable and moderately successful member of society. It is for boarder and dayboy a soul destroying institute in which he who loses his identity is defended, and he who retains his identity is branded as a REBEL and is earmarked and frequently criticised.
>
> *Boy, eighteen*

Others put it less abstractly:

> The system does not agree with me – it causes me much unhappiness. It is OUT-DATED in the modern world today even in my $2\frac{1}{2}$ years here I have seen ideas changes and boys revolt against the dictatorial authority of the Victorian age. 'The Public School' boy is now as 'with it' as anyone – yet any attempt at this is banned. No smoking, no drinking, I cannot see my family very often – they won't (my parents) be alive for ever – would it really hurt my education to be at a school for day boys? I do not like the place or the way it is run as a whole. It is high time for changes – it is 1966 not 1866.
> *Boy, seventeen, public school*

> Individuals are not catered for in this school – anything different is stamped on. I loathe this place – I want to get out and *be myself*.
> *Boy, seventeen, public school*

In the effort to retain identity, some rebels virtually provoke martyrdom:

> The best thing would be that I should be expelled – I would then be a martyr (to myself) and prove to myself that I have the courage to do what I think.
> *Boy, seventeen, public school*

Some get expelled without seeking it. Here is one boy's account of why he left a famous public school in the sixth form. He settled happily at another school.

> I came here from X School a year ago, having been there two years. During the last year the system sickened me so much that my work fell off, and I became nervously affected (ie acute depressions). I had one friend who was even more emotional in this way than myself, and he ran away early in the term and walked 60 miles home. I was asked to leave towards the end of the term, because my views were very much against the school. The depressing thing was that they looked for some fault in me and I was convinced it was there despite my reason. I believe that a school like that which can be so blind to

faults in itself (the complete lack of personal interest in the pupils, the insensitivity of the older boys and prefects to the younger boys) should not exist. *Boy, seventeen, progressive school*

That his new school suited *his* personality does not mean that it suits all others, as one whom it does not suit points out:

> Last holidays I visited a place for difficult children, the headmaster was telling us some of the cases of children that were there. A lot of them behaved exactly like the people here!
>
> But still this is probably a wonderful place for the right person! (God help them) – not me. *Boy, seventeen, same school*

For some, the expressive concern of schools amounts to an intolerable infringement of their autonomy:

> I hate the place – being spied on and one's life being pried into by housemasters and others. *Boy, seventeen, public school*

It is denominational or religiously associated schools which have the greatest expressive emphasis and which generate clearly among their pupils the most widespread and the most intense commitment. Among a minority, however, they produce the most extreme alienation of all:

> We are treated like children, we are locked up and never see a girl. There's too much fucking religion. The priests aren't priests, they wear cassocks and that's about all apart from being bloody hypocrites. They lecture about how bad homosexuality is, but what do they do to prevent it? Lock us away from girls. The rules are petty, the headmaster is a blaspheming Jew. Our lockers are searched, the dirty sneaky slimy priests spy on us and enjoy giving us the cane, for no reason at all. This is not an exaggeration. These are the raw facts of a Borstal which costs £500 a year. Also the 6 head prefects were expelled last term. Shows how good their choice is.
>
> *Boy, seventeen, public school*

These then are the basic kinds of adaptation that children make to the particular school societies they find themselves in. But what of their broader experience as boarders? What is their assessment of the benefits or otherwise of *residential* education? With their verdicts on the value of this educational method which we have explored through their eyes in the preceding chapters, we end this book.

The large majority of senior boys and girls think the merits of boarding outweigh the disadvantages, though most also stress the disadvantages and ask if they are always necessary. Of the detailed disadvantages which many find, we shall say nothing more here: the boarders' previous writings have illustrated most of them. Here we keep to fundamental ones. Without doubt, the most fundamental disadvantage, from which so many others derive and which most senior pupils experience in some form and often acutely, is the sense of isolation, of being cut off from ordinary, everyday life and society in a small unnatural community. Many seniors express this feeling by analogy – a very common one – with other custodial institutions, such as prisons:

> The cooped-up prison typed feeling. I regard this school as an open prison.
> *Boy, eighteen, state boarding school*

> It makes me feel like a convict let out on parole in the holidays.
> *Boy, seventeen, independent school*

> The cut-off feeling, bolted and barred by well-meaning restrictions and people from the life and experience which other blokes of my age lead. Do boarding schools have to be so much like prisons?
> *Boy, seventeen, independent school*

Sometimes the analogy is with other total societies:

> This place is like a 13th century monastery, except those old monks *wanted* to be cut off from the world and we do not.
> *Boy, sixteen, state boarding school*

Some of the constituents of this feeling of 'cut-offness' stand out. For some it is the unreality of one-class boarding society, as for this girl at a progressive school:

Fetid social atmosphere, being stuck with same people for 5+ years. Insularity again – theoretical preparation for 'big wide world' but we're *very* feather-bedded and our rat-race is only 100 yds. with no hurdles. As everyone is so rich, we little realise emotionally the real state of the world even in *slightly* poorer people than ourselves.

Girl, sixteen, progressive school

or these boys who fear they are being damaged by the class character of the tiny society:

I am cut off from civilisation, other people. The public school system is a breeding ground for snobbery, and you are really *forced* into being a snob. *Boy, seventeen, public school*

I dislike being here because other people dislike me because I have been or am at the present here.

Boy, eighteen, public school

Others feel cut off from their contemporaries outside and rendered inferior to their style of life, like this boy at an integrated, charity-based school:

Another disadvantage of coming to a school like this is the clothes the day clothes which we wear all the time except Sundays are of very poor quality. One feels a fool to go out in the town with baggy trousers and a thread bear jacket. And, very short hair. At home at end of term you feel out of place with your mates who go to day schools. They have got long hair while yours is still round your ears. And being away from girls for so long makes some blokes afraid to mix with them when he gets home.

Boy, seventeen, integrated school

Frustration – nothing but idiots in trousers, where are the bits of skirt?? *Boy, seventeen, public school*

The lack of variety in the boarding community also contrasts with the life outside:

Seeing the same drips day-in day-out.

Boy, sixteen, state boarding school

Your topics of conversation are cut down to girls, the latest scandal, the latest complaints.

Boy, sixteen, independent school

In this narrow community things get out of perspective.

Boy, seventeen, public school

The monotonous routine of life also contrasts with the changing styles and experiences of outer life:

> Routine – you might as well be dead as lead the same life day after day as we do for twelve weeks on end.
>
> *Boy, seventeen, public school*

Others see difficulties of adjustment later caused by their isolation now, like this boy at a state boarding school:

> I don't think it helps being shut away from the outside world – by this I mean having a school right out in the country where you are not experiencing enough of the outside world. When I leave school, although I shall have a stable educational background I think the change from the safety of a Boarding School to the harsh reality of the 'big bad world' will be a step that will take some getting used to.
>
> *Boy, sixteen*

or this girl at a progressive school who notes how, from some kinds of school, the old pupils tend to reproduce the society of the school:

> Relationships become fantastically serious and people become more sensitive than they should be – when they go out into the big wide world they tend to stick together because they have lost all the security of X. I often meet two old X's out in London together at theatres, etc.
>
> *Girl, seventeen, progressive school*

For some, the small inescapable world produces an almost palpable sense of being stifled or shaped and pressured:

> The cumulative effect is like being in a mould so that you feel you are being pushed into a certain pre-ordained shape. Some people like myself have tended to rebel against this mechanical and conscienceless social stratification only to find with horror that one is rebelling against everything so we have nothing constructive to feel proud of. So whatever you do the system can impinge on you.
> *Boy, seventeen, public school*

> I have existed in this environment for $5\frac{1}{2}$ years. I consider myself lucky to still be able to write with a clear head. This length of time makes the circle around me seem tighter. Prolonged contact with other creatures of much the same species will, I am certain, influence the whole future of my existence. This is really the tragedy of the closed circle, the miniature society of the boarding school. My attitude to others has been perverted. *Boy, seventeen, public school*

As part of this 'cut-offness' comes the sense of isolation from the home, of loss there that many boarders feel they experience as one of the greatest disadvantages of their life. We have already discussed this in detail elsewhere, and it needs only to be recalled here in general.

> The disadvantages are sometimes it can be hard on a boy when perhaps his parents are ill and he can't go and see them and also a boy misses the home affection that his parents give him when he's away from them.
> I am very lonely when I go home because there is no-one around. Our holidays seem to be good at the start but after a few days I wish I was back at school with my friends.
> *Boy, seventeen, independent school*

One more personal experience exemplifies this common feeling: here is a girl at a progressive school:

> After a break I have a tutorial. I can't and don't talk about anything

very personal in my tutorials. I used to want to, desperately, but now I don't. This may be because I am leaving at the end of this term and therefore problems concerned with school don't seem so urgent. One of the reasons I am leaving is because I have been at boarding school since I was ten and that's enough. I think this is the only boarding I would want to be at, but even here can't compensate for missing family life. This is an individual thing, I know quite a few people here who are never homesick and have no wish to be at home. My home isn't ideal but I do still get very homesick and its always a wrench coming back. I dread leaving in a way, boarding school can give tremendous, if only temporary, security.

Girl, eighteen

'Cut off' and 'cooped up', separation from home – the next commonly expressed disadvantage relates to the pressures of life in a small enclosed society. Sometimes it is physical:

I can't relax, there is nowhere absolutely silent.

Boy, seventeen, public school

There is no privacy – only the lavatory. *Boy, sixteen, public school*

At other times it is the pressure of reputation:

You are judged on things of the past by the head, the housemaster and everyone, your past is ever present inside these walls. 'You are your reputation' – it's horrible. *Boy, seventeen, public school*

The omnipresence of the hierarchy of authority might produce this kind of reaction:

It has given me an inner hatred of all forms of so called 'authority'. Life in the holidays it doesn't stop. When I go to work somewhere labouring I hate taking orders from these people of a lesser intellectual category than myself. It also makes one go against the Police (I don't like policemen). In English the other day we were asked to define 'to obey' no one gave a satisfactory answer and we were told that it meant 'to submit'. Well I deeply resent that for I do not feel that I am submitting to masters just because I try to turn up to lessons on time. I do it because I don't want to get listed.

Boy, seventeen, integrated school

But perhaps the greatest pressure is the subjection twenty-four hours a day, seven days a week to external rules, the lack of freedom and of autonomy which residential life at many schools entails at present:

Ever since I have been here restrictions have become harsher and harsher. It is hard to believe that when one is free from this place one can do what one likes, surely this vast change is not right. Especially for boys over 17.

Boy, seventeen, public school

The rules, like not going outside the school grounds after dark annoy me. I have to work here whether I feel inspired or not, and am not allowed to work when I feel inspired, as we work at prep at a fixed time. I think a day school education is much better, into making one into a responsible citizen, and should be chosen – if possible. *Boy, seventeen, coeducational school*

The fundamental lack of self-direction in schools which boast of fostering 'independence' puzzles and troubles many senior pupils:

When one has been here for 12 weeks everyone is really 'cheesed' off because we're not given enough freedom, ie we are not allowed to go down to a cafe in the town on a Sunday or a weekday. There are also too many seemingly unnecessary regulations like having to be out of the dormitory by a certain time which tends to make life one long routine and one long hurry. When we do get spare time over the weekends, there is nothing really to do except go for a walk or play friendly games on the field between ourselves. There is no doubt about it that boarding school does mean tending to lose a lot of freedom. *Boy, seventeen, public school*

Some envy the day boys their apparent autonomy:

I find that I envy young people who go home every day after school and find they are free to do as they wish; to go out, or stay in, and at all times, to relax. To go somewhere and feel free and quiet, from sight and hearing of anybody; without a care or worry of anybody or anything; to sit and think because you want to.

Boy, sixteen, independent school

And one state day-boy boarding at a public school sums up some of the anxieties of boarders on this score:

From what I saw of a public school, I got the impression that it was rather like a zoo in so much as the occupants were perfectly happy because they knew no better. It seemed to me that I am better off through having so much extra freedom (not being forced to do prep for instance – what else is there to do here? and taking my own decisions, under guidance about how much I shall drink, whom I shall associate with, and what I spend my money on). I feel that a person of intelligence, with reasonably enlightened parents, can emerge from a grammar school with just as much 'character' as the public school products. I get the impression that public school is a let-out for parents who can't be bothered to train their children or even in several cases which made me feel deeply moved, for parents who just find their children a nuisance and don't want them around.

The feeling of lack of freedom produces states of mind which some feel to be part of the disadvantages of boarding. They feel that hothouse living forces them to extremes of reaction even in the holidays.

Being away from the outside for so long makes you crave even more for a few of the vices. This becomes self evident when you talk to other boys, go to the school dance, go on holiday, etc., etc.

Boy, seventeen, state boarding school

or during term:

It brings out extremes in my character which I would prefer to remain hidden (bad moods and temper). I don't want to grow too cynical, but this school does seem to encourage cynicism.

Boy, seventeen, public school

It forces you either to conform absolutely or to go to an extreme of individualism. *Boy, seventeen, public school*

A minority in whom this extreme reaction takes place think the principal disadvantages which we have now summarized outweigh any possible advantages – they long to escape, and their attitude is summed up by this boy:

God I shall never forget what life is like at this place. Christ that f— name makes me cringe. When I am out of this place I will not come back. When you leave you are given a bible, but Christ it's a bit late isn't it? *Boy, eighteen, independent school*

So much for the disadvantages. For some pupils, the boarding experience produces such an inextricable mixture of gain and loss that it is impossible to separate the two: a few of their often moving comments deserve to appear as a whole. Most of them are state boarders, boys with day-school backgrounds, who seem to be able to assess their experience in a clearer perspective than boys who are reared in a tradition of boarding. Here is one to whom the loss seems to outweigh the gain:

It has brought something out of me that might have remained dormant for years if I had remained under the wing of my mother. But also it has isolated me from most of my friends, made me an oddity and a virtual outcast. It makes home more appreciated, but makes walking down the street, for instance, seem like to what it must seem to a newly released prisoner – a breath of fresh air – a taste of freedom – something unreal. This is, I think, why many boys rebel in the holidays, going to the opposite extreme of dress, behaviour and respectability – often verging on the delinquent – which *has* happened to some old boys. Hatred of discipline is something this school has given me – also a desire to go to the opposite extreme

from the Victorian respectability that reigns here – for the rest, this school has brushed off on me a kind of social sterility and isolation.
Boy, seventeen, state boarding school

Another sees the benefits but also the deprivations which the toughening life has created:

Boarding school has given me another world to live in. A world which is totally different to the one I used to know all about. It has created a horrible gap between my parents and myself, and now I find it really difficult to communicate with my mother, which of course leaves me in a state of nagging frustration. Living with other boys has made me mentally harder and more resilient to mental blows, it has also given me confidence within the community. Being in charge of 60 boys I can reprimand or encourage with some degree of confidence. This I hope will stand me in good stead. But it has cut me off from the opposite sex, and although I am lucky enough to have a girl friend close by, I feel rigid and socially stiff in her presence and this I'm sure has had an adverse effect upon our relationship. I feel a fear of going out into the world merely because I am not prepared, socially. This school has taken no steps to make any boys socially confident. But the lonely spare time has given me a chance to analyse my feelings over and over again, and I am glad, for this has given me a chance to write poetry, which releases much of the tension of school life. *Boy, eighteen, state boarding school*

Yet another notices this combination of social incapacity combined with increased sensitization to individual expression:

Thus the school has deprived me of a social tongue and given me a sensitivity towards words and music and an apathy towards outside life and social events. I hate mixing with adults and find the masters extremely stiff and death like, although I will probably end up as a master myself. But not here, that's for sure.
Boy, seventeen, state boarding school

At a Quaker coeducational school a girl sums up the mixture which residence has brought her, the removal from some pressures at the cost of exposure to other pressures:

The Advantages of Boarding:
I can travel alone on a train without feeling the fear of imminent rape. I can live for three months on the ridiculous sum of £3.10.0.

I did not have to live with my parents between the ages of 11–15 when I loathed them – at times I still feel this advantage.

In a co-ed school one sees boys eating, playing hockey, hears them swear and thus becomes discriminating.

I have learned to suffer cold, Quaker meeting, loneliness and boredom with the patience of Boaz. I have learned the value of a person in whom one can trust – such people are rare.

The Disadvantages:
I constantly worry about my mother who is always ill, it seems a shame I should be away from her, I never know how she really is, or how much longer she has!

I am in love, and am frightened by the pressures about me. I have learned not to respect people. One is removed from religion in a Quaker school. There is no privacy.

Constantly living with diverse people lots of whom are loathesome is a huge strain.
Girl, eighteen

From these few mixed and problematic verdicts, we turn to the positive ones. Whatever the demerits the senior boys and girls see in boarding and so vociferously express, the balance, in their opinion, comes down emphatically in favour of the experience they have undergone.

The first advantage which the vast majority feel is that it has taught them a deep tolerance by constant exposure to a wide range of other people.

Before I came to boarding school I was quite fat and did not care much about life in general.

Now I am reasonably built have many interests in life and am fairly good at sport. This I can only attribute to the fact that I have come to this school and that I have to rely on my own initiative instead of that of my parents.

For me at this school, I have learned the meaning of tolerance and charity, and I feel as if I have completely lost the mean streak that I had in me before I came here. I and most of my friends can certainly take a lot. *Boy, seventeen, state boarding school*

Its tolerance – this school accepts every type of boy – madman or genius – as long as he doesn't either annoy or disturb others.
Boy, seventeen, public school

The company, because there are all sorts of interesting and congenial people, and the fact that eccentrics (people often call me that) are laughed with, rather than, at (excuse the English here!) and are tolerated by the staff. *Boy, seventeen, public school*

It teaches someone independence and a sense of responsibility. As the school is a microcosm, it binds people together whether they like it or not and teaches them to tolerate each other.
Boy, seventeen, public school

Likewise boarding removes the social distinctions which matter so much in the outer world. Inside the school people are judged on what they are, whether at an integrated school:

There is certainly *not* a lack of contact with people of different backgrounds. I find there are all kinds of social backgrounds in the school. What is good is that everyone has to live at the same level and has the same opportunities. Being born of well off parents doesn't make any difference whatsoever; people wear the same clothes, eat the same food as everybody else regardless of any social background. *Boy, seventeen, integrated school*

or like this boy from a comprehensive staying at another public school:

There was none of the snobbery I had feared – less than at my day school. At the day school you knew whether they lived in the posh districts or not, what sort of house and car their parents had, boys stuck together according to where they went home and this followed social differences. At the boarding school you never *knew* where they came from, or what their houses were like. You just acted on what they were like as people. *Boy, eighteen, public school*

The second benefit which most boarders claim is a sense of independence.

It has toughened me mentally and physically. One meets more fists than mother's kisses.

Made me a fitter member of the community. I have learnt that one needs courage to face life to the full and appreciate the rights and wrongs offered by society as a whole. Discipline, manners and self-confidence have all been given to me by the school.

Taught me the meaning of physical courage and spirit on the games field. It is not skill or talent that matter, rather it is the attitude and courage shown.

Boy, seventeen, state boarding school

Another state boarder speaks for a majority of his kind:

It is now that I realise that my whole future was started with that decision and I am extremely glad that I made it. Never before have I found my feet in life, been able to hold responsibility and respect, and most of all been able to understand what it is like to do something for yourself. The school has given me something that *no* other school could have given me, and for that I am very grateful.

Boy, sixteen, state boarding school

and a public school boy for a majority of his:

Only like this can one gain what a school has to offer – one can give far more and gets far more. The discipline of boarding is very good for one. One has to face up to life and to one's fellows and even to oneself in a way which one might not have to at home.

Boy, seventeen, public school

Yet another boy notes how it has freed him from over-dependence on his parents.

> I would never have dared to argue with my parents before I came here, or with any other adult for that matter. I would never have dared to come home late. Then my parents sent me to boarding school and I have grown in mind quicker over the last few years than I ever knew I could. At a boarding school like this you have to fend for yourself and make your own decisions do things at your own discretion and decide yourself what you think of the school with all its petty rules and in turn of the great outside. My mother cannot understand what has happened to me she does not know how I can just stand and say 'No'. I've done it myself for quite some time now. Parents do not realise that you have stood alone and their once dependent children have suddenly grown up.
>
> *Boy, seventeen, state boarding school*

Many find other advantages in being away from parents:

> I like being able to play a lot of music. I like the fact that, even if we are punished for a serious offence, our parents will never know.
>
> *Boy, seventeen, public school*

Another at a progressive school claims that his independent life at school, away from the limitations of home, has opened up the way for creative fulfilment – a claim which earlier quotations from all kinds of schools have borne out.

> One advantage: the way you grow up here *is* all done by yourself and your surroundings *here*; not at home, not by parents. I can attribute very little of my personality to my parents. My years of formation were spent here at school. I've found that I get these creative urges (I mean it) here at school, and not at home. Here I find myself, in the evening, sitting down and writing a story or a poem, or a little essay on the three asterisks after 'f' (f***) which I could do at home but I don't. Have you been down to the art block? You see we've got plenty of materials to do what we like.
>
> *Boy, seventeen, progressive school*

The third benefit of boarding as the children see it is the material advantages which these schools confer. They might be long-term career advantages described by this public school boy:

> The name 'Lanchester' is a great asset for life.
> *Boy, eighteen, public school*

or this secondary modern girl who feels that boarding has enhanced her chances too:

> I now have the chance to be a typist when I was at my other school I could have got no further than shop assistant.
> *Girl, sixteen, integrated school*

Other children, chiefly state boarders, many of whose homes are in unattractive environments, stress what the sheer physical space, setting or beauty of their schools have meant to them. Here is one boy from east London, boarding at a maintained school in a sumptuous eighteenth-century mansion in East Anglia:

> I leave in four weeks time and have been very happy here. I don't want to leave. I feel very grateful. Just you try living in Bethnal Green instead of watching it on TV or reading those sociological books about it by people who take care to live in Hampstead. I'll never live in as lovely a house as this again; the grounds, the trees, the birds, the space here – all these things have helped me. The people too – they're kind and interesting. *Boy, eighteen*

A younger boy from a similar background finds the setting of his secondary modern boarding school an asset:

> The school is situated in the countryside where rivers are many. It gives you a chance to get some fresh air and just to sit fishing quietly with another boy. *Boy, fifteen, state boarding school*

The many facilities – sporting, cultural and academic – which boarders have at their disposal all and every day naturally appear among the material advantages:

The opportunities it gives people. I have taken up many new interests eg climbing, the organ. It tolerates and tries to care and nourish individuals.
Boy, seventeen, public school

This place has *made* me musically – practice rooms, instruments, groups to play with in evenings and weekends, masters who are first rate and spend lots of time helping and playing with us, old B (the Housemaster) dead keen – he takes us up to operas, lends us his tremendous stereo and records and has musical evenings, well-known performers come and play and sing and talk informally. This school has brought out an interest in me which I might never have discovered.
Boy, seventeen, public school

Frankly I like games best – sounds hearty doesn't it? You've got those pitches nearby, keen and good coaches, the courts, etc. You can play and train every day, five minutes away from your room. Its developed my skill and I'm glad about coming here.
Boy, seventeen, integrated school

The impact of boarding on work is only partly a material benefit, but many children claim it as one of the great advantages. Less able children, those who failed the 11+ perhaps, stress that the boarding school with its more intensive tuition not only offers renewed academic prospects but renews self-respect – it is a community which offers many other avenues for achievement and high status outside the academic sphere.

I failed the 11+ and thought I would have no future. Since I've been here I've got some O levels but that's not all: boarding teaches you that those things aren't all that matter. I'm house prefect and captain of hockey. You learn that the best people aren't always the best brains.
Boy, seventeen, state boarding school

For others the school itself provides academic stimulants:

I like many friends and company because I feel that at least I belong somewhere other than home. I want to distinguish myself academic-

ally and as a fencer. I feel that I progress here and stagnate at home.
Boy, seventeen, public school

When a junior, I always knew senior boys who would take a *purely* academic interest in you – parents would not provide that.
Boy, seventeen, public school

or physical or organizational opportunities for academic fulfilment:

I find it easy to work here. No time is wasted on travel, TV, fleapit pictures, etc. I have a permanent wish to do something constructive and this helps. *Boy, seventeen, public school*

I certainly think that I have every opportunity to work. I have a study, effectively soundproofed, splendid lectures, teachers always on hand. The one drawback is that I have other commitments. Although I can find the time to do academic work, I find that I am very tired by running three societies as well. I said on the questionnaire that the school seemed to be very capable of keeping me occupied. I can only say that if I can run three societies and get three A levels, I will have gained a lot!! *Boy, seventeen, public school*

The other material benefits are too numerous to illustrate and some are idiosyncratic:

I love the baked beans every Friday (true).
Boy, seventeen, public school

From the material to the *im*material advantages – the benefits gained by living in a community where expressive values or opportunities are all-pervasive:

It has given me a good sound basis on which to live and from which to take example. *Boy, seventeen, public school*

You learn to discriminate – living so close to so many people and so many attitudes to life. Things are *concentrated* in a boarding school,

even exaggerated: you can't evade ugly aspects of life, or morality, which you could outside.
Boy, eighteen, state boarding school

I disagree with the school on most things. But it *has* definite (fuddy duddy) views on most things. I'm grateful in a way – because its made me, by reacting, *think* and find myself.
Boy, seventeen, public school

Others find in the community a real security:

Boarding school has given me a sense of security. The meals, the games, the common room and relaxation and the pleasant grounds, all this encloses round one and directs one through the term. The first day of term one walks through the front door and adopts a completely different 'closed-in-secure' attitude right through the term and when it ends it leaves you as one goes off to holiday.
Boy, sixteen, state boarding school

And many claim to have learnt in practice the meaning of responsibility in the broad scope which residence gives for its exercise:

Its been hard. Being a prefect and all that looks nice – but if you take it seriously as I do, its far from easy. Its not just difficulties over discipline and all that. Its the fact that in a boarding school you have power to really hurt or help people, its balancing the staff against the boys, the rules against individuals, the past against the present, your own wishes against someone else's needs. This year has been an education in itself. I feel 25 years the wiser.
Boy, eighteen, public school

But, in conclusion, underlying all these individual advantages, there is something which most feel but find it difficult to express, an underlying sense of being part of a community, an entity which enlarges the self in a union with others. Some see it in individual relationships:

The sport means much to me, but, more important, I have found the most wonderful friend I could find anywhere.
Boy, seventeen, public school

Others in a general way:

> Good friends and close, friendly staff. The splendid games facilities – I play to my heart's content. You couldn't get all this anywhere else.
> *Boy, seventeen, public school*

> I like being able to get things done which I am unable to do in other circumstances. Here I have a number of intelligent friends, lots of ideas, co-operative authority, what more could I want?
> *Boy, eighteen, state boarding school*

Others have a mystical sense of belonging to something bigger than themselves, yet which somehow enables them to *be* themselves:

> Its history and beauty: I look out over school yard and know that I am part of a community which has gone on for 500 years and that those who are dead are still influencing me now through a pattern of life and all these lovely old buildings. But here and now I feel part of something larger than myself which yet exists for me alone. In a community there is a fulness of life which can become *your* fulness of life – if you try.
> *Boy, seventeen, public school*

Less mystical souls feel this sense of community in more concrete terms:

> The sense of community or companionship you have – you feel it most after a school play, show, concert. It makes you very happy.
> *Girl, eighteen, progressive school*

> I get a feeling of togetherness and I have lots of friends whereas at home I have few. I learn a lot by observation when living with other boys. Its a good experience.
> *Boy, seventeen, independent school*

We sum up the advantages of boarding as seen by boarders and conclude this book with the words, not of a sophisticated sixth-former, but of a fourteen-year-old girl at a state secondary modern boarding school. Her simple words express in summary the benefits which most children feel that their experience has brought them.

> It took me about a week to get the position of the buildings, and at the end of the week I had about a week of homesickness and crying, but now I never cry for home. It is lovely here and I am never bored like I was at home: there are so many good things to do. You learn to live with everybody and enjoy small, almost childish things that you felt you had grown out of at home, such as running through fallen leaves. You tend to lose your being one separate person and become part of everyone else, their expressions of speech, the way they laugh, the things they do. You learn how much you love your parents and family. And you learn to fend for yourself.

Index

Absconsion, 327-9
Academic work, 23, 24, 27, 28, 30, 31, 36, 51, 52-4, 55, 56-7, 84, 338; attitudes to, 396-8; benefits, 427-9; discussed, 98-108; problems of, 303-5, 321, 389; *see also*: lessons, vocational training
Activities, extra-curricular, 33, 51, 70, 83, 86, 89-92, 163-4, 399, 431; benefits of, 427-9, 431; discussed, 130-32; problems of, 100-101; *see also*: facilities, games, music
Adaptations, discussed, 394-5, 416-17; *see also*: conformity, ritualism, retreatism, innovation, alienation and rebellion
Adolescence, complexities of, 38-9; groups in, 263-4; sex in, 332-3
Alienation, discussed, 409-10; forms of, 263, 284-8, 290-91; in norms, 250-2, 256; *see also*: rebels
Arriving at school, 65-7; reception on arrival, 67-77
Assimilation, 243-5; *see also*: arriving at school
Authority, *see* power, punishment, hierarchy

Beagling, 124-5, 326

Beating, 181, 187-91, 195, 202-8; *see also*: punishments
'Beauchamp Manor', extracts from, 21-5, 138-9, 147-8
Bed, discussed, 147-9; going to, 25, 39, 42, 56, 57-8, 310
Boarding education, alleged advantages of, 414, 423-32; alleged disadvantages of, 413-21; alleged effects of, 44, 51, 81, 84-5, 98-100, 222-9, 234-41, 314-20, 349-51, chap. 13, *passim*; extent of, 20; 'need' for, 43, 61, 63; pupils' expectations of, 49, 64-7; pupils' reasons for, 60-63; varied effects of, 421-4; variety within, 20-58, chaps. 5 and 6, *passim*; *see also*: coeducational schools, day schools, independent schools, integrated schools, preparatory schools, progressive schools, public schools, state schools
'Bolshies', 263, 410, 411
Bounds, 275-6
Bullying, 69, 75-6, 203, 254, 257-9, 264, 313-14

Campaign for Nuclear Disarmament, 307-8
Ceremonies, 142-3, 144-5, 165-9

Index

Chapel, *see* religion

Chaplain, *see* religion

Christian names, significance of, 317–18, 357

Classes, *see* academic work, lessons, prep

Cliques, *see* élites, groups, relations

Coeducational schools, adaptations in, 402; alleged advantages of, 391–3; alleged disadvantages of, 339–41, 385–92; amount, 377; comparison with single-sex schools, 43–4, 348, 392; description, 40–43, 44–5, 49, chap. 12 *passim*; illicit activity in, 386–7; pastoral care in, 320, 324; policies in, 377–80; problems of, 387; relations in, 38, 40–43, 107–8, 270–72, 380–82, 383–5; sexual relationship, 346, 384, 385; weekends in, 137–8, 141, 382–3; *see also*: heterosexual relations, progressive schools, Quaker schools, sex, single-sex schools

Combined Cadet Force, 30, 132–4, 408

Community, spirit of, 397–8, 400–401, 429–32

Competition, problems of, 305–8; uses of, 153–4

Conformity, 246–8, 307; defined, 394–5; discussed, 396–401

Control, general, 418–21; by prefects, 179–83, 184–92, 202–9; by pupils, 256–9, 309–11; by school, 210, 211–13, 307–9; *see also*: freedom, power, prefects, pupils' society, relations, rules

Corporal punishment, *see* beating, punishment

Cricket, 128–9, 130; *see also*: games

'Cromwell College', extracts from, 43–4, 89, 93–4, 204, 226–7, 234

Dames, *see* matrons

Dances, 336–8, 342, 382–3

Day pupils, 33, 156; alleged advantages of, 220–22, 419–21; policies towards, 218; problems of, 218–21

Day schools, compared with public schools, 81–6; compared with boarding schools, 170, 203, 210–12, 218–19, 238, 243, 295–9, 330–31, 332–4, 345–6, 395, 409

Domestic work, 35, 96–7

Dress, 32–3, 43, 211–12, 252, 415

Drinking, 196–7, 208, 270, 275

Drugs, 279–80, 329–30

Eccentrics, *see* retreatists

Élites, mentioned, 138, 259–60

Emotions, effects of boarding on, 315–20; norms about, 248, 256; *see also*: heterosexual relations, homosexuality, self-control

Examinations, 101, 103, 105, 329, 396, 397, 398, 405

Expressive ends, defined, 395; discussed, chap. 13 *passim*.

Facilities, 99–100, 309, 427, 429, 431

Fagging, 31, 67, 83, 139, 140, 156, 158, 165, 185–91, 201, 202, 298, 358, 398; absence of, 47; discussed, 77–81, 158–9; functions of, 59, 185

Family, effects of boarding on, 77, 234–41; missing it, 49, 56, 69–70, 76, 295–6; pupils' relations with, 228–9, 321; *see also*: home, parents

Favouritism, 306–7

Fees, 146

Food, 24, 25, 29, 31, 35, 36, 37, 40, 46, 50, 52, 53, 54, 57, 72, 83, 107–8, 309, 429; discussed, 108–11

Freedom, 32, 34, 45, 73; absence of, 45, 83, 84, 87–92, 418–21; of interests, 210–12; of movement, 48, chap. 7, *passim*; of relations, 218–24; *see also*: control, dress, rules

Friendships, discussed, 288–93, 310, 311, 430; effect of boarding on, 222–30; *see also*: heterosexual relations, homosexuality, pupil society, relations

Games, 29, 53; compulsion, 27, 40, 94–6, 408; described, 88–91, 139–40; discussed, 121–30, 428, 431; excess of, 82; and House, 153–4, 164, 165; and licence, 215; non-compulsory, 57; organization, 31; views on, 21–2, 94–5, 128; *see also*: cricket, rugby, rowing

Gambling, 278–9

Girls, *see* coeducational schools, heterosexual relations, homosexuality, single-sex schools

Gossip, 310–11

Groups, 259–65

Haircuts, 110

Half-term, 143–4

Headmasters, described, 50, 52, 94, 97, 140, 157, 174, 409; interviewed, 15; pastoral role, 327–8, 354; satirized, 146–7; wives, 321; *see also*: staff–pupil relations

Headmasters' Conference, the, 13

Heterosexual relations, 23, 40–43, 214, 250, chaps. 11 and 12, *passim*; alleged effects of segregation, 338–49; boy friends, 39–43, 96, 107–8, 137–8, 142, 217–18; dances, 337–8, 342, 382; girl friends, 22, 23, 40–43, 48, 78, 137, 210, 217, 292, 315–16; lack of, 84, 85, 408, 415; in holidays, 224, 296–7; illicit activities, 385–7; kinds of relations, 380–82, 383–5; norms governing, 252–3, 389–91; schools' policies towards, 211, 212, 217–18, 334–7, 338, 377–81; sexual acts, 96, 273, 384–6; slang of, 270; various problems of, 386–7; *see also*: coeducational schools, homosexuality, relations, sex

Hierarchy, breakdown of, 182; in House, 156–60, 163–4, 165–6, 185–91, 201–2; hostility to, 418; *see also*: power, prefects

Hitch-hiking, 142

Holidays, friendships in, 222–9; pupils' behaviour in, 85, 227–9, 420; relations in, 238–41, 341; sex in, 345; start of, 233–5

Home, contact with, 23, 47, 228–33; contrast with school, 100, 325, 399–400, 425, 432; homeliness of schools, 47, 70; lack of contact with, 81–2, 233–41, 417; returning to, 232–4; *see also*: family, holidays, parents

Homesickness, 70, 73, 77, 234, 240, 295, 432

Homework, *see* prep

Homosexuality, 22, 23, 24, 84, 139, 140, 147, 155, 161–2, 189, 190,

203, 227, 250, 253, 256; alleged causes of, 334, 349–54; amount of, 356, 373–6; between staff and pupils, 46, 74, 299–301, 367; 'big-boy' and 'small-boy', 365–70; compensations of, 370–73; controls over, 258, 351; effects of, 372; groups and, 292; kinds, physical, 360–63; emotional, 364–6; masturbation, 349, 361; new boys and, 68; norms governing, 250, 253, 367–70, 390–91; preoccupation with, 368–70; schools' policies towards, 322, 353–5, 359; slang concerning, 267, 269, 270; worries over, 298–300, 354; *see also*: coeducational schools, heterosexual relations, single-sex schools

House, the, chap. 5, *passim*; ceremonies in, 165–9; competition in, 153–4; emphasis on, 83, 150–52, 307, 398; music in, 131, 165, 167, 187; problems in, 159–63, 312–13; satires, 145–7, structures, 156–8, 165–6; values of, 67–8, 134, 151–3, 157, 164–5, 167, 187–8, 192, 398, 407; variety in, 151–7; *see also*: housemasters, power, prefects

House captains, *see* prefects

Housefathers, 33, 57, 114

Housemasters, criteria for, 162–3; described, 25, 26, 29, 30, 88, 93, 140, 141, 157, 167, 310, 355; interviewed, 15; pastoral role of, 318–27, 354; relations with, 99, 162–3, 176–7, 283, 284, 285, 288; role of, 174; *see also*: house, staff, staff–pupil relations

Housemothers, 37, 39, 96, 98, 148

'In-crowds', *see* élites

Independence, 425–6

Independent schools, control in, 301; definition of, 13 note 2; sample of, 15; weekends in, 137, 141

Informal society, *see* pupils' society

Initiation rites, 245–7

Innovators, defined, 394–5; discussed, 195–6, 407–10

Instrumental ends, defined, 395; discussed, chap. 13 *passim*

Integration, between social classes, 33–4, 46, 47; effects of, 45; in public schools, 81–6, 312; *see also*: integrated schools, public schools

Integrated schools, 424; definition of, 13 note 2, 20; description of, 45–7; drugs in, 279; norms of pupils in, 250–51; ritualism in, 401

Intelligentsia, 262; *see also*: Élites

Isolates, *see* outcasts

Jealousy, 310

'Lady Margaret Foundation', extracts from, 45–6, 74, 204, 245, 274

Language, private, *see* slang

Lessons, described, 22–3, 27, 30, 35–7, 38, 50, 51, 52–8, 55, 56–7, 82, 368–70; discussed, 98–108; *see also*: academic work, prep

Libraries, 85, 98; *see also*: facilities

Maids, 323, 335–6

Maintained schools, *see* state boarding schools

Matrons, 31, 72, 93, 97, 111, 178, 269, 285, 287, 288, 324–5

Merton, R. K., 395
Music, 25, 130–31, 136, 140–41, 214, 428

New boys, *see* arriving at school, boarding education, pupils' expectations of
Night-wandering, 276–7
Norms, of pupils, 248–57

Outcasts, 264–5; described, 311–14, 327
Outings, 213–15

Parents, 23, 322; choice of boarding, 60, 69; effects on relations with, 334–41, 316, 319, 412, 423, 426, 432, 'need' for boarding, 61, 405; visits by, 142–4; *see also*: family, home
Parties, house, 145–7
Pastoral care, 25, 39, 47, 102, 118–19, 161, 183–4, 194, 231–2, 283–4, 292, 294–5, 354, 417–18; discussed, 320–27
Pets, 56, 57, 124–5, 326–7
Pin-ups, 348–9
Plundering, 278
Power, of pupils, importance of, 170–73, 418; nature of, 178–9; problems of, 194–200, 306; scale of, 173–9
Prefects, attitude to, 34; compensations of, 171–3, 201–2; criteria for, 192–5; differing views of, 178–80, 430; norms of, 254; power of, 83, 170–72, 173–9, 185–92; problems of, 194–200, 306; role of, 26, 48, 83, 157–9, 160–62, 185–92; sanctions of, 202–8; state schools, 51, 172, 178, 179, 191; tasks of, 182–4, 213; *see also*: power, punishment
Prep, 27, 30, 42, 55, 92; effects of boarding on, 99–101
Preparatory schools, sample, 15, 16, 20; descriptions, 52–8; holidays, 233–4; lessons, 103–4; relations with family, 237, 240; religion in, 112
Privacy, absence of, 28, 100, 289–90, 309, 418; value of, 38, 99
Privileges, 201–2, 408
Progressive schools, adaptations in, 402, 406–7, 412–13, 426; assimilation in, 243–7; attitudes to, 377; control in, 301; day pupils in, 219–22; drugs in, 279, 280; effects on in holidays, 225–6; groups in, 260–61 lessons at, 106–68, 304; norms in, 252, 254, 256–7; choice of, 62; power in, 173, 191–2; punishment in, 208–9; religion in, 114; sample of, 15, 16; sex in, 385–6; staff–pupil relations in, 282, 284; *see also*: coeducational schools, 'Stanton School'
Public schools, adaptations in, 397–403, 407–10, 411–15; assimilation in, 243–6; change in, 88, 120, 128, 133, 181, 182, 194, 200, 338, 357, 407–8; comments of integrants in, 81–6, 420, 424–5; control in, 301, 409; day pupils in, 219–22; definition of, 13 note 2; descriptions of, 26–32; drugs in, 280; effects on family, 236–7; groups in, 259–64; moderation in, 267; norms of pupils in, 248–50; power in, 172–209; punishment in, 202–9; reasons for boarding at, 62–4;

religion in, 112–14, 118, 119, 399, 400, 401, 408; sample of, 15, 16; self-control in, 314–19; staff–pupil relations in, 282–3; weekends at, 135–6, 139–41; values of, 151–2, 192, 315–19, 395, 398, 399, 429–31; variety within, 71; *see also*: house, housemaster, power, prefects

Public Schools Commission, 216

Punishments, attitudes to, 46, 386; methods of, 43–4, 84; by prefects, 83, 179–84, 185–91, 195–6, 202–9; *see also*: bullying, prefects

Pupils' society, assimilation, 243–7; cliques in, 259–65, 310; controls of, 256–9; language of, 266–70; norms of, 249–57, 289, 314–20; pressures of, 246–8, 308–20; relation to official system, 242–3, 265; relations to staff, 281–8; relations within, 288–93, 322–4, 339–40, 410–11, 429; underlife, 271–80; *see also*: élites, controls, heterosexual relations, homosexuality, relations

Quaker schools, 32, 42, 43–4, 422–3; control in, 301; emotion in, 320; pastoral care in, 323; religion in, 114, 117–18; sex in, 348; *see also*: coeducational, progressive schools

Qualifications, 396–7

Rebels, 263, 307–8; defined, 394–5; discussed, 409–14

Relations, among pupils, 54–5, 74–5, 181–4, 252–7, 259–65, 288–93, 339–40, 411, 429, 430–31; *see also*: bullying, friendships, staff–pupil relations

Religion, chapel, 22, 26–7, 29, 43, 114–15, 118–20, 139, 140, 216, 407, 408; chaplains, pastoral care of, 145–6; satirized, 84; discussed, 111–20; pupils' attitudes to, 84, 116–20, 398, 399, 401, 402, 407; prayers, 27, 30, 115–17, 257; religious instruction, 23, 116–17; talks, 216–17

Reputation, its functions, 247, 256, 257, 418

Research, methods of, 11–19, 333–4; team referred to, 89, 105, 106, 108, 114, 216, 222, 288, 326

Responsibility, 430

Retreatists, 312–14, 327, 423; defined, 394–5; discussed, 402–7

Rising, descriptions, 21, 26, 28, 31, 35, 53; discussed, 92–7

Ritualism, defined, 394–5; discussed, 401–2

Routine, 82, 88, 148; described, 87; effects of, 302, 416

Rowing, 122, 123, 140; *see also*: games

Rugby, 121, 127–8; *see also*: games

Rules, 195–200, 201–9, 210–13, 301, 302–3, 407, 419–21

Running, 128; *see also*: games

Running away, *see* abscondion

St Augustine, 399

Sampling of schools, 12–14; *see also*: research, methods of

Security, 430

Self-control, 312, 357–8, 373; discussed, 314–19, 343; *see also*: emotions

Sex, 332–6; attitudes in general to, 85, 147, 308; *see also*: coeducational schools, heterosexual relations, homosexuality, single-sex schools

Single-sex schools, alleged strengths and weaknesses of, 339–51; *see also*: coeducational schools, heterosexual relations, homosexuality

Slang, 59–60; kinds and uses of, 266–70

Smoking, 105, 111, 149, 196–7, 203–4, 273–4

Smuggling, 272

Snobbery, 415; absence of, 82, 424–5

Social distance and prefects, 197–200

Social service, 132–4

Staff, as teachers, 99, 102; expectation of, 281; general, 52, 280–81, 285–8; interviewed, 15–16; power of, 179; *see also*: housefathers, housemasters, housemothers, matrons, staff–pupil relations

Staff–pupil relations, 29, 32–3, 39–40, 50, 51, 53–4, 84, 85, 108, 109–10, 317, 399, 400, 410–11; effect of boarding on, 99–100, 214–15, 281–8, 431; language and, 267–72; *see also*: staff, pastoral care, pupil society

Staff wives, 282–3

'Stanton School', extracts from, 34–9, 106–7, 136–7, 141, 261, 291

State boarding schools, adaptations in, 396–7, 401, 402, 403–5, 427; assimilation to, 243–5; contact with home, 228–33; control in, 301; description of, 47–52; goals in, 396; 'need' and, 61; power in, 174–5, 178, 179, 191; religion in, 115, 119; staff–pupil relations in, 284; sample of, 15–16

Status, problems of, 415–16; *see also*: prefects, power

Stealing, 33, 41, 46, 278

Studies, 290, 292, 293, 313

Suicide, 330

Surnames, 317–18

Teaching, 102; *see also*: academic work, lessons, staff

Tolerance, 423–4

'Tormouth School', extracts from, 56–7, 97–8

Tutors, 39; in houses, 156, 157, 162, 167, 175; *see also*: housemasters

Underlife, 272–80

Valentines, 382

Visitors, 215–17

Vocational training, 49–50

Weather, its effect, 222

Weekends, descriptions of, 57, 382; discussed, 134–42; expectations of, 56

Writings, how gathered, 13–19

Youth culture, and school controls, 210–11; *see also*: pupil society

More about Penguins and Pelicans

Penguinews, which appears every month, contains details of all the new books issued by Penguins as they are published. From time to time it is supplemented by *Penguins in Print*, which is a complete list of all available books published by Penguins. (There are well over four thousand of these.)

A specimen copy of *Penguinews* will be sent to you free on request. For a year's issues (including the complete lists) please send 30p if you live in the United Kingdom, or 60p if you live elsewhere. Just write to Dept EP, Penguin Books Ltd, Harmondsworth, Middlesex, enclosing a cheque or postal order, and your name will be added to the mailing list.

Note: *Penguinews* and *Penguins in Print* are not available in the U.S.A. or Canada

Educating the Intelligent

Michael Hutchinson and Christopher Young

If the Battle of Waterloo was won on the playing-fields of Eton, it is equally true that Britain's destiny is today being hammered out in the classrooms of secondary schools all over the country. Recent controversies have raised many questions about the direction which is being taken by secondary education. Is it correctly orientated for the needs of modern society or does it tend to 'level downwards'? Should more encouragement be given to pupils who are above the average intelligence? Ought we deliberately to train an élite?

The two authors of this constructive and absorbing book have had many years' experience as teachers. After exposing some of the serious inadequacies of the present curriculum in secondary schools, they go on to analyse the basic educational needs of the intelligent child. They then outline an alternative curriculum which would both meet these needs and be practicable within the average secondary school. In addition, they discuss fully the sixth-form syllabus, the examination system, university selection, and the choice, training, and remuneration of teachers.

Education

W. O. Lester Smith

Intended for the general reader, this book attempts to provide an account of modern trends in educational theory and practice, and it reviews current problems.

It presents for the reader's consideration most of the fundamental issues under discussion today in educational circles – aims and principles, the interaction of home and school, the curriculum, the significance of the neighbourhood, problems of control and administration, equality of opportunity, the education and status of teachers, the organization of secondary education, the influence of the Churches and voluntary societies, and the educational needs of an industrial society.

A brief survey of this kind can be a dreary catalogue if it is not selective, and for that reason there are some important omissions. It has been assumed that many readers will wish to study more closely aspects and issues that particularly interest them, and throughout there are references to relevant literature, including many books to which the author is specially indebted. A reading list has also been appended in the hope that it will prove helpful. Several revisions have been made in this reprint, to bring the book up to date.

'Cool, unbiased, objective, tolerant' –
The Times Educational Supplement

Education for Tomorrow

John Vaizey

Education for Tomorrow first appeared in 1962 as a Penguin Special which quickly sold out. Some of the forecasts and concepts formulated by John Vaizey at that time have since become commonplaces of the educational world and found their way into official reports.

The importance of education, for the country's future, is now (almost to the surprise of the academic world) generally recognized. In this Pelican, which is a revised and expanded edition of the Penguin Special, John Vaizey surveys the present state of English education against the background of the new society now emerging. In a series of chapters he points to the many changes which will be needed – greater equality of opportunity, more teachers, increased Higher Education, modern teaching methods, a balanced partnership between Ministry, local authority, teachers, and parents – if Britain is to hold her position in an age of science and specialization.

A Parents' Guide to Education

E. B. Castle

Does a child's home environment determine his intelligence score? What sort of people are teachers? Is there a real parents' choice? What is a school for?

These are some of the questions which parents face, and which are answered in this clear and readable guide to education by the author of *Ancient Education and Today*. Always conscious of the ideals of schooling, this is yet a realist's book and illustrated by personal experience.

E. B. Castle begins by tracing the most formative ideas in the British tradition of education, and describes how they have influenced teaching methods and teachers' attitudes towards children. He goes on to discuss social problems such as equal educational opportunity and the effect of environment on intelligence. Later chapters deal with the future of schools, what type of people the staff should be, and the internal organization of a school.

Written primarily for parents, to introduce them to teachers, school governors, and administrators, this book also introduces teachers to themselves and young teachers to their profession.

Also available
Ancient Education and Today

A Guide to English Schools

Tyrrell Burgess

Third Edition

Education today claims more from the nation's budget than defence. Conscious that 'children get a better chance nowadays', more and more parents feel an increasing need to explore all the possibilities that exist for schooling.

In this Pelican, Tyrrell Burgess provides a straightforward and up-to-date guide to schools of all kinds in England and Wales, together with an outline of their administration and structure. Nursery schools, primary schools, comprehensive, secondary modern and grammar schools are all factually described, as well as the preparatory and public schools of the private domain. In addition the author summarizes the facilities for further and higher education.

Parents – particularly of children approaching the age of five – will find this book a useful map of a territory where such signposts as 'multilateral' and 'direct-grant' tend to confuse the most eager explorer.

The Comprehensive School

Robin Pedley

Second Edition

Britain's educational system will soon be based firmly on the comprehensive school, and in this new edition of an already successful Pelican the Director of the Exeter University Institute of Education gives a clear and critical picture of the comprehensive as it operates in England and Wales today. Professor Pedley first describes just what the 11+ is and does. Then, after dispelling the bogey that comprehensive schools need at least two thousand pupils in order to function, he goes on to demonstrate, by statistics, that those in existence are already rivalling the tripartite system in academic achievements. Finally, and most important, he argues that a good comprehensive school can both focus and mirror a community as can no other school.

Of all our educational establishments the comprehensive school is the least understood. This book, which contains a glossary of educational terms and a summary of country-wide plans for reorganization, offers to interested readers – especially parents – all the facts.